AN ACCOUNT

OF

THE POLYNESIAN RACE

ITS ORIGIN AND MIGRATIONS

AND THE

ANCIENT HISTORY OF THE HAWAIIAN PEOPLE
TO THE TIMES OF KAMEHAMEHA I.

BY

ABRAHAM FORNANDER,

CIRCUIT JUDGE OF THE ISLAND OF MAUI,'H.I.
KNIGHT COMPANION OF THE ROYAL ORDER OF KALAKAUA.

VOL. II.

British Library Cataloguing-in-Publication Data
A catalogue record for this book is available from the
British Library

PREFACE.

In issuing this, the second volume of " An Account of the Polynesian Race," &c., and the " Ancient History of the Hawaiian People," the author gratefully acknowledges the kind reception which the first volume received. It was a hazardous undertaking to publish a work of that kind ten thousand miles away from the author's residence, with no opportunity of revising the sheets as they came from the press, or preparing an index when the volume was finished. The well-known ability and care of his publishers, the world-known Messrs. Trübner & Co., grappled bravely and successfully with the difficulties of a MS. which, owing to peculiar circumstances, had not been clean copied for the press before it was sent away. To Stephen Spencer, Esq., formerly Chief Clerk to the Interior Department of the Hawaiian Government, and now residing in London, the author is under great obligations for the kind and vicarious supervision that he gave to the proof-reading, and for the thoroughly faultless rendition of the Polynesian words, phrases, and entire chants occurring in the work.

To the gentlemen who compose the staff of such leading literary journals as the "Westminster Review," the "British Quarterly Review," and the "Academy," the author sends his warm *Aloha* for the notices of kindness and encouragement with which they met his efforts to bring the Polynesian folklore within the zone of scientific research; to collect the broken and distorted rays of that folklore into one historical focus; and, by following the indications thus obtained, to seek the homesteads of the earlier Polynesians, where they themselves say that they ought to be found.

The author may have startled some and shocked others by seeking a Polynesian ancestry beyond the Malay Archipelago; but their own undoubted folklore, their legends and chants, gave no warrant for stopping there. They spoke of continents, and not of islands, as their birthplace. They referred to events in the far past which have hitherto been considered as the prehistoric heirlooms of Cushites and Semites alone. And the language in which that folklore is conveyed, whatever its subsequent modifications and admixtures, will be found, on a critical examination, to be fundamentally Arian of a pre-Vedic type before the inflections were fully developed or generally adopted. If the author has not in every instance secured the consensus of his reader to those conclusions, which to him seem the only possible ones, from the data that he has collected, the fault must be ascribed to the author and not to the data. He may have failed in his manner of presenting them; they still remain, a now imperishable heirloom of the Polynesian race, to await a more skilful expounder, and to challenge any attempt to deprive that race of its inheritance in the Arian blood and the Cushite civilisation.

In the present volume the author has endeavoured to present the ancient history of that branch of the Polynesians which took up its abode on the Hawaiian Islands. In entering the wilderness of a hitherto untrodden field, and the almost impenetrable jungle of traditions, legends, genealogies, and chants, the author has had no easy task in reducing his materials to historical sequence, precision, and certainty. The difficulties he has had to contend with hardly any but Polynesian scholars can fully appreciate, and how far he has succeeded he respectfully leaves to the Hawaiians themselves to decide.

The author had originally sketched out for himself as a portion of this work—or rather as an appendix to the first volume—a comparative glossary of the Polynesian and Arian dialects in confirmation of their affinity. But the closer and the more critically that subject was approached, the greater and the more numerous became the points of contact, and what had been intended for a few pages has unavoidably swollen to the size of a volume, and as such will be issued in separate form if life and health are granted the author.

ABR. FORNANDER.

LAHAINA, *December* 1879.

ORIGIN AND MIGRATIONS

OF

THE POLYNESIAN RACE.

PART II.

In the first part of this work I have attempted to trace the origin of the Polynesian Race by following strictly the plain lead of its own folklore and the obvious inductions which the scattered fragments of that lore suggest. To recapitulate in an inverse order the findings to which that folklore has led, I would briefly say that I have found a vague, almost obliterated, consciousness in some of their legends that the head, and front, and beginning of the Polynesians lay in a white (the Arian) race; and I found this consciousness confirmed by referring to the language, probably the oldest Arian form of speech, and to the Arian numeral system, as well as to some customs and modes of thought exclusively Arian. I found in their legends proofs, many and distinct, that at this remote era the Polynesians must have come into long and intimate contact with the early Cushite, Chaldeo-Arabian civilisation, of which so many and so exceedingly interesting fragments yet remain in their folklore. I found that during or after this period of Cushite contact the Polynesians must have amalgamated, as greatly as their Vedic

A

brethren did afterwards, with the Dravidian peoples south
of Chaldea in India.   I next found that, whatever the
manner or the occasion of their leaving India, though
they probably followed in the wake of the great Chaldeo-
Arabian commerce of that period, they had occupied the
Asiatic Archipelago from Sumatra to Luzon and Timor.
I have found no time of their arriving in the archipelago,
but I have found from their own genealogies and legends
that, approximatively speaking, during the first and second
centuries of the Christian era many and properly organised migrations of the Polynesians into the Pacific Ocean
took place from various points of the archipelago; a
period coincident with the rise and development of the
Hindoo and Malay invasions of Sumatra, Java, &c.   I
found, moreover, that though there is nothing to indicate
that some of these migratory expeditions may not have
pushed on to some of the eastern, northern, or southern
groups of the Pacific now held by the Polynesians, yet
that their general rendezvous during this migratory period
was on the Fiji group, and principally on the west side
of *Viti-levu;* that they were of superior cultivation to the
Papuans then and now inhabiting that group; that they
stayed there long enough to introduce a large amount of
their vocables into the Fijian language, and no inconsiderable part of their legends and customs in the Fijian folklore; and that when finally, after several generations of
séjour, they were expelled from the Fiji group, they
scattered over the Pacific, taking up their present positions on the principal groups, either simultaneously or
by stages from group to group, or in both ways; and I
have shown that that branch of the Polynesian family
from which the oldest ruling line of Hawaiian chiefs
claim descent arrived at the Hawaiian group during the
sixth .century of the Christian era, and, in the utter
absence of legendary information, is supposed to have
lived secluded and isolated from its cousins in the South.
Pacific for twelve to fourteen generations, or until a

period which, for convenience, I have designated as that of *Maweke* and *Paumakua,* or about the close of the tenth or beginning of the eleventh century A.D.

So far the previous volume has carried the reader. It is known in most cases, and presumed in all, that by the time indicated above all the principal groups had been occupied and peopled by the Polynesians migrating thither, partly during, mostly after, their *séjour* on the Fiji group. There are few data to determine the order of their going; whether the more distant groups were not settled upon as early, or nearly as early, as those nearer to the Fiji group. Mr. Horatio Hale, of the " United States Exploring Expedition," argues a successive distribution of the Polynesian race, after leaving the Fiji group, from the corruption of language and the affinity of dialects; and intimates that the Samoan group was the mother group and the keynote of Polynesian migrations within the Pacific; that having first settled on the Samoan, when this group became over-peopled, it threw off new migrations to the Society group, which, in its turn, when overstocked, started expeditions to the Paumotu and the Marquesas, and that these, in their turn, relieved themselves of a too-redundant population by migratory expeditions to Easter Island and the Hawaiian group, and he allows over three thousand years for this gradual process of redundancy and relief.

The dialectical variations of the different Polynesian groups, and their linguistic corruption from a once common form of speech, are patent enough to him who takes an interest in examining the subject; but it is far from patent, and cannot be proved, that these variations are the result of a process of sequences; in other words, that the Tahitian is a dialect of the Samoan, the Marquesan is a dialect of the Tahitian, and the Hawaiian is a dialect of the Marquesan, and so on in other directions. There are shades of affinity that appear to link one dialect to another more than to the rest; but there are also shades of divergence so great and glaring that they cannot be explained except on the hypothesis that they existed of old, and were brought with the Polynesians from their various habitats in the Asiatic Archipelago when first they entered the Pacific.

I believe it is now well understood among the best philologists of Europe that the ancient High and Low German, the Saxon and the old Norse, were not successive dialects, formed the one upon the other, but contemporary and coexistent varieties of the Teutonic or Gothic stock when first it entered Europe; and by the same law I claim that the Polynesian dialects are older than their appearance in the Pacific, though the variations may have widened and the peculiarities attached to each may have hardened through lapse of time and through isolation; and, consequently, that the lines of distribution within the Polynesian area cannot safely be argued according to the apparent affinity or divergence of the different dialects. It is, geographically speaking, probable, and as a matter of fact not to be disputed, that the early Hawaiians arrived at their group *via* Tahiti and the Marquesas; though there is nothing to disprove that some of those emigrants came from Samoa direct, as it is known to Hawaiian scholars to have been the case during the period upon which we are now entering, five hundred years later. There is an amount of archaic forms of speech and archaic meanings of vocables in each dialect, that have been altered or become obsolete in the others; thus showing that each dialect was coeval with the others. And in further disproval of Mr. Hale's theory of derivation, the three dialects that are farthest away from what is considered the common centre or source, the Hawaiian, the Easter Island, and the New Zealand are the least corrupted from what undoubtedly was the common mother tongue of the Polynesians before their migration into the Pacific, and much less so than the supposed mother form, the Samoan. Moreover, the legends and traditions of the pre-Pacific life of the Polynesian race have been preserved in a fuller, better, and purer condition on the Marquesan and Hawaiian groups than on the Tahitian, Samoan, or Tongan, where they are found distorted or frittered away, if found at all, or else entirely forgotten.

I have referred to this subject somewhat at length to justify me in assigning as old, or nearly as old, a residence of the Hawaiians on their group as the Tongans, Samoans, Tahitians, and Marquesans on their groups respectively ; and to confirm the correctness of Hawaiian traditions and genealogies, which carry their principal line of chiefs, known and admitted to have lived and flourished on the Hawaiian group, up to *Nanaulu,* or some forty-three generations ago, with the reservation always understood of any previous chance emigrants, of whom tradition makes no mention.

During that long period, of which *Nanaulu* may be considered as the initial point, and extending for thirteen or fourteen generations, or between four and five hundred years, I find nothing in Hawaiian legends, except the bare genealogical tree, to indicate even the faintest ripple of national life and existence. If the epigram be true that " happy is the nation that has no history," the Hawaiians must have been eminently happy during this period. Human and organic nature were, however, probably the same then as now, and wars and contentions may occasionally have disturbed the peace of the people, as eruptions and earthquakes may have destroyed and altered the face of the country. The traditions of such events were forgotten through lapse of time, or absorbed in and effaced by the stirring events which ushered in and accompanied the new era at which we have now arrived. But in spite of the din and stir of the succeeding epoch, in spite of the lapse of time and increasing decadence and savagery of the people, some relics still remain of the *Nanaulu* period to attest the condition and activity of the people of that period. Such are the *Heiaus* (temples) of the truncated pyramidal form found in various places of the group, and the best preserved specimen of which that I have seen is the Heiau of *Kumakaula* at Kaimu, district of Puna, Hawaii. Such are the *Pohaku-a-Kane*, referred to on p. 46, vol. i., and which retained their sanctity to comparatively modern times. Such are the fishponds—*Loko-ia*—of Cyclopean structure along the coast of Molokai and in some other places, of which tradition has no other account than that they were the work of the *Menehune* people, one of the ancient names of the Polynesians, thus showing that they were executed previous to the *Maweke-Paumakua* period and the arrival of the southern expeditions, after which that name, as a national appellation, disappeared from Hawaii. Such are the *Kumuhonua, Welaahilani,* and *Kumuuli* legends and genealogies referred to in the first volume, and which, however much shorn, distorted, and overlaid by subsequent innovations, still found shelter and adherents among the *Maweke* descendants, and have survived in part to the present time.

About the commencement of the eleventh century, after a period of comparative quiet and obscurity, the Polynesian folklore in all the principal groups becomes replete with the legends and songs of a number of remarkable men, of bold expeditions, stirring adventures, and voyages undertaken to far-off lands. An era of national unrest and of tribal commotion seems to have set in, from causes not now known, nor mentioned in the legends. In all the legends and traditions relating to this period that have come under my cognisance, I have been unable to discover any allusions which might indicate that pressure from without by some foreign foe was the primary cause of this commotion; and I am inclined to believe that it arose spontaneously from over-population, or perhaps, in a measure, from elemental casualties, such as desolating volcanic eruptions, subsidence of peopled areas, or the like. Be the cause what it may, a migratory wave swept the island world of the Pacific, embracing in its vortex all the principal groups, and probably all the smaller. Chiefs from the southern groups visited the Hawaiian group, and chiefs from the latter visited the former, accompanied by their relatives, priests, and retainers, and left indelible traces of their *séjour* and permanent settlement on the genealogies of succeeding chiefs, in the disuse of old and substitution of new names for places and landmarks, in the displacement of old and setting up of new tutelar gods, with enlarged rites of worship and stricter tabus. In as far as the Hawaiian group partook of this ethnic convulsion, it continued for seven or eight generations, though there is ground for believing that among the southern groups it continued several generations later, and only finally closed with the emigration from Sawaii, Samoan group, to New Zealand, about fifteen generations previous to 1850,[1] or at the close of the fourteenth or commencement of the fifteenth century A.D.

[1] In "Polynesian Researches," Rev. Mr. Ellis mentions that the Tahitians have genealogies going back upward of a hundred generations, but that only thirty of them can be considered as accurate and reliable. Those thirty generations bring us up to that period of tribal commotion of which I am now treating, when the aristocracy in almost all the groups took, so to say, a new departure. Mr. De Bovis, in his "Etat de la Société Taitienne a l'arrivée des Européens," mentions twenty-four generations of chiefs on Raiatea and Borabora, from *Raa*, the progenitor, to *Tamatoa*, the then (1863) reigning chief of Raiatea. The establishment of this line of chiefs on Raiatea coincides in a remarkable manner as to name, time, and some other circumstances with the well-known Hawaiian chief *Laa*, surnamed *Mai-kahiki*, with whom, or perhaps with whose sons, closed the Hawaiian period of this interoceanic communication. In the Hervey group, at Rarotonga, the chief, *Makea*, reckoned himself as the twenty-ninth descendant from the time when the two united expeditions from Samoa and Tahiti, under the leaderships of *Karika* and *Tangia*, arrived and established themselves by subduing the previous inhabitants. The Marquesan chiefs of Hivaoa, after counting one hundred and forty-eight generations from the beginning of things, commence a new series from *Matapa*, and count twenty-one generations to the present time. The *Mangarewa* or *Gambier* islands count twenty-five generations since *Teatumoana* arrived there from foreign lands.

It has been objected by not a few writers to the long voyages of the Polynesians, either on their first entering the Pacific or at this period of tribal commotion and unrest, that they could not possibly be performed in their frail canoes, incapable of containing stores and provisions for a long voyage, and for want of astronomical and nautical knowledge of those who navigated them. Those writers judge the Polynesians as they found them one hundred years ago, isolated, deteriorated, decaying. Had those writers been acquainted with Polynesian folklore, they would have learnt that, at the time we are now speaking of, the Polynesians were not only possessed of open canoes, hollowed out of a single tree, and seldom used except for coasting or fishing excursions, but of vessels constructed from planks sewn or stitched together in a substantial manner, pitched and painted, decked over, or partly so, and with a capacity of hold sufficient to contain men, animals, and stores for any projected voyage;[1] that they possessed a respectable knowledge of the stars, their rising and setting at all times of the year, both in the Southern and Northern Hemisphere; that they were acquainted with the limits of the ecliptic and situation of the equator; that they possessed the keenest eyesight and a judgment trained to estimate all appearances indicating the approach of

---

[1] Rev. J. Williams relates that during his residence at Tahiti there arrived at Papeete, about 1819-20, from Rurutu, one of the Austral group, 700 miles distant, a large canoe, planked up and sewed together, whose hold was twelve feet deep. This peculiar method of planking up or sewing together the different pieces of which the large seagoing canoes in olden times were made prevailed throughout Polynesia, and is still retained at the Navigators, Paumotu, and other groups, besides in Micronesia, and is still customary among the Buguis of Celebes and Ceram. In the Hawaiian group this manner of making large canoes was not wholly discarded as late as the middle of the last century; for it is credibly reported by some of the old natives, whose grandparents lived at the time and saw it, that the principal war-canoe, or admiral's ship, of *Peleioholani*—the famous warrior-king of Oahu, who died about eight years before the arrival of Captain Cook —was a double canoe built in that manner; its name was "*Kaneaaiai*," and that on *Peleioholani's* expeditions it carried on board from one hundred and twenty to one hundred

land, by flight of birds and other signs; and with all this a courage, hardihood, and perseverance that never failed them at critical moments. And when to this be added that seven or eight hundred years ago the Pacific Ocean probably presented a different aspect as regards islands and atolls than it now does—the legends speaking of islands both large and small in the track of their voyages, of which now no trace exists—surprise ceases when one finds on the traditional record accounts of voyages undertaken from Hawaii to Marquesas, Tahiti, Samoa, or *vice versa.*

As little as the legends speak of the cause or causes which led to this ethnic or tribal movement and intercommunication after so long a period of comparative quiet, as little do they mention the causes which led to its discontinuance after more than two hundred years' duration. It is permitted, therefore, to suppose that, among other causes, not the least potent was the subsidence and disappearance of some of those islands which had served as landmarks and stopping-places on previous voyages.

What the conceptions of the ancient Hawaiians of this and subsequent periods were in regard to the geography of the Pacific may be gathered from the following chant of *Kamahualele,* the astrologer and companion of *Moikeha,*

and forty men, besides provisions, water, stores, armament, &c. Of the enormous size of the double canoes that were fashioned out of a single tree, some idea may be formed from a specimen still existing—at least it was a few years ago when the author visited the locality—near the south point of Hawaii. It was said to have been one of a double canoe belonging to *Kamehameha I.*, and it measured one hundred and eight feet in length. Its mate had decayed and disappeared, and this giant relic of ancient shipbuilding was also hastening to decay. In the New Zealand legends collected by Sir George Grey we read of a Samoan expedition of five large double canoes, the *Arawa, Tainui,* &c., decked over, or partly so, containing the different chiefs and their families, their retainers and their families, provisions, animals, &c., which were bound to New Zealand, the *Ao-tea-roa* of the legend, who found the land they were bound to, and, disembarking, settled there; that some of them returned to the Samoan group, and finally came back and remained permanently on New Zealand.

the grandson of *Maweke,* on his return from Tahiti to
Hawaii. As he approached the latter island the seer
and prophet exclaimed :—

Here is Hawaii, the island, the man,
Eia Hawaii, he moku, he kanaka,
A man is Hawaii,—E.
He kanaka Hawaii,—E.
A man is Hawaii,
He kanaka Hawaii,
A child of Kahiki,
He kama na Kahiki,
A royal flower from Kapaahu,
He pua Alii mai Kapaahu,
From Moaulanuiakea Kanaloa,
Mai Moaulanuiakea Kanaloa,
A grandchild of Kahiko and Kapulanakehau,
He moopuna na Kahiko laua o Kapulanakehan,
Papa begat him,
Na Papa i hanau,
The daughter of Kukalaniehu and Kauakahakoku.
Na ke kama wahine o Kukalaniehu laua me Kauaka-
hakoko.
The scattered islands are in a row,
Na pulapula aina i paekahi,
Placed evenly from east to west,
I nonoho like i ka Hikina, Komohana,
Spread evenly is the land in a row
Pae like ka moku i lalani
Joined on to Holani.
I hui aku, hui mai me Holani.
Kaialea the seer went round the land,
Puni ka moku o Kaialea ke kilo,
Separated Nuuhiwa, landed on Polapola :
Naha Nuuhiwa, lele i Polapola :
O Kahiko is the root of the land,
O Kahiko ke kumu aina,
He divided and separated the islands.
Nana i mahele kaawale na moku.
Broken is the fish-line of Kahai,
Moku ka aholawaia a Kahai,
That was cut by Kukanaloa :
I okia e Kukanaloa :
Broken up into pieces were the lands, the islands,
Pauku na aina na moku,
Cut up by the sacred knife of Kanaloa.
Moku i ka ohe kapu a Kanaloa.

O Haumea Manukahikele,
O Haumea Manukahikele,
O Moikeha, the chief who is to reside,
O Moikeha, ka Lani nana e noho,
My chief will reside on Hawaii—a—
Noho kuu Lani ia Hawaii—a—
Life, life, O buoyant life !
Ola, Ola, o kalana ola !
Live shall the chief and the priest,
Ola ke Alii, ke Kahuna,
Live shall the seer and the slave,
Ola ke Kilo, ke Kauwa,
Dwell on Hawaii and be at rest,
Noho ia Hawaii a lu lana,
And attain to old age on Kauai.
A kani moopuna i Kauai.
O Kauai is the island—a—
O Kauai ka moku—a—
O Moikeha is the chief.
O Moikeha ke Alii.

In the chant of *Kahakukamoana*, a famous high-priest of olden times, though several generations later than this migratory period, mention is made of Hawaii as having arisen from the dark—from the deep—and forming one of " the row of islands of *Nuumea*, the cluster of islands reaching to the farthest ends of Tahiti."[1] And giving the same indefinite origin to Maui and the other islands under the paraphrases of natural births, the chant refers to some of the principal chief families from *Nuumea, Holani, Tahiti,* and *Polapola* who settled on the other islands of the Hawaiian group, and are thus poetically said to have given birth to them. Thus *Kuluwaiea*, the husband, and *Hinanui-a-lana*, the wife, are said to be the parents of Molokai, which is called " a god, a priest, the

---

[1] *Ea mai Hawaii-nui-akea !*
Ea mai loko, mai loko mai o ka
  po !
Puka ka moku, ka aina,
Ka lalani aina o Nuumea,
Ka Pae aina o i kukulu o Kahiki.

Rising up is Hawaii-nui-akea !
Rising up out of, out of the night
  (Po)!
Appeared has the island, the land,
The string of islands of Nuumea,
The cluster of islands stretching to
  the farthest ends of Tahiti.

first morning light from Nuumea."[1] Lanai is said to
have been an adopted child of a chief from Tahiti, whose
name, if the transcript of the chant is correct, is not
given, but whose epithet was "the spatterer of the red
or dirty water," *Ka haluku wai ea.* Kahoolawe is said to
be the child of *Keaukanai,* the man, and *Walinuu,* the
wife, from Holani; and the epithet of the island-child is
"the farmer"—*he lopa.* Molokini has no separate settlers,
but is called the navel-string—*Iewe*—of Kahoolawe.
Oahu is attributed to *Ahukini-a-Laa,* a son of the
famous *Laa-mai-kahiki,* who was fourth in descent from
Paumakua of the southern *Ulu-puna* branch, and his
wife's name is given as *Laamealaakona.* The epithet of
Oahu is *he Wohi,* a royal title assumed only by the Oahu
chiefs of the highest rank until comparatively modern
times. *Ahukini-a-laa* is said in the chant to have come
from foreign lands, *mai ka nanamu,* from Apia, Samoan
group, though the verse makes a pun on the word, and
from the deep sea of Halehalekalani.[2] Kauai is said to
have been begotten by *Laakapu,* the man, and *Laamealaakona,* the wife, thus having the same mother as Oahu.
Finally, *Wanalia,* the husband, from Polapola, and his
wife, *Hanalaa,* were the parents of Niihau, Kaula, and
Nihoa, the last and westernmost islands of the group.

A remarkable fragment has been preserved of the chant
of *Kaulu-a-kalana,* a famous navigator of this period.

---

[1] *Na Kuluwaiea o Haumea he kane,*   To Kuluwaiea of Haumea, the hus-
Na Hinanui-a-lana he wahine,   band,
Loaa Molokai, he Akua, he Ka-   To Hinanui-a-lana, the wife,
  huna,   Was born Molokai, a god, a priest,
He pualena no Nuumea.   The first morning light from Nuumea.

[2] *Ku mai Ahukinialaa,*   Up stands Akuhinialaa,
He Alii mai ka nanamu,   The chief from the foreign land,
Mai ka Api o ka ia,   From the gills of the fish,
Mai ke ale poi pu o Halehaleka- From the overwhelming billows of
  lani,   Halehalekalani,
Loaa Oahu he Wohi,   Born is Oahu the Wohi,
He Wohi na Ahukini-a-Laa,   The Wohi of Ahukinialaa,
Na Laamealaakona he wahine. And of Laamealaakona the wife.

Whether he belonged to the southern, *Ulu,* line of chiefs, or to the northern, *Nana-ulu,* line, is not clear, but that he lived or settled on Oahu seems to be admitted; and he is referred to in several legends of this period as contemporary with *Moikeha, Luhaukapawa,* the famous priest and prophet, and other prominent personages of both lines. In his chant he mentions a number of lands and islands visited by him, some of which occur under the very same names as those earlier homesteads of the Polynesian race of which I have treated in the beginning of the first part of this work, and to which the legends of *Kumuhonua* and *Hawaii-loa* refer. The majority of the lands visited by Kaulu I have, however, been unable to identify. Wawau of the Tonga group and Upolo of the Samoan are clearly distinguishable as parts of his periplus. I quote the fragment in full:—

> I am Kaulu,
> *O Kaulu nei wau,*
> The child of Kalana,
> *O ke kama o Kalana,*
> The sacred rest,
> *O ka hiamoe kapu,*
> The sea-slug,
> *Ka auwaalalua,*
> The great slinger (expert with the sling).
> *Ke keele maaalaioa.*
> Rainbow colours, morning light,
> *O kuulei, o pawa,*
> He (is the one) who spreads them out,
> *Ka mea nana i hoolei,*
> Kaulu ashore, E, Kaulu at sea,
> *Kaulu mauka, E Kaulu makai,*
> E. Kaulu—E—He is the Kiwaa,
> *E Kaulu—E—Kiwaa*[1] *ia,*
> E. Kaulu—E—a fleet is he.
> E. *Kaulu—E—auwaa ia.*[2]
> He has landed on (visited) Wawau,
> *O lele aku keia o Wawau,*

---

[1] *Kiwaa* was the name of a very large bird.

[2] Analogous to the English expression, "he is a host in himself."

Upolu, Little Pukalia,
  O Upolu, O Pukalia iki,
Great Pukalia, Alala,
  O Pukalia nui, O Alala,
Pelua, Palana, Holani,
  O Pelua, O Palana, O Holani,
The Isthmus, Ulunui, Uliuli,
  O ke Kuina,[1] *O Ulunui, O Uliuli,*
Melemele, Hiikua, Hiialo,
  O Melemele, O Hiikua, O Hiialo,
Hakalauai ;—who has spanned the heaven,
  O Hakalauai- ; apo ka lani,
Spanned the night, spanned the day,
  Apo ka po, apo ke ao,
Spanned the farthest ends of Kahiki ;
  Apo Kukuluo Kahiki ;
Finished (explored) is Kahiki by Kaulu,
  Pau Kahiki ia Kaulu,
Finished is Kahiki by Kaulu,
  Pau Kahiki ia Kaulu,
To the coral reefs where the surf is roaring.
  I Koa o Halulukoakoa.
From the time perhaps of Ku,
  Mai ke au paha ia Ku,
From the time perhaps of Lono,
  Mai ke au paha ia Lono,
Broken has been the sacred shell,
  I Wahia ai ka Pumaleolani,[2]
The shell-fish, the porpoise,
  O ka pupu, O ka Naia,
The garlands for the back, the garlands for the breast,
  O ka lei Kua, O ka lei Alo,
The altar, the altar of that one,
  O ka lele, O ka lele o Kela,
Hakuhakualani is my father,
  Hakuhakualani kuu Makuakane,

---

[1] I have rendered *Kuina* by "isthmus;" it may be a proper name of a place or land, but the prefixed article, *ke,* seems to indicate otherwise. *Kuina* is a poetical phrase for an isthmus, its literal meaning being a "junction," the place where two things meet, a seam between two cloths, &c. What particular isthmus is here referred to it is difficult to say.

[2] *Pumaleolani* was the name of a large shell or conch, on which the highest chiefs alone were privileged to blow; and it was tabu for any inferior to touch or break it. Thus the sense of this and the two preceding lines is that from the most ancient times the tabus have been broken and authority disregarded.

The altar, the altar of this one,
O ka lele, O ka lele o keia,
Hakuhakualani is my mother.
Hakuhakualani kuu Makuahine.
Falling are the heavens, rushing through the heavens
Lele ka oili o ka lani, lele i ka lani
Falls the dismal rain, rushing through the heavens
Lele ka ua lokuloku, lele i ka lani
Falls the heavy rain, rushing through the heavens
Lele ka ua hea, lele i ka lani
Falls the gentle rain, rushing through the heavens
Lele ka ua huna, lele i ka lani
Soars the dragonfly, rushing through the heavens,
Lele ka pinaohaololani, lele i ka lani,
Passed away has this one to Moanawaikaioo.
O lele aku keia o Moanawaikaioo.
The strong current, the rolling current, whirl away,
O ke au miki, o ke au ka, e mimilo ai,
It will be overcome by you,—
E make ai ia oe,—
Passing perhaps, remaining perhaps.
E lele paha, e ku paha.

Another ancient Hawaiian bard sung about these foreign regions :—

The noisy sea (around) the island,
Kai wawa ka moku,
The sea of burning coals,
Kai lanahu ahi,
The azure blue sea of Kane.
Kai popolohua mea a Kane.
The birds drink (of the waters) in the Red Sea,
Inu a ka manu i ke kai-ula,
In (the waters of) the Green Sea,
I ke kai a ka omaomao,
Never quiet, never falling, never sleeping,
Aole ku, aole hina, aole moe,
Never very noisy is the sea of the sacred caves.
Aole wawa loa kai a ke ana oku.[1]

Though the legends of *Hema* and of *Kahai* are undoubtedly of southern origin, yet, as evidences of the

---

[1] Where these red or green or otherwise described seas may have been situated it is now hardly possible to determine ; but they certainly were beyond the area of the Pacific Ocean, and in so far attest the distant voyages of the Polynesians of this epoch.

great nautical activity, and the expeditions to far-off foreign lands of this period, the following extracts may be quoted. The chant says of *Hema* :—

> Hema went to Kahiki to fetch the red fillet (circlet or
>   ring),
> *Holo Hema i Kahiki, kii i ke apo-ula,*[1]
> Hema was caught by the Aaia,
> *Loaa Hema, lilo i ka Aaia,*[2]
> He fell dead in Kahiki, in Kapakapakaua,
> *Haule i Kahiki, i Kapakapahaua,*
> He rests in Ulu-paupau.
> *Waiho ai i Ulu-paupau.*[3]

According to the legend, his son *Kahai* started in search of his father or to avenge his death, and the chant describes his expedition :—

> The rainbow is the path of Kahai ;
> *O ke anuenue ke ala o Kahai ;*
> Kahai arose, Kahai bestirred himself,
> *Pii Kahai, Koi Kahai,*
> Kahai passed on on the floating cloud of Kane ;
> *He Kahai i ke Koi ula a Kane ;*
> Perplexed were the eyes of Alihi ;
> *Hihia i na maka o Alihi ;*[4]

---

[1] Other versions of the legend say that Hema went to *Kahiki* to receive the tribute or tax due at the birth of his son, *Kahai*, which tax was called *Palala ;* those legends stating that Hema's wife was from Kahiki.

[2] The *Aaia*, or *Aaia-nuke-a-kane*, is the name of a large sea-bird with white feathers, but in the old legends was a fabulous bird, a messenger of Kane, and dedicated to him.

[3] For explanations of *Kapakapa-ua* and *Ulu-paupau*, see vol. i. pp. 15, 23, 134. According to the chant, *Hema* attempted to revisit those legendary homes of his race and was lost by the way ; and according to the legend of his son, *Kahai*, the voyage of the latter was equally disastrous, at least he never returned.

[4] According to the New Zealand legend of *Kahai* or *Tawhaki*, after he

and his brother *Karihi* had avenged their father's death upon the *Pona-turi* tribe—a race living below the sea in the daytime and on shore at night ("Polynesian Mythology," by Sir G. Grey)—they started to climb up to heaven in search of *Kahai's* celestial wife. *Karihi* slipped and fell back on the earth, and saw, with wonder and amazement, his brother succeeding in getting up into heaven. Hence doubtless the expression in the chant, "perplexed, bewildered, were the eyes of *Alihi*." The Hawaiian legends make no mention of *Kahai's* brother, but this line in the chant confirms the identity of the Hawaiian *Kahai* with the New Zealand, or rather Samoan, *Tawhaki*, and the importation of the legend by the southern emigrants.

Kahai passed on on the glancing light,
Ae Kahai i ke anaha,
The glancing light (on) men and canoes;
He anaha ke kanaka, ka waa ;
Above was Hanaiakamalama,
Ilunao Hanaiakamalama,[1]
That is the road to seek the father of Kahai ;
O ke ala ia i imi ai i ka makua o Kahai ;
Go on over the deep blue ocean,
O hele a i ka moana wehiwehi,
And shake the foundations of heaven.
A halulu i Hale-kumu-kalani.
Inquiring are the retainers of the God,
Ui mai kini o ke akua,
Kane and Kanaloa are asking
Ninau o Kane o Kanaloa [2]
For what purpose is your large travelling party,
Heaha kau huakai nui,
O Kahai, that has come hither?
E Kahai, i hiki mai ai ?
I am seeking for Hema,
I imi mai au i ka Hema,[3]
There in Kahiki, there in Ulupaupau,
Aia i Kahiki, aia i Ulupaupau,

---

[1] *Hanaiakamalama* was the sobriquet of *Hema's* mother, *Hina*. She is said to have been disgusted with her children *Puna* and *Hema*, and to have gone up to the moon to live, but in the act of ascending, her husband, *Aikanaka*, caught her by the leg and tore it off, on account of which she was called *Lono-moku*, "the maimed or crippled Lono." Mr. S. B. Dole, in his translation of this chant published in the "Hawaiian Club Papers," Boston, 1868, gives *Hanaiakamalama* as the "Southern Star." I am not aware of any other legends or chants where this word is used to designate the "Southern Star," or rather the Southern Cross, which was a well-known and important constellation to Polynesian navigators. Its application to the moon was more usual, and in this case would imply that *Kahai* sailed under the protection of his grandmother, who dwelt in the moon.

[2] The placing of *Kanaloa* in the same category of gods as *Kane* shows the southern taint of the chant, although Hawaiian bards, in adopting and rearranging the legend, gave to their own ancient god *Kane* the pre-eminence by placing his name before that of *Kanaloa.*

[3] Here is a play upon the word *Hema*, which was the name of *Kahai's* father, and, with the accent on the first syllable, signifies "the south." From the whole tenor and drift of the literature of this period, I am convinced that the article *ka* before Hema is a Hawaiian alteration in aftertimes, to produce a double meaning, and convey the idea, from a Hawaiian point of view, that while *Kahai* was seeking his father *Hema*, he was also seeking him in places situated at the south of the Hawaiian group.

B

There at the Aaia constantly breathed on by Kane,
Aia i ka Aaia, haha mau ia a Kane,
Reaching to the farthest ends of Kahiki.
Loaa aku i kukulu o Kahiki.

Another extract from the chants of this period preserved by Hawaiian bards shows that the Hawaiian group was well known to the southern tribes of the Pacific. It is a portion of the chant of *Makuakaumana,* the priest who accompanied *Paao,* the southern prince and high priest, on his voyage to establish a new dynasty on Hawaii after the fall of *Kapawa.* *Paao* had offered the throne to *Lono Kaeho,* but he after a while refused, and recommended that *Pili,* surnamed *Kaaiea,* be sent. Following is the portion of the chant preserved; *Makuakaumana* is supposed to be addressing *Lono Kaeho*—

E Lono, E Lono !—E ! E Lonokaeho !
E Lono, E Lono—E ! E Lonokaeho !
Lonokulani, Chief of Kauluonana !
Lonokulani, Alii o Kauluonana !
Here are the canoes ; get on board,
Eia na waa ; kau mai a-i,
Come along, and dwell in Hawaii-with-the-green-back,
E hoi, e noho ia Hawaii-kua-uli,
A land that was found in the ocean
He aina loaa i ka moana,
That was thrown up from the sea,
I hoea mai loko o ka ale,
From the very depths of Kanaloa,
I ka halehale poi pu a Kanaloa.[1]
The white coral in the watery caves
He Koakea i halelo[2] *i ka wai,*
That was caught on the hook of the fisherman,
I lou i ka makau a ka lawaia,
The great fisherman of Kapaahu,
A ka lawaia nui o Kapaahu,
The great fisherman, Kapuheeuanu.
A ke lawaia nui o Kapuheeuanuu-la.[3]

---

[1] This expression refers again to the southern legend that the islands were fished up from the ocean by *Kanaloa.*

[2] Abbreviation from "Halelelo," caves in the sea.

[3] The foregoing lines refer to a legend which states that *Kapuheeuanuu,* a fisherman of *Kapaahu* in Kahiki, being out fishing, caught a lump of coral on his hook. His priest advised him to perform certain religi-

The canoes touch the shore, come on board,
   A pae na waa, kau mai,
Go and possess Hawaii, the island ;
   E holo, e ai ia Hawaii he moku ;
An island is Hawaii,
   He moku Hawaii,
An island is Hawaii, for Lonokaeho to dwell on.
   He moku Hawaii, no Lonokaeho e noho.

Numerous other extracts of ancient legends and chants may be quoted from Hawaiian folklore alone to prove, not only the knowledge, in a general way, of each other's existence, possessed by the Polynesian tribes, but also the intimate and frequent connection between them at this period. Whatever the causes that led to its discontinuance, the fact of its once having existed can no longer be doubted. And the criticism which rests content with the apparent difficulty of navigating the Pacific Ocean in small vessels, without compass, and what may now be considered competent nautical knowledge, has simply failed to inform itself of the conditions and circumstances under which those voyages were undertaken, as well as of the then intellectual status of those who performed them. Certainly the difficulty of the Polynesians navigating the Pacific in their large canoes of that period, whether single or double, was no greater than that of the Norsemen navigating the Atlantic to Iceland, Greenland, and Vinland, or penetrating up the Mediterranean in their " sneckas "

ous rites over the coral and throw it back into the sea, where it would grow into an island and be called *Hawaii-loa ;* and it happened accordingly. Next time the fisherman caught another lump of coral, which in the same manner was sanctified and called *Maui-loa ;* and thus on different occasions the whole Hawaiian group was fished up out of the ocean by *Kapuheeuanuu.* The reference to *Kapaahu,* as being the place where the fisherman belonged, stamps the legend as of southern origin, it being the place in Kahiki whence, according to the legends, *Moikeha* and *Laamaikahiki* departed on their return to Hawaii. From that time Kapaahu became the name of several lands on the Hawaiian group. I have been unable as yet to ascertain if any district or land on any of the southern groups still retains the name of Kapaahu. In Hawaiian legends it is intimately connected with that southern migratory period, as one of the chief places to which and from which the naval expeditions of those days were fitted out.

and "drakes;" nor was the nautical knowledge of the latter any greater than that of the former. We believe the Icelandic folklore which tells of exploits and voyages to far distant lands; why then discredit the Polynesian folklore which tells of voyages between the different groups, undertaken purposely and accomplished safely both in going and returning?[1]

Among the several southern chief families which at this period established themselves on the Hawaiian group, it is now almost impossible to determine the priority of arrival. The *Nana* family, of which *Kapawa* was the last reigning chief on Hawaii, and predecessor to *Pili*, was probably among the earliest arrivals. I have shown (vol. i. p. 200) that this family has been misplaced on the Hawaiian genealogies. *Nanamaoa*, or *Nana-a-Maui*, as he is called in some genealogies, could not possibly be the son of *Maui-a-kalana*, and at the same time the grandfather, or even great-grandfather, of *Kapawa*. I am led to assume, therefore, that *Nanamaoa* was the first of his family who arrived from one or the other of the southern groups and established himself on the Hawaiian group. His son, *Nanakaoko*, was a chief of considerable note on the island of Oahu. He and his wife, *Kahihiokalani*, are by the oldest, and by all the legends, acknowledged as having built the famous and in all subsequent ages hallowed place called *Kukaniloko*, the remains of which are still pointed out about three-fourths of a mile inland from the bridge now crossing the Kaukonahua stream in Ewa district, island of Oahu. Chiefs that were born there were "born in the purple," and enjoyed the dis-

----

[1] The reader will bear in mind the size of the vessels with which Columbus started to discover the new world. Even Drake's celebrated South Sea expedition was composed of vessels the largest of which was only one hundred tons and the smallest was but fifteen tons, the other three ranging at eighty, fifty, and thirty tons.

tinction, privileges, and tabus which that fact conferred.[1]
So highly were those dignities and privileges prized, even
in latest times, when the ancient structure and surroundings had fallen in decay, that *Kamehameha I.*, in 1797,
previous to the birth of his son and successor, *Liholiho
K. II.*, made every arrangement to have the accouchement
take place at Kukaniloko ; but the illness of Queen *Keopuolani* frustrated the design.

Notwithstanding the royal genealogies of both Hawaii
and Maui have expunged the name of *Nanakaoko's* son
Kapawa from their lists, substituting the name of *Helei-
pawa*, and have misplaced *Nanakaoko* some seventeen
generations ahead of his actual time, yet Oahu and Kauai
genealogies, though equally misplacing the *Nana* family
in the series, acknowledge *Kapawa* as the son of *Nanakaoko;* and while the legends—which either come down
contemporary with and independent of the genealogies,
or else are a sort of running commentary upon them—
make brief mention of *Kapawa*, they are positive and
plain on three episodes of his life, which, if we recognise
him as the contemporary of *Paumakua*, have all the air of
probability, and doubtless are historically true, but which,
if referred to fifteen or seventeen generations earlier,
would bring us away from the Hawaiian group altogether,
and land us in that nebulous region of myth and legend
which characterises the whole southern element, at least
in Hawaiian tradition, from the time of *Ulu* up to this
migratory period now under consideration. Those three
events in *Kapawa's* life were, that he was born at *Kukaniloko* aforesaid;[2] that he was buried at *Iao*, an equally

[1] Here was kept the sacred drum, *Hawea*, which announced to the assembled and expectant multitude the birth of a tabu chief.

[2] Some legends call *Kapawa* a chief of Wailua district, island of Oahu. As he was born at Kukaniloko, his youth may have been passed at Wailua, and hence the epithet of " Ke Alii o Wailua." Oahu legends make no further mention of *Kapawa*, or of his subsequent career; but Hawaii legends declare distinctly that he was the predecessor of *Pili* as chief over Hawaii, and that for his bad government or other wickedness he had been deposed or expelled. Even the notice of his death and burial at Iao comes to us through the *Paao* and *Pili* legends.

hallowed burying-place of ancient chiefs situated in the valley of Wailuku on the island of Maui; and that he was the last sovereign or supreme chief of the island of Hawaii previous to the arrival of *Pili,* surnamed *Kaaiea.*

Kapawa is the first Hawaiian chief whom tradition mentions as having been buried at *Iao;* but as no allusion is made anywhere to him as the founder of that sacred burial-place, the presumption is that it was instituted previous, though by whom or when is now unknown. During this period, however, and in after ages, it was considered as great an honour to be buried at *Iao* as to have been born at *Kukaniloko.* What the particular crimes of *Kapawa* may have been which lost him the sovereignty of Hawaii, tradition does not mention. Whatever they were, if any, it is presumable that they were imputed to him by those who succeeded him; and it is equally probable that *Paao,* that southern chief and high priest who constituted his own family as a hereditary priesthood on Hawaii, had more or less to do with the downfall of *Kapawa.* On the expulsion or death of *Kapawa, Paao* sent to "Kahiki" for some one of the southern chiefs to come and take possession of the vacant sovereignty. *Lonokaeho* was first applied to, but refused; and then *Pili Kaaiea* was advised to go, and he came to Hawaii, and by the assistance of *Paao* was established as the territorial sovereign of that island, *Paao* remaining his high priest. And from *Pili* the ruling Hawaiian chiefs, down to the *Kamehameha* family, claimed their descent; and, as if conscious of their usurpation or intrusion upon the domestic line, their genealogists and bards in subsequent ages were always trying to connect *Pili* with the indigenous chiefs on the Maui line from *Paumakua* and *Haho;* and the occasional matrimonial alliances of those *Pili* descendants with Oahu or Kauai chiefs or chiefesses of the ancient *Nanaulu* line were always considered an honour, and dwelt on with no small emphasis in the Meles (songs) and legends.

The next families of note derived from this southern immigrating element of this period were the two *Paumakuas*, the one claiming descent from *Puna* and the other from his brother *Hema*, both of the *Ulu* line. The former family spread over Oahu and Kauai, the latter on Maui and Hawaii. The Oahu *Paumakuas* may have arrived in the time of the grandfather *Newalani*,[1] or even earlier; certain it is that the *Paumakua* of this branch was born on Oahu, at Kuaaohe in Kailua, Koolaupoko, that he died on Oahu, and was buried at Iao on Maui. The Maui *Paumakuas*, on the other hand, probably did not arrive earlier than the time of the father, *Huanuikala-lailai*, if *Paumakua* himself was not the first arrival of that family, along with his brother *Kuheailani*. And though the Maui and Hawaii dynasties ever kept the *Paumakua*, whom they claimed as ancestor, distinctly descending on the *Hema* branch of the *Ulu* line, yet they never scrupled in after ages to appropriate to him the legends and events connected with the Oahu *Paumakua*,

---

[1] To judge from an ancient legend, *Newalani* had another son beside *Lonohoo-Newa*, the father of *Pauma-kua*. This son was called *Kahano-a-Newa*, and is mentioned as the *Kahu* (guardian or foster-father) of *Kahihi-ku-o ka-lani*, whom there is reason to believe was the same as *Kahihio-ka-lani*, the wife of *Nanakaoko* and mother of *Kapawa*. If so, it establishes beyond a doubt the contemporaneity and relationship of *Kapawa* and *Paumakua*, as well as their southern extraction. With a singular blending in after ages of ancient reminiscences and ancient myths, the legend speaks of this *Kahano-a-Newa* as a great sorcerer—a prominent characteristic of most of the southern celebrities—who "stretched out his hands to the farthest bounds of Kahiki, and on them," as on a bridge, "came the *Menehune* people to Oahu;" and the places assigned them to live in were Kailua in the Koolau district, and Pauoa and Puowaina in the Kona district; and it is said that they were introduced to be the servants of *Kahihi-ku-o ka-lani*, and that they were employed to build the Heiaus of Mauiki, Kaheiki, Kawaewae, Eku, Kamoalii, and Kuaokala. It is further stated, probably in reference to some remarkable eclipse, that "when the sun vanished and the earth became dark, *Kahano* brought the sun back again." It is impossible to determine the date of this legend, but the ancient national appellation of *Menehune* must have become obsolete long before that, and forgotten by the compiler. The mention of the *Menehune* as servants of a chiefess of known southern extraction marks the legend as a product of that southern element, especially Tahitian, where *Menehune* had become the name for the lowest labouring class of the people.

and which apparently they borrowed from Kauai and Oahu sources. And when in later times, previous to the discovery of the islands by Captain Cook, and subsequently during the long reign of *Kamehameha I.*, the Hawaii and Maui dynasties had gained a decided preponderance and political supremacy, their versions of legends and genealogies passed undisputed, and it became treason to criticise them. Hence no little confusion in the national records and great embarrassment to the critical student who endeavours to elicit the truth from these conflicting relics of the past. Fortunately, both Oahu and Kauai genealogies have survived, and by their aid, and by the legends attached to them, it is possible to disentangle the apparent snarl of the various versions, and reduce the pretensions of the Hawaii and Maui genealogists and bards to limits conformable with historical truth.

Thus brought to the test, and divested of the embellishments of the raconteurs and the poetical frenzy of the bards, the Hawaiian folklore of this period establishes the following main facts :—That the family of the Oahu *Paumakua*, the son of *Lonohoonewa*, had been in the country for two if not three or more generations before *Paumakua* was born ; that the family of the Maui *Paumakua*, the son of *Huanuikalalailai*, probably arrived with the said *Paumakua* himself ; that the voyages to foreign lands, exploits, and adventures promiscuously ascribed by later legends to *Paumakua*, the ancestor of the Maui and Hawaii chiefs, in reality belong to the Oahu *Paumakua* of the *Puna* branch on the *Ulu* line.[1]

The various legends referring to this *Paumakua* relate

[1] There was a legend from which S. M. Kamakau culled the notice that *Huanuikalalailai* was buried at Niuula, Honokohau, Maui, and that he was the ancestor ("Kupuna"), or, according to the genealogies, the great-grandfather, of the famous *Kana* and *Niheu-Kalohe*, of whom more hereafter. I know not the origin of the other legend which Kamakau strangely mixes up with the foregoing, and which says that *Huanuikalalailai*—so called by the people for his liberal and good government, but whose proper name was *Hua-kama-pau*—was an Oahu chief who ruled in Honolulu and Waikiki, and was born at Kewalo,

more or less of his wanderings in foreign lands; how he circumnavigated the world ("*Kaapuni Kahiki*"), meaning thereby all foreign lands outside of the Hawaiian group. One of these legends relates that on his return from one of his foreign voyages he brought back with him to Oahu two white men, said to have been priests, *Auakahinu* and *Auakamea*, afterwards named *Kaekae* and *Maliu*, and from whom several priestly families in after ages claimed their descent and authority. The legend further states that *Paumakua* on the same occasion also brought a prophet ("*Kaula*") called *Malela*, but whether the latter was also a white man the tradition is not so explicit. Another legend relates that when *Paumakua* returned from foreign voyages he brought with him three white persons, called *Kukahauula*, *Kukalcpa*, and *Haina-Pole*, a woman, The latter legend, however, appears to me to be a Maui or Hawaii *réchauffée* of the original Oahu legend, and for this reason, that in all subsequent times no Maui or Hawaii priestly family traced their descent to either *Kaekae* or *Maliu*, which, with perhaps one or two exceptions on Kauai, flourished exclusively on Oahu.

The white foreigners who came with *Paumakua* are in the legend said to have been "*Ka haole nui, maka alohilohi, ke a aholehole, maka aa, ka puaa keokeo nui, maka ulaula*" ("Foreigners of large stature, bright sparkling eyes, white cheeks, roguish, staring eyes, large white hogs[1] with reddish faces"). A fragment of an ancient chant referring to this occurrence has been preserved, and reads—

> *O Paumakua, ka lani o Moenaimua,*
> O Paumakua, the lord of Moenaimua,

---

between these two places; but in view of the foregoing observations, and the fact that the Ohau and Kauai genealogies do not know him, I look upon it as one of many other similar attempts on the part of Hawaiian bards to give him and other dubious names on the *Ulu-Hema* line an in-digenous *locus standi* when their foreign pedigrees, whether Tahitian or Samoan, had been forgotten or obscured.

[1] It is not uncommon in the ancient Meles to find the word *Puaa* (lit. "hog") applied to persons. It was a poetical and sacerdotal expression.

O ke Alii nana i hele ke Kahiki,
O the chief who went to Tahiti,
A Kahiki i ke kaiakea,
Tahiti in the open ocean,
O mimo, o momi, o ka mamio,
The gentle, the precious, the prosperous,
O ka ia mailoko,[1] *o ka Auakahinu*
(And) the fish within (were) Auakahinu,
O Auakamea ia lani.
(And) Auakamea the noble.

There is a discrepancy in the Oahu genealogies leading up to *Paumakua.* Some of them make *Moenaimua* his son and *Kumakaha* his grandson; others pass over *Moenaimua* in silence and make *Kumakaha* the son of *Paumakua.* Judging from analogy on other well-known genealogies of much later age, I am inclined to think that both *Moenaimua* and *Kumakaha* were the sons of *Paumakua*, and introduced successively by bards in after times with that persistent vanity of making the line of descent as long as possible which characterised the entire fraternity of Hawaiian genealogists and bards.

Besides his extensive voyages to foreign countries, and his introduction of the two priests of an alien race, said to be white, and that some legends ascribe the custom and ceremony of circumcision to *Paumakua*—a fact disputed by others—little is known of his reign and influence on the island of Oahu. A reference to the genealogical table will show that he was the ancestor in the fourth generation of the famous *Laa-mai-kahiki*, from whom every succeeding generation of chiefs took a special pride in claiming their descent.

Giving thus all due credit to the *Paumakua* of the *Puna* line, whom the Oahu and Kauai chiefs exalted and glorified as their ancestor, there is little to tell of the Maui *Paumakua* of the *Hema* line, the son of *Huanui-kalalailai*, and brother of *Kuheailani.* Through his son

---

[1] A poetical phrase signifying that the fish that he caught, the treasure he found in his net on his voyage, were the foreigners *Auakahinu* and *Auakamea.*

Haho and grandson *Palena* he became the great-grandfather and progenitor of the noted *Hanalaa,* whom both the Maui and Hawaii chiefs contended for as their ancestor under the varying names of *Hanalaa-nui* and *Hanalaa-iki,* asserting that *Palena* was the father of twins who bore those names. Up to the time of the conquest of the islands, the Maui chiefs claimed *Hanalaa-nui* as their ancestor, and assigned *Hanalaa-iki* to the Hawaii chiefs; but after the conquest by *Kamehameha I.,* the claim of the Hawaii chiefs prevailed, and no genealogy recited after that ventured to give Maui the precedence in the claim upon the two brothers.

Here, again, the Oahu traditions come in as an umpire to settle the contention which for so many generations disturbed the peace and ruffled the temper of its windward neighbours, and destroy the illusion of the *Hanalaa* twins, into which even the Maui genealogists had fallen while hotly contending for their own priority over the Hawaii branch. This Oahu tradition is contained in an ancient chant or genealogical register, evidently once the property of the powerful *Kalona* families on Oahu, who claimed descent from *Maweke* as well as from *Laamaikahiki,* and who must reasonably be supposed competent to discriminate between the *Paumakua,* from whom their own *Laamaikahiki* descended, and this *Paumakua,* from whom the Maui *Hanalaa* descended. This register, while observing the requirements of chronology and contemporaneity, as mostly all the *Nanaulu* registers do, brings the *Piliwale* branch of the *Kalonas* up to this Maui *Paumakua,* descending from him through *Haho, Palena, Hanalaa, Mauiloa, Alo, Kuhimana,* &c., to *Mailikukahi,* the father of the *Kalonas.* This chant says nothing of two *Hanalaas;* it knows but one; and when the undisputed fact is taken into consideration that *Pili,* from whom the Hawaii chiefs reckon their lineal descent, was an emigrant chief from the southern groups, the attempt to piece his lineage on to already existing Hawaiian lines becomes too palpably untrue to deserve any notice. The chant or register referred to is probably not much later in time than the reign of *Kalaimanuia* on Oahu, the grand-daughter of *Piliwale*, or twelve generations ago; but it is invaluable as a protest from olden time, and from those who in later ages were generally admitted as the best informed, against the exaggerated inflations and unscrupulous interpolations practised on the national registers by genealogists and bards in the service of Hawaii and Maui chiefs.

But though this Maui *Paumakua* is not remembered in song or legend for anything remarkable that he did or performed, yet his son, the afore-mentioned *Haho*, has gone down to posterity and been remembered by all succeeding ages throughout the group as the founder of the *Aha-Alii*, an institution which literally means "the congregation of chiefs," and, in a measure, may be compared to a heralds' college; and to gain admission into which it was incumbent on the aspirant to its rank and privileges to announce his name, either personally or through an accompanying bard, and his descent, either lineal or collateral, from some one or more of the recognised, undisputed ancestors ("*Kupuna*") of the Hawaiian nobility, claiming such descent either on the *Nanaulu* or *Ulu* line. "Once a chief always a chief," was the Hawaiian rule of heraldry, and no treason, crime, or lesser offence ever affected the rank or dignity in the *Aha-Alii* of the offender or of his children. There was no "bill of attainder" in those days.

There were gradations of rank and tabu within the *Aha-Alii*, well understood and seldom infringed upon. No chief could fall from his rank, however his possessions and influence might vane; and none could rise higher himself in the ranks of the *Aha-Alii* than the source from which he sprang either on mother's or father's side; but he might in several ways raise the rank of his children higher than his own, such as by marriage with a chiefess of higher rank than his own, marrying with a sister, or by their adoption into a family of higher rank than that of the father.

The privileges and prerogatives of the *Aha-Alii* were well defined and universally known, both as regards their intercourse with each other and their relation to the commonalty, the *Makaainana*. Their allegiance or fealty to a superior chief was always one of submission to superior force, of personal interest, or of family attachment, and continued as long as the pressure, the interest, or the attachment was paramount to other considerations; but the slightest injury, affront, or slight on the part of the superior, or frequently the merest caprice, would start the inferior chief into revolt, to maintain himself and his possessions by arms if able, or he fled to some independent chief of the other islands, who almost invariably gave him an asylum and lands to live on until a change of affairs made it safe to return to his former home.

A chief of the *Aha-Alii*, if taken captive in war, might be, and sometimes was, offered in sacrifice to the gods, but he or his family were never made slaves if their lives were spared. And if the captive chief was of equal or higher rank than his captor, he invariably received the deference and attention due to his rank, and his children not unfrequently found wives or husbands in the family of the conqueror. A chief of the *Aha-Alii* was of right entitled to wear the insignia of his rank whenever he pleased: the feather wreath, the *Lei-hulu*—the feather cloak or cape, the *Ahu-Ula*—the ivory clasp, the *Palaoa;* his canoe and its sail were painted red, and he wore a pennon at the masthead.

Among the members of the *Aha-Alii* it was not unusual that two young men adopted each other as brothers, and by that act were bound to support each other in weal or woe at all hazards, even that of life itself; and if in after life these two found themselves, in war time, in opposing ranks, and one was taken prisoner, his life was invariably spared if he could find means to make himself known to his foster-brother on the opposite side, who was bound to obtain it from the captor or the commanding chief. And there is no instance on record in all the legends and traditions that this singular friendship ever made default.

Such were some of the leading features of the *Aha-Alii*, which all existing traditions concur in asserting was instituted by *Haho* about twenty-five generations ago. It arose, probably, as a necessity of the existing condition of things during this migratory period, as a protection of the native aristocracy against foreign pretenders, and as a broader line of demarcation between the nobility and the commonalty. It lasted up to the time of the conquest by *Kamehameha I.*, after which this, as so many other heathen customs, good, bad, or indifferent, gradually went under in the light of newer ideas, new forms of government, and new religion. At present there is no Aha-Alii, though there is a "House of Nobles," in which the foreign-born number ten to nine of the native-born, and few of these latter recall to the minds of the common people the great historical names of former days, the great feudal lords on this or that island, who, still within the memory of yet living people, could summon a thousand vassals or more to work their fields and do their bidding.

Nothing remarkable has been retained upon Hawaiian traditions about *Kuheailani*, the brother of this Maui *Paumakua*. His son, *Hakalanileo*, appears to have become lord of some lands in the Hilo district of Hawaii, and married a chiefess of southern descent named *Hina*, or, in some legends, *Hoohoakalani*, whose mother, *Uli*, came from Kahiki by some one or other of those southern expeditions of the period. The abduction and recovery of this Lady *Hina* or *Hooho* is the subject of one of the most popular legends of olden time. Though this legend is bristling with marvellous and fabulous exploits, yet doubtless an historical basis underlies the superstructure of later times, and is confirmed by other legends of contemporary and later date. When stripped of their poetical and fictitious drapery, the facts appear to have been these :—

At the time of *Hakalanileo*, the son of *Kuheailani*, there lived on the island of Molokai a powerful family of the ancient native chiefs. Tradition has not preserved the pedigree of this family beyond that of the father of the subject of this legend, but its connection with the ancient *Nanaulu* line is frequently affirmed. The father of this family was *Kamauaua*,[1] who seems to have been the superior chief of Molokai. Among his several sons, the second, *Keoloewa*, succeeded his father in the sovereignty of the island, and married *Nuakea*, the granddaughter of *Maweke*, and daughter of *Keaunui*, and sister of *Lakona*, all famous and powerful chiefs on Oahu. The eldest son of *Kamauaua* was called *Kaupeepee-nui-kauila*, and he dwelt on [a promontory or mountain-neck called Haupu, situated on the north side of Molokai.[2] This promontory was strongly fortified by art as well as by nature, and was in those days considered impregnable. From this stronghold *Kaupeepee* sallied forth in search of adventures, possibly plunder, and on one of his excursions off the coast of Hilo he saw and became enamoured of the beautiful *Hina*, the wife of *Hakalanileo*. To see and to desire to possess was the logical operation of the chieftain's mind. He succeeded in carrying off the lady, and returned with her without mishap to his mountain eyrie. So skilfully laid were the plans of *Kaupeepee*, and so well executed, that the bereaved husband was for a long

---

[1] The children of *Kamauaua* and his wife *Hinakeha* were *Kaupeepee-nui-kauila, Keoloewa, Haili*, and *Ulihala-nui*. The adventures of the first will be treated of immediately ; the second was noted as the head and progenitor of numerous powerful families throughout the group, whose pedigrees reach up to him and his wife *Nuakea* ; the third I have only encountered once in the traditions referring to this family, and then he is quoted as an ancestor of *Kanikaniaula*, one of the wives of *Kakaalaneo* of Maui and mother of the famous *Kaululaau* ; of the fourth no further mention has been preserved.

[2] Between Pelekunu and Waikolo.

time ignorant of what had become of his wife or who was her abductor. He travelled over Hawaii and Maui, seeking and inquiring, but got no tidings of the lost one. Years rolled on, and the young sons of *Hina*, having grown up to manhood, took up the search which their father had abandoned. These sons were called *Kana* and *Niheu-Kalohe*. They are said to have been instructed by their grandmother, *Uli*, in all the arts of sorcery and witchcraft, for which the southern immigrants were noted and feared by the previous inhabitants of the Hawaiian group. The sons soon discovered where their mother was kept captive, and measures were taken for her liberation. *Kaupeepee* was warned by his *Kaula*, or prophet, *Moi*, the brother of *Nuakea*, the wife of his brother *Keoloewa*, that bad days were approaching, and that the sons of *Hina* were coming to the rescue of their mother. Secure in his mountain fastness, the chief scorned the advice and defied the sons of the outraged lady. On the episodes and details of the war that ensued I will not dwell. They are so mixed up with the fabulous and supernatural, that it is almost impossible to disentangle a thread of truth in the whole account. But of the result of the war there is no doubt whatever. By force, by stratagem, by treachery, or by all combined, the fortress was taken and demolished, *Kapeepee* slain, the Lady *Hina* delivered and returned to *Hakalanileo*, and the prowess and skill of the southern element in this expedition retained upon the songs and sagas of all succeeding generations.

The embellishments of the marvels and of the skill and adroitness which adorn this legend, indicate that the form it now possesses was given to it in much later times, probably during the period of Hawaiian intellectual activity which characterised the nearly contemporary reigns of the *Kawulos* on Kauai, the *Kakuhihewas* of Oahu, the *Kamalalawalu* of Maui, and the *Keawenuiaumi* of Hawaii and his children, when so many of the old traditions and still older myths received a new dress and a new circulation among the court circles and the commonalty of those days.

The two heroes of the legend, *Kana*—who is said to have disdained the use of canoes, and, by a faculty peculiar to himself, like the joints of a telescope or a Japanese fishing-rod, could walk with his head above the water through the deepest ocean—and his brother *Niheukalohe*, renowned for his cunning, his skill, and his trickery, left no progeny to claim their honours; and though *Hakalanileo* and *Hina* had three other children mentioned in the tradition, viz., *Kekahawalu, Kepani*, and *Haka*, yet in all my collections of Hawaiian genealogies I have found none and heard of none that ascended to either of *Hakalanileo's* children.

Before referring to *Pili*, surnamed *Kaaiea*, from whom the principal chief families on Hawaii claimed descent to present times, the family and legend of *Paao* arrests our attention.

Forty years ago there were two sets of traditions current regarding *Paao*. They were nearly similar in most points, but differed in some essentials. The one legend, collected and referred to by David Malo, the Hawaiian antiquarian, states that *Paao* came from "Wawao;" that having quarrelled with his brother *Lonopele*, he left and proceeded to Hawaii, where he established himself in the capacity of a high priest; and finding the island in a state of anarchy and without a sovereign chief "on account of the crimes of *Kapawa*, the chief of Hawaii," he sent back (another legend says he went back himself) to his native island, inviting some chief there to come and take possession of Hawaii. To which invitation *Pili* responded, and, having arrived at Hawaii, was confirmed in the government by *Paao*, whose family, after him, remained the high priests of the reigning chiefs of Hawaii, until after *Kamehameha I.* The other legend, collected and referred to by S. M. Kamakau, another Hawaiian antiquary, states that *Paao* came from " *Upolo,*" though he possessed lands at " *Wawao,*" and in the islands still farther south; that having quarrelled, as above mentioned, with his brother *Lonopele,* he left in company with *Pili-kaaiea, Pili's* wife *Hinaauaku,* his own sister *Namauuo-malaia,* and thirty-five others, relatives and retainers, and after a long and dangerous voyage, arrived at the island of Hawaii, where he established himself in the district of Kohala, and *Pili* became sovereign chief of the island of Hawaii. It is possible that *Paao, Pili,* &c., came from Wawao, one of the Tonga group, as the legend quoted by D. Malo asserts; but I think it hardly probable, for reasons that I will now set forth. Counting the greater distance from Wawao to the Hawaiian group as nothing to the adventurous spirits of those times, yet the legend quoted by Kamakau covers the whole ground when it states that *Paao,* a native of Upolo in the Samoan group, " owned lands in Wawao and in the islands farther south." The continued intercourse between the Tonga and Samoan groups is well ascertained from the earliest times, and it would have been nothing unusual for a Samoan chief to own lands in the Tonga or Hapai groups. The cause of *Paao's* departure from Upolo to seek a new establishment in other lands, as narrated by Hawaiian tradition, bears so strong a resemblance to the Samoan legend brought by the first emigrants to New Zealand, and narrated by Sir George Grey in his " Polynesian Mythology and Ancient Traditional History of the New Zealand Race," London, John Murray, 1855, page 202, &c., that it is easy to recognise that both legends are but different versions of one and the same event. The Hawaiian version, whatever embellishments it may have received in subsequent ages, came substantially to Hawaii during this migratory period we are now considering, from twenty-one to twenty-seven generations ago, and is quoted as an explanation of why

Paao left Upolo in the Samoan group. The New Zealand version goes back, at best, only fifteen generations on New Zealand soil, and is offered as an explanation of why the Samoan chief *Turi* left Hawaiki (Sawaii) for New Zealand, but how many generations that legend may have been current in the Samoan group before the departure of *Turi* there is no means of knowing. Thus, whatever credibility may attach to the legend as an historical relic, yet the similarity of the cast of the drama in each, and the fact of its being avowedly derived, both in New Zealand and Hawaii, from Samoan sources, would seem to confirm that one of the Hawaiian legends which claims *Paao* and *Pili* and their companions as coming from the Samoan group, notably the island of Upolo.

The only other places in the Samoan group mentioned in the Hawaiian legends of *Paao* which may help to identify the particular place from which *Paao* came, are called "the mountains of Malaia" and "the cliff of Kaakoheo," the latter overlooking the beach from which *Paao* took his departure. Whether any such mountain and cliff still exist by those names on the island of Upolu or any of the Samoan islands, I am unable to say. Samoan archæologists may be able to throw light on that subject.

Paao is said to have made his first landfall in the district of Puna, Hawaii, where he landed and built a Heiau (temple) for his god and called it *Wahaula*. The ruins of this Heiau still remain a short distance south of the village of Kahawalea in Puna,[1] but it is almost impossible now to say what portions of it date back to the time of *Paao*, seeing that it was almost entirely rebuilt by *Imaikalani*, a noted chief over the Puna and Kau districts *tempore Keawenui-a-umi*, some twelve or thirteen generations ago, and was again repaired or improved in the time of *Kalaniopuu*, who died 1782. It was the very last Heiau that was destroyed after the tabus were abrogated by *Kamehameha II.* in 1820. It was built in the

[1] On the land called Pulama.

quadrangular or parallelogram form which characterised all the Heiaus built under and after the religious régime introduced by *Paao*, and in its enclosure was a sacred grove, said to have contained one or more specimens of every tree growing on the Hawaiian group, a considerable number of which, or perhaps their descendants, had survived when last the author visited the place in 1869.

From Puna *Paao* coasted along the shores of the Hilo and Hamakua districts, and landed again in the district of Kohala, on a land called Puuepa, near the north-west point of the island, whose name, "*Lae Upolu*," was very probably bestowed upon it by *Paao* or his immediate descendants in memory of their native land. In this district of Hawaii *Paao* finally and permanently settled. Here are shown the place where he lived, the land that he cultivated, and at Puuepa are still the ruins of the Heiau of *Mookini*, which he built and where he officiated. It was one of the largest Heiaus in the group, an irregular parallelogram in form, with walls more than twenty feet high and fully eight feet wide on the top; its longest sides are two hundred and eighty-six and two hundred and seventy-seven feet, and the shorter one hundred and thirty-six and one hundred and eighteen feet. The stones of which it is built are said to have come from Niulii, a land in Kohala, nine miles distant from Puuepa; and, as an instance of the density of population at that time, tradition says that the building-stones were passed by hand from man to man all the way from Niulii, a feat requiring at least some fifteen thousand working men at three feet apart. Ten years ago, when I visited the place, the walls of the Heiau were still unimpaired. The then Circuit Judge of that part of the island, Mr. Naiapaakai, who was well conversant with the ancient lore of the district, and who accompanied me to the ruins, showed me a secret well or crypt in the south side of the walls, east of the main entrance, several feet deep, but now filled up with stones and boulders of similar nature to those that com-

pose the wall. Having climbed on the top of the wall
and removed the stones out of the well, we found at the
bottom two *Maika* stones of extraordinary size, which
were said to be the particular *Ulu* which *Paao* brought
with him from foreign lands, and with which he amused
himself when playing the favourite game of *Maika*. These
stones were as large as the crown of a common-sized hat,
two inches thick at the edges and a little thicker in the
middle. They were of a white, fine-grained, hard stone,
that may or may not be of Hawaiian quarrying: I am not
geologist enough to say. I have seen many *Maika* stones
from ancient times, of from two to three inches diameter,
of a whitish straw colour, but never seen or heard of any
approaching these of *Paao* in size or whiteness. Though
they are called the *Maika* stones of *Paao*—" *Na Ulu a
Paao* "—yet their enormous size would apparently forbid
their employment for that purpose. If Maika stones, and
really intended and used for that purpose, there could be
no conceivable necessity for hiding them in the bottom of
this crypt or well in the wall of the Heiau. In this un-
certainty the legend itself may throw some light on the
subject when it says that " *Paao* brought two idols with
him from Upolu, which he added to those already worshipped by the Hawaiians." Though almost every legend
that treats of *Paao* more or less mentions the changes
and innovations which he effected in the ancient worship,
yet no tradition that I have heard mentions the names of
those two idols or where they were deposited. May not,
then, these so-called Maika stones of *Paao*, so carefully
hidden in the walls of the Heiau, be those idols that *Paao*
brought with him ? Their presence there is a riddle ;
and the superstitious fear with which they are treated or
spoken of by the elder inhabitants of the district evinces
in a measure the consideration in which they were anciently held, that certainly would never have been bestowed on a chief's playthings like actual Maika stones.
When the tabus were abrogated, when the Heiaus were

doomed, when Christian zealots proved the genuineness
of their new faith by burning the objects of faith of their
fathers, and when the ancient gods were stripped of their
kapas and feathers and their altars overturned, then many
a devotee, a *Kahu* or servant of special Heiaus or individual gods, hid the object of his adoration in caves, in
streams, in mountain recesses, in the mud of swamps or
other unfrequented places, in hopes of the better days
which never came. Thus many a Kahu died and made
no sign, and the idol he cherished has only been discovered by accident. And so these stones, if they were
the idols of *Paao,* may have been hidden at some previous
time of change or improvement in the Heiau or its culte
—perhaps when it was repaired by *Alapai-nui* of Hawaii,
the stepson and usurping successor of *Keawe,* the great-
grandfather of *Kamehameha I.*—or when the tabus were
abolished and Christianity introduced in 1820–30.

The priesthood in the family of *Paao* continued until
the last high priest on Hawaii, *Hewahewanui,* joined *Liho-
liho Kamehameha II.* and *Kaahumanu* in abrogating the
tabus. Several families at this day claim descent from
Paao.

That both *Pili* and his wife *Hinaauaku* were of foreign
birth, probably from Upolu of the Samoans, there can be
no doubt. The name of his wife, *Hina,* with the sobriquet *auaku,* is a thoroughly southern name, a common
and favourite appellation of female chiefs on the *Ulu* line,
both on the *Hema* and *Puna* branches, but was utterly
unknown or discontinued among the members of the
Nanaulu line (the Hawaiian) from the days of *Kii,* the
father of both *Ulu* and *Nanaulu.*

Of *Pili's* exploits scant mention is made in the legends
beyond the main fact that he established himself and his
family firmly on the island of Hawaii.

The genealogical tree published by David Malo, and quoted on page 191, vol. i., represents *Pili* as the father of *Koa*, the grandfather of *Ole*, and great-grandfather of *Kukohou*. I believe this to be another interpolation in subsequent ages, when the memory of the names alone were retained and the order of succession more or less forgotten. Judging from analogy of other genealogies, *Koa* and *Ole* may have been brothers of *Pili*; or *Koa*, *Ole*, and *Kukohau* may all have been sons of *Pili*. There are no legends serving as commentaries to their genealogy, and the Meles are silent respecting them. Moreover, the names of their wives, *Hina-aumai*, *Hina-mailelii*, *Hina-keuki*, are all of southern extraction, and indicate a simultaneous arrival. *Kukohou* may have been the son of *Pili*, and his wife the daughter of some other southern chief who accompanied *Pili* to Hawaii; but that *Koa*, *Ole*, and *Kukohou* were son, grandson, and great-grandson of *Pili*, as the Hawaiian genealogy current at the court of *Kamehameha*, and quoted by David Malo, has it, I think historically impossible. I have shown that the most sober and trustworthy traditions concur in making *Pili* the successor of *Kapawa* as sovereign chief of Hawaii, and that *Pili* either accompanied or followed *Paao* to Hawaii, not as explorers or first discoverers, but when the Polynesian migratory wave was at its full height, and the Hawaiian group was already well known to southern chieftains and their wise men and bards. *Pili* therefore must have been contemporary with the grandchildren of *Maweke* of the *Nanaulu* line, established on Oahu and Kauai, with *Keoloewa* of Molokai, with *Haho* of Maui. When to this is added the undisputed, and by the *Pili* descendants never-forgotten fact, that *Kanipahu* of the *Pili* posterity married *Hualani*, the great-granddaughter of *Nuakea*, who was granddaughter of *Maweke* and wife of *Keoloewa*, there is no room on a correct pedigree for *Koa* and *Ole* as being son and grandson of *Pili*.

Of *Kanipahu's* father, *Kaniuhu*, the legends are silent,

but of *Kanipahu* himself we gather the following from
his legends:—

Beside *Hualani*, of Molokai and Oahu descent above
mentioned, he also married *Alaikauakoko*, who at one time,
whether previously or subsequently cannot now be ascertained, was the wife of *Lakona*, the son of *Nawele*, who
was the great-grandson of *Kumuhonua* the brother of
Moikeha. With the latter he had a son, *Kalapana*, surnamed *Kuioiomoa* ; with the former he had four children,
called *Kanaloa, Kumuokalani, Laaikiahualani,* and *Kalahuimoku.* Up to this time the *Pili* family does not
appear to have been so firmly seated in the sovereignty of
Hawaii, but that occasional disturbances occurred with
the ancient chief families of the island. It is related that
a scion of one of those families named *Kamaiole* had
revolted against *Kanipahu*, and, being successful, had
driven him out of Hawaii. *Kanipahu* left his sons with
some trusted friend in the secluded valley of Waimanu,
Hamakua district, and sought refuge for himself on the
island of Molokai, where, at Kalae, he lived as a simple
commoner, doing his own work and carrying his own
burdens. Years rolled on, and *Kamaiole* ruled Hawaii
with such oppressiveness and severity that the people at
length became wearied and disgusted with his sway, and
went to the head of the *Paao* family, the high priest of
Hawaii, for advice and aid. The priest sent messengers
to *Kanipahu* on Molokai asking him to return to Hawaii
and resume the government. *Kanipahu* refused, as the
legend says, because he was ashamed of the hump on his
shoulders contracted during the many years of hard and
toilsome labour that he had lived on Molokai, but he
directed the messengers to go to Waimanu, where they
would find his son *Kalapana*, on whom he devolved the
war with *Kamaiole* and the government of Hawaii. On
the receipt of this information from *Kanipahu* the high
priest sent for *Kalapana*, who raised an army among the
discontented and gave battle to the usurper at a place

called Anaehoomalu in Kekaha, North Kona. *Kamaiole* was defeated and slain, and *Kalapana* was installed sovereign chief of Hawaii. *Kanipahu* remained on Molokai, and died there.

As *Kanipahu* was contemporary with *Laa-mai-kahiki* at the close of this migratory period, I will leave the *Pili* family at present, in order to notice some other prominent men of southern descent whose names have been preserved on the national legends.

Among those, the one whose fate probably arrested most attention, and served as a warning in after ages when chiefs ventured to oppose the priesthood, was *Hua*, with the sobriquet of *a-Kapuaimanaku*, in distinction from *Hua-nui-kalalailai*, the father of the Maui *Paumakua*. In the royal genealogies of both Hawaii and Maui this *Hua* is placed as third in ascent from *Paumakua*, to whom he is represented as having been the great-grandfather; but when the legends referring to him are critically scanned, and regard had to the contemporaneity of the other personages therein mentioned, his proper place would be three generations later than *Paumakua*. It is probable that he belonged to that southern *Hua* family from which *Paumakua* and *Haho* descended. He is said to have been king of Maui, and lived principally at Hana, Kauwiki. The earliest remembered war between Maui and Hawaii is said to have been conducted by him, who invaded Hawaii, and at Hakalau, in the district of Hilo, thoroughly defeated the Hawaii chiefs. The Hawaiian legends call that war by the name of *Kaniuhoohio*. One time, while residing on East Maui, *Hua* got into a dispute with his priest and prophet, *Luahoomoe*, about some birds called "Uwau," and became so angry that he resolved upon the death of the priest. *Luahoomoe*, conscious of the fate that awaited him, gave directions to his two sons, *Kaakakai* and *Kaanahua*, how to escape the vengeance of the king. In due time, according to ancient custom, the house of *Luahoomoe* was burnt by order of the king, and the refractory priest was killed. His sons and some of his household escaped to one of the mountain-peaks called Hanaula. But the vengeance of *Luahoomoe* and the king's punishment for slaying a priest were swift in coming and terrible in their consequences. No sooner was *Luahoomoe* consumed by the fire of his burning house than the streams of water ceased running, the springs dried up; no rain fell for three years and a half, and famine and desolation spread over the islands. *Hua* and his people perished miserably, and the saying survives to this day, *Nakeke na iwi a Hua i ka la*—"rattling are the bones of Hua in the sun"—as a warning to wicked people, implying that no one survived the famine to bury *Hua* or hide his bones;—the greatest disgrace of ancient times.

The legend further tells that the drought and famine spread to the other islands, and that *Naula-a-Maihea*, the famous prophet and seer who dwelt at Waimalu, Ewa district, Oahu, became concerned for the fate of the entire Hawaiian people. Seeing no signs of rain on the Kauai mountains, and none on the Kaala mountains of Oahu, he looked towards Maui, and there on the peak of Hanaula he saw a dark spot where the rain was concentrated. He knew at once that there the sons of *Luahoomoe* had taken up their abode, and he proceeded thither with offerings of a pig, fowl, &c., to appease their anger and procure rain. The sons of *Luahoomoe*, seeing *Naula* arriving, descended from the mountain and met him in Kula. The meeting was cordial; rain followed, and the country was relieved of the curse which followed *Hua's* wicked attempt on the life of a priest.

Naula-a-Maihea is said to have accompanied *Laa-mai-kahiki* from Kahiki, the southern groups. He was noted and feared as a sorcerer and a prophet, traits strongly characteristic of the priestly class of the southern immigrants. He built a Heiau at Waimalu, Ewa, Oahu, the foundation of which may still be seen. The legend mentions that, starting at one time from Waianae, Oahu, for

Kauai, his canoe was upset; that he was swallowed by a whale, in whose stomach he crossed the channel between Oahu and Kauai, and was vomited up alive and safe on the beach at Waialua, Kauai. If this is not a remnant of ancient myths and legends brought with them by the Polynesians from their trans-Pacific ancient homes, localised in new habitats and adapted to the most noted prophet of the times, it is at least a remarkable coincidence with the Jewish legend of the prophet Jonah.

Among other southern families of note who arrived at the Hawaiian group during this migratory period, though now it is impossible to place them in their proper order, the legend mentions *Kalana-nuunui-kua-mamao*, and *Humu*, and *Kamaunua-niho* who came from Kahiki (the southern groups), and landed at Kahahawai in Waihee, Maui. *Aumu* soon returned to Kahiki, being discontented with *Kalana*, who had taken *Kamaunuaniho* for wife. They had a daughter named *Hina*, who became the wife of *Olopana* (not the brother of *Moikeha*, the grandson of *Maweke*), who had arrived from Kahiki and settled at Koolau, Oahu. To this *Olopana* is attributed the Heiau of Kawaewae at Kaneohe, Oahu. *Olopana's* brother *Kahikiula* came with him from Kahiki. Both these families are said to have come from places in Kahiki called "Keolewa," "Haenakulaina," and "Kauaniani."

With this family of *Olopana* is connected the legend of *Kamapuaa*, whom story and fable have exalted into a demigod, assuming the nature of a man or that of a gigantic hog as suited his caprice. There was doubtless a historical foundation for the legend of *Kamapuaa*. He is reported to have been the son of *Kahikiula* (*Olopana's* brother) and *Hina*, *Olopana's* wife. He offended his uncle *Olopana* and rebelled against him, and after various battles was taken prisoner and condemned to be sacrificed, but by the advice and assistance of *Lonoaohi*, the chief priest of *Olopana*, he surprised and slew his uncle in the very Heiau where he himself was to have been sacrificed. After that *Kamapuaa* left Oahu and went to Kahiki, where he married, and, acquiring renown for his prowess, dwelt a considerable time.

It is extremely difficult to advance an opinion as to whether the combats and adventures of *Kamapuaa* with *Pele*, the reputed goddess of the volcano Kilauea, have any historical foundation, or are merely pure fiction of later ages, embodying some hidden and half-forgotten religious tenets of opposing creeds. Though *Pele* was universally acknowledged as the goddess of volcanoes, and of Kilauea in particular, yet her worship in the Hawaiian group is only subsequent to this migratory period and the arrival of the southern immigrants. Her culte was unknown to the purer faith of the older inhabitants of the *Nanaulu* line, and her name had no place in the *Kane* doxology. Yet, to the careful observer of the ancient Hawaiian legends of this period, various circumstances combine together to produce the impression, almost of certainty, that among the immigrants of this period arriving from the southern groups was one particular family, afterwards designated as that of *Pele*, with her brothers and sisters; that they established themselves on Hawaii at or near the volcano of Kilauea; that becoming powerful, they became dreaded and identified with the volcano near which they resided; and that in course of time the head of the family, under the name of *Pele*, was regarded as the tutelary deity of that and other volcanoes. The minute and variedly narrated adventures of *Pele* herself and her sister *Hiaka-i-ka-pole-o-Pele* leave but little doubt on the critical student's mind that, at the time when the facts connected with these personages had become historically mouldy and passed into legends, they were still regarded as originally mortal beings, but by common consent ex-, alted in the category of *Au-makua* (spirits of deceased ancestors), and feared and worshipped as such. Viewed in that light, there is some sense and some historical foundation for the legends which relate that *Kamapuaa* went to Hawaii to court *Pele*, how he was refused and waged war upon her, and how, after a drawn battle, a compromise was effected. The metaphysical and theological notions associated with the legends of *Pele* appear to me to be partially due to the fertile imagination of priests and bards, as the actual, corporeal existence of *Pele* receded in the shadowy past, and partially also to be remnants of an older creed which had collected around the legend of *Pele* when their own appropriate associations and *point de mire* had been forgotten or distorted.

Another notability of southern extraction who arrived at the Hawaiian group during this period is *Luhaukapawa*. He was the "*kilo-kilo*," astrologer, navigator, and priest of *Kaula-a-kalana*, the famous Oahu chief who visited so many foreign lands, and who is said to have been the grandson of *Hina-i-kapaikua*, the wife of *Nanamaoa*, and consequently contemporary with the *Paumakuas* and with the children of *Maweke*. What southern group was his birthplace is not known, but he returned with *Kaulu-a-kalana* to Oahu and settled there. Some legends attribute to *Luhaukapawa*, in a general way, the introduction of the tabus; but it is most probable that he only enforced their stricter observance, and perhaps added some new regulations previously unknown to, or not in use among, the Hawaiians. He must have attained a remarkable old age, for he is said to have been still alive in the time of *Mualani*, the great-granddaughter of *Maweke* from his son *Kalehenui*, and who was an Oahu chiefess.

There was at this period one powerful family on the island of Kauai known as the *Puna* family, which probably belonged to this oft-mentioned southern *Ulu* line of emigrants, though their pedigree is nowhere mentioned in the traditions now remaining. Tradition mentions three of that name, viz., *Puna-nui-kaianaina*, *Puna-kai-olohia*, and *Puna-aikoai*, the latter of which was contemporary with *Moikeha*, who, on his return from Kahiki,

married *Puna's* daughter *Hinauulua,* or, as she is also
called, *Hooipo-kamalanae.* This family may possibly have
descended from the same *Puna* branch of the *Ulu*
southern line as the Oahu *Paumakua* family; and as the
first name known to Hawaiian tradition, that of *Puna-nui-
kaianaina,* was also probably the first arrival at the
Hawaiian group from the south, he would be contemporary with *Newalani,* the grandfather of *Paumakua,* and
thus among the first immigrants of this period. I am
inclined to think that this *Puna* family originally came
from the Marquesan group, inasmuch as on a Marquesan
genealogy of a Hivaoa (St. Dominica) chiefess I find that
about thirty-twó generations ago there were a number of
Punas, with various sobriquets to distinguish them, on
the said genealogical tree, evidently showing it to have
been a family name, and I hold it quite probable that
Hawaiian immigrants bearing that name came from that
direction and from that family.

Doubtless many other southern chiefs visited the Hawaiian group and established themselves there, but time
has blotted their names from the traditional record, and
the fame of their exploits has not come down to after
ages—" *carent quia saero vate* "—or, having been mixed
up and absorbed in the native population at an early
period, they lost their southern individuality. The combined influence, however, of all these expeditions, large
and small, known and unknown, on the condition of the
previous Hawaiians, amounted almost to a social revolution, and was deep-felt and lasting. I shall refer to the
changes introduced during this period at the conclusion
of this section of Hawaiian history.

If Hawaiian traditions are remarkably redundant with
the brilliant exploits of princely adventurers from the
southern groups, who flocked to this country, or by some

means or other insinuated themselves or their descendants on vacant thrones and in prominent positions, they are equally redundant, if not more so, with the adventures and achievements of Hawaiian chiefs of the original *Nanaulu* line, who roamed over the southern and south-western groups of the Pacific in quest of fame, of booty, or of new homes. Many of these returned to their native homes laden with rich and curious knowledge of foreign manners and foreign modes of thought, and thus aided not a little in overlaying the ancient condition, social, political, and religious, with the more elaborate but grosser southern cultus and more despotic rule of government.

About the time, probably a generation earlier, of the *Paumakuas, Kapawa*, and *Paao* who have been referred to in previous pages, there lived on Oahu a chief by the name of *Maweke*. He was the son of *Kekupahaikala* (k) and *Maihikea* (w), and the lineal direct descendant from *Nanaulu*, the brother of *Ulu*, from whom the southern chiefs claimed their descent. He lived twenty-seven generations ago, counting on the direct line through the Oahu chiefs his descendants, or from twenty-six to twenty-eight gene-rations ago, counting on the collateral Hawaii and Maui lines of chiefs, or approximatively about the earlier and middle part of the eleventh century. Nothing worthy of note is related by the traditions about *Maweke*, but it is remarkable that he is the first on the *Nanaulu* line, counting downward, from whom any collateral branches have descended to our days. No doubt there were col-lateral offshoots of the *Nanaulu* line before his time. The *Hikapoloa, Kamaiole*, and others on Hawaii; the *Kamauaua* on Molokai; the *Wahanui* on Oahu; the *Kealiiloa, Pueo-nui*, and *Keikipaanea* on Kauai, and several others to whom the legends refer, were not southerners of the *Ulu* line, but it is nowhere stated through whom, on the *Nanaulu* line above *Maweke*, they descended. It does appear as if those families and many other collaterals above *Maweke* had been merged, absorbed in, and eclipsed by the southern element, and in process of time lost the memory of their connection with the *Nanaulu* line, while the *Maweke* family was strong enough to not only retain its own individuality and its ancient genealogy to the latest times unruffled by southern contact, but also to absorb and subordinate to itself several of those southern invaders whose descendants in after ages counted it no small honour to be able, through the marriage of some of their ancestors, to claim connection and descent from this powerful *Nanaulu Maweke* family.

Tradition records that *Maweke* had three sons, *Mulielealii*, *Keaunui*, and *Kalehenui*, whose lines, with numerous collaterals, have descended to our days. The *Kalehenui* family appear to have chiefly resided on the Koolau side of the island of Oahu, while the favoured residence and patrimonial estates of the *Keaunui* family appear to have been in the Ewa, Waianae, and Waialua districts of the same island. The particular district occupied by *Mulielealii* is not well defined in the legends. As the descendants of one of his sons, *Kumuhonua*, are found for several generations afterwards in possession of the district of Kona, Oahu, it may be supposed to have been their heritage after the death of *Maweke*.

On the deeds and exploits of *Mulielealii* and *Kalehenui* personally the legends are silent. But to *Keaunui*, the head of the powerful and celebrated Ewa chiefs, is attributed the honour of having cut a navigable channel near the present Puuloa saltworks, by which the great estuary, now known as "Pearl River," was in all subsequent ages rendered accessible to navigation. Making due allowance for legendary amplification of a known fact, the estuary doubtless had an outlet for its waters where the present gap is; but the legend is probably correct in giving *Keaunui* the credit of having widened it and deepened it, so as to admit the passage of canoes, and even larger vessels, in and out of the Pearl River estuary. Among the most noted of *Keaunui's* children were *Lakona*, the great progenitor of the Ewa chiefs, *Nuakea*, the wife of the Molokai *Keoloewa-a-kamauaua*, and *Moi*, the prophet and seer of *Kaupeenui*, the brother of *Keoloewa*.

Nothing very remarkable is related of the descendants of *Kalehenui* during this period, except that tradition informs us that during the time of *Mualani*, the grand-daughter of *Kalehenui*, while she and her husband *Kaomealani* lived at Kaopulolia in Kaneohe, Oahu, there arrived at the promontory of Mokapu, in Kaneohe aforesaid, a vessel with foreigners (white people—*haole*) on board. Tradition gives the vessel's name as *Ulupana*, and of the crew are mentioned the chief or captain, *Mololana*, and his wife, *Malaea*, and three other persons. Whether they remained in the country or left again is not known.

We now come to the *Mulielealii* branch of the *Maweke* family, which occupies so great a portion of the ancient legends of this period. *Mulielealii* is said to have had three sons and one daughter. The former were *Kumuhonua*, *Olopana*, and *Moikeha*; the latter was named *Hainakolo*.

Kumuhonua seems to have remained in possession of the patrimonial estates on Oahu, and possibly of the nominal sovereignty of the island. He had four sons, *Molohaia*, *Kahakuokane*, *Kukawaieakane*, and *Elepuuka-honua*. The genealogies of none of these has been preserved except the last, which descends to the time of *Haka*, a noted Ewa chief who lived at Lihue, and was the last Oahu sovereign of the *Kumuhonua* branch, having been succeeded in the sovereignty by *Mailikukahi* of the *Moikeha* branch.

The two other sons of *Mulielealii*, viz., *Olopana* and *Moikeha*, appear to have established themselves on Hawaii, where *Olopana* ruled the valley of Waipio and adjacent country, and *Moikeha*, if not co-ordinate with his brother in power, was at least his highest subject and most trusted friend. Here *Olopana* married *Luukia*, granddaughter of *Hikapoloa*, chief of Kohala Hawaii, and *Mailelavlii*, his

wife, from Kona Hawaii—both descended from the ancient
Hawaiian *Nanaulu* line—and begat a daughter named
Kaupea.

How long *Olopana* dwelt in Waipio is not mentioned,
but the legend states that after a while heavy storms,
floods, and freshets desolated the valley and compelled
the inhabitants to seek refuge in other places. *Olopana*
and his family, accompanied by his brother *Moikeha* and
his family, embarked on their canoes and sailed for Kahiki,
where they arrived safely, and where, according to the
legend, *Olopana* obtained the sovereignty of a district or
section of land called " Moaulanuiakea," and where *Moikeha,* still the right-hand man of his brother, built a sumptuous residence and Heiau for himself, called " Lanikeha."
On this voyage *Moikeha* took with him, as an adopted son,
the young chief *Laa*—who then must have been but a
child—the son of *Ahukai,* who was the great-grandson of
the Oahu *Paumakua,* and who in the chants is called
" Chief of Kapaahu and Lord of Nualaka."

> *Ke 'lii no Kapaahu*
> *He Lani no Nualaka.*

It would be interesting to know, if possible, on which
of the southern or south-western groups of the Pacific
Olopana and *Moikeha* landed and established themselves.
The word " Kahiki," from a Hawaiian point of view, com-
prises any and every group from Easter Island to the
farthest west, even far into the present Malaysia. Not
being able to define the particular place, it may be assumed with a considerable degree of certainty to have
been on one of the Society or Georgian groups. The
Hawaiian legends mention only three names of places in
connection with these voyages of *Moikeha,* of *Kila,* or of
Laa-mai-kahiki, and they were *Moa-ula-nui-akea,* the
name of a land or district where *Olopana* dwelt, *Lanikeha,*
the name of the residence and Heiau of *Moikeha,* and
Kapaahu, the name of a neighbouring mountain, where

Laa-mai-kahiki was stopping when *Kila* was sent to bring
him back to *Moikeha*. My own limited knowledge of
names of places, ancient or present, in the Society group,
prevents me from positively identifying either of these
names, and thus settle the question. But the whole tenor
of the Hawaiian legends would seem to indicate the
Society group as the objective point of these voyages of
Moikeha, Kila, Laa, and others referring to the same localities. The name of the district or section of country over
which *Olopana* is said to have ruled in Kahiki was in
Hawaiian *Moa-ula-nui-akea*. Analysing this word, it
consists of one appellative, *Moa*, and three adjectives or
epithets, *ula, nui, akea,* " red, great, open, or wide-spreading." As the adjectives may or may not have been
original at the place to which they were applied, and
probably arose in the eulogistic tendency of those who
cherished its memory, and in the magnifying disposition
of the bards of subsequent ages, there remains the word
Moa as an index for our research. In the island of
Raiatea, Society group, one of the entrances leading to the
bay on which Opoa was situated was anciently, and is
possibly still, called *Ava-Moa*, " the sacred harbour " or
entrance. This, then, may be the place which Hawaiian
legends so highly extolled as the splendid domain of
Olopana and of *Laa*. *Moa*, which in Tahitian means
" sacred," and was originally a distinctive epithet of that
particular harbour, became in Hawaiian and to Hawaiian
emigrants a local name, adorned with other though analogous epithets. When, moreover, we consider that Opoa,
to which this " sacred entrance," this *Ava-Moa*, conducted
the voyager, was the seat, cradle, and principal sanctuary
of the entire Society group, the Tahitian Mecca, in fact,
there are reasonable grounds for assuming that the *Moaula, &c.,* of the Hawaiian legends refers to the *Ava-Moa*
of Raiatea, Society group. It is true that the Hawaiian
legends referring to this period make no mention of Opoa,
its Morae or temple, nor to its presiding deity, *Oro*. But

according to Tatutian legends and traditions, the Morae of
Opoa was built and dedicated to *Oro* by *Hiro*, whom their
genealogies make the twentieth before the late Queen
Pomare, and who, according to the same genealogies, was
the great-grandson of *Raa ;* whereas the Hawaiian *Laa*
flourished twenty-three generations ago, and his foster-
father, *Moikeha*, at least two generations earlier. Hence
the legends of *Moikeha* and his contemporaries are silent
on the Morae of Opoa and its famous god *Oro*.

Of the mountain of *Kapaahu* I have been unable to
obtain any information. It is to be hoped that some
Tahitian archæologist may take the trouble to ascertain
if any of the mountains of Raiatea, especially in the
neighbourhood of Opoa, ever bore the name of Kapaahu.

According to the legend, *Olopana* and *Moikeha* lived
harmoniously in their new domain for a long time, until
jealousy and envy actuated a Tahitian chief named *Mua*
to slander *Moikeha* and prejudice him in the eyes of
Luukia, the wife of *Olopana*. Unable to clear himself of
the slander and to convince *Luukia* of its malice, life
became irksome to *Moikeha*, and he concluded to seek
diversion by returning to his native land. His canoes
were equipped forthwith under the superintendence of
Kamahualele, his astrologer and seer (*Kilokilo*), and, with
a goodly company of chiefs, retainers, and relatives, they
set sail for Hawaii. It was on this occasion, as they
approached the island of Hawaii, that *Kamahualele* is
said to have chanted the verses quoted on page 10. The
legends differ somewhat as to the names of the followers
of *Moikeha*, but they all agree that a number of places in
the Hawaiian group were named after such or such companions of *Moikeha*, who were permitted to land here and
there as the fleet coasted along the island shores, and who
succeeded in establishing themselves where they landed.
Thus were named the land of *Moaula* in Kau, Hawaii, the
capes of *Haehae* and *Kumukahi* in Puna, the district of
Honuaula on Maui, capes *Makapuu* and *Makaaoa* on Oahu.

One legend says that *Moikeha's* priest was called *Mookini*, and that he and another follower named *Kaluawilinau* landed at Kohala, Hawaii. It may have been so, but the inference drawn by the native Hawaiian mind, that the famous Heiau of Mookini in Kohala was called after this companion of *Moikeha*, is an evident anachronism, as *Paao* who built the Heiau preceded *Moikeha* in time of arrival at Hawaii; and it is not probable that the *Paao* and *Pili* joint interest in Kohala would then, or in after-times, permit their special and sacred Heiau to be named after a chance passenger in the fleet of *Moikeha*; the more so as the former sprang from the Samoan group, and the latter came from the Society group. There was, doubtless, a Heiau in Puuepa, Kohala, near the shore, called Moo-kini, the ruins of which still remain, but it was much older than the one which *Paao* built, and probably gave its name to the latter. Another of the companions of *Moikeha* was the famous *Laamaomao*, who by subsequent generations was worshipped as an *Aumakua*, and exalted as a demigod, a Hawaiian Æolus, from whose *Ipu* or calabash the imprisoned winds went forth at his bidding, in force and direction to suit the wishes of the devotee. He is said to have taken up his abode near a place called Hale-a-Lono, a well-known hill and landmark on Kalua-koi, island of Molokai. No incident is recorded during the voyage from Kahiki to Hawaii, and having passed through the Hawaiian group, making the different debar-cations above mentioned, *Moikeha* arrived one evening off the island of Kauai, and anchored his canoes outside of Waialua and the surf of Makaiwa, or, as others say, off Waimahanalua in Kepaa, the neighbouring land, where the *Puna* family of chiefs held their court. Early next morn-ing, with his double canoe dressed in royal style (*Pulou-lou-Alii*), *Moikeha* went ashore and was cordially received by the chiefs of the district. According to one tradi-tion, *Puna* had two daughters, *Hooipo i Kamalanae* and *Hinauu* or *Hinauulua*, who fell in love with *Moikeha*, and whom he married ; another tradition only mentions *Hooipo i Kamalanae* as his wife. On the death of *Puna, Moikeha* became the principal chief (*Alii nui*) of Kauai, and remained there the balance of his life. With these two wives *Moikeha* had the following children mentioned in the legends, viz.:—*Hookamalii, Haulanuiaiakea, Kila, Umalehu, Kaialea, Kekaihawewe,* and *Laukapalala,* all boys. Not much is said of *Hookamalii* in the legends. It would appear that he settled in the Kona district of Oahu, where his grandfather, *Muliele-alii,* had held possession, and is reported to have resided at Ewa. His son *Kahai* is said to have made a voyage to Kahiki, and from Upolu in the Samoan group brought a species of bread-fruit tree, which he planted at Puuloa. The great-granddaughter of *Hookamalii,* called *Maelo,* married *Lauli-a-Laa,* the son of *Laa-mai-kahiki,* whom *Moikeha* took with him to the Society group, and from this union descended the great *Kalona* families on Oahu, which spread their scions over the entire group.

The second son of *Moikeha* was *Haulanuiaiakea.* He followed his father in the supremacy of Kauai. I have been unable to recover any complete genealogy of his descendants, but it was universally conceded that *Kapoleikauila,* the wife of *Kalanikukuma,* a descendant of *Laa-mai-Kahiki's* second son, *Ahukini-a Laa,* was the lineal descendant of *Haulanuiaiakea.* It probably was so, for it is undeniable that that union increased immensely the tabu and aristocratic rank of *Kalanikukuma's* two sons, *Kahakumakalina* and *Ilihewalani.*

The third son of *Moikeha* was *Kila.* He makes a more conspicuous figure in the ancient legends than his other brothers. I possess two legends relating to *Kila.* One is very copious and detailed, but shows evident marks of the embellishments of later narrators; the other is more succinct. They differ in several material points, and thus induce me to believe that the one is not a copy of the other, but that both sprang from independent sources. Com-

paring the two together, and with other legends referring
to this period, the historical facts appear to be these:—
After *Moikeha* had been many years residing at Waialua
as chief ruler of Kauai, and when his sons were grown-up
men, a strong desire took possession of him to see once
more his foster-son *Laa*, whom, on his departure from
Kahiki, he had left with his brother *Olopana*, and whom
Olopana had adopted as his heir and successor. Either
Moikeha was too old, or from other causes unable to
undertake the voyage himself, and *Kila* was commissioned
to go to Kahiki to Moa-ula-nui-akea and bring *Laa* with
him to Kauai. The double canoes were fitted out and
equipped for the long voyage; several, if not all, of *Kila's*
brothers went with him; and, finally, *Moikeha's* own
astrologer (Kilokilo) and friend, *Kamahualele*, who came
with him from Kahiki, was ordered to accompany *Kila* as
special counsellor and chief navigator. When all were
ready the expedition started. After passing through the
Hawaiian group, and taking its departure from the south
point of Hawaii, it stood to the southward, and in due
time arrived at Kahiki. Whether, as the one legend has
it, *Laa* returned with *Kila* to the Hawaiian group, saw his
foster-father, *Moikeha*, visited the other islands, and finally
returned to Kahiki; or, as the other legend has it, *Laa*
remained in Kahiki until after the death of *Olopana*,
and then proceeded to Hawaii with his own canoes,
accompanied by his priest, his astrologer, his master of
ceremonies, his drummer, his prophet, and forty other
attendants, the fact is none the less certain that *Laa*
came to the Hawaiian group and stayed there for some
time, principally on Oahu at Kualoa. Here he married
three wives—*Hoakanuikapuaihelu*, daughter of *Lonokaehu*
from Kualoa, *Waolena* from Kaalaea, and *Mano* from
Kaneohe. All the ancient traditions retain the fact of
this triple marriage, and that each one of those three
ladies was delivered of a son on one and the same day,
and from each of these three sons it was the glory and

pride of the aristocracy on Oahu and Kauai to trace their descent. These sons of *Laa-mai-Kahiki* were respectively called *Lauli-a-Laa, Ahukini-a-Laa*, and *Kukona-a-Laa. Pakui*, a noted bard and priest in the time of *Kamehameha I.*, in his version of the ancient chant of the creation of the islands and the origin of the nobility, thus sings:—

> *O Ahukai, O Laa-a, O Laa-a,*
>> O Ahukai, O Laa-a, O Laa-a,
> *O Laa-mai Kahiki ke Alii,*
>> O Laa from Tahiti, the chief,
> *O Ahukini-a-Laa,*
>> O Ahukini-a-Laa,
> *O Kukona-a-Laa,*
>> O Kukona-a-Laa,
> *O Lauli-a Laa, makua,*
>> O Lauli-a Laa, the father,
> *O na pukolu a Laa-mai-Kahiki,*
>> The triple canoe of Laa-mai-Kahiki,
> *He mau hiapo kapu a Laa,*
>> The sacred firstborn (children) of Laa,
> *Hookahi no ka la i hanau ai.*
>> Who were born on the same one day.

The legend adds that after *Moikeha's* death *Laa* returned to Tahiti and lived and died there. It then narrates the adventures of *Kila* and his troubles with his brothers in a rather prolix and marvellous manner; but the result seems to be, comparing the two legends together, that *Kila* abandoned the island of Kauai and established himself on Hawaii, where he obtained possession of the valley of Waipio, the former land of his uncle *Olopana;* and from him several Hawaii families claimed descent, notably *Laakapu*, the wife of *Kahoukapu, Kapukamola*, the wife of *Makakaualii*, and *Piilaniwahine*, the wife of *Kamalalawalu* of Maui.

Of *Mulielealii's* daughter *Hainakolo* a legend still exists. She is said to have married a southern chief named *Keanini,* whom she accompanied to his home in Kuaihelani; that the marriage was not a happy one; that *Hainakolo* returned to Hawaii while her brother *Olopana* still resided there;

that she met with a tragical end, and that her spirit still haunts the mountains and precipices around the valley of Waipio. This legend is very much overlaid with the fabulous and fanciful, but the historical kernel of it still confirms the prevalence of the long voyages and social intercourse of the Polynesian tribes during this period. *Hainakolo's* son is called *Leimakani*, from whom some Hawaiian families claimed descent.

Among other Hawaiian chiefs who during this period of unrest and tribal commotion visited foreign lands, the legends have retained the name of *Wahanui*, a chief from Oahu. He is not claimed as a scion of the powerful *Maweke* family, and was probably a descendant of some one of *Maweke's* ancestors, though the connection is now lost and forgotten. His expedition visited the southern groups first, and having seen them all (" *Ua pau ka Hema* "), it started for the islands in the west, and from there returned to the Hawaiian group. It is said that he brought many strange and curious things with him from the foreign lands that he had visited, and among others are mentioned the *Kanaka-pilikua*, a dwarfish people, whom he landed on Kauai, and who, on account of their swiftness, became famous as runners.

Kaumailiula was another Hawaiian chief whose adventures in foreign lands (*Kahiki*) formed the subject of contemporary gossip and of subsequent legend. He was the grandson of *Hikapaloa*, the noted Hawaiian chief from Kohala of the *Nanaulu* line, and brother to *Luukia*, the wife of *Olopana*. He married his niece *Kaupea*, Olopana's daughter, who had come on a visit to Hawaii while her parents still were living in Kahiki. Misunderstandings possibly arose between husband and wife, and *Kaupea* returned to her parents in Kahiki, where she gave birth to a daughter afterwards named *Kamakaokeahi*. Hearing of this by other arrivals from Kahiki, *Kaumailiula* started to recover and bring back his daughter. His adventures on this voyage, and his narrow escape from being sacrificed in Kahiki for having inadvertently broken the tabus, and his successful return with his daughter to Hawaii, are the theme of the legend and the traditional data in support of the frequent and intimate intercourse between the Hawaiian and the southern groups at this period.

With *Laa-mai-Kahiki* closes this period of oceanic travel, migrations, and intercourse so far as the Hawaiian group was concerned; at least no name has come down upon the traditions, legends, or genealogies of any Hawaiian chief who undertook such a voyage to the southward, or of any southerner that arrived at the Hawaiian group after that time. While the exploits and adventures of the many who failed to establish themselves and perpetuate their names on the genealogies of the country have faded from the national memory, or are only alluded to in connection with some other more prominent figure, yet sufficiently many succeeded in making themselves famous among their contemporaries and sending their names and their exploits down to posterity as a cherished heirloom through unbroken generations, and thus—in spite of the marvellous accretions which the legends gathered as they passed from father to son—attesting the historical truth of the fact, the time, and the character of this singular episode in Hawaiian and Polynesian national life.

I have formerly stated that Polynesian legends furnish no clue as to the causes which set this migratory vortex in motion within the Polynesian area of the Pacific. No more do they give an inkling of what led to its discontinuance. To the Hawaiian people it was an era of activity and enterprise, an awakening from a sleep of fifteen generations, not devoid of the peculiar danger of being swamped or absorbed in this ethnic whirl. Its traces, however, were deep and indelible. It modified the ancient customs, creed, and polity. It even affected the speech of the people, and as late as fifty years ago it was easy to distinguish a native from the leeward islands from one of the windward by his manner of pronouncing the letters *k* and *l*, which Kauai and Oahu natives, adopting the Tahitian style, pronounced *t* and *r*. Since the conquest of Oahu by *Kamehameha I.* in 1796, and the cession of Kauai in 1809, the fusion of the people of the leeward and windward isles of the group has been so great as to nearly obliterate the ancient difference of speech between them.

To this period Hawaiian tradition assigns the introduction of the four-walled, more or less oblong, style of Heiau (temple), instead of the open truncated pyramidal structure of previous ages, indicating a great change in the ceremonial of the religion and a tendency to exclusiveness unknown before. Under the old, the previous régime, the Heiau of the truncated pyramid form, with it presiding chief, officiating priests, and prepared sacrifice, were in plain open view of the assembled congregation, who could hear the prayers and see the sacrifice, and respond intelligently to the invocations of the priest. Under the innovations of this period, the presiding chief, those whom he chose to admit, and the officiating priests, were the only ones who entered the walled enclosure where the high-places for the gods and the altars for the sacrifices were erected, and where the prayers and invocations were recited, the congregation of the people remaining seated on the ground outside the walls, mute, motionless, ignorant of what was passing within the Heiau until informed by the officiating priest or prompted to the responses by his acolytes.

To this period may also be assigned the introduction and adoption of several new gods in the Hawaiian pantheon. That the Hawaiians previous to this venerated and prayed to the spirits of departed ancestors—*Aumakua* —is abundantly shown from their legends and traditions;

but I have found no indications to show that these were looked upon in any other light than as tutelar genii and family intercessors with the great omnipotent gods *Kane, Ku,* and *Lono,* to whom alone Heiaus were raised, and to whom alone, singly or jointly, the public ceremonial of worship was addressed. During and following this migratory period, however, several varieties of the great gods begin to appear in the legends of the people, unknown to the former creed and culte. Originally, perhaps, they were considered as manifestations of the various attributes and powers of the three primeval gods; but if so, the original conception had been worn down by time and defaced by usage, until, at the time we now speak of, those deified attributes had been exalted to the position of independent godheads, receiving separate worship, and as such were introduced by the southern emigrants for the acceptance and worship of the Hawaiians. We thus find varieties of *Kane,* such as *Kanemakua,*[1] *Kanepuaa,*[2] *Kane-i Ka-pualena,*[3] and eight or ten others of that class, generally known as *Kane-nuiakea.* We thus find the varieties of *Ku,* such as *Ku-ula,*[4] *Ku-ka-oo,*[5] *Ku-kaili-moku,*[6] and others. We thus find *Lono-a-kihi,*[7] *Lono-i-ka-ou-alii,*[8] and several others in more or less vogue. To this period belongs the introduction of

[1] One of the gods worshipped by fishermen, especially at the season of catching Malolo (flying-fish).

[2] The god of husbandry.

[3] Lit. "Kane with the yellow flower." The particular god worshipped by *Kawelo-a-Mahunalii,* the great Kauai chief who flourished some eight or nine generations ago.

[4] Another god worshipped by the fishermen throughout the group. His wife's name was *Hina* — which of itself shows their southern origin; and when the god proved unpropitious, the fishermen prayed to her to intercede with her husband.

[5] A god of husbandry.

[6] A feather god, chosen by *Umi* and by *Kamehameha I.* as their particular tutelar god, generally worshipped as a god of war. According to Rev. Mr. Ellis's "Polynesian Researches," vol. i. p. 276, *Tuiri* was one of the ancient war-gods in Tahiti, "a deity of the first rank, having been created by *Taaroa* before *Oro* existed."

[7] The eel god.

[8] The particular god which *Laamai-Kahiki* brought with him from Raiatea, and which was deposited in the Heiau of his foster-father, *Moikeha,* at Wailua, Kauai.

the *Pele*[1] family of divinities, male and female, and the transformation of the Hawaiian fallen angel, *Kanaloa*,[2] the prince of darkness and chief of the infernal world, to a rank almost equal with *Kane, Ku,* and *Lono.* To the influence of this period may be attribted the increased stringency of the tabus, and probably the introduction, or at least more general application, of human sacrifices. In support of this surmise, I may state that in all the legends or allusions referring to the period previous to this migratory epoch I have found no indications of the practice of human sacrifices, though they may have existed; but subsequent to this period the inhuman practice becomes progressively increasing, until in the latter days of paganism hardly any public affair was transacted without the inevitable preamble of one or more human victims.

[1] This family of gods consisted of *Pele*, the presiding goddess, whose especial abode was in the crater of the volcano of Kilauea, and her five brothers and eight sisters. They ruled over all volcanic phenomena, and they were considered as a cruel, capricious, and vengeful set of gods. Their names will indicate their attributes and functions, as well as the peculiar process by which, with an ignorant people, natural phenomena become exalted into special deities, and the " nomen " of one age becomes the " numen " of another. The five brothers were *Kamoho-alii*, the royal Moho; *Kapoha-i-kahi-ola*, the explosion in the place of life; *Ke-ua-a-ke-po*, the rain of night; *Kanehekili*, Kane the thunderer; *Ke-o-ahi-kama-kaua*, the fire-thrusting child of war. The eight sisters were *Makole-wawahi-waa*, red-eyed canoe-breaker; *Hiaka-wawahi-lani*, Hiaka the heaven-rending; *Hiaka-noho-lani*, Hiaka the heaven-dwelling; *Hiaka-kaalawa-maka*, Hiaka who turns her face; *Hiaka-i-ka-poli-o-Pele*, Hiaka on the bosom of Pele; *Hiaka-kapu-enaena*, Hiaka of the burning consuming tabu; *Hiaka-ka-*

lei-ia, Hiaka adorned with garlands; *Hiaka-opio*, Hiaka the young one. Rev. Mr. Ellis translates *Hiaka* (*Hii-aka*) with " cloud-holder." I think the better rendering would be "twilight-bearer." In Tahitian *Ata* sometimes has the sense of a " cloud," but in Hawaiian never. In all the Polynesian dialects, *Ata, Aka,* has one common sense, " shadow " of a person or thing. In a majority of the dialects *Ata* also has the sense of "twilight," the particular lighting up of the sky which precedes or follows the rising or setting of sun or moon; and in this sense it would appropriately convey the idea of the lurid light which accompanies an eruption of the volcano. As the name of the goddess was probably imported along with the culte of *Pele*, it may assist us in tracing the direction from whence it came to Hawaii to know that in Samoan *Ata* means " twilight; " *Ata ata*, "the red sky after sunset;" in Marquesan *Ata-ua* means the morning "twilight," "aurora."

[2] For my remarks upon *Kanaloa*, see vol. i. pp. 83, 84.

To what extent the previous Hawaiian social customs
were affected by this prolonged intercourse with their
southern cousins, it is extremely difficult now to state
from any allusions that may be found in the legends or
Meles. What the peculiar style of garment worn by
Hawaiian females may have been before this time, I am
unable to say, and there is nothing in the traditions to
indicate; but all the legends concurrently testify that the
style of garment known as the "*Pau*," consisting of five
thicknesses of kapa or cloth, and reaching from the waist
to the knee, was first introduced and rendered fashionable
in Hawaii by *Luukia*, the wife of *Olopana*, who, as previously stated, established himself as a supreme chief on
one of the Society group, probably Raiatea. Could the
ancient bards and raconteurs of legends be interrogated
how *Luukia* could have introduced the fashion of this
garment on Hawaii, seeing that she never returned there
after she and her husband and *Moikeha* left Waipio,
their probable answer would be that to *Luukia* belonged
the credit of the invention, and that her daughter *Kaupea*
brought the pattern of it to Hawaii when she visited her
mother's family, and became the wife of her uncle *Kaumailiula*. In the Hawaiian group the pattern remained
in its original comparative simplicity, and to this very
day the manufacturers of kapa make them fivefold, from
no other motive than because the "*Pau*" of *Luukia* was
of five thicknesses.

Among the improvements or additions to the ancient
musical instruments of the Hawaiians which are assigned
to this period is that of the large drum, "*Kaeke*," made
from the hollowed trunk of a large cocoanut-tree and
covered with shark skin. It was beaten by hand, and
was first introduced in the group by *Laamaikahiki* when
he returned from Kahiki. It was said to have been preserved at the Heiau of Holoholoku, Wailua, Kauai, until
comparatively modern times. From *Laamaikahiki's* time

to the introduction of Christianity, the use of this kind of drum became general over the group, and every independent chief, and every " *Heiau Pookanaka* "—where human sacrifices were offered—had its own "*Kaekeeke*" and drummer.

The "*Puloulou*," bundles or balls of either black or white kapa, tied to staffs and erected in front of the dwellings of the high chiefs, priests, and of the Heiaus, as signs of tabu, are said to have been introduced by *Paao*, the high-priest of Hawaii, who, there is reason to believe, came from the Samoan group. The "*Puloulou*" are still preserved in the national coat of arms as insignia of the ancient tabu.

Some prayers current amongst the priests and the people, which evidently go back to this period of disturbance and innovation on the old creed and old modes of thought for their origin, may be found in Appendix No. I.

In the polity of government initiated during this period, and strengthened as ages rolled on, may be noted the hardening and confirming the divisions of society, the exaltation of the nobles and the increase of their prerogatives, the separation and immunity of the priestly order, and the systematic setting down, if not actual debasement, of the commoners, the *Makaainana.* From this period dates the *Aha-Alii*, that peculiar organisation of the Hawaiian peerage referred to on previous pages, that zealous and watchful " Committee on Nobility," before whom every stranger aspirant to its prerogatives and privileges must recite his *Naua,* his pedigree and connections, and whom no pretensions could dazzle, no imposture deceive. The obligation was imperative on the highest as well as the lowest chieftain, whenever, passing beyond his own district or island where personally known, he visited a strange place or island where doubts might arise as to his identity. Thus when *Lono-i-ka-makahiki*, the son of *Keawe-nui-a-umi* and suzerain lord of the whole island of Hawaii, after the unpleasant affair with his wife *Kaiki-lani-wahine alii o Puna* at Kalaupapa on Molokai—to which we shall refer in its proper place—visited the court of *Kakuhihewa* of Oahu incognito, a sort of " Chevalier Noir " in that gay, luxurious, and illustrious rendezvous, to which all the restless spirits of the group repaired in search of dissipation or distinction, he was promptly challenged, although his high rank was surmised from his surroundings, and obliged to satisfy the *Aha-Alii* or its committee as to who he was and whence descended.

At this period commenced the development of the idea of a sovereign lord or king, *Ka-Moi*, over each of the principal islands of the group. Previously it appears that each chief was entirely independent of every other chief, and his authority was co-extensive with his possessions. When the legends referring to that time speak of an *Alii-nui* of Kauai or an *Alii-nui* of Hawaii, it simply means that he was the most powerful chief on that island for the time being, and by inheritance, conquest, or marriage had obtained a larger territory than any other chief there. But after this period the word *Moi* appears in the legends and Meles, indicating that the chief who bore that title was, by some constitutional or prescriptive right, acknowledged as the suzerain lord of his island, the *primus inter pares* of the other chiefs of said island, to whom the latter owed a nominal, at least, if not always a real, allegiance and fealty. Nor were the territorial possessions and power of the acknowledged *Moi* always the source of this dignity, for the legends relate several instances where the wealth in lands and retainers of a Moi were inferior to some of the other chiefs, who nevertheless owed him allegiance and followed his banner. Thus *Keawemauhili*, the twice-tabued ·chief of Hilo, though he acknowledged *Kalaniopuu* of Hawaii as his suzerain, and assisted him in his wars with Maui, was far the more powerful in terri-

torial wealth and resources, and he refused to acknowledge *Kamehameha I.* as his *Moi* or sovereign for many
years. Thus *Kuahuia,* the grandson of *I,* chief of Hilo,
three generations earlier than *Keawemauhili,* did for many
years set the whole strength of the nominal sovereign of
Hawaii at defiance; that sovereign and titular *Moi* being
Keakamahana, great-granddaughter of *Keawe-nui-a-umi,*
and grandmother to *Keawe,* surnamed *i-Kekahi-alii-o-ka-
moku* ("the one chief of the island"), from whom the
Kamehameha dynasty descended. Thus the East Maui
chiefs, though generally acknowledging the line of *Piilani*
as the rightful possessors of the dignity and pre-eminence
as *Moi,* sovereigns of Maui, were frequently too powerful
to be coerced; and similar instances were not scarce on
the other islands.

Though the dignity of *Moi* was generally hereditary,
yet several cases are recorded in the legends where the
Moi was deposed from his office and dignity by the other
chiefs of his island and another *Moi* elected by them.
Thus *Haka* on Oahu, in whose line—the *Maweke-kumu-
honua*—the Moi-ship had been retained for many previous generations, was deposed by the Oahu chiefs and
Mailikukahi of the *Maweke-Moikeha* line elected in his
place. Thus *Kumahana,* the grandson of *Kualii* and son
of *Peleioholani,* was deposed by the Oahu chiefs, and
Kahahana, son of *Elani,* of the Ewa line of chiefs, elected
in his place. Thus after the death of *Keawe* of Hawaii,
his son and successor to the title of " *Moi,*" *Kalani-nui-
amaomao,* was deposed and killed by his cousin *Alapainui*—the son of *Keawe's* half-sister *Kalanikauleleiaiwi*—
who, although he usurped the authority and dignity of
Moi of Hawaii, was none the less so recognised by the
very son of the deposed monarch, by the rest of his
family, and by all the other chiefs of Hawaii, and retained the authority for many years until his death.

Whatever disadvantages might arise under the government of a sovereign whose individual possessions and

power were inadequate to give weight to his commands, or who had failed to secure the good-will and co-operation of the quasi-independent chiefs and feudatories of his island, yet on the whole the institution of a recognised political head and umpire between turbulent and contending chiefs was a great advantage, in so far as it tended to make a political unit of each island, and in a measure to check the condition of anarchy into which the people apparently had fallen, consequent upon this period of invasion, disruption, and commingling of elements of varying culture and conflicting pretensions. It enabled each island to combine its forces for purposes of defence, and it required a *Moi* of more than common ability and force of character to induce his chiefs to join him in an aggressive war upon another island.

I have referred to the institution of a *Moi*, the recognition of one sovereign chief, however limited his authority, on each island, as a consequence and a political result of this migratory period. My reason for so doing is not the *post hoc, propter hoc,* argument of some; but because in all the legends and chants that have come under my inspection referring to this very period and to times preceding, I have never discovered the slightest mention of the name of *Moi*, nor any allusion to an institution at all corresponding. When the migratory wave had passed, and the commotions incident to it had subsided, this was one of the fruits it brought with it, and it grew out of the altered condition of society. The very word itself, if it existed at all in the Hawaiian dialect, was never applied in the sense which it afterwards acquired. We look in vain through the Hawaiian dialect for any radical sense of the word *Moi*. It has but one concrete meaning, that of sovereign ; whereas in the sister dialect of Tahiti it has the radical sense of "the heart of a tree," "the pith," and in the duplicated form *Moi-moi* means "aged, stricken in years, principal, steady old man." Hence I look upon this word as imported into the Hawaiian, and employed to distinguish the status and functions of that particular chief from that of the other independent chieftains of the various districts of an island,—the *Alii-ai-moku*, as they were called.

I am inclined to think that the oldest Hawaiian designation of the highest rank of chiefs was *Hau*,[1] which word meets us with nearly the same meaning in the Samoan and Fijian *Sau*, the Tongan and Tahitian *Hau*, the Rorotonga and Mangarewa *Au*, the New Zealand *Whaka-hau*, for I have found it applied to the independent district chiefs of an island as well as to the Moi or titular sovereign of the island ; but the title of *Moi* was never applied to a district chief since Moi-ship was instituted.

HAWAII.

When the islands had somewhat recovered from the shock of the preceding migratory period, about three generations after *Laamaikahiki*, there lived a chief on Hawaii who was the Moi of that island, and grandson of *Kalapana* of the southern *Pili-kaaiea* line, which came in the time of *Paao*, and had obtained the titular sovereignty of the island of Hawaii. The name of this chief was *Kalau-* Kalaunuio-*nuiohua.* He is represented in the legends as a warlike hua. and enterprising prince, and having confirmed his sway on Hawaii, he felt ambitious of extending it over the neighbouring islands. His warriors and his fleet were collected, and invaded the island of Maui, where *Kamaluohua* was the reigning or principal chief. A battle was

[1] In the excellent Hawaiian Dictionary of Hon. Lorrin Andrews, this word is rendered *Haui*. The word had become obsolete long before Mr. Andrews wrote, and was only met with in ancient chants, and there joined to the epithet *Ka-lani*. The latest of these chants was composed by *Keaulumoku*, the son of *Kauakahiakua*, of the Maui royal family, and half-brother to *Kanekapolei*, the wife of *Kalaniopuu*, king of Hawaii about the year 1784. I am inclined to think that Mr. Andrews was misled by the spelling of those who reduced that chant to writing. *Hau-i-ka-lani* would seem to me to be the better way of spelling the word with which the chant of *Keaulumoku* opens.

fought, in which *Kamaluohua* was defeated and taken
prisoner. Elated with the first success, *Kalaunuiohua*
invaded the island of Molokaï, where *Kahokuohua* was
the principal chief or Moi. After another obstinate battle
Kahokuohua was conquered, and surrendered himself to
the victor. *Kalaunuiohua* now aimed at subjugating the
entire group, and hastened to Oahu, taking his royal
prisoners with him. It is doubtful if Oahu had any recognised Moi or titular sovereign at the time. The invasion of
Kalaunuiohua must have occurred while *Moku-a-Loe* ruled
over the Koolau division and *Kahuoi* ruled over the Kona
division of that island; for, without attacking either of
those chiefs, *Kalaunuiohua* landed his forces at Waianae
and gave battle to *Huapouleilei*, principal chief of the
Ewa and Waianae division of the island. Again victory
perched on *Kalaunuiohua's* banners, and *Huapouleilei* was
defeated and captured. What steps, if any, *Kalaunuiohua*
might have taken to consolidate his conquests is not
mentioned in the legend. At least he did not stop to
subdue the other portions of Oahu, but after the victory
at Waianae set sail for the island of Kauai with the three
captive kings in his train. At this time *Kukona*, the great-
grandson of *Ahukini-a-Laa*, was the Moi or sovereign of
Kauai. *Kalaunuiohua* made his descent on the coast of
Koloa, and in that neighbourhood was met by *Kukona*
and all the Kauai chiefs. A desperate engagement ensued
in which *Kalaunuiohua* was thoroughly defeated, himself
taken prisoner by *Kukona*, and his fleet surrendered.
Having delivered his country from the invader, *Kukona*
immediately set the three captive princes at liberty, and
furnished them with the means of returning to their own
possessions, but he kept *Kalaunuiohua* a close prisoner for
a long time; the legend says for several years. At length
negotiations were entered into with the Hawaii chiefs for
the release of their Moi, and, though the conditions are
not mentioned in the legend, the result proved favourable
to *Kalaunuiohua*, and he was allowed to return to Hawaii,

where he ended his days without indulging in more warlike adventures.[1] *Kalaunuiohua's* wife was *Kaheka*, with
whom he is said to have had a son, *Kuaiwa*, who succeeded him, and a daughter, *Kapapalimulimu*, from whom
descended *Henaiakamalama*, the wife of *Makaoku*, one of
the sons of *Kihanuilulumoku* of Hawaii.

During this period there lived on Hawaii a prophetess,
or " *Kaula*," called *Waahia*, who in some way was connected with the expeditions of *Kalaunuiohua*, or with the
negotiations for his release; but the legend merely refers
to her as a person whose fame was too well known at the
time the legend assumed its present form to require anything more than a passing allusion. Her fame and her
prophecies, their fulfilment or their failures, are now, however, completely faded from the popular mind, and even
the well-stored memory of the late Hon. S. M. Kamakau,
from whom I received the legend, could tell nothing about
her, though he admitted that the *Wanana o na Kaula*,
" the sayings or predictions of the prophets," when preserved, formed a most valuable contribution towards understanding and elucidating the ancient legends purporting
to treat of this or that dynasty of chiefs.

In the time of *Kalaunuiohua* the priestly power had
not yet been firmly established, for the legends represent
him as a chief who had no fear of the priesthood, but
killed both priests and prophets when it suited his humour.
No doubt the priesthood was struggling for ascendancy
even then, and it is instructive to remark how, here in the
Pacific, the heathen priests and their kindred bards consigned to odium the chiefs that thwarted or ill used them,
as Christian priests and monks, the historiographers of
their times in Europe, besmeared the memory of naughty
kings who opposed their doings or frustrated their designs.

Of *Kalaunuiohua's* son *Kuaiwa*, who followed his father Kuaiwa.
as sovereign of Hawaii, not much is related except that,

[1] This war is remembered in the legends as the war of *Kawelewele.*

from his peaceable character, he is held up as a contrast to his warlike father. *Kuaiwa* had two wives, *Kamuleilani* and *Kamanawa*. The former descended from *Luaehu*, of the southern *Ulu* stock of chiefs, who arrived with or about the time of *Laamaikahiki;* the latter descended from *Maweke* of the *Nanaulu* line, through his son *Keaunui* and granddaughter *Nuakea*. By reference to the genealogical tables, it will be seen that *Kamanawa's* great-grandmother *Hualani*, on the *Maweke* line, was the Molokai wife of *Kanipahu* of the *Pili* line of Hawaii chiefs. With *Kamuleilani Kuaiwa* had three sons, *Kahoukapu*, *Hukulani*, and *Manauea*, and with *Kamanawa* he had one son, *Ehu*, all of whom became noted heads of numerous aristocratic families.

Kahoukapu. — *Kahoukapu* seems to have followed his father *Kuaiwa* in the sovereignty of Hawaii. No wars nor misfortunes disturbed his reign, at least the report of none has come down to our time. His wife was *Laakapu*, who was descended from *Kila*, son of *Moikeha*, and grandson of *Maweke* on the original *Nanaulu* line. Only a portion of her pedigree has been preserved. *Laakapu*, with another husband named *Kanalukapu*, became the ancestress of the famous *Mahi* family on Hawaii.[1] She had also another son named *Hilo-a-Laakapu*, who, in conjunction with two other Hawaii chiefs, *Hilo-a Hilo-kapuhi* and *Punaluu*, and *Luakoa*, a Maui chief, invaded the island of Oahu, but were defeated and slain by *Mailikukahi*, the then sovereign of Oahu.

Kauholanuimahu. — *Kauholanuimahu* was the son of *Kahoukapu* and *Laakapu*,[2] and followed his father as *Moi* or sovereign of Hawaii. No mention occurs in the traditions of any wars between Hawaii and Maui during this and the preceding reign, nor of any conquests made; yet the tradition is posi-

---

[1] S. M. Kamakau states that the *Mahi* family descended from *Kuaiwa's* son *Hukulani*. Kamakau does not give the pedigree; but, if so, it must have been on the side of *Kanaloanoo*, the father of the *Mahis*.

[2] *Kahoukapu* is said to have had another son named *Kukaohialaka* (Legend of Keamalu).

tive, and has not been contradicted, that *Kauholanuimahu* resided a great portion of his time at Honuaula, Maui, where he exercised royal authority, and, among other useful works, built the fishpond at " Keoneoio," which still remains. During one of his long séjours on Maui, his wife *Neula* remained on Hawaii and took another husband, whose name has not survived in Hawaiian legend. The new husband and rival revolted from *Kauholanui* and assumed the government of Hawaii. Informed of the treachery and the revolt, *Kauholanui* hastened back to Hawaii, suppressed the rebellion,. and slew his opponent. After that *Kauholanui* remained on Hawaii until his death.

Kauholanui's wife, *Neula,* is said in some traditions to have been a Maui chiefess; if so, the district of Honuaula may have been her patrimonial estate, and that may account for the frequent and protracted residences there by *Kauholanui.*

Kauholanui-mahu was contemporary with the *Kakaalaneo* family on Maui, with the *Kalonas* on Oahu, and with *Kahakuokane,* the grandson of *Manokalanipoo* of Kauai. *Kiha-nui-lulu-moku* was the son of *Kauholanui-* Kiha-nui *mahu* and *Neula,*[1] and succeeded his father as Moi of lulu-mok Hawaii. His principal residence was at Waipio, district of Hamakua, where the Moi of Hawaii seem to have preferred to dwell from the days of *Kahaimoelea.* *Kiha,* though no wars or conquests are reported as occurring during his reign, is represented in the legends as a strong, powerful, and industrious chief, who made himself respected and obeyed at home, and held in high estimation by his neighbours. Hawaiian priests and bards of later ages embellished his legend with marvels, and witchery, and superhuman adventures, a certain proof of the high esteem in which he was held by his contemporaries and

[1] *Kauholanui* is said in some of the old chants to have had another son named *Kaohuwale.* Mele of *Kaaika-* *walu*, MS. Collection of L. Andrews, No. 41.

their posterity. He is eulogised as a chief of a peaceful disposition, but at the same time always ready to keep peace between the subordinate chieftains by force if necessary. Agriculture and industry received his attention, and the island of Hawaii is represented as prosperous and contented during his reign.

A curious and much-prized memento of *Kiha* has come down to our times. It was the celebrated war-trumpet of *Kiha*—" *Kiha-pu* "—whose notes, when blown upon, were said to have been audible from Waipio to Waimea, a distance of ten miles. It was a large nautilus shell, of a kind seldom if ever found now in this group, and inlaid, after the custom of those days, with the teeth of rebel or opposing chiefs slain in battle. It had been preserved as an heirloom in the *Kamehameha* branch of *Kiha's* descendants, and was, with many other relics of the Hawaiian heathen time, sent to the Paris Exhibition of 1865. It now adorns the Royal Hawaiian Museum. Many a weird tale is still told by some of the older people of the miraculous properties of the said shell or trumpet, how it was found, and of its power over the *Kini Akua*, "the host of gods or genii," when properly blown.

Kiha lived to a very old age and died at Waipio. His first wife was his own aunt, *Waoilea*, the sister of *Neula*, his mother, with whom he had *Lilou*, who succeeded him as Moi of Hawaii. He also had three other sons, either with *Waoilea* or with some other wife whose name has not been preserved. Their names were *Kaunuamoa, Makaoku*, and *Kepailiula*, the second of whom became chief of the Hilo district, and married *Hinaiakamalama*, sixth in descent from *Kalaunuiohua*. In his old age *Kiha* took a new wife named *Hina-opio*, with whom he had a son, *Hoolana*, who appears to have been provided for in the Puna district, where the family remained for four generations, until *Kuikai* removed to Molokai, married *Kumakakaha*, the daughter of *Kalani-Pehu*, the then most potent chief of that island, and became the ancestor of the well-known *Kaiakea* family, the head of which still survives in the author's daughter.[1]

Liloa followed his father *Kiha* as sovereign of Hawaii, Liloa. and kept his court at Waipio. He is represented as an affable, jolly monarch, who frequently travelled over the island, kept the other chiefs quiet, and protected the land-holders. After his reign the glories of Waipio declined. It had been built up and delighted in as a royal residence from the time of *Kahaimoelea*, and the tabus of its great Heiau (temple) were the most sacred on Hawaii, and remained so until the destruction of the Heiau and the spoliation of all the royal associations in the valley of Waipio by *Kaeokulani*, king of Kauai, and confederate of *Kahekili*, king of Maui, in their war upon *Kamehameha I.* in 1791. It is not known by whom this Heiau, called *Pakaalana*, was built, but it existed before *Kiha's* time; and so did the sacred pavement leading to the enclosure where the chief's palace or mansion—called "*Haunoka-maahala*"—stood, though its name has come down to

[1] The high consideration in which the *Kaiakea* family was formerly held throughout the group may be inferred from the connections it formed by its marriages. *Kuikai*, as above stated, married the daughter of *Kalanipehu;* his son *Kanehoalani* married *Kawakaweloaikanaka*, daughter of the famous *Kawelo-peekoa* of Kauai. His grandson *Kukalanihoouluae* married *Ainlei*, granddaughter of *Iukteleele*, of the *Liloa-Hakau* and *Keawenui-a-Umi* branches of the Hawaii chiefs; and *Kaiakea* himself married *Kalanipoo-a-Peleioholani*, daughter of *Kukuiaimakalani*, who was daughter of *Kualii* of Oahu, and own sister to *Peleioholani*, who died about eight years before the discovery of the Hawaiian group by Captain Cook. *Kaiakea's* son *Kekuelikenui*, the grandfather of the author's wife, was a staunch and personal friend of *Kamehameha I.*, who, referring to the unsettled state of the group, the

treachery and anarchy prevailing at the time, remarked that "*Kekuelike's* house was the only place where he could sleep with his *malo* off," that is, that he could sleep undressed without fear of violence or treachery. It was to *Kekuelike's* place at Kalamaula, Molokai, that the Maui royal family, including *Kalola* and *Keopuolani*, afterwards *Kamehamehu's* wife, fled for refuge after the disastrous battle of Iao in Wailuku. As an instance of the dense population, even a few years previous to *Kamehameha's* death, the author has often been told by a grand-niece of *Kekuelike*, who was a grown-up girl at the time, that when the chief's trumpet-shell sounded, over a thousand able-bodied men would respond to the call, within a circle described by Palaau, Naiwa, Kalae, and Kaunakakai. Those lands together cannot muster a hundred men this day.

our days as the *Paepae-a-Liloa.* The tabued *Nioi,* a *Liloa,* or pepper tree, was also uprooted at the same time by this sacrilegious *Kaeokulani.* *Liloa's* first wife was *Pinea* or *Piena,* a Maui chiefess, with whom he had a son, *Hakau,* and a daughter, *Kapukini.* Later in life, while travelling near the borders of the Hamakua and Hilo districts,[1] he spied a young woman, of whom he became deeply enamoured, and whom he seduced, and the fruit of which liaison was a son, whom the mother named *Umi,* and who afterwards played so great a rôle in the annals of Hawaii. The mother of *Umi* was named *Akahiakuleana,* and though in humble life, she was a lineal descendant in the sixth generation from *Kalahui-moku,* the son of *Kanipahu,* with *Hualani* of the *Nanaulu-Maweke* line, and half-brother to *Kalapana,* the direct ancestor of *Liloa.* When parting from *Akahiakuleana,* *Liloa* gave her the ivory clasp (Palaoa) of his necklace, his feather wreath (Lei-hulu), and his *Malo* or waist-cloth,[2] and told her that when the child was grown up, if it was a boy, to send him with these tokens to Waipio, and he would acknowledge him. The boy grew up with his mother and her husband, a fine, hearty, well-developed lad, foremost in all sports and athletic games of the time, but too idle and lazy in works of husbandry to suit his plodding stepfather. When *Umi* was nearly a full-grown young man, his stepfather once threatened to strike him as punishment for his continued idleness, when the mother averted the blow and told her husband, " Do not strike him ; he is not your son ; he is your chief ;" and she then revealed the secret of his birth, and produced from their hiding-place the keepsakes which *Liloa* had left with her. The astonished stepfather stepped back in dismay, and

[1] The legend says that he had been to Koholalele in Hamakua to consecrate the Heiau called *Manini,* and that, passing from there, he stopped at Kaawikiwiki, and at the gulch of Hoea, near Kealakaha, he fell in with *Akahiakuleana.*

[2] One legend has it that, instead of the *Lei, Liloa* gave her his *Laau-palau,* a short instrument for cutting taro tops, a dagger.

the mother furnished her son with means and instruction for the journey to Waipio. Two young men accompanied him on the journey, *Omaukamau* and *Piimaiwaa,* who became his constant and most trusted attendants ever after. Arrived in Waipio valley, they crossed the Wailoa stream, and *Umi* proceeded alone to the royal mansion, not far distant. According to his mother's instructions, though contrary to the rules of etiquette observed by strangers or inferior visitors, instead of entering the courtyard by the gate, he leaped over the stockade, and instead of entering the mansion by the front door, he entered by the back door, and went straight up to where *Liloa* was reclining and set himself down in *Liloa's* lap. Surprised at the sudden action, *Liloa* threw the young man on the ground, and, as he fell, discovered his Malo and his ivory clasp on the body of *Umi.* Explanations followed, and *Liloa* publicly acknowledged *Umi* as his son, and even caused him to undergo, *pro forma,* the public ceremony of *Oki ka piko* in token of his recognition and adoption.[1]

Umi's position was now established at the court of *Liloa,* and, with the exception of his older brother *Hakau,* whose ill-will and jealousy his recognition by *Liloa* had kindled, he soon became the favourite of all. When *Liloa* was near dying, he called the two sons before him, and publicly gave the charge of the government of Hawaii, the position of Moi, to *Hakau,* and the charge of his God— that is, the maintenance of the Heiaus and the observance of the religious rites—to *Umi,* telling the former, "You are the ruler of Hawaii, and *Umi* is your man," equivalent to next in authority.

The legends make no mention of any wars or contentions having occurred during *Liloa's* long reign to disturb the tranquillity of Hawaii.

---

[1] The ceremony of Oki ka piko, "cutting the naval string," was one of the most important proceedings attending the birth of a high chief's child. It was always, if possible, performed at the Heiau with much pomp and ceremony, the sacred drum beating and prayers offered up by the officiating priests.

Liloa's high-priest was · *Laeanuikaumanamana*, great-grandson of *Kuaiwa* through his son *Ehu*, and he received as a gift in perpetuity from *Liloa* the land in Kona district called Kekaha, which, through all subsequent vicissitudes of wars and revolutions, remained undisturbed in *Laeanui's* family until the time of *Kamehameha I.*

After *Liloa's* death *Hakau* became the Moi and chief ruler of Hawaii. He appears to have been thoroughly wicked, cruel, and capricious. I have found no legend in which he is mentioned that has a single good word to say in his behalf. No doubt much allowance must be made from the fact that nearly all the legends relating to him emanated from and were handed down by his opponents, the family of *Umi* and their descendants. Yet making allowance for the exaggeration of his faults, enough remains to load his memory with odium. He was rapacious and extortionate beyond endurance of either chiefs or people. He had the silly vanity of fancying himself the handsomest man on the island of Hawaii, and could brook no rival in that matter. If he even heard a man praised for his good looks, he would send for him and have him killed. He dismissed, disrated, and impoverished all the old and faithful counsellors and servants of his father, chiefs, priests, or commoners, and surrounded himself with a crew of sycophants and time-servers as cruel and as treacherous as himself. He missed no opportunity to thwart his brother *Umi*, and openly reviled him for his low birth, insisting that his mother was a woman of low degree. *Umi*, unable to bear the taunts of his brother, and not prepared to come to an open rupture with the tyrant, absented himself from the court of *Hakau*, and quietly left Waipio with his two friends, *Omaukamau* and *Piimaiwaa*. On the road he was joined by *Koi*, and these four travelled through Hamakua without stopping at Kealahaka, where *Umi's* mother lived, but proceeded at once to Waipunalei, near Laupahoehoe in the Hilo district, where, being unknown to the people, they concluded to stop, and being kindly received by the farmers' families, they lived there for some time, associating themselves with the farmers, assisting them in their labours on the land or at fishing or bird-catching. After a while *Umi* was recognised by *Kaoleioku*, a priest of much influence and power in that part of the country. *Umi* and his friends now removed to *Kaoleioku's* estate, and active preparations were entered into for the overthrow of *Hakau*. Men were collected from the villages around, and measures taken to ensure a successful revolt. The plot, doubtless, spread into Waipio, for under the gloss of the legend the fact shines out that two of the principal priests and former counsellors of *Liloa*, named *Nunu* and *Kakohe*, disgusted with the tyranny of *Hakau*, and under pretext of a journey to Hilo, secretly went to *Kaoleioku's* residence to confer with him and *Umi* and ascertain the strength of the conspirators. Deeming *Umi's* forces inadequate to cope with those of *Hakau* in open combat, they advised a stratagem and promised to aid it. Returned to Waipio, the priests attended on *Hakau*, who asked them if they had seen *Umi* on their journey to Hilo. They frankly told him that they had seen *Umi* at *Kaoleioku's* place, and advised *Hakau* to lose no time to send his men to the mountain to get fresh feathers wherewith to dress his tutelar god (*Kauila i ke Akua*). *Hakau*, somewhat surprised, reminded the old priests that the *Kauila Akua* was only done when war was imminent or on some other public emergencies. The priests then told him that *Umi* was collecting men and preparing to rebel at no distant time. Somewhat shaken by this recital, *Hakau* concluded to follow the priests' advice, and the day after the approaching festival of *Kane* was fixed upon, when *Hakau* was to send all his available household men and retainers to the mountain to hunt the birds from which the proper feathers were to be obtained. That was the very day which had been previously agreed upon between the two priests and *Kaoleioku* and *Umi* for an attack upon *Hakau*. The plot succeeded. *Umi* and his followers descended into the Waipio valley, found *Hakau* nearly alone and killed him, and *Umi* was proclaimed and installed as Moi or sovereign of Hawaii. No other blood was shed but that of *Hakau*, and the lives of his wife and daughter were spared ; in fact, in after life *Hakau's* granddaughter *Haukanuinonakapuakea* became one of the wives of *Umi's* son *Keawenui-a-Umi*.

Hakau's wife was *Kukukalani-o-pae*[1] and his daughter's name was *Pinea*.

MAUI.

Among the Maui chiefs from the close of the migratory period—say *Laamaikahiki* to *Piilani*, the contemporary of *Umi* and his father *Liloa*—not many names arrest the attention of the antiquarian student. The position of " Moi " of Maui appears to have descended in the line of *Haho*, the son of *Paumakua-a-Huanuikalalailai*, though, judging from the tenor of the legends, East Maui, comprising the districts of Koolau, Hana, Kipahulu, and Kaupo, was at times under independent Mois. The legends mention six by name, from *Eleio* to *Hoolae*,[2] the latter of whom was contemporary with *Piilani*, and whose daughter married *Piilani's* son, *Kiha-a-Piilani*. Their allegiance to the West Maui Mois was always precarious, even in later times. The island of Molokai does not appear to have acknowledged the sway of the

[1] Probably a daughter, at least belonging to the family of *Pae*, a famous priest and high chief in the time of *Liloa*. It is reported that after *Liloa's* death *Pae* took the bones of the defunct chief, and, sailing round the south point of Hawaii, stood up along the Kona shore, and sunk the bones in deep water off Kekaha. *Pae* had another daughter named *Hoe-a-Pae*, who was the mother of *Piimauilani*(*w*), whose descendants still survive.

[2] These names were *Eleio*, *Kalaehaeha*, *Lei*, *Kamohohalii*, *Kalaehina*, and *Hoolae*, each one succeeding the other. They generally resided at Hana, where the fortified hill of Kauiki was considered an impregnable fortress. I have a legend which mentions some transactions between *Eleio* and *Kakaalaneo*, the son of *Kaulahea I.*, but, if the legend may be trusted, *Eleio* must have been very old at the time. Whether this *Eleio* of Hana family descended from

Moi of Maui during this period, and for some time after, but obeyed its own independent chiefs, the ancestors of *Kalanipehu* and descendants of *Keoloewa* and *Nuakea.* The island of Lanai, however, and its chiefs, though often in a state of revolt, appear always to have recognised the Moi of Maui as their suzerain.

From the time of *Mauiloa,* third from *Haho* and contemporary with *Laamaikahiki,* to the time of *Kaulahea I.,* there must have been troublous times on Maui, and much social and dynastic convulsions, to judge from the confusion and interpolations occurring on the royal genealogy of this period. I have shown it to be nearly historically certain that the Oahu and Maui *Paumakuas* were contemporary, and it will be seen in the sequel that it is absolutely certain that *Kawaokaohele* on the *Paumakua-haho* line was contemporary with *Kalamakua, Piliwale,* and *Lo-Lale* on the *Maweke* line of Oahu chiefs, as well as on the Oahu *Paumakua* line through *Lauli-a-Laa;* and yet the Maui royal genealogy, as recited at the court of *Kahikili II.* at the close of the last century, counts thirteen generations between *Mauiloa* and *Kaulahea I.,* or sixteen generations between *Mauiloa* and *Kawaokaohele,* whereas the *Maweke* and Oahu *Paumakua* genealogies count only seven from *Laamaikahiki* to *Keleanohoanaa-piapi,* the sister of *Kawaokaohele.* Even the contemporary Hawaii royal genealogy from *Kaniuhi* to *Kiha-nui* counts only seven generations. Evidently the Maui genealogy has been doubled up by the insertion of contemporary chieftains, who probably divided the rule of

some of the southern immigrant chiefs or from the ancient *Nanaulu* line, I have not been able fully to ascertain. The ever more or less uncertain state of allegiance of the Hana chiefs to the Maui sovereign, and their frequently independent political status, would seem to have been born of some radical ancient antagonism. The old legends mention incidentally that *Kanaloa* and *Kalahuimoku,* two of the sons of *Hualani,* the wife of *Kanipahu,* and fifth in descent from *Maweke,* settled at Kauwiki in Hana. While the Hawaii chiefs retained the pedigree of the younger brother whose grand-daughter *Kamanawa* married *Kuaiwa,* the Moi of Hawaii, the descendants of the older brother, have dropped out of memory. *Kanaloa* may have been the great-grandfather of *Eleio.*

the island. The Oahu and Hawaii genealogies convict
the Maui genealogy of error. To this confusion may be
ascribed the fact that the same event is in different
legends said to have happened in the time of *Kamaloahua*
and of *Wakalana*, and that *Luakoa* of Maui, who in
company with *Laakapu's* of Hawaii sons made war on
Mailikukahi of Oahu, is placed the sixth in order above
Kakae and *Kakaalaneo*, who, through their grandsons
Kawaokaohele and *Luaia*, were the undoubted contemporaries of *Mailikukahi*. Moreover, *Kahokuohua*, who
figures on the Maui royal genealogy as the seventeenth
from *Paumakua* and a son of *Loe*, was a Molokai chief,
contemporary with *Kamaloohua* of Maui, with *Kalaunuiohua* of Hawaii and with *Kukona* of Kauai.

In reconstructing the Maui royal genealogy for this
period, I have, therefore, preferred to follow the *Kalona*
register referred to on page 27, and the ascertained contemporaneity of Maui chiefs with those of the other islands
whose places on their respective genealogies are undisputed and historically certain.

Looking down the line of these Maui chiefs, I have
found nothing but the names to distinguish the lives of
Mauiloa, Alo or *Alau*, and *Kuhimana*. The son of *Kuhi-*
mana was *Kamaloohua*, of whom mention is made on
page 67, and who was attacked, defeated, and taken
prisoner by *Kalaunuiohua* of Hawaii, carried captive in
the conqueror's train to Kauai, and there liberated by
Kukona after the crushing defeat of *Kalaunuiohua*. The
above-mentioned *Kalona* register indicates that *Kuhi-*
mana had a daughter named *Waohaakuna*, through whom
Mailikukahi of Oahu became connected with the Maui
line of chiefs. She does not appear by that name on the
Kakuhihewa pedigree, though, according to ancient custom,
it was very common for high chiefs to be known by several
names.

While *Kamaloohua* ruled over the greater part of Maui,
a chief who was doubtless a near relation, and was called

Kamaloo-
hua.

Wakalana, ruled over the windward side of the island and resided at Wailuku. During his time tradition records that a vessel called "*Mamala*" arrived at Wailuku. The captain's name is said to have been *Kaluiki-a-Manu,* and the names of the other people on board are given in the tradition as *Neleike, Malaea, Haakoa,* and *Hika.* These latter comprised both men and women, and it is said that *Neleike* became the wife of *Wakalana* and the mother of his son *Alo-o-ia,* and that they became the progenitors of a light-coloured family, "*poe ohana Kekea,*" and that they were white people, with bright, shining eyes, "*Kanaka Keokeo, a ua alohilohi na maka.*" The tradition further states that their descendants were plentiful in or about Waimalo and Honouliuli on Oahu, and that their appearance and countenances changed by intermarriage with the Hawaiian people. As the time of *Kamaloohua* and *Wakalana* was at least twenty generations ago, or about the middle of the thirteenth century, it is evident that no Europeans traversed the Pacific Ocean at that time, and that these white or light-coloured foreigners probably were the crew of some Japanese vessel driven out of her course, and brought by winds and currents to these shores, as is known to have happened at least in two instances since the islands were discovered by Captain Cook, and may have happened at other unrecorded times previous to the event now referred to. That the Hawaiian natives regarded these castaways as of an alien race is evident; and the impression of astonishment and wonder at their light complexions remained on the traditional record long after their descendants had become absorbed by, and become undistinguishable from, the original native inhabitants. Another version of the same tradition, while substantially the same as the foregoing, differs somewhat in the names of the new arrivals; and the event is ascribed to the time of *Kamaloohua,* while the other ascribes it to the time of *Wakalana.* As *Kamaloohua* and *Wakalana* were contemporary, and as the main fact is identical in

both versions, this difference rather confirms than weakens
the truth of the narrative, inasmuch as it goes to show
that the remembrance of the event had come down on
two different streams of tradition, one reckoning time by
the reign of *Kamaloohua*, the other by that of *Wakalana*.

After the reign and times of *Kamaloohua* nothing
worthy of note has been recorded of the Maui chiefs until
we arrive at the time of *Kakae* and *Kakaalaneo*, the sons
of *Kaulahea I.*, three generations after *Kamaloohua*. Of
Kakae personally nothing is remembered.[1] His wife's
name was *Kapohauola*, and she was probably the same
Kapohauola who at one time was the wife of *Ehu*, the
son of *Kuaiwa*, on the Hawaii *Pili* line, and thus establishes the contemporaneity of these chieftains. *Kakae's*
son was *Kahekili I.*, who is known to have had two
children, a son named *Kawao Kaohele*, who succeeded him
as Moi of Maui, and a daughter named *Keleanohoanaapiapi*,
who was successively the wife of *Lo-Lale*, son of *Kalona-
iki*, and of *Kalamakua*, son of *Kalona-nui*, on the Oahu
Maweke line.

Kakae's brother, *Kakaalaneo*, appears, from the tenor
of the legends, to have ruled jointly with *Kakae* over the
islands of Maui and Lanai. He was renowned for his
thrift and energy. The brothers kept their court at
Lahaina, which at that time still preserved its ancient
name of Lele, and tradition has gratefully remembered
him as the one who planted the bread-fruit trees in
Lahaina, for which the place in after times became so
famous. A marvellous legend is still told of one of
Kakaalaneo's sons, named *Kaululaau*, who, for some of
his wild pranks at his father's court in Lahaina, was
banished to Lanai, which island was said to have been
terribly haunted by ghosts and goblins—" *Akua-ino.*"
Kaululaau, however, by his prowess and skill, exorcised

Kakae and
Kakaalaneo.

[1] He was surnamed *Kaleo-iki*, and was considered as deficient in mental qualities. Some traditions state that *Luaia* was his grandson, but all the genealogies that I have seen or heard make *Luaia* the grandson of *Kakaalaneo*, and I have followed the latter.

the spirits, brought about quiet and order on the island, and was in consequence restored to the favour of his father.[1] It is said that *Kaululaau's* mother was *Kanikaniaula*, of the Molokai *Kamauaua* family, through *Haili*, a brother of *Keoloewa*.

With another wife, named *Kaualua*, *Kakaalaneo* had a son, *Kaihiwalua*, who was the father of *Luaia*, who became the husband of the noted *Kukaniloko*, daughter of *Piliwale*, the Moi of Oahu, son of *Kalona-iki*, and brother of *Lo-Lale* and *Kamaleamaka*.[2]

During the reign of *Kawaokaohele*, the son of *Kahikili I.*, and grandson of *Kakae*, the island of Maui appears to have been prosperous and tranquil. No wars with neighbouring islands or revolts of turbulent chieftains at home have left their impress on the traditional record. *Kawaokaohele's* wife was *Kepalaoa*, whose pedigree is not remembered, but who was probably some Maui chiefess. Kawaokhele.

The manner in which *Kawaokaohele's* sister, *Kelea*, surnamed "*Nohoanaapiapi*," became the wife of the two prominent Oahu chiefs above mentioned is characteristic of the times, and was a favourite subject of bards and raconteurs in after ages. The tradition regarding her may be abridged as follows:—

There lived at this time at Lihue, Ewa district, Oahu, a chief named *Lo-Lale*, son of *Kalona-iki*, and brother of *Piliwale*, the reigning Moi of Oahu. He was a bachelor and a man of an amiable temper. His brothers and the friendly neighbouring chiefs became very anxious that he should take unto himself a wife. Apparently no suitable match for so high a chief could be found on Oahu, or none had succeeded in captivating the fancy of *Lo-Lale*. In this case a bride must be sought for abroad, and a

[1] One legend mentions six children of *Kaululaau* by name—*Kuihiki*, *Kuiwawau*, *Kuiwawau-e*, *Kukahaulani*, *Kumakaakaa*, and *Ulamealani*. No further record of them occurs, however.

[2] *Kakaalaneo* is also said to have had a daughter named *Wao*, who caused the watercourse in Lahaina called "Auwaiawao" to be dug and named after her.

proper canoe, with trusty messengers, was fitted out at
Waialua to visit the windward islands and report upon
the beauty and rank of the chiefesses there. The canoe
first visited Molokai, but not satisfied with their inquiries,
the messengers proceeded to Lanai, and being equally
unsuccessful there, they sailed to Hana, Maui, intending
to cross over to Hawaii. At Hana they heard that *Kawaokaohele*, the Moi of Maui, was at that time stopping with
his court and his chiefs at Hamakuapoko, regulating the
affairs of the country, and enjoying the cool breezes of
that district, and the pleasure of surf-bathing, and that
with him was his sister *Kelea*, the most beautiful woman
on Maui, and the most accomplished surf-swimmer.
Hearing this, the messengers turned back from Hana and
arrived with their canoe on a fine morning off Hamakuapoko. On that very morning *Kelea* and her attendants
had gone down to the beach to enjoy the sport of surf-
bathing. Swimming out beyond the surf, she encountered
the canoe, and was at first somewhat surprised and startled
at seeing strangers in it, but being reassured by their
kindly speech, and being invited to come on board, the
messengers offered to ride the canoe ashore through the
surf—a sport as exciting as that of swimming on the surf-
board. *Kelea* accepted the invitation, and gallantly the
canoe shot over the foaming surf and landed safely on the
beach. All sense of danger or mistrust being dispelled,
the princess accompanied the canoe again out over the
surf, and again rode successfully ashore over the breakers,
the attendants hurraing lustily at the brave and fearless
style in which the canoe was handled. The messengers
having by this time ascertained who their illustrious
guest was, invited her to another trip through the roaring
surf. Thoughtlessly she consented, and the canoe pulled
out beyond the surf, watching for a good, high, combing
roller of the sea to start in with. At this moment a
squall or a whirlwind suddenly struck the canoe, coming
from off the shore, and away sped the canoe with its fair

and involuntary passenger over the broad ocean. When the storm subsided, the shores of Maui were far distant, and the messengers started for Waialua, Oahu, where they arrived safely. From Waialua *Kelea* was taken up to Lihue, where *Lo-Lale* received her with the regard due to a chiefess of her rank, and as she did not commit suicide, it may be inferred that she became reconciled to her lot and accepted him as her husband. And as no invasion of Oahu was ever attempted by *Hawaokaohele*, or vengeance exacted for the abduction of his sister, it is probable, though the legend says nothing about it, that the affair was diplomatically settled to the satisfaction of all parties.

For several years *Kelea* lived with *Lo-Lale* at Lihue, and bore to him three children, named *Kaholi-a-Lale, Luliwa-hine*, and *Luli Kane*. But the inland situation of Lihue, at the foot of the Kaala mountains, and far away from the sea, became wearisome and monotonous to the gay and volatile temper of *Kelea*. She informed her husband of her intention to leave, and reluctantly he gave his consent, knowing well that the prerogatives of her rank gave her the privilege of separation if she wanted it. His grief at parting has been preserved by the tradition in the form of a chant, the following portion of which alone has been remembered :—

> *Aloha kóu hoa i ka puali,*
>> Farewell, my partner on the lowland plains,
> *I ka wai o Pohakea,*
>> On the waters of Pohakea,
> *He luna o Kanehoa,*
>> Above Kanehoa,
> *He Lae ino o Maunauna.*
>> On the dark mountain spur of Maunauna.
> *O Lihue, ke hele ia!*
>> O Lihue, she has gone !
> *Honi aku i ke ala o ka Mauu,*
>> Sniff the sweet scent of the grass,
> *I ke ala o ke kupukupu,*
>> The sweet scent of the wild vines,

E linoia ana e ka Waikoloa,
  That are twisted about by (the brook) Waikoloa,
E ka makani he Waiopua-la,
  By the winds of Waiopua,
Kuu pu——a!
  My flower!
Me he pula la i kuu maka,
  As if a mote were in my eye,
Ka oni i ka haku onohi,
  The pupil of my eye is troubled,
Ka wailiu I kuu maka. E auwe áu-e!
  Dimness (covers) my eyes. Woe is me! Oh!

Leaving Lihue, *Kelea* descended to Ewa, and skirting the head of the lagoon by way of Halawa, arrived at the mouth of Pearl river opposite Puuloa, and found a crowd of idlers, nobles and retainers of *Kalamakua,* the high chief of that region, disporting themselves in the surf. Borrowing a surf-board from one of the bystanders, *Kelea* jumped in the sea and swam out beyond the breakers and joined the company of the other surf-bathers. When the surf broke at its highest they all started for the shore, and *Kelea* excelled them all, and was loudly cheered for her daring and skill. *Kalamakua,* being at the time in a neighbouring plantation, heard the loud uproar of voices from the shore, and inquired what the cause of it was. He was told that a beautiful woman from Lihue had beaten all the Halawa chiefs at surf-swimming, and hence the loud and continued cheering. Satisfied in his own mind that but one woman at Lihue could perform such a feat, and that she must be his cousin, *Lo-Lale's* wife, the Maui chiefess, *Kalamakua* went at once to the beach, and threw his *kihei* (mantle) over *Kelea* as she touched the shore, returning from another victorious trip through the surf. Explanations followed, and *Kelea* was borne home in state to the residence of *Kalamakua* in Halawa, and became his wife. With him she remained to her death, and bore him a daughter, called *Laielohelohe,* who in early youth was betrothed and subsequently married to her cousin *Piilani* of Maui, the son of *Kelea's* brother, *Kawaokaohele.*

Kawaokaohele was succeeded as Moi of Maui by his son *Piilani*, who, through his good and wise government, and through his connection with the reigning chief families of Oahu and Hawaii, brought Maui up to a political consideration in the group which it never had enjoyed before, and which it retained until the conquest by *Kamehameha I.* consolidated the whole group under one rule. During *Piilani's* reign, and perhaps during that of his father, the Hana chiefs acknowledged the suzerainty of the Moi of Maui, and *Piilani* made frequent tours all over his dominions, enforcing order and promoting the industry of the people. One of his daughters, named *Piikea*, became the wife of *Umi*, the son of *Liloa*, the Moi of Hawaii, and through her great-grandson, *I*, became the ancestress of the present sovereign of the Hawaiian group, *Kalakaua.*

Piilani's children with *Laielohelohe* were *Lono-a-Pii*, who succeeded him as Moi of Maui; *Kiha-a-Piilani*, who was brought up to the age of manhood among his mother's relatives on Oahu; the daughter *Piikea*, just referred to; and another daughter, *Kalaaiheana*, of whom no further mention occurs. With another wife, named *Moku-a-Hualeiakea*, a Hawaii chiefess of the *Ehu* family, he had a daughter, *Kauhiiliula-a-Piilani*, who married *Laninui-a-kaihupee*, chief of Koolau, Oahu, and lineal descendant of *Maweke* through his son *Kalehenui.* And with still another wife, named *Kunuunui-a-kapokii*, whose pedigree has not been preserved, he had a son, *Nihokela*, whose eighth descendant was *Kauwa*, grandmother of the late King *Lunalio* on his father's side.

OAHU.

On Oahu, at the close of the migratory period, after the departure of *Laamaikahiki*, we find his son, *Lauli-a-Laa,* aelo.

married to *Maelo*, the sixth in descent from *Maweke*, and daughter of *Kuolono*, on the *Mulielealii-Moikeha* line. They probably ruled over the Kona side of the island, while *Kaulaulaokalani*, on the *Maweke-Kalehenui* line, ruled over the Koolau side, and *Lakona*, also sixth from *Maweke*, on the *Mulielealii-Kumuhonua* line, ruled over Ewa, Waianae, and Waialua districts, and in this latter line descended the dignity of Moi of Oahu. Tradition is scanty as to the exploits of the Oahu Mois and chieftains, until

aka.

we arrive at the time of *Haka*, Moi of Oahu, chief of Ewa, and residing at Lihue. The only genealogy of this chief that I have, while correct and confirmed by others from *Maweke* to *Kapae-a-Lakona*, is deficient in three generations from *Kapae-a-Lakona* to *Haka*. Of *Haka's* place on the genealogy there can be no doubt, however, as he was superseded as Moi by *Mailekukahi*, whose genealogy is perfectly correct from the time of *Maweke* down, and conformable to all the other genealogies, descending from *Maweke* through his various children and grandchildren. Of this *Haka*, tradition records that he was a stingy, rapacious, and ill-natured chief, who paid no regard to either his chiefs or his commoners. As a consequence they revolted from him, made war upon him, and besieged him in his fortress, called Waewae, near Lihue. During one night of the siege, an officer of his guards, whom he had ill-treated, surrendered the fort to the rebel chiefs, who entered and killed *Haka*, whose life was the only one spilt on the occasion. Tradition does not say whether *Mailikukahi* had a hand in this affair, but he was clamorously elected by the Oahu chiefs in council convened as Moi of Oahu, and duly installed and anointed as such at the Heiau (temple).

Haka's wife was *Kapunawahine*, with whom he had a son, *Kapiko-a-Haka*, who was the father of two daughters —*Kaulala*, who married *Kalaniuli*, a Koolau chief, and became the ancestress of the royal *Kualii* family on Oahu. —and *Kamili*, who married *Ilihiwalani*, son of *Kala iku-*

kuma, of the Kauai royal family, from whom *Kaumualii,* the last independent Kauai king, descended.

Mailikukahi was the son of *Kukahiaililani* and *Koka-lola.* His father was fourth in descent from *Maelo* and her husband *Lauli-a-Laa,* and he thus represented both the *Maweke* and *Paumakua* families; a fact which gave him and his descendants no little importance among the Hawaiian aristocracy.

Mailikukahi is said to have been born at Kukaniloko, and thus enjoyed the prestige of the tabu attached to all who were born at that hallowed place. After his installation as Moi he made Waikiki in the Kona district his permanent residence, and with few exceptions the place remained the seat of the Oahu kings until Honolulu harbour was discovered to be accessible to large shipping.

On the Oahu legends *Mailikukahi* occupies a prominent place for his wise, firm, and judicious government. He caused the island˙to be thoroughly surveyed, and the boundaries between the different divisions and lands to be definitely and permanently marked out, thus obviating future disputes between neighbouring chiefs and land-holders. He caused to be enacted a code of laws, in which theft and rapine were punishable with death. He also caused another ordinance to be enacted and proclaimed, which the legend says found great favour with both chiefs and commoners, namely, that all first-born male children should be handed over to the Moi, to be by him brought up and educated. He was a religious chief withal, built several Heiaus, held the priests in honour, and discountenanced human sacrifices. The island of Oahu is said to have become very populous during his reign, and thrift and prosperity abounded.

I have before (p. 70) referred to the expedition by some Hawaii chiefs, *Hilo-a-Lakapu, Hilo-a Hilo-Kapuhi,* and *Punaluu,* joined by *Luakoa* of Maui, which invaded Oahu during the reign of *Mailikukahi.* It cannot be considered as a war between the two islands, but rather as a

Mailiku-kahi.

raid by some restless and turbulent Hawaii chiefs, whom the pacific temper of *Mailikukahi* and the wealthy condition of his island had emboldened to attempt the enterprise, as well as the *éclat* that would attend them if successful, a very frequent motive alone in those days. The invading force landed at first at Waikiki, but, for reasons not stated in the legend, altered their mind, and proceeded up the Ewa lagoon and marched inland. At Waikakalaua they met *Mailikukahi* with his forces, and a sanguinary battle ensued. The fight continued from there to the Kipapa gulch. The invaders were thoroughly defeated, and the gulch is said to have been literally paved with the corpses of the slain, and received its name, "Kipapa," from this circumstance. *Punaluu* was slain on the plain which bears his name, the fugitives were pursued as far as Waimano, and the head of *Hilo* was cut off and carried in triumph to Honouliuli, and stuck up at a place still called *Poo-Hilo.*

Mailikukahi's wife was *Kanepukoa*, but to what branch of the aristocratic families of the country she belonged has not been retained on the legends. They had two sons, *Kalonanui* and *Kalona-iki*, the latter succeeding his father as Moi of Oahu.

Kalona-iki.   *Kalona-iki* appears to have followed in the footsteps of his father, and observed the laws and policy inaugurated by him. The island was quiet and continued prosperous. No attacks from abroad, no convulsions within, have been remembered in the legends during his time. His wife was *Kikinui-a-Ewa.* Her parents are not mentioned, but it is said that she belonged to the great family of *Ewa-uli-a-Lakona*, the great-grandson of *Maweke. Kalona-iki's* children, as known, were *Piliwale, Lo-Lale,* and *Kamaleamaka.* The first succeeded him as Moi, the second we have already referred to, and of the third nothing more is known.

Piliwale.   Of *Piliwale's* reign no legends remain, and it may be presumed that the country enjoyed the same tranquillity and good fortune which had attended the reigns of his father and grandfather. His wife was *Paakanilea*, but of what descent is now not known. They had two daughters, one named *Kukaniloko*, who succeeded her father as Moi of Oahu, the other named *Kohipalaoa*, who married *Kaholi-a-Lale*, her cousin, and son of *Lo-Lale* and *Keleanohoana-apiapi*.

Of *Kukaniloko's* reign the legends are equally meagre, Kukan loko. except that she is frequently referred to as a great and powerful chiefess, who kept the country quiet and orderly. Her husband was a Maui chief named *Luaia*, grandson of *Kukaalaneo*. They had two children, *Kalaimanuia*, a daughter, and *Kauwahimakaweo*, of whom nothing further is known.

MOLOKAI.

The island of Molokai during this period, from *Laa-maikahiki* to *Kukaniloko* and her contemporary *Piilani*, presents no legendary lore of historical importance except the disaster which befell its principal chief, *Kahokuohua*, from the invasion of *Kalaunuiohua*, the Moi of Hawaii, referred to on page 67. The possession of the island had not yet become a political bone of contention between the Oahu and Maui kings, and its internal affairs apparently did not attract the attention of the neighbouring islands. Among the local legends of the island referring to the early part of this period is one which mentions *Kupa* as having been a brother of *Laamaikahiki*, and as having come with him from Tahiti, and become a principal chief of the eastern portion of Molokai. He is said to have resided at Mapulehu, and he and his household were destroyed and drowned by an extraordinary waterspout or freshet coming down the mountain and flooding the valley. It is also said that the Heiaus of Kahakoililani at Waialua, and of Iliiliopae at Mapulehu existed at this time, though the building of the latter has also been attributed to later times.

KAUAI.

On the exploits and achievements of the Kauai sovereigns and chiefs during this period the ancient legends are very incomplete. The line of sovereigns or Mois seems to have been kept, without exception, in that branch of the *Laamaikahiki* family which descended through his second son, *Ahukini-a-Laa*. How the dynastic differences between the older and powerful *Puna* and *Maweke* families, separately or jointly through *Moikeha's* children, and the comparatively later *Laa-maikahiki* descendants, were settled so as to confirm the sovereignty in the line of the latter, I have found no record of. Certain it is that the older lines had not become extinct, for their scions were referred to in much later times as enjoying a degree of tabu and consideration which greatly enhanced the dignity of the *Ahukini-a-Laa* descendants when joined with them in marriage.

Ahukini-a-
Laa, &c.

Of *Ahukini-a-Laa* no legend remains. His wife was *Hai-a-Kamaio*, granddaughter of *Luaehu*, one of the southern emigrant chiefs during the previous period. Their son was *Kamahano*, of whom nothing also is known, except that his wife's name was *Kaaueanuiokalani*, of unknown descent, and that their son was *Luanuu*. Equally curt notice remains of the reign of *Luanuu*. His wife's name on the genealogy is *Kalanimoeikawaikai*, but she could hardly have been the same who figures on the *Muliele Kumuhonua* genealogy as the wife of *Nawele*, the grandson of *Elepuukahonua*, the latter being fifth from *Maweke*, while the former was eighth from *Maweke* on the contemporary line of *Paumakua*. *Luanuu's* son was

Kukona.

Kukona, of whom mention has already been made in narrating the war of invasion undertaken by *Kalaunuiohua*, the sovereign of Hawaii, p. 67. It would appear that during these three generations from *Laamaikahiki* to *Kukona*, Kauai, its government and chiefs, had been living apart, or not mingled much with the chiefs or events on the other islands. Indigenous Kauai legends referring to this period have perished, and up to *Kukona's* time naught but the royal genealogy remains. But the war with the Hawaii chief, and the terrible defeat and capture of the latter, as well as *Kukona's* generous conduct towards the Oahu, Molokai, and Maui chiefs who fell into his hands after the battle, brought Kauai back into the family circle of the other islands, and with an *eclat* and superiority which it maintained to the last of its independence. *Kukona's* wife was *Laupuapuamaa,* whose ancestry is not known, and their son and successor was *Manokalanipo.*

Manokalanipo has the characteristic honour among the Hawaiians of having had his name affixed as a sobriquet to the island over which he ruled, and in epical and diplomatic language it was ever after known as " Kauai-a-Manokalanipo." He was noted for the energy and wisdom with which he encouraged agriculture and industry, executed long and difficult works of irrigation, and thus brought fields of wilderness under cultivation. No foreign wars disturbed his reign, and it is remembered in the legends as the golden age of that island.

The wife of *Manokalanipo* was *Naekapulani.* What lineage she sprang from is not known with any certainty. She was probably of Kauai birth, and one legend calls her *Naekapulani-a-Makalii,* indicating that *Makalii* was her father; and other legends speak of *Makalii* as a chief of Waimea, Kauai, though nothing is said whether he belonged to the *Maweke-Moikeha* line, or to that of *Laamai-kahiki.*[1] The children of *Manokalanipo* and his wife were *Kaumaka-mano, Napuu-a-mano* and *Kahai-a-mano.*

No special legend attaches to *Kaumaka-a-mano,* nor to his wife *Kapoinukai.* Their son was *Kahakuakane,* of whom nothing remarkable has been remembered in the

Manoka-lanipo.

Kaumaka-a-mano.

Kahakua-kane

<hr />

[1] In the "Mele inoa" (Family Chant) of *Kiha-a-Piilani* it is said that her name was *Noho-a-Makalii,* and that *Manokalanipo* had also another wife called *Pulanaieie.*

legends. *Kahakuakane* had two wives. With the first, named *Manokaikoo*, he had a son and successor called *Kuwalupaukamoku;* with the second, named *Kaponaenae*, he had two children called *Kahekiliokane* and *Kuonamauaino*. Though no legend or genealogy, that I have seen, state explicitly who were the parents or ancestors of either of the two wives of *Kahakuakane*, yet, judging from their names, and guided by the prevalent custom in such cases among the Hawaiian chiefs, it is very probable that the first was a granddaughter of *Manokalanipo*, and thus a cousin to her husband, and that the second was a sister of *Kahekili I*. of Maui, and daughter of *Kakae* and *Kapohauola*. And I am strengthened in the correctness of this suggestion by the fact that the granddaughter of this *Kahekiliokane* was sought for, and became the wife of *Lono-a-Pii*, the son of *Piilani* of Maui, thus returning to the family from which she sprang with the Kauai blood superadded.

No incidents in the reign of *Kahakuakane*, nor in that of his son *Kuwalupaukamoku*, have been retained on the traditional record. The wife of the latter was *Hameawahaula*, but her parentage is not given.

Kuwalu-
paukamo-
ku.

Kuwalupaukamoku's son was *Kahakumakapaweo*, contemporary with *Piilani* of Maui, with *Liloa* of Hawaii, and with *Kukaniloko* of Oahu. He is remembered with great renown and affection throughout the group, not only as a good, wise, and liberal sovereign, but also as the ancestor, through his grandchildren, *Kahakumakalina* and *Ilihiwalani*, of numerous aristocratic families from Hawaii to Niihau, who in after ages took a special pride in tracing themselves back to the high and pure-blooded tabu chiefs of Kauai.

Kahakuma
tapaweo.

During these nine generations from *Laamaikahiki*, the island of Niihau bore about the same political relation to the Moi of Kauai as the island of Lanai did to the Moi of Maui—independent at times, acknowledging his suzerainty at others. No historical event connected with Niihau during this period has been preserved, nor any genealogy of its chiefs. Springing from and intimately connected with the Kauai chiefs, there was a community of interests and a political adhesion which, however strained at times by internal troubles, never made default as against external foes.

Thus, after all allowance made for the marvellous and the palpably fabulous in the legends, and after comparing the legends and scraps of tradition, in prose or verse, of each island together, as well as with those of the other islands, the foregoing may be considered as the residuum of historical truth regarding the period just treated of. After the great excitement, the wild adventures, and restless condition attending the migratory period, which may be considered as closed with *Laamaikahiki*, a reaction of solitariness, quiet, and, so to say, darkness set in over the entire group, during which, with a very few exceptions, each island appears to have attended to its own affairs, and enjoyed that repose which leaves so little to chronicle in song or legend, and whose history may be condensed in an epigram.

We now approach the last period of Hawaiian ancient history before the conquest of the group by Kamehameha I. It was an era of strife, dynastic ambitions, internal and external wars on each island, with all their deteriorating consequences of anarchy, depopulation, social and intellectual degradation, loss of knowledge, loss of liberty, loss of arts. But, as the moral shadows deepen on the picture, the historical figures emerge in better view, and enable us to give a clearer synopsis of this period than of the foregoing.

HAWAII.

We again commence our review with this island, not because of any political preponderance that it may have exercised over the other members of the group—for its ascendancy only comes in at the closing scene of this period—but on account of its geographical position solely, it being the most eastward.

After the overthrow and death of *Hakau*, the son of *Liloa*, referred to on p. *78*, his brother, *Umi-a-Liloa*, became the Moi of Hawaii, the titular sovereign of the island. So great had been the discontent and disgust of the entire people, chiefs, priests, and commoners, with the tyrannical and unusually barbarous rule of *Hakau*, that, as a matter of political reaction and as an expression of relief, the great feudatory chiefs in the various districts of the island cordially received and freely acknowledged the sovereignty of *Umi* as he made his first imperial tour around the island shortly after his accession to power.

This journey, however, was stained by an act of cruelty which even those rough times felt as such and recorded. When *Umi* had fled from his brother *Hakau's* court, and was living at Waipunalei, in the Hilo district, unknown and in disguise, he and his friend, *Koi*, attended a surf-swimming match at Laupahoehoe. A petty chief of the district, named *Paiea*, invited *Umi* to a match, and offered a trifling bet, which *Umi* refused. *Paiea* then offered to bet four double canoes, and *Umi*, at the request, and being backed up by his friends, accepted the bet. *Umi* won the bet, but in coming in over the surf, by accident or design, *Paiea's* surf-board struck the shoulder of *Umi* and scratched off the skin. *Umi* said nothing then, but when he had attained to power and was making his first tour around the island, on arriving at Laupahoehoe he caused *Paiea* to be killed and taken up to the Heiau at Waipunalei to be sacrificed to his god.

Kaoleioku, the priest who assisted *Umi* in his revolt against *Hakau*, became *Umi's* high priest and chief counsellor, and through *Umi's* acknowledgment of the services rendered him, the priesthood advanced a large step in its status and pretensions.

Though *Liloa* had formally and publicly acknowledged *Umi* as [his] son, and *Umi's* prowess and accomplishments had vindicated his assumption of power, yet doubtless not a few of the higher chiefs, while acknowledging the pure descent of *Umi's* mother, considered her rank as so much inferior to that of *Liloa*, as to materially prejudice the rank of *Umi* himself in his position as Moi and as a chief of the highest tabu. To remedy this so far as his children were concerned, *Umi* took his half-sister, *Kapukini*, to be one of his wives, and thus their children would be "*Alii Pio*," chiefs of the highest grade. Moreover, on the advice of *Kaoleioku*, the high-priest, *Umi* resolved to send an embassy to Maui to solicit the hand of *Piikea*, the daughter of *Piilani*, the Moi of Maui, and of *Laielohelohe*, the grand-daughter of the Oahu *Kalonas*. Such a union, it was thought, would not only bring personal *éclat* to *Umi*, but also produce more intimate relations between the Hawaii sovereigns and those of the other islands. Forthwith a proper expedition was fitted out, and *Omaokamau* was sent as ambassador. The expedition landed at Kapueokahi, the harbour of Hana, where *Piilani* held his court at the time. *Umi's* offer was laid before *Piilani*, and met a favourable acceptance from both him and his daughter, and the time was arranged when she was to leave for Hawaii. At the appointed time *Piilani* sent his daughter over to Hawaii, escorted as became her rank and dignity. The legend says that four hundred canoes formed her escort. She landed at Waipio, where *Umi* resided, and, according to the etiquette of the time, she was lifted out of the canoe by *Omaokamau* and *Piimaiwaa* and carried on their locked hands into the presence of *Umi*. The legend adds, that shortly after these nuptials *Piilani* of Maui died, and his son, *Lono-a-Pii*, succeeded him.

When *Kiha-a-Piilani*, the younger brother of *Lono-a Pii*, had to flee from Maui, he sought refuge with his sister, *Piikea*, at the court of *Umi*. Here his sister advocated his cause so warmly, and insisted with *Umi* so urgently, that the latter was induced to espouse the cause of the younger brother against the older, and prepared an expedition to invade Maui, depose *Lono-a Pii*, and raise *Kiha-a-Piilani* to the throne of his father. Having received favourable auguries from the high-priest, *Kaoleioku, Umi* summoned the chiefs of the various districts of Hawaii to prepare for the invasion of Maui. When all the preparations were ready, *Umi* headed the expedition in person, accompanied by his wife, *Piikea*, and her brother, *Kiha-a-Piilani*, and by his bravest warriors.

Crossing the waters of "Alenuihaha" (the Hawaii channel), the fleet of *Umi* effected a landing at Kapueokahi, the harbour of Hana, Maui, where *Lono-a-Pii* appears to have continued to reside after his father *Piilani's* death. Having failed to prevent the landing of *Umi's* forces, *Lono-a Pii* retired to the fortress on the top of the neighbouring hill called Kauwiki, which in those days was considered almost impregnable, partly from its natural strength and partly from the superstitious terror inspired by a gigantic idol called *Kawalakii*, which was believed to be the tutelar genius of the fort. *Umi* laid siege to the fort of Kauwiki, and, after some delay and several unsuccessful attempts, finally captured the fort, destroyed the idol, and *Lono-a Pii* having fallen in the battle, *Kiha-a-Piilani* was proclaimed and acknowledged as Moi of Maui. Having accomplished this, *Umi* and his forces returned to Hawaii.

Though the legend from which the foregoing episode of *Umi's* reign is taken is probably incorrect when it refers to *Imaikalani*, the blind warrior chief, as fighting on the side of the Maui sovereign, *Lono-a Pii*, unless there were two of the same name and both affected by blindness, yet inasmuch as it has preserved a portion of a chant purporting to be a *Mele inoa* (a family chant) of *Kiha-a-Piilani*, which chant bears intrinsic evidence of not having been composed any later than in the time of *Keawe* and *Kalanikauleleiaiwi*, or about two hundred years ago, in so far it is valuable as showing that at that time *Lauli-a-Laa's* mother (*Hoakanuikapuaihele*) was said to be the daughter of *Lonokaehu*, and that the latter or his ancestors came from " Wawaụ " in the southern groups. That legend ends with the return of *Umi* from the war with Maui.

In the legend of *Kihapiilani* it is said that *Hoolae*, the chief of Hana, commanded the fortress of Kauwiki, and that *Lono-a Pii* was at Waihee at the time; that *Hoolae* escaped at the capture of the fort, but was pursued and overtaken on Haleakala, and there slain by *Pimaiwaa ;* and that *Umi's* army proceeded from Hana to Waihee, where a final battle was fought with *Lono-a Pii*, in which. he was killed. But whatever the discrepancies in detail between the two legends—the first being confessedly of Hawaiian growth, and the second probably of Maui origin —the historical result set forth by both cannot well be called in question.

After *Umi* returned from the war with Maui, he turned his attention to the domestic affairs of the island. Some legends refer to difficulties between *Umi* and *Imaikalani*, the powerful blind chief of Kau and parts of Puna, and though others intimate that *Piimaiwaa* was despatched to bring the obstinate old chief under subjection, yet it is not clear that any open rupture occurred between *Umi* and his great feudatory during their lifetime.

In the " *Récits d'un Vieux Sauvage pour servir à l'Histoire ancienne de Hawaii*" M. Jules Remy has evidently been misled by the venerable savage *Kanuha*, who related to him the legend of *Umi*, when he says that *Umi's* last rival and opponent on Hawaii "was his cousin *Keliiokaloa*," whom he fought and slew on the high plateau between the Hualalai and Maunaloa mountains, and erected the memorial stone-piles on that spot now known as the *Ahua-a-Umi* in commemoration of that event. As the tales related to M. Remy have been translated into English by Prof. W. T. Brigham (Boston, 1868), and may be read by many people even here, who have not the means of critically examining the merits of a legend, it may be proper in this place to correct the error into which M. Remy has been led.

The genealogical tree of *Umi* is one of the best preserved in the group, for his descendants were numerous and powerful, and spread themselves over all the islands. I have a large number of pedigrees of those families descending from *Umi*, and they all concur in asserting that *Keliiokaloa* was Umi's oldest son, and all the legends in my possession referring to the time of *Umi* and that of his children and grandchildren also concur in making *Keliiokaloa* the son and successor of *Umi* as Moi of Hawaii. Thus supported, I venture to say that there must have been some confusion as to names in the mind of the ancient Hawaiian who told M. Remy the tale of *Umi*. If there had been contest between *Umi* and a chief of the Kona district, that chief could have been none other than *Hoe-a-Pae*, the son of *Pae*, who was the counsellor and friend of *Liloa*, and who is said to have buried his bones in the deep sea off the *Hulaana*, between Waimano and Pololu, on the north-east coast of Hawaii; or, as another legend has it, off Kekaha on the Kona coast. But the legends, which I have collected and carefully compared, make no mention of such a civil war, nor that the *Ahua-a-Umi* were erected to commemorate this war.

It is doubtless true that *Umi* discontinued the permanent residence of the Hawaii sovereigns at Waipio. The reasons why are not very explicitly rendered. It is advanced in some legends that it was in order to check the rapacity of the nobles and retainers attending his court while held in that rich and densely peopled valley of Waipio, and that that was the reason which led him to establish his residence on that great and comparatively barren plateau where the *Ahua-a-Umi* were reared, far from the fruitful and ordinarily inhabited portions of the island, choosing to live there on the income or tribute brought him by the chiefs and the landholders of the various districts. And thus the six piles of stones were reared as peaceful mementoes and rallying-points, each one for its particular district, while the seventh pile indicated the court of *Umi* and its crowd of attendants.

Perhaps also another reason for *Umi's* removal from Waipio was the desire to live conveniently near to the rich fishing-grounds of the smooth sea off the Kona coast, the "*Kai Malino o Kona,*" which from time immemorial had filled the minds of the chiefs of the eastern and northern parts of the island with golden dreams of a luxurious life, and which continued to be a constant cause of bitter feuds between those who coveted its possession. But though *Umi* deserted Waipio and established his royal camp or headquarters at the *Ahua-a-Umi,* he did by no means withdraw himself from the active supervision of the affairs of his kingdom. He frequently visited the different districts, settled disputes between chiefs and others, and encouraged industry and works of public utility.

It is presumed that *Umi's* life passed tranquilly after his removal from Waipio; at least no wars, convulsions, or stirring events have been recorded. In making his tours around the island, *Umi* erected several Heiaus, distinguished from the generality of Heiaus by the employment of hewn stones. Such, among others, are the Heiau of *Kukii,* on the hill of that name, overlooking the warm springs of Kapoho, in the district of Puna; and of *Pohaku Hanalei,* in the district of Kau, above the wooded belt of the mountain. A number of hewn stones of this period —at least tradition, by calling them the *Pohaku Kalai a Umi* ("the hewn stones of Umi"), does so imply—were found scattered about the Kona coast of Hawaii, specially in the neighbourhood of Kailua, and, after the arrival of the missionaries (1820), furnished splendid material wherewith to build the first Christian church at Kailua.

Umi is reported to have been a very religious king, according to the ideas of his time, for he enriched the priests, and is said to have built a number of Heiaus; though in the latter case tradition often assigns the first erection of a Heiau to a chief, when in reality he only rebuilt or repaired an ancient one on the same site.

M. Jules Remy, in his collection of Hawaiian legends before referred to, thinks that the cruciform pavement observed in some of the Heiaus said to have been built by *Umi* is an indication of the advent and influence of the shipwrecked Spaniards, whose arrival he places in the reign of *Umi*. The author of this work is personally cognisant of the great interest and zeal in Hawaiian archæology evinced by M. Remy during his séjour in these islands; but the limited data at the command of M. Remy have led him into a wrong conclusion. For, first, the overwhelming majority of traditions still extant, referring to the advent of the shipwrecked foreigners about this time, place the event in the time of *Keliiokaloa*, the son of *Umi*, and not in that of *Umi* himself. Second, as *Keliiokaloa* did not become Moi of Hawaii until after his father's death, and as, according to Hawaiian custom, when an event is said to have transpired during the time or reign of such or such a chief, its proper and traditional meaning is that it transpired while such a chief was the Moi or sovereign, or at least most prominent chief on his island; it follows that the event so universally ascribed to the time or reign of *Keliiokaloa*—"*i ke au o k*"—could not possibly be, and was not by the ancients construed to mean, the time of *Umi*. Third, the cruciform pavement or division of the ground-floor, though found in some of the Heiaus on Hawaii ascribed to *Umi*, and very rare on the other islands, was neither exclusively peculiar to Hawaii nor to the time of *Umi;* for the Heiau of Iliiliopae, in Mapulehu valley on Molokai, was certainly not built by *Umi*, inasmuch as it was generations older than the time of *Umi*.

In the domestic relations of *Umi*, though blessed with
a number of wives, as became so great a potentate, yet he
knew how to keep his house in order, and no discords or
family jars have been reported. He is known to have
had at least six wives, viz.—(1.) *Kulamea*, whose family
and descent are not reported, and who was the mother of
Napunanahunui-a-Umi, a daughter; (2.) *Makaalua*, whose
family has not been remembered, and who was the mother
of *Nohowaa-a-Umi*, a daughter; (3.) *Kapukini*, a half-
sister of *Umi*, and daughter of *Liloa* with *Pinea*, and who
was the mother of *Kealiiokaloa*, a son, *Kapulani* or *Kapukini*, a daughter, and *Keawenui-a-Umi*, a son; (4.) *Piikea*,
the daughter of *Piilani*, the Moi of Maui, and who was
the mother of *Aihakoko*, a daughter, and *Kumalae*, a son;
(5.) *Mokuahualeiakea*, descended from the great *Ehu* family
in Kona, and who previously is said to have been the wife
of *Piilani* of Maui. She was the mother of *Akahiilikapu*,
a daughter. (6.) *Henahena*, said to be descended from
Kahoukapu of Hawaii. She was the mother of *Kamolanui-a-Umi*, a daughter. There is one legend which
mentions a seventh wife, named *Haua*, but her descent
and her children are unknown, and her name is not mentioned on any of the genealogies that I possess.

Of these eight children of *Umi*, *Kealiiokaloa* first, and
Keawenui-a-Umi afterwards, succeeded their father as
sovereigns of Hawaii. Of *Napunanahunui-a-Umi* not
much is known, except that the lands generally known
as " Kapalilua," in south Kona, Hawaii, were given by
Umi to this daughter in perpetuity, and through all the
vicissitudes and violence of subsequent reigns remained
in the possession of her descendants to the days of *Kamehameha*, when *Keeaumokupapaiaaheahi*, the son of *Keawepoepoe* and *Kumaiku*, and grandson of *Lonoikahaupu*,
possessed them, they having descended through his
mother's, *Kumaiku's*, ancestors, *Ua*, *Iwakaualii*, *Iama*,
&c., for eight generations. Of *Nohowaa-a-Umi* nothing
more is known. Of *Piikea's* children the legends refer to

the tragical end of *Ainakoko,* near Kalepolepo, on Maui, but no details of her sad fate have come down to the present time, so far as the author has been able to learn. *Kumalae,* however, the son of *Umi* and *Piikea,* is well known as the grandfather of *I,* of Hilo, and head of the present reigning family of *Kalakaua.* Of *Akahiilikapu* it is related that *Kahakumakaliua,* son of *Kalanikukuma,* the Moi of Kauai, travelling through the group for pleasure and observation, arrived at the court of *Umi,* and, charmed with this daughter of *Umi,* asked and obtained her for wife. Another legend says that *Akahiilikapu* went visiting the islands, and that having arrived at Kauai, there became the wife of *Kahakumakaliua.* Judging from the intrinsic merits of each legend, I consider the former as the correct version of the affair. Certain it is that *Akahiilikapu* accompanied her husband to Kauai and gave birth to two children, a daughter named *Koihalauwailaua*—or popularly, *Koihalawai*—and a son named *Keliiohiohi.* After some time spent on Kauai, and for some reasons which have not been handed down, *Akahiilikapu* returned to Hawaii with her children, and *Kahakumakaliua* remained on Kauai. Of *Kamolanui-a-Umi* it is known that she became one of the wives of *Keawenui-a-Umi,* and was the mother of *Kapohelemai,* the wife of *Makua-a-Kumalae,* and mother of *I.* *Kamolanui* had also another daughter named *Kanakeawe,* who was the mother of *Kapukamola,* the wife of *Makakaualii,* and mother of *Iwikauikaua.* This *Kanakeawe* is said also at one time to have been the wife of *Kaihikapu-a-Kahuhihewa* of Oahu.

The legend which M. Remy relates of the disposition of the remains of *Umi* is probably correct, for it is corroborated by other legends; and it so strikingly illustrates the custom of those times in regard to the funeral of high chiefs, that I take the liberty to quote it verbatim:—
" *Umi,* some time before his death, said to his old friend *Koi,* 'There is no place, nor is there any possible way, to

conceal my bones. You must disappear from my presence. I am going to take back all the lands which I have given you around Hawaii, and they will think you in disgrace. You will then withdraw to another island, and as soon as you hear of my death, or only that I am dangerously sick, return secretly to take away my body!'

" *Koi* executed the wishes of the chief, his *aikane* (friend). He repaired to Molokai, whence he hastened to set sail for Hawaii as soon as he heard of *Umi's* death. He landed at Honokohau. On setting foot on shore he met a Kanaka in all respects like his dearly-loved chief. He seized him, killed him, and carried his body by night to Kailua. *Koi* entered secretly the palace where the corpse of *Umi* was lying. The guards were asleep, and *Koi* carried away the royal remains, leaving in their place the body of the old man of Honokohau, and then disappeared with his canoe. Some say that he deposited the body of *Umi* in the great *Pali* (precipice) of Kahulaana, but no one knows the exact spot; others say that it was in a cave of Waipio at Puaahuku, at the top of the great Pali over which the cascade of Hiilawe falls."

This extreme solicitude of concealing the bones of defunct high chiefs was very prevalent in the Hawaiian group, and I have found indications of the same custom in other groups of Polynesia. The greatest trophy to the victor, the greatest disgrace to the vanquished, was the possession of the bones of an enemy. They were either simply exhibited as trophies, or they were manufactured into fish-hooks, or into arrow-points wherewith to shoot mice. Hence various expedients were resorted to to effectually prevent the bones of a high chief ever becoming the prey of any enemies that he may have left alive when he died. One of the most trusted friends of the deceased chief was generally charged with the duty of secreting the bones (*Hunakele*), and the custom prevailed till after the time of *Kamehameha I*. This custom applied, however, more particularly to prominent warrior chiefs, whose deeds in life may have provoked retaliation after death. Generally the custom in chief families was to strip the flesh off the corpse of a deceased chief, burn it, and collect the skull, collar-bones, arm and leg bones in a bundle, wrap them up in a tapa cloth, and deposit them in the family vault, if I may so call it, a house especially devoted to that purpose, where they were guarded with the utmost care, some trusty Kahu or attendant of the family always being present night and day, who in time of danger immediately conveyed them to some safe and secret hiding-place.

During *Umi's* reign the following chiefs have been recorded as the district chiefs, the "Alii-ai-moku," of Hawaii:—*Wahilani* of the Kohala district; *Wanua* of Hamakua; *Kulukulua* of Hilo; *Huaa* of Puna; *Imaikalani* of Kau; and *Hoe-a-Pae* of Kona. During his and their lifetime peace and quiet obtained on Hawaii.

Kealiio-
kaloa.

When *Umi* died he was succeeded as Moi of Hawaii by his oldest son, *Kealiiokaloa.* Not much is said of him in the legends, and his reign apparently was of short duration. Whether he died from sickness, or, as one legend has it, was treacherously assailed and killed by some rebellious chief, he is remembered as an unpopular king, and the only event of note connected with his reign is the arrival on the coast of Kona of some shipwrecked white people.

The legend of that event is well known, and has several times been stated in print. Its main features are the following:—

"In the time of *Kealiiokaloa*, king of Hawaii and son of *Umi*, arrived a vessel at Hawaii. *Konaliloha* was the name of the vessel, and *Kukanaloa* was the name of the foreigner (white man) who commanded, or to whom belonged the vessel. His sister was also with him on the vessel.

" As they were sailing along, approaching the land, the vessel struck at the Pali of Keei, and was broken to pieces by the surf, and the foreigner *Kukanaloa* and his sister swam ashore and were saved, but the greater part of the crew perished perhaps; that is not well ascertained.

" And when they arrived ashore, they prostrated themselves on the beach, uncertain perhaps on account of their being strangers, and of the different kind of people whom they saw there, and being very fearful perhaps. A long time they remained prostrated on the shore, and hence the place was called ' *Kulou*,' and is so called to this day.

" And when evening came the people of the place took them to their house and entertained them, asking them if they were acquainted with the food set before them, to which they replied that they were; and afterwards, when breadfruit, ohia, and bananas were shown to them, they expressed a great desire to have them, pointing to the mountain as the place where to get them. The strangers cohabited with the Hawaiians and had children, and they became ancestors of some of the Hawaiian people, and also of some chiefs."—" *Moolelo Hawaii*," *by D. Malo.*

That such an event as the arrival of shipwrecked white people really transpired there is no reasonable ground for doubting. It was generally so received throughout the group previous to its discovery by Captain Cook; and as the first echoes of the event grew fainter by the lapse of time, some of the other islands set up claims to have this identical event occurring on their shores. Thus the Maui version of the event, while retaining the name of the vessel and the name of the commander, relegates the occurrence to the time of *Kakaalaneo*, king of Maui; changes the locality of the wreck from the Kona coast of Hawaii to Kiwi in Waihee, Maui, and enters into a number of details unknown or forgotten in the Hawaii tradition. There was a tradition in later times on Kauai also that such an event had happened on their shores.

Taking the Hawaii tradition to be the original and correct version of this event, let us first ascertain to what period, if not to what particular year, Hawaiian chronology assigns it, and then inquire how far it may with probability be confirmed by outside contemporary historical evidence. Hawaiian chronology counts by generations, not by reigns nor by years. In computing long genealogies, thirty years to a generation will be found approximately correct. *Keliiokaloa*, it will be seen by all the genealogies that lead up to him directly, as well as by the genealogies of his contemporaries in the other islands of the group, is the eleventh generation back of the present one now living. But the present generation—and for illustration we take his present majesty, *Kalakaua* — was born in 1836. Eleven generations, or 330 years back of 1836, bring us to A.D. 1506 as the year of *Keliiokaloa's* birth. If we count by the line of her Highness *Ruth Keelikolani*, the great-granddaughter of *Kamehameha*, and who was born in 1826, we come to the year 1496 as the probable birth-year of *Keliiokaloa;* and considering that he was the oldest of *Umi's* children, the latter year is probably the more correct. When *Umi* died and *Keliiokaloa* succeeded to the government of Hawaii, the latter was certainly about twenty-five or thirty years old, which brings us to a period between 1521–1526 A.D. But his reign is everywhere said to have been of short duration, certainly not exceeding ten years. We have, then, from Hawaiian authority, established the fact that the arrival of the shipwrecked foreigners—white people—took place between the years 1521–1530 A.D. No legend states whether it was in the early or latter part of his reign, but as he is reported to have reigned but a few years before his brother succeeded him, we may be justified in taking a middle term, and say that it happened between 1525–1528.

In Burney's "Discoveries in the South Seas," vol. i. p. 148, we read, in substance, that on October 31, 1527, three vessels left a port called Zivat Lanejo, said by Galvaom to be situated lat. 20° N. on the coast of New Spain, for the Moluccas or Spice Islands. The vessels were called the "Florida," with fifty men, the "St. Iago," with forty-five men, and the "Espiritu Santo," with fifteen men. They carried thirty pieces of cannon and a quantity of merchandise, and they were under the command of Don Alvaro de Saavedra. These vessels sailed in company, and when they had accomplished 1000 leagues from port, they were overtaken by a severe storm, during which they were separated. The two smaller vessels were never afterwards heard of, and Saavedra pursued the voyage alone in the "Florida," touching at the Ladrone Islands.

A thousand Spanish or Portuguese leagues are equal to nearly fifty-eight equatorial degrees. Now allowing that Saavedra's logbook was perfectly correct as regards the 1000 leagues that the vessels kept company, saving and excepting always what allowance should be made for the westerly current, and that Galvaom is also correct as regards the latitude of Zivat Lanejo, the port of departure, it becomes evident that Saavedra's fleet must have been somewhere within 200 miles, probably to the westward and southward, of the Hawaiian group when the storm overtook it. And, to judge from the period of the year when the fleet left New Spain (October 31), that storm must have been what in this group is well known as a Kona storm—a southerly or south-westerly gale with heavy squalls of rain. In that position and under those circumstances, if unable to weather the gale by lying-to, and obliged to scud, a vessel would almost necessarily run ashore on the western coast of Hawaii. That one vessel, at least, about that time was wrecked on Hawaii, and two, if not more, people saved, Hawaiian tradition bears ample testimony to ; and Spanish records furnish us with the further testimony that at that time, in that vicinity, and during a severe storm, there were not one only, but three Spanish vessels likely to be shipwrecked, and that two of the three were never afterwards heard of. They may have foundered in open sea, but Hawaiian tradition is positive, and cannot be refuted, that one at least was wrecked on the Kona coast off Keei, and that two of its crew, if not more, a man and a woman, were saved.

Moreover, as there can be now no doubt that the foreigners referred to in the Hawaiian tradition were "Haole"—white people—and as no white people except Spanish subjects were cruising in the Pacific at that time, the conclusion becomes almost irresistible that the said foreigners were a portion of the crew or the passengers on board of one or the other of the lost vessels under Saavedra's command.

The names preserved in Hawaiian tradition of the vessel and of the saved man, "Konaliloha" and "Kukanaloa," are Hawaiian names, and furnish no indications of their nationality.

It may reasonably be assumed, in the absence of proof to the contrary, that the influence exercised by these foreigners over the people among whom they were cast was very limited. No traces of such influence can now be found in the religion, knowledge, customs, or arts of the Hawaiians, as practised from that time till now. They were either too few, or too ignorant, or too unpretending, to become reformers, or to impress themselves for good or for bad upon the national mind, and with the exception of the blood that they transmitted through their descendants to our days, little is known of them or ascribed to them beyond the fact of their arrival.

It has been said that the feathered headdress or helmet, the *Mahiole*, worn by the chiefs when dressed for battle, or in gala array, was an invention of this period, and attributable to these foreigners. But the *Mahiole*, as a part of a chief's apparel, is mentioned in legends older than the time of *Umi;* and besides, such feathered helmets were worn by Tahitian chiefs when Wallis and Bougainville first made their acquaintance.

The wife of *Keliiokaloa* was *Makuahineapalaka*,[1] and their son was *Kukailani*, who became the father of *Maka-*

---

[1] Her family or descent is nowhere mentioned.

kaualii, and grandfather of *Iwikauikaua,* a prominent and turbulent chief in his day, and grandfather of *Keaweke-kahialiiokamoku* and his sister *Kalanikauleleiaiwi.*

After the death of *Keliiokaloa* there supervened a season of internal war, anarchy, and confusion, which has left its blurred image on the traditions of the country, for they are neither copious nor clear in regard to it. Yet reading the legends of the time with a tolerably correct conception of the customs and condition of men and things, and knowing that those ancient legends frequently merely hint at an event instead of describing it, because it was well and commonly known at the time the legend was composed or was popularly recited, it would appear that at *Kealiiokaloa's* death the great district chiefs of the island of Hawaii refused to acknowledge the sovereignty or Moiship of *Keawenui-a-Umi,* the younger brother of *Kealiiokaloa.* War followed, but the revolted chiefs seem to have been deficient in organisation or co-operation, for *Keawenui-a-Umi* defeated each and all of them, killed them, and kept their bones—bundles referred to on page 105—as trophies. In the legend and chant of *Lonoikama-kahiki,* the son of *Keawenui,* the names of the six district chiefs whom his father defeated are given : *Palahalaha,* son of *Wahilani* of Kohala; *Pumaia,* son of Wanua of Hamakua ; *Hilo-Hamakua,* son of *Kulukulua* of Hilo ; *Lililehua,* son of *Huaa* of Puna; *Kahalemilo,* son of *Imai-kalani* of Kau; *Moihala,* son of *Hoe-a-Pae* of Kona.

After these revolted chiefs had been subdued and disposed of,[1] *Keawenui* restored order and quiet in the island of Hawaii, on the pattern of his father, *Umi. Keawenui* is said to have been of a cheerful and liberal disposition, and not only frequently travelled around his own dominions of Hawaii, but also visited the courts of the sovereigns of the other islands. His visit to Maui, and

Keawenui-a-Umi.

---

[1] In the legend of *Lonoikamakahiki* the son of *Keawenui-a-Umi,* it is said that the revolted chiefs were con- quered and captured in a severe battle fought at Puumaneo, in Kohala district.

his sumptuous entertainment by *Kamalalawalu*, the Moi of Maui, is particularly described. One of his most trusted friends and " *Puuku* " (royal treasurer) was a man named *Pakaa*, who for many years had served him faithfully and well. But at the court of *Keawenui*, as at many other courts, jealous and intriguing rivals conspired the downfall of *Pakaa*, and after a while they succeeded. *Pakaa* fled to Molokai to escape the anger of *Keawenui*, and lived there in retirement and disguise. *Pakaa's* wife is said to have been *Hikauhi* of Molokai, daughter of *Hoolehua* and *Iloli*, who lived at Kaluakoi, which may have been the reason of his fleeing there for shelter and safety. Some time after *Pakaa's* flight—how long is not stated, but several months may be inferred—*Keawenui* discovered that the accusations brought against *Pakaa* had been unjust and malicious, and, filled with sorrow and regret for the loss of his old friend and the injustice done him, he resolved to seek him in person and be reconciled to him. The account of this voyage of discovery by *Keawenui-a-Umi* was a favourite subject for listening ears in the olden time, and particularly interesting as giving a detailed relation of all the winds, their names and localities, that ever blew on the coasts and the mountains throughout the group. It is a chant of over four hundred lines, embodied in the legend, and supposed to have been recited by *Ku-a-Pakaa*, the son of Pakaa.[1]

After *Keawenui's* reconciliation with *Pakaa*, no further event of note during his reign has been recorded in the traditions. His principal residence seems to have been at Hilo.

Keawenui-a-Umi has been greatly blamed by some

---

[1] To Hawaiian scholars it may suffice to indicate the chant by its opening lines :—

Kiauau ! kiauau ! kiauau !
Hiki ka ua, ka makani, ka ino,

No Puulenalena, no Hilo no, &c.
Softly ! softly ! softly !
The rain is coming, the wind and bad weather,
From Puulenalena* of Hilo.

* The name of a cold wind from the mountains back of Hilo and the neighbourhood of the volcano.

genealogists for his numerous amours with women of low
degree and with the daughters of the common people,
thereby impairing the purity of the aristocratic blood and
giving rise to pretensions that in after ages it became
difficult to disprove. This objection dates back to the
turbulent times of the early part of the reign of *Kamehameha I.*, and has been repeated since, but may have
been of older origin. Admitting, however, that *Keawenui's*
amours were not always conformable to the rules of Hawaiian heraldry, yet it is due to the memory of this great
chief and to historical truth to state that during the
present century, and in all the legends of the times preceding it, I have found no name or family claiming
descent from him and setting up pretensions accordingly,
unless they were actually and historically descended from
some one of his five wives, all of whom were of high and
undoubted aristocratic families. These five wives were—
(1.) *Koihalawai* or *Koihalauwailaua*, daughter of his sister
Akahiilikapu and *Kahakuma Kaliua*, one of the tabu
chiefs of Kauai. With this wife *Keawenui* had four
children, three sons and a daughter : *Kanaloakuaana,
Kanaloakuakawaiea, Kanaloakapulehu*, and *Keakalaulani*.
(2.) *Haokalani*, of the *Kalona-iki* family on Oahu, or from
the great *Ehu* family on Hawaii through *Hao-a-kapokii*,
the fourth in descent from *Ehunui Kaimalino ;* the fact
is not very clearly stated, though the presumption, from
allusions in the legends, is in favour of the former. Her
son was the celebrated *Lonoikamakakiki*. (3.) *Hoopiliahae*,
whose parentage is not stated,[1] but whose son, *Umiokalani*, allied himself to the Maui chiefess *Pii-maui-lani*, and
was the father of *Hoolaaikaiwi*, mother of the widely-
known and powerful *Mahi* family on Hawaii. (4.)
Kamola-nui-a-Umi, the half-sister of *Keawenui*. Her
daughter was *Kapohelemai*, who became the wife of her

---

[1] I have but one genealogy in which *Huanuikalalailai*, through his son,
her parentage is referred to, and there *Kuhelaui*, the brother of the Maui
she is said to be a descendant of *Paumakua*.

cousin *Makua* and mother of *I*, from whom the present reigning family descends. (5.) *Hakaukalalapuakea*, the granddaughter of *Hakau*, the brother of *Umi*. Her daughter was *Iliilikikuahine*, through whom more than one family now living claims connection with the line of *Liloa*. All the legends mention a son of *Keawenui* named *Pupuakea*, who was endowed with lands in Kau, but none of the legends that I possess mention who his mother was. He remained true to *Lonoikamakahiki* when all the world forsook him, and was treated by *Lono* as a younger brother or very near kindred.

There can be little doubt that *Keawenui* himself, as well as the public opinion of the chiefs and landholders of Hawaii, considered his occupancy of the dignity and position of Moi of Hawaii as an usurpation of the rights of his nephew, *Kukailani*, the son of *Keliiokaloa*; and this was probably the cause of the commotion and uprising of the great district chiefs in the early part of *Keawenui's* reign. Thus, when *Keawenui* was on his deathbed, he solemnly, and in the presence of his chiefs, conferred the sovereignty, the dignity, and prerogatives of Moi on *Kaikilani*, the daughter of *Kukailani*, and who was the joint-wife or successive wife of his two sons, *Kanaloa-kuaana* and *Lonoikamakahiki*. This *Kaikilani*, whose full name was *Kaikilani-nui-alii-wahine-o-Puna*, must not be mistaken, as several later genealogists have done, for another wife of *Lonoikamakahiki* called *Kaikilanimai-panio*, and who was the daughter of *Kaeilaunui* and his wife *Kauluoaapalaka*, a descendant of the great *Ehu* family through *Laeanuikaumanamana*, the high-priest in the time of *Kihanui* and *Liloa*. *Kaikilani-alii-wahine-o-Puna* had three children with *Kanaloa-kuaana*, but had no children with *Lonoikamakahikii*; whereas *Kaikilanimai-paneo* had two sons with the aforesaid *Lonoikamakahiki*.

The legends are rather minute in detailing the early life and training of *Lonoikamakahiki*, how he was instructed, and became a great proficient in all the athletic and war-

Kaikilani and Lonoi-kamaka-hiki.

like exercises of the time; how he was endowed with great powers of conversation and argumentation; how he was a zealous worshipper of the gods, having in early life been deeply affected, when on a visit with his father to Hilo, by the austere and venerable aspect of *Kawaamau-kele*, the high-priest of Hilo, whose long hair, reaching down to his knees after the fashion of high-priests, inspired him with awe and terror, and who afterwards told him his fortune.

For some time after the accession of *Kaikilani* as Moi, though the government of the island was carried on in her name, yet *Kanaloakuaana* appears to have acted as a Regent or Prime Minister and as a special guardian of his younger brother, *Lonoikamakahiki*. After a while, *Kanaloakuaana* instituted a formal examination or trial of *Lonoikamakahiki* as to his qualifications as a warrior, a counsellor, and chief, and the latter having come out victorious in all the trials, *Kaikilani* was advised to share the throne and dignity with *Lonoikamakahiki*, and thenceforth the latter was hailed as Moi of Hawaii.

For several years peace and prosperity prevailed on Hawaii and concord in the royal family. Having regulated the government satisfactorily, and having no wars or rebellions to contend with, *Lonoikamakahiki* concluded to visit the other islands, especially Kauai, in search of some famous kind of wood of which spears were made. His wife *Kaikilani* accompanied him. Among his outfit on the occasion are mentioned the royal *Hokeo*,[1] called "*Kuwala-wala*," and the royal *Kahili*,[2] called "*Eleeleualani*."

Lonoikamakahiki and his suite stopped at Lahaina, but

---

[1] The *Hokeo* was a large, high, and straight calabash, in which the wardrobe of chiefs and other valuables were packed, as in a trunk. This particular "Hokeo" was famous for containing the bundles of bones of the six rebel chiefs of Hawaii whom his father, *Keawenui-a-Umi*, had slain.

[2] The *Kahili* was an ensign of chiefship and royalty. It was composed of select birds' feathers closely tied on to a flexible handle or staff, and varying in size from two to three feet long for daily use, to twelve or fifteen feet in length for processions and grand occasions.

Kamalalawalu, the Moi of Maui, was absent visiting other parts of the island, and *Lono* proceeded on towards Oahu. Being overtaken by bad and stormy weather, *Lono* put in to Kalaupapa, on the north-west side of the island of Molokai, for shelter; hauled up his canoes, and remained the guest of the Kalaupapa chiefs until better weather should permit him to leave.

To beguile the time while thus windbound, *Lonoikama-kahiki* and *Kaikilani* frequently amused themselves with a game of "*Konane,*" resembling the game of draughts, played on a checkered board with white and black squares. One day while thus occupied, seated in the open air, the faint sound as of some one hailing from the top of the overhanging Pali of "*Puupaneenee*" reached the players. Again the hail was repeated, and distinct and clear these words came down on the astounded ears of Lono:—
"*E, Kaikilani alii wahine o Puna—E, E aa mai ana ia oe kou ipo; o ke ku a Kalaulipali, o Uli, o Heakekoa!*" ("Ho, Kaikilani! your lover Heakekoa, the son of Kalau-lipali and Uli, is longing for you.") By her confusion and her attempts to divert the attention of *Lono, Kaikilani* confirmed him in his suspicions; and enraged at the infidelity of his wife, as well as at the audacity of the lover thus publicly to affront him, he snatched up the Konane board and struck *Kaikilani* so violent a blow on the head that she fell senseless and bleeding on the broad flag-stones[1] where they had been sitting. Full of his angry feelings, the chief ordered his canoes to be launched, and, sternly forbidding *Kaikilani* to follow him, set sail for Oahu that same day.

It is said in the legend that this passionate exhibition of her husband's love, and the finding herself left alone and forbidden to accompany him, produced such revulsion

[1] Tradition has preserved, and the old inhabitants, on the author's first visit to the place, pointed out the very broad stone on which *Lono* and *Kaikilani* were said to have been sitting and playing when the game was so fatally interrupted. The place was called "Pikoone," and is near the harbour of Kalaupapa.

in the mind of *Kaikilani* as to entirely break off her fondness for *Heakekoa* (if she really ever had had any such), who disappears, and is not further heard of in the legends. As soon as she had recovered from the wound inflicted by the Konane-board she sorrowfully returned to Hawaii. Meanwhile the news of the tragical episode at Kalaupapa had preceded her arrival at Hawaii. The island was filled with consternation ; the chiefs took counsel together how to avenge the reported death of *Kaikilani* and the indignity offered her ; all the brothers of *Lonoikamakahiki*, and all the district chiefs except *Pupuakea* of Kau, joined in the revolt, *Kanaloakuaana* again assuming the regency and organising measures to intercept and slay *Lonoikamakahiki* should he attempt to land on the coast of Hawaii. When *Kaikilani* arrived at Kohala from Molokai, she learned the news of this great revolt, and, with all the ardour of her old love for *Lono* reawakened, and only anxious for his safety, she quietly re-embarked and sailed for Kau, avoiding the rebel chiefs, and placing herself in communication with *Pupuakea*, the only chief of note that still adhered to the fortunes of *Lonoikamakahiki*. Under his advice and with his assistance men were assembled and measures taken to recover the lost supremacy of *Lono*. In view, however, of the superior forces and personal character of the revolted chiefs, it was thought that *Lono's* presence was absolutely needed as a counterpoise before commencing active hostilities. In this dilemma *Kaikilani* resolved to go to Oahu and personally acquaint her husband with the state of affairs on Hawaii, and by this proof of her returned love endeavour to win back his affections and induce him to return. She sailed ; how she succeeded will be seen in the sequel.

When *Lonoikamahiki* left Kalaupapa on Molokai he started with only one canoe, leaving the rest of his retinue to follow when ready. *Lono* went straight to Kailua, in Koolaupoko district, Oahu, where *Kakuhihewa*, the Moi of Oahu, then held his court, the name of the royal resi-

dence being " Kamooa." As Lono's canoe approached the
shore, *Lanahuimihaku*, a chief and a priest who had formerly been in the service of *Keawenui-a-Umi*, and was
well versed in all the lore of the Hawaii chiefs, but who
was now a counsellor under *Kakuhihewa*, recognised the
canoe, the sail, and the insignia, and informed *Kakuhihewa* that one of *Keawenui's* sons was approaching.
Kakuhihewa received him royally and cordially. Food
was prepared in abundance and a house set apart for his
reception. An incident that occurred the first night of
Lono's stay ashore will in a measure show the manners of
the time, and may well be worth repeating.

After *Lono* had left his royal host in the evening and
retired to rest, either that the thoughts of the Kalaupapa
affair troubled his mind, or that the heat of the night
made it uncomfortable to sleep in the house, he got up
and went down to the beach to sleep in his canoe, where
the cool breeze off the sea would fan and refresh him.

While there, another double canoe arrived during the
night from Kauai, having on board a chiefess named
Ohaikawiliula, bound to Hawaii on a visit. *Lono* accosted
the stranger, inquired the news from Kauai, and in course
of conversation learned that a new *Mele* or chant had just
been composed in honour of this chiefess's name; that it
was only known to a few of the highest chiefs on Kauai,
and had not yet become public. Prompted by curiosity
and a natural bent for acquiring all sorts of knowledge,
Lono entreated the chiefess to repeat the chant, which she
complaisantly did, and *Lono's* quick ear and retentive
memory soon caught and correctly retained the whole of
it. The chant was well known to Hawaiians of the last
generation, and many of the present may recall it to
mind by hearing the first line:

> *Kealialia liu a Mana.*[1]
> The salt pond of Mana.

---

[1] For what remains of this chant, see Appendix No. 2.

His expected sleep on the beach having been thus interrupted, *Lono* returned to the house and slept soundly till late in the morning.

Kakuhihewa, having enjoyed an uninterrupted night's rest, rose early next morning and repaired to the seashore for a bath, according to the custom. He there found the canoe of the Kauai chiefess just getting ready to leave. Saluting the stranger, he also inquired the latest news from Kauai, and received the same information that *Lono* had received during the night, of which fact, however, *Kakuhihewa* was ignorant. Having repeated the chant to *Kakuhihewa*, and he having committed it to memory, the Kauai chiefess made sail and departed, and *Kakuhihewa* returned to his palace much pleased at the opportunity of puzzling his guest, when he should awake, with the latest news from Kauai. When *Lono* finally awoke and made his appearance, *Kakuhihewa* challenged him to chant the latest Mele from Kauai. Without hesitation *Lono* complied, and recited the chant correctly from beginning to end, to the great discomfiture and perplexity of *Kakuhihewa*.

Lonoikamakahiki remained a long time a guest of *Kakuhihewa*, and their adventures, excursions, amusements, and betting exploits are related at great length in the legends, but they are so greatly exaggerated, so mixed with the marvellous, and withal so confused as to sequence of time, that it is hardly possible to eliminate any historical fact from them, except the general one that during this time "les rois s'amusaient." It was during this period also that *Lono* exhibited the trophies of his father (the bundles of bones referred to on a former page) and chanted the names of the slain chiefs. Yet, though there was no doubt in *Kakuhihewa's* mind that *Lono* was a chief of very high rank on Hawaii, and probably one of *Keawenui-a-Umi's* sons, still his real name and position appear not to have been known to *Kakuhihewa* nor to his grand counsellor *Lanahuimihaku*, and the latter did not scruple openly to call *Lono* an *Alii inoa ole*, "a nameless chief," to which taunt *Lono* merely replied that if ever *Lanahuimihaku* fell in his power he would flay him alive.

One day when *Lonoikamakahiki* and *Kakuhihewa* were playing Konane, *Kaikilani* arrived from Hawaii. Going up to the enclosure of the palace and perceiving *Lono* inside occupied at the game and with his back towards her, she commenced chanting his *Mele inoa*—"the chant of his name"—in the well-known strain :—

> *O Kahikohonua ia Elekau Kama,*
> *O Halalakauluonae,*" &c., &c.

At the very first intonation of the chant *Lono* knew who the singer was, and remembering the unpleasant affair at Kalaupapa, resolutely kept his seat without looking round to the singer. But as stave after stave of the chant rolled over the lips of *Kaikilani*, and allusions to common ancestors and scenes endeared to both came home to the obdurate mind of her husband, the stern heart relented; yet, mastering his emotions until she had finished, he turned around, and in reply chanted her own name. This was the token of his forgiveness and reconciliation, and gladly *Kaikilani* sprang to her husband and was again tenderly saluted by him.

This mutual public recognition between the two sovereigns of Hawaii solved the mystification and the incognito of *Lono's* presence at *Kakuhihewa's* court, which form so large a portion of the legend.

Informed by *Kaikilani* of the revolt on Hawaii, *Lonoikamakahiki* left Oahu at once, crossed the channels of the group, and avoiding the Kohala coast, where the rebels were in force, sailed to Kealakeakua, and sent messengers to Kau to acquaint *Pupuakea* of the arrival of himself and *Kaikilani*. *Pupuakea* responded promptly, and, taking a mountain road above the coast villages, he joined *Lono* and the forces that the latter had collected in Kona at Puuanahulu, on a land called Anaehoomalu, near the boundaries of Kohala and Kona. The rebel chiefs were encamped seaward of this along the shore. The next day *Lono* marched down and met the rebels at a place called Wailea, not far from Wainanalii, where in those days a watercourse appears to have been flowing. *Lono* won the battle, and the rebel chiefs fled northward with their forces. At Kaunooa, between Puako and Kawaihae, they made another stand, but were again routed by *Lono*, and retreated to Nakikiaianihau, where they fell in with reinforcements from Kohala and Hamakua. Two other engagements were fought at Puupa and Puukohola, near the Heiau of that name, in both of which *Lono* was victorious. His brother *Kanaloakapulehu* was taken prisoner, slain, and sacrificed at the Heiau, but *Kanaloakuakawaiea* escaped with the scattered remnant of the rebel forces. The rebels now fled into Kohala, and were hotly pursued by *Lonoikamakahiki*. Several skirmishes were fought during the pursuit; at Kaiopae, where *Kanaloakuakawaiea* was slain; at Kaiopihi, and finally at Puumaneo, on the high lands above Pololu, where the last remnant of the rebel force was conquered and slain, and the island returned to its allegiance to *Lono* and *Kaikilani*.

Although *Kanaloakuaana*, the eldest brother of *Lono*, was the originator and prime mover in this revolt, there is nothing said in the legends as to how he escaped condemnation and death, and they are equally silent about the youngest brother, *Umiokalani*. They probably made separate peace and submitted to *Lono*, for we find them, a few years afterward, on good terms with their brother *Lono*, and acting under him in his war with *Kamalalawalu* of Maui.

Having restored peace and order on Hawaii, *Lono* went

round the island consecrating Heiaus as acknowledgment to the gods for his victories. The following Heiaus are mentioned:—"Muleiula," in Apuakehau, Kohala; "Puukohola," at Kawaihae; "Makolea," in Kahaluu Kona. After leaving the latter place, one of the rebel chiefs named *Kapulani* was caught and brought to *Lono*. He was condemned to death, and ordered to be sacrificed at the Heiau the next morning; but during the night he was set at liberty by *Kalanioumi*, *Lono's* niece, and one of the daughters of *Kaikilani* and *Kanaloakuaana*. *Kapulani* escaped into Kau, and was not further molested.

After this *Lonoikamakahiki* and *Kaikilani* made a visit to Maui. *Kamalalawalu*, the Moi of Maui, held his court at Hana at that time, and thither the royal visitors repaired. They were sumptuously entertained, and when their visit was ended they returned to Hawaii. *Kamalalawalu* must have been very advanced in years at that time, as he was a contemporary of *Keawenui-a-Umi*, and his sons were man-grown when *Lono* visited Maui.

Not long after the return of *Lono* to Hawaii, *Kamalalawalu*, either stimulated by ambition or misled by false reports as to the strength and resources of Hawaii, formed the resolution to invade that island and conquer it. Orders were issued to prepare the fleet and collect men for the invasion. The priests and soothsayers were given to understand that the king expected favourable auguries, and, afraid of their lives, they framed their answers to suit his wishes. One only among the subservient crowd lifted a warning and protesting voice against the mad enterprise. That man was *Lanikaula*, a high-priest from Molokai, whose tomb and grove may still be seen near the north-east point of that island. His warning was unheeded; yet, when the fleet was ready and *Kamalalawalu* was stepping on board, *Lanikaula* implored him to desist in a "Wanana," or prophecy, which has been preserved, and which commences—

Koae[1] *ula, Ke Koae Kea,*
Koae lele pauma ana,
Kiekie i luna Ka hoku
Haahaa i áu Ka Malama.
The red Koae, the white Koae,
The Koae soaring, pushing (upward)
High above are the stars,
Lowly am I the gazer.

The only answer the irate monarch vouchsafed was, "When I return I will burn you alive." *Kamalalawalu's* fleet landed without opposition near Puako, a few miles south of Kawaihae. *Kanaloakuaana* was at the time at Waimea, and hearing of *Kamalalawalu's* landing on the coast, he started off with what forces he had to check his advance until *Lonoikamakahiki*, who was then at Kohala, could arrive. At Kaunooa he met *Kamalalawalu*, who was marching inland. A battle ensued. The Maui forces greatly outnumbered those of *Kanaloakuaana*, who was utterly defeated and himself taken prisoner at Kamaka-hiwa, in Puako, where his eyes were put out, and then he was slain.

This wanton cruelty inflicted on *Kanaloakuaana* appears to have been looked upon by his contemporaries as a touch beyond the ordinary barbarity of Hawaiian warfare, for not only was the place where it occurred called after the black eyes (Ka-maka-hiwa) of the unfortunate chief, but the bards embalmed his memory and his tragical end in a Mele or chant, which has been partly preserved till the present time, and in the Hawaiian anthology was known as "*Koauli.*"

After this first success *Kamalalawalu* marched boldly inland, and took up a position in Waimea, at a place called Hokuula. Here he awaited the arrival of *Lono's* forces. A second battle was fought, and *Kamalalawalu* was defeated with great slaughter. Among the slain were *Kamalalawalu* and *Makakukalani*, his nephew and gene-ralissimo; his son *Kauhi-a-Kama* escaped to Kawaihae,

---

[1] A species of bird found in the mountains.

where he was aided to cross over to Maui by one *Hinau*, one of *Lono's* officers, who had taken a liking to him, and who accompanied him to Maui.

Though it is very probable that *Lonoikamakahiki* made a visit to Kauai after this war with the Maui king, and it may be accepted as a fact that he did so, yet the romance of the expedition may be called in question; that, having started with a grand retinue, as became so great a chief, immediately on his arrival at Kauai he was deserted by all, from the highest to the lowest, of his retainers, and left to pursue his way alone, and that he would have perished had not a Kauai man named *Kapaihiahilina* been moved by compassion for the forsaken chief, and accompanied him through his perilous journey among the mountain wilds of Waialeale[1] in search of a real or imaginary place called "Kahihikalani;" that having accomplished his journey and returned to Hawaii, he heaped honours and distinction on this *Kapaihialina*, and the romance of the latter's disgrace and restoration to favour. The adventures related are certainly in keeping with the spirit of the time, and there can be no doubt that in his day and by his contemporaries *Lonoikamakahiki* was looked upon as a Hawaiian Richard Cœur de Lion, whose name and whose deeds the bards passed down to after-

[1] I know that the romantic episode of *Lonoikamakahiki's* visit to Kauai, and the rise and vicissitudes in the fortunes of his friend *Kapaihiahilina*, have by some been attributed to *Kalaninuiamamao*, five generations after the time of *Lonoikamakahiki*. But I cannot find that such an application of the legend dates higher than the time of the conquest of the group by *Kamehameha I.*, or thereafter. It is very probable that *Kalaninuiamamao* visited Kauai as well as Oahu, where he fell in with *Kamakaimoku*, and engaged her to come to Hawaii as his wife; but in critically examining the two legends, it becomes pretty conclusively evident that the *Lonoika-* *makahiki* legend is the older and the original one, after and on which the *Kalaninuiamamao* legend was modelled. *Kalaninuiamamao* being close upon our own times, and the granduncle of *Kamehameha I.*, it is hardly conceivable that his deeds and adventures should have been set back in time, and assigned to so remote an ancestor as *Lonoikamakahiki*, whereas there is both probability and precedent in favour of the presumption that—both having visited Kauai—the adventures of *Lono* were borrowed, so to say, or assigned by time-serving bards or priests to embellish the Kauai voyage of *Kalaninuiamamao*.

times, and whose more romantic adventures, embellished by fervent imaginations, were rehearsed by professional storytellers, and continued to delight chiefs and commoners even down to our own days, when so much of the ancient poetry of Hawaiian life has been wrung out of it by the pressure of a new civilisation, leaving the more repulsive features which it partially covered protruding in the day, to be wept over or to be hooted at as suits the humour of the beholder.

Returned from the Kauai expedition, *Lonoikamakahiki* passed the balance of his days in peace on his own island of Hawaii.

The children of *Kaikilani-Alii-Wahine-o-Puna* with *Kanaloakuaana* were a son, *Keakealanikane*, and two daughters, *Kealiiokalani* and *Kalani-o-Umi*. She had no children with *Lonoikamahiki*, as previously stated. With his other wife, *Kaikilanimaipanio*, *Lono* had two sons, one called *Keawehanauikawalu* and the other *Kaihikapumahana*, from both of whom her Highness *Ruth Keelikolani* is the descendant on her father's and mother's sides. The first was the husband of *Akahikameenoa*, the daughter of *Akahiilikapu* and *Kahakumakalina*, referred to on page 104. The second, who, according to the Oahu legends, was born while *Lono* was sojourning at the court of *Kakuhihewa*, and was called after *Kakuhihewa's* favourite son *Kaihikapu*, was the husband of *Aila*, a Kauai chiefess of the great *Kealohi* family, and thus became the great-grandfather of *Lonoikahaupu*, on whom the Kauai sovereignty finally settled after the close of the civil wars between the members of the *Kawelo* family.

To this period of *Lono's* reign belongs the episode of *Iwikauikaua*, another knight-errant of this stirring time. *Iwikauikaua* was the son of *Makakaualii*, who was the younger and only brother of *Kaikilani-Alii-Wahine-o-Puna*. His mother was *Kapukamola*.[1] The direct legends con-

[1] A daughter of *Kanakeawe*, who was the daughter of *Kamolanui-a-Umi*. The other children of *Maka-* *kaualii* were *Kapukini*, a daughter, *Keawe* and *Umikukailani*, sons, and *Pueopokii*, a daughter.

cerning him have mostly perished, but enough remains referring to him in other legends to give us glimpses of his character and a few data of his life.

Though nearly related to the reigning family of Hawaii, yet, being the son of a younger brother, without feudatorial possessions in his own right, a tabu chief by birth, but with no land to back the title except what his aunt's bounty might provide, brought up to, and master of, all the princely exercises of the time, he sought his fortune as other chiefly scions had to do.

During the time of the revolt of *Kanaloakuaana* and the Hawaii chiefs against *Lonoikamakahiki*, it would appear that *Iwikauikaua* was already a grown-up young man, for he is reported as having espoused the cause of *Lono* and his aunt *Kaikilani*. During some of the battles of that civil war *Iwikauikaua* was taken prisoner by *Kanaloakapulehu* and condemned to be sacrificed at the Heiau. When standing on the steps of the altar, he asked the officiating priest to allow him to utter a prayer to the gods before he was slain. The priest consented, but told him if his prayer was bad—that is, if it was interrupted or attended by unfavourable omens, and thus repudiated by the gods—he would surely die that day; but if not, he would be reprieved. *Iwikauikaua* chanted his prayer, and it appears to have been successful, for his life was spared. This prayer, addressed to *Ku*, to *Uli*, and to *Kama*, has been preserved. It is replete with archaic expressions and now obsolete words, and is probably as old as the times it represents.

After this narrow escape *Iwikauikaua* went to Oahu, and there became the husband of *Kauakahikuaanauakane*, daughter of *Kakuhihewa's* son *Kaihikapu*. He is next heard of in the legends as having visited Maui, where one of his sisters, *Kapukini*, was the wife of the Moi *Kauhi-a-Kama*, and another sister, *Pueopokii*, was the wife of *Kaaoao*, the son of *Makakukalani*, and head of the Kaupo chief families who descended from *Koo* and

Kaiuli. He finally returns to Hawaii, where he becomes the husband of *Keakamahana*, the daughter of his cousins *Keakealanikane* and *Kealiiokalani*, and who at their death became the Moi of Hawaii.

When *Lonoikamakahiki* and *Kaikilani*, his wife, died, they were succeeded as Moi of Hawaii by *Kaikilani's* son *Keakealanikane*. We have no legends of his reign, as we have of the preceding, and infer that it was un- Keakealani-
kane.
eventful as regards himself. Though no open revolt has been recorded, yet there is little doubt that the feudal bonds in which the district chiefs were held by the strong hand of *Lonoikamakahiki* were greatly loosened during this reign, and thus the great houses of *I* in Hilo and of *Mahi* in Kohala, with large territorial possessions, were enabled to assume an attitude little short of political independence, and which, in the reign of his grandchild *Keakea-laniwahine*, ripened into civil war.

Keakealanikane's wife was his sister *Kealiiokalani*, and their daughter and successor as Moi was *Keakamahana*, Keakama-
hana. whose recognised husband was *Iwikauikaua* above referred to. They had also another daughter named *Kalai-kiiki*, who became the wife of *Ahulililani*, a chief of Puna, and mother of *Kuikai*, referred to on pp. 72 and 73 note. Though the genealogical Meles speak in the highest laudatory terms of *Keakamahana*, yet there is little left to mark her reign on the historical page.

The most prominent figures about the time of *Keaka-mahana* was probably *Kanaloauoo*, the renowned chief of Kohala, and his three sons, all named *Mahi*, though with different sobriquets, — *Mahiolole*, *Mahikuku*, *Mahikapa-lena* or *Mahiopupeleha*. *Kanaloauoo* had two wives from the reigning Maui dynasty; first, *Kapuleiolaa*, who was a descendant of *Lonoapii*; second, *Kihamoihala*, who was a great-granddaughter of *Kamalalawalu*. With the first he had a daughter named *Kapaihi*; with the second he had the son *Mahikapalena*. The families from both these children remained on Maui, and do not appear to have settled on Hawaii or taken part in its politics. Returning from Maui to Kohala, of which district *Kanaloauoo* was the ruling chief, the " *Alii-ai-moku*," he took for wife *Hoolaaikaiwi*, a daughter of *Umiokalani* and *Piimauilani*, and granddaughter of *Keawenui-a-Umi*. With this last wife he had the two sons *Mahiolole* and *Mahikuku*.

The only husband known of *Keakamahana* was *Iwikauikaua*, above referred to, and with him she had a daughter called *Keakealaniwahine*, who succeeded her mother as Moi of Hawaii. With his other wife, the Oahu chiefess *Kauakahi-kuaanaauakane*, *Iwikauikaua* had a son, *Kaneikaiwilani*, who became one of the husbands of his half-sister *Keakealaniwahine*, and with another wife named *Kapukiniakua* he had a daughter called *Kamakahauoku*.

Keakealani-
wahine.
The reign of *Keakealaniwahine* was a troubled one. The great house of *I*, in whose family the chieftainship of the Hilo district had been vested since the days of their ancestor *Kumalae* the son of *Umi*, had grown to such wealth, strength, and importance, as to be practically independent of even the very loose bonds with which the ruling district chiefs were held to their feudatory obligations. The representative of this house as district chief of Hilo at this time was *Kuahuia*, the son of *Kuaana-a-I*, and grandson of *I*. What led to the war, or what were its incidents, has not been preserved on the traditional records, but it is frequently alluded to as a long and bitter strife between *Kuahuia* and *Keakealaniwahine;* and though tradition is equally silent as to its conclusion, it may be inferred that the royal authority was unable to subdue its powerful vassal from the fact that at the death of *Keawe*, *Keakealani's* son and successor, we find that *Mokulani*, the son of *Kuahuia* was still the principal chief—"*Alii-ai-moku*"—of Hilo. It is on record that *Mahiolole*, the powerful district chief of Kohala, was the chief counsellor and supporter of *Keakea-*

laniwahine, which fact, independent of other causes, may account in a measure for the intimacy of *Keakealani's* daughter, *Kalanikauleleiaiwi,* and *Mahiolole's* son, *Kauaua-a-Mahi.*

Keakealaniwahine had two husbands. The first was *Kanaloaikaiwilewa,* or, as he is called in some genealogies, *Kanaloakapulehu.* His pedigree is not given in any genealogy or legend that I have met with, but he was probably a descendant of *Lonoikamakahiki's* brother with the same name. The other husband was *Kaneikaiwilani,* who was the son of *Iwikauikaua* and *Kaukahikuaanaauakane.* With the first, *Keakealani* had a son named *Keawe;* with the second, she had a daughter named *Kalanikauleleiaiwi.*

Keawe, surnamed "*ikekahialiiokamoku,*" succeeded his Keawe. mother, *Keakealaniwahine,* as the Moi of Hawaii. He is said to have been an enterprising and stirring chief, who travelled all over the group, and obtained a reputation for bravery and prudent management of his island. It appears that in some manner he composed the troubles that had disturbed the peace during his mother's time. It was not by force or by conquest, for in that case, and so near to our own times, some traces of it would certainly have been preserved on the legends. He probably accomplished the tranquillity of the island by diplomacy, as he himself married *Lonomaaikanaka,* the daughter of *Ahu-u-I,* and he afterwards married his son *Kalaninuiomamao* to *Ahia,* the granddaughter of *Kuaana-a-I* and cousin to *Kuahuia's* son, *Mokulani,* and thus by this double marriage securing the peace and allegiance of the Hilo chiefs. The other districts do not seem to have shared in the resistance made by the Hilo chiefs to the authority of the Moi, at least the name of no district chief of note or influence has been recorded as having been so engaged.

Three short generations had passed between the time of *Lonoikamakahiki* and the present *Keawe,* and the "iron-hand" policy of the former, as of his father, *Keawenui-a-*

Umi, had been exchanged for the "velvet-glove" state-craft of the latter.   But the iron hand, though nude and rude, kept the turbulent district chiefs in subjection, or forcibly ejected them if contumacious ; whereas the velvet glove was deficient in grip, and the great feudal vassals became practically independent, and their allegiance grew into a question of interest, rather than one of constitutional obligation.   Under these conditions it is much to the credit of *Keawe* that he gathered up in a firmer hand the loosened reins of government, and during his lifetime ruled the island peaceably and orderly, without rebellion, tumult, or bloodshed occurring to be chronicled in song or legend.

There can be little doubt that Keawe's half-sister, *Kalanikauleleiaiwi,* was, during the ancient regime, considered as co-ordinate with her brother as Moi of Hawaii, though she is not known to have been actively occupied in any matters of government.   The legends refer to her as his equal on the throne ; and at the time, and by posterity, she was held to be of higher rank than *Keawe,* owing to her descent, on her father's side, from the Oahu dynasty of *Kakuhihewa.*

Keawe's wives were—(I.) *Lonomaaikanaka,* a daughter of *Ahu-a-I* and of *Piilaniwahine.*   The former belonged to the powerful and widely spread *I* family of Hilo ; the latter was the daughter of *Kalanikaumakaowakea,* the Moi of Maui.   With her *Keawe* had two sons, *Kalaninuiomamao* and *Kekohimoku.*[1]   (2.) *Kalanikauleleiaiwi,* his half-sister, as before stated.   With her he had *Kalanikeeaumoku,* a son, and *Kekelakekeokalani,* a daughter.   (3.) *Kanealae,*[2] a daughter of *Lae,* chief of the eastern parts of

[1] Some genealogies state that *Keawe* and *Lonomaaikanaka* had also a daughter named *Kauhiokaka ;* others state that she was the daughter of *Lonomaaikanaka* with a previous husband named *Hulu.* We are inclined to hold with the latter authorities in this case, for the reason that the chronological necessities of *Kauhiokaka's* descendants require it.

[2] She afterwards became the wife of *Kekaulike,* the Moi of Maui, with whom she had a daughter named *Luahiwa.*

Molokai. With her he had *Hao, Awili, Kumukoa,* sons, and *Kaliloamoku,* a daughter. (4.) *Kauhiokaka,* daughter of *Lonomaaikanaka* and *Hulu.* With her he had a daughter named *Kekaulike,* who became one of the wives of her half-brother *Kalaninuiomamao,* and was the mother of the celebrated *Keawemauhili,* chief of Hilo. *Keawe* had two other wives, though, strange to say, their names have perished from the traditional record. With the one he had two sons, *Ahaula* [1] and *Kaolohaka-a-Keawe,* [2] whose descendants were conspicuous enough in after-history; with the other he had a son, *Kanuha,* who is said to have built the city of refuge, the "*Puu-honua,*" known as the *Hale-o-Keawe,* at Honaunau in the South Kona district.

Kalanikauleleiaiwi, the half-sister of *Keawe,* had four husbands :—(1.) *Kaulahea,* the Moi of Maui. This union must have taken place in her early youth, and tradition is silent as to the causes which led to her leaving *Kaulahea* and returning to Hawaii. With him she had a daughter, *Kekuiapoiwanui,* who remained on Maui and became the wife of her half-brother, *Kekaulike.* (2.) *Keawe,* the Moi of Hawaii, above referred to. (3.) *Kauaua-a-Mahi,* son of *Mahiolole,* the great Kohala chief. With him she had two sons, *Alapainui* and *Haae !* [3] (4.) *Lonoikahaupu,* one of the tabu chiefs of Kauai, and a descendant of *Kahaku-*

[1] He was one of the husbands of the noted Maui chiefess, *Kaupeka-moku,* and father of *Kaiana - a - Ahaula,* who played so prominent a part during the early years of the reign of *Kamehameha I.,* and who was killed in the battle of Nuuanu, Oahu, 1796.

[2] From him descended *Kaikioewa,* the governor of Kauai during portion of the reign of *Kamehameha III.,* and whose daughter *Kuwahine* was mother of *Leleiohoku I.,* governor of Hawaii in 1848. From him also descended *Koakanu,* who was the father of the chiefess *Liliha,* and grandfather of her numerous children, *Abigail, Jane Loeau, Kailinaoa, Koa-*

kanu, Pelekaluhi, Mary Ann Kili-wehe, et als., some of whom survive to this day.

[3] I possess one genealogy which asserts that *Haae* was the son of *Kauaua-a-Mahi* and *Kapoomahana,* who was a great-granddaughter of *Kalakauaehu-a-Kama,* one of the sons of *Kamalalawalu* of Maui. I have not been able to decide upon the merits of these two genealogies. The former appears to have been followed by those who claimed descent through *Kamakaeheukuli,* the one daughter of *Haae,* while the latter has been followed by those who claim through *Kekuiapoiwa II.,* the other daughter of *Haae.*

makapaweo through *Ilihiwalani* and *Kealohikanakamaikai.* With him she had her last and youngest son, *Keawepoepoe*, who was the father of *Keeaumoku-papaiahiahi*,
Kameeiamoku, and *Kamanawa*, who, together with *Keawe-
a-Heulu*, were the four principal chiefs that assisted
Kamehameha I. to conquer and consolidate the group
under one dominion, and who became his counsellors and
ministers after the conquest. *Lonoikahaupu* afterwards
returned to Kauai, and with his Kauai wife, *Kamuokau-
mehiwa*, became the great-grandfather of *Kaumualii*, the
last independent sovereign of Kauai, of whom the present
Queen-consort, *Kapiolani*, is the granddaughter.

Though nothing is positively said in the legends on the
subject, yet it may credibly be inferred that during his
lifetime *Keawe* had established his eldest son, *Kalaninuiamamao*, as " *Alii-ai-Moku*," principal chief of Kau, and
his other son, *Kalanikeeaumoku*, as principal chief of
Kona, and probably portions of Kohala, for we find that
while both were living in their respective districts a
quarrel arose between them, and that *Kalaninuiamamao*
was killed, or caused to be killed, by *Kalanikeeaumoku* ; [1]
and we find further that at *Keawe's* death, *Mokulani*, who
ruled over Hilo, Hamakua, and part of Puna districts,
declared himself independent of *Kalanikeeaumoku*, who
apparently was unable to enforce his claims as Moi of
Hawaii, but who, nevertheless, claimed lordship over the
Kona and Kohala districts. When *Keawe* died, *Alapainui*,
the rightful heir of the Kohala district, as representative
of the *Mahi* family, was sojourning at the court of *Kekaulike*, the Moi of Maui, on a visit to his half-sister *Kekuiapoiwanui*, the wife of *Kekaulike.* Hearing of the troubles
on Hawaii, he hastened back to Kohala, assembled the
warriors, vassals, and retainers of his house, made war on

[1] One version of the *Kalaninuiamamao* legend states that he was
deposed (" Wailana ") by the land-
holders — " Makaainana "—of Kau,
who were a notoriously and prover-
bially turbulent people, frequently
deposing, and even slaying, their chiefs,
when, either from popular caprice or
personal tyranny, they had become
unpopular.

Kalanikeeaumoku first, who was worsted in battle and slain, and then on *Mokulani,* who shared the same fate. In consequence of these victories *Alapainui* declared himself as Moi of Hawaii, and the island submitted to his sway.

Having established himself as sovereign or Moi of Hawaii, *Alapainui* assumed the lordship, in his own person, of the Kohala and Kona districts, while, for political reasons, doubtless, the chieftainship of the Hilo district, with its outlying possessions, was retained in the person of *Mokulani's* daughter and only child, *Ululani,* with whom it afterwards passed over to *Keawemauhili,* the son of *Kalaninuiamamao.* The Kau district seems in a measure to have escaped the troubles and changes incident to the interregnum and civil war after *Keawe's* death, for we find that when *Kalaniopuu,* the son of *Kalaninuiamamao,* was grown up, he assumed the lordship of it as his patrimonial estate, and it passed as such from him to his son, *Keoua-Kuahuula,* who retained it until his death in 1791. Alapainui.

While these intestine commotions were occurring on Hawaii, harassing the country people and weakening the power of the chiefs, *Kekaulike,* the Moi of Maui, judging the time opportune for a possible conquest of Hawaii, assembled his forces at Mokulau, Kaupo district, Maui, where he had been residing for some time, building the Heiaus Loaloa and Puumakaa at Kumunui, and Kanemalohemo at Popoiwi. When his forces and fleet were ready, *Kekaulike* sailed for the Kona coast of Hawaii, where he harried and burned the coast villages. *Alapainui* was then in Kona, and, assembling a fleet of war canoes, he overtook *Kekaulike* at sea, fought a naval engagement, beat him, and drove him off. Retreating northwards, *Kekaulike* landed in several places, destroying villages in Kekaha, cutting down the cocoa-nut trees at Kawaihae, and plundering and killing along the Kohala coast, and finally returned to Mokulau, Maui, intending to invade Hawaii with a larger force next time.

Hearing of the depredations committed by *Kekaulike* on the Kohala coast, *Alapainui* hurried back to Kohala, and concluded to forestall *Kekaulike* by invading Maui, and thus carry the war home to *Kekaulike's* own dominions. For that purpose all the great feudal chiefs and their vassals were summoned to assemble at Kohala along the shore from Koaie to Puuwepa, with their men and war-canoes, and *Alapainui* established his own head-quarters at Kokoike, near Upolu, the north-west point of Hawaii.

It is related of *Alapainui*, that when he obtained the sovereignty of Hawaii, he caused the oldest sons of *Kalaninuiamamao* and of *Kalanikeeaumoku* to be brought to him and kept at his court. The legends say that he did so out of kindness and love to the young chiefs, his near relatives, though it may have been, and possibly was, for political reasons—the keeping them about his person to prevent them from hatching treason and revolt in the provinces. These two chiefs were the afterwards well-known *Kalaniopuu*, Moi of Hawaii at the time of Captain Cook's arrival, and *Kalanikupuapaikalaninui*, generally known by his shorter name of *Keoua*, who was the father of *Kamehameha I.* But whether from policy or affection —and the two motives are so frequently blended in life— the fact is none the less that these two princes were the nearest and most trusted about the person of *Alapainui* at this time, and for many years subsequent.

Kamakaimoku was the mother of these two princes, and a sketch of her life may serve to illustrate the freedom of manners and the liberty of selecting their husbands accorded to chiefesses of high rank during the ancient régime.

Kamakaimoku's mother was *Umiula-a-kaahumanu*, a daughter of *Mahiolole*, the frequently referred to Kohala chief, and *Kanekukaailani*, who was a daughter of *I* and *Akahikameenoa;* consequently, according to the Hawaii peerage, she was a cousin to *Alapainui*, and a chiefess of the highest rank. Her father was *Kuanuuanu*, an Oahu chief, and in her childhood and youth she was brought up by her father on Oahu, her mother having gone back to Hawaii and espoused *Kapahi-a-Ahu-Kane*, the son of *Ahu-a-I*, and a younger brother of *Lonomaaikanaka*, the wife of *Keawe*. With *Kuanuuanu Umiulaakaahumanu* had another child, a son named *Naili*, who remained on Oahu, and followed his father as chief over the Waianae district. With *Kapahi-a-Ahukane* she had a son named *Heulu*, who was the father of *Keawe-a-Heulu*, one of *Kamehameha I.'s* doughty counsellor chiefs, from whom the present dynasty descends in the fourth degree. When grown up, *Kamakaimoku* was seen by *Kalaninuiamamao* on his visit to Oahu, and sent for to be his wife. Living with him at the court of *Keawe*, she bore him a son, *Kalaniopuu*, who afterwards became the Moi of Hawaii. This union was not of long duration, for within a year or two she left *Kalaninuiamamao* and became the wife of his brother, *Kalanikeeaumoku*, and to him she bore another son, *Kalanikupuapaikalaninui Keoua*, the father of *Kamehameha I.* How long she remained with *Kalanikeeaumoku* is not known positively, but she is next referred to as the wife of *Alapainui*, with whom she had a daughter, *Manona*, grandmother of the celebrated *Kekuaokalani*, who, at the abolition of the tabus in 1819, after *Kamehameha's* death, took up arms in defence of the old gods and the old religion.

While *Alapainui* was staying at Kohala superintending the collection of his fleet and warriors from the different districts of the island preparatory to the invasion of Maui, in the month of "*Ikuwa*," corresponding to November of present reckoning, there was born on a stormy night a child whose career in after life so greatly influenced the destiny of the entire group of islands and the conditions of its people. That child was *Kamehameha I.*, and we thus obtain another approximate chronological starting-point, whether counting backward or forward; for when

Kamehameha died in 1819 he was past eighty years old. His birth would thus fall between 1736 and 1740, probably nearer the former than the latter. His father was *Kalanikupua-keoua,* the half-brother of *Kalaniopuu* above referred to, and grandson of *Keawe;* his mother was *Kekuiapoiwa II.,* a daughter of *Kekelakekeokalani-a-keawe* and *Haae,* the son of *Kalanikauleleiaiwi* and *Kauaua-a-Mahi,* and brother to *Alapainui.*

It is related of *Kamehameha I.* that on the night of his birth, amidst the din, confusion, and darkness of the storm, he was stolen from his mother's side by a chief called *Naeole,* lord of Halawa in Kohala. At first all search after the missing child proved unsuccessful, but finally he was discovered with *Naeole,* who apparently compromised the affair in some way with the parents; for instead of being punished as a kidnapper, he was allowed to retain the child and become his "kahu" (nurse or guardian), and with him *Kamehameha* remained until he was five years old, when he was taken to *Alapainui's* court and there brought up.

When all the preparations for the invasion of Maui were completed, *Alapainui* set sail with his fleet and landed at Mokulau, in the district of Kaupo on Maui. He met no resistance, but learned that *Kekaulike* had died but a short while previous; that his body had been removed to the sepulchre of Iao in Wailuku, and that *Kamehamehanui,* the son of *Kekaulike* and *Kekuiapoiwa,* had, by orders of the late king, succeeded him as Moi of Maui. On hearing this news *Alapainui's* anger relented, and moved by feelings of affection for his sister *Kekuiapoiwa* and his nephew *Kamehamehanui,* he refrained from acts of hostility, and met the young Moi and his mother with the rest of the royal family at Kiheipukoa, where peace was concluded and festive reunions took the place of warlike encounters.

While here, tidings arrived from Molokai that *Kapiiohokalani,* the son and successor of *Kualii,* the Moi of

Oahu, had invaded the island of Molokai with a large force, and that several of the chiefs there were in great distress, having taken refuge in fortified mountain localities, while their possessions on the lowlands and their fishponds were ravaged and destroyed by the Oahu invaders, who were said to have made their headquarters at Kalamaula and occupied the country from Kaunakakai to Naiwa.

When this intelligence reached *Alapainui*, having no occupation for his army and fleet on Maui, he concluded to go to Molokai to the assistance of the distressed chiefs there; the more so as some of them were his near relatives, being the sons and grandsons of *Keawe* of Hawaii with his Molokai wife, *Kanealai*. Leaving Maui, he crossed the Pailolo channel, and landed his fleet on the Molokai coast from Waialua to Kaluaaha. Having landed his army, he marched to Kamalo, and at Kapualei he met the forces of *Kapiiohokalani*. An obstinate fight ensued, which lasted for four days, without any decisive result; but as *Kapiiohokalani* retreated to Kawela, it is presumed that he suffered most. On the fifth day the battle was renewed at Kawela, extending as far as Kamiloloa. The Hawaii troops being ranged along the seashore, and the auxiliary Molokai chiefs descending from the uplands with their men, *Kapiiohokalani* was hemmed in between them, and, after a severe fight from morning till far in the afternoon, he was completely routed with great loss of life, and himself slain. Those who escaped from the battle immediately evacuated Molokai and fled back to Oahu.

Among the more illustrious of the Oahu chiefs who partook in this battle under *Kapiiohokalani* were *Kauakahialiikapu, Kuihewakaokoa, Kaihikapu-a-Mahana, Kaweloikiakulu, Lononuiakea*, who are said to have commanded the left wing of the Oahu army, and *Kahoowahakananuha, Kahooalani, Hua*, and *Mokokalai*, who commanded the right wing; the centre being commanded by *Kapiiohoka-*

lani in person. *Kalanikupua-keoua* and *Kalaniopuu* commanded under *Alapainui*.

This famous battlefield may still be seen in the place described, where the bones of the slain are the sports of the winds that sweep over that sandy plain, and cover or uncover them, as the case may be. The numerical strength of the two opposing armies is not mentioned in the legends; but to judge from the multitude of bones and the number of skulls that are bleaching in the sun when a strong north wind has removed their sandy covering, the numbers engaged on each side must have been reckoned by thousands.

With rare forbearance in a barbarous chief, *Alapainui* neither annexed Molokai to Hawaii nor covered annexation by the name of protectorate; but reinstated the chiefs who had suffered from *Kapiiohokalani's* oppression, and allowed them to manage their own affairs, domestic or foreign, according to ancient custom. The possible conquest of Oahu, however, the hereditary kingdom of *Kapiiohokalani*, arose as a bright vision on *Alapainui's* mind after the brilliant victory at Kawela, rendered more probable, perhaps, from the number of Oahu chiefs that had been killed in the battle, and the fact that *Kapiiohokalani's* son and successor, *Kanahaokalani*, was but a young boy, some six years old, thus inferring a regency, discord, and weakness in the Oahu government.

Stopping on Molokai only long enough to refresh his men and repair his own losses, *Alapainui* started with his fleet for the conquest of Oahu. Attempting to land at Waikiki, at Waialae, at Koko, and at Hanauma, *Alapainui* found the young Oahu king's regency fully prepared to meet the emergency; and baffled and repelled at all these places, he sailed round the east side of the island and effected a landing at a place called Oneawa, in Kailua, district of Koolaupoko. Though unable to prevent his landing on that side of the island, the Oahu forces, after crossing the Pali of Nuuanu in great haste, succeeded in limiting the operations of the war to a mere series of skirmishes, thus protracting the contest for nearly a month.

Immediately on the arrival of *Alapainui's* fleet on the coasts of Oahu, messengers were, sent to the young king's uncle, *Peleioholani*, who at that time held the sovereignty over the western portion of Kauai, to come to the assistance of the Oahu chiefs. With the least possible delay *Peleioholani* started with a fleet and a number of warriors for Oahu, and joining their forces, took supreme command of the young king and his chiefs.

Among the Oahu chiefs was one *Naili*, chief of Waianae, brother of *Kamakaimoku*,[1] the mother of *Kalaniopuu* and *Keoua*, and a cousin of *Alapainui*. It is not known on whose suggestion he acted, but being so nearly related to the principal Hawaii chiefs, he was considered the fittest man to approach *Alapainui* with overtures of peace. Advancing to the outposts of the Hawaii army in Kaneohe, he encountered *Kalaniopuu* and *Keoua*, and having made himself known to them, they conducted him to the headquarters of *Alapainui* at Waihaukalua, near the shore. He was cordially received, and *Alapai* expressed his willingness to meet and confer with *Peleioholani* with a view of terminating the war. It was agreed that the Hawaii fleet should move to a place called Naonealaa, in Kaneohe, and that *Alapainui* alone should go ashore unarmed, while *Peleioholani* on his part would advance from the lines of his army equally alone and unarmed.

The meeting took place as arranged. The two sove-

[1] It is stated in the legend which I am following that at this time *Kamakaimoku* was living at Waikele, in Ewa district.

It is further intimated in some legends that *Kamakaimoku* had cohabited with *Peleioholani* before she went to Hawaii to be the wife of *Kalaninuiamamao*, and that she was *enceinte* at that time with *Kalaniopuu*, who was born in Kau, on Hawaii. It may have been so, but the report was probably gotten up by the opponents of *Kamehameha I.*, in the early years after the death of *Kalaniopuu*, when he was contending with *Keoua Kuahuula*, the brother of *Kiwalao*, and son of *Kalaniopuu*, for the supremacy of Hawaii.

reigns met on the beach, and acknowledging each other's rights and dignities, a peace was concluded, and *Alapai* gave orders to evacuate Oahu.

On his return *Alapainui* rested his fleet at Molokai, and after assisting the chiefs there to settle up their affairs and establish friendly relations with those of Maui and Lanai, he sailed for Maui.

Arrived at Lahaina, *Alapainui* was informed that *Kauhiaimokuakama*, also known as *Kauhipumaikahoaka*, the eldest son of the late *Kekaulike* and his wife *Kahawalu*, had risen in arms against the authority of his brother *Kamehamehanui*, whom *Kekaulike* on his death-bed had appointed Moi of Maui. It is said that *Alapainui* offered to mediate between the two brothers, and that if *Kauhi* would meet him at an appointed place, and terms could be agreed upon, then he (*Alapai*) would remove *Kamehamehanui* to Hawaii and leave *Kauhi* in possession of the government of Maui. *Kauhi*, on the advice of his counsellors, rejected the offer, thinking it was a ruse to get him in *Alapai's* power, and in answer made a furious attack on *Kamehamehanui's* forces in Lahaina, defeated and dispersed them, and obliged *Kamehamehanui* to flee on board of *Alapai's* fleet for safety.

Alapai, not feeling ready for a new war after the losses sustained in the various battles on Molokai and on Oahu, returned to Hawaii to prepare a fresh force for the war with *Kauhi*, and took *Kamehamehanui* with him to Hawaii.

In the following year, say 1738, *Alapainui* returned to Maui with a large fleet, well equipped, accompanied by *Kamehamehanui*. With headquarters at Lahaina, his forces extended from Ukumehame to Honokawai. Meanwhile *Kauhi* had not been idle during the absence of *Alapai*. Besides his own forces and the chiefs that adhered to him, he had sent presents and messages to *Peleioholani*, now king of Oahu, to come to his assistance, which that restless and warlike prince accepted, and landing his fleet at Kekaha, encamped his soldiers about Honolua and Honokahua.

It is said that *Alapai* proceeded with great severity against the adherents of *Kauhi* in Lahaina, destroying their taro patches and breaking down the watercourses out of the Kauaula, Kanaha, and Mahoma valleys.

Though details of this war are not given in the legend, yet the following facts may be gathered from scattered passages, viz., that *Alapai* arrived at Lahaina with his fleet before *Peleioholani* had landed at Kekaha; that *Kauhi*, being unable to cope alone with the large force under *Alapainui*, retreated to the uplands and ravines back of Lahaina, where he was kept in check by a corps of observation; that *Peleioholani*, after landing and finding *Kauhi* in this position, resolved to march to his relief, and by engaging *Alapai's* forces in a general battle, enable *Kauhi* to descend and form a junction with his Oahu allies.

To this effect *Peleioholani* advanced to Honokawai, where he found a detachment of *Alapai's* army, which he overthrew and drove back with great loss to Keawawa. Here they rallied upon the main body of the Hawaii troops. The next morning *Alapai* had moved up his whole force, and a grand battle was fought between the Oahu and Hawaii armies. The fortune of the battle swayed back and forth from Honokawai to near into Lahaina; and to this day heaps of human bones and skulls, half buried in various places in the sand, attest the bitterness of the strife and the carnage committed. The result was probably a drawn battle, for it is related that, after great losses on both sides, the two kings—*Alapainui* and *Peleioholani*—met on the battlefield, and, instead of coming to blows, they saluted each other, and, considering their mutual losses on behalf of others, they made a peace between themselves and renewed the treaty of Naonealaa on Oahu.

Kauhiaimokuakama was captured during this battle, and it is said that he was killed by drowning by order of *Alapai*. No other opposition being made to *Kamehamehanui*, he resumed the position of Moi of Maui, which he held to his death, several years afterwards.

After this *Peleioholani* returned to Oahu, stopping first on the Koolau side of Molokai, and *Alapainui* returned to Hawaii.

Having achieved fame and consideration by his foreign expeditions, *Alapai* now occupied himself with the affairs of his own island, making frequent circuits and visiting the different districts ; and when not thus occupied he resided with his court at Hilo. Nothing appears to have troubled the peace and tranquillity of his reign until about the year 1752.

During said year *Kalanikupua Keoua*, the half-brother of *Kalaniopuu* and father of *Kamehameha I.*, died after a severe illness at Piopio, near Wailoa in Waiakea, Hilo district. *Kalaniopuu* was then at Kalepolepo, and rumours having been circulated attributing the death of *Keoua* to *Alapai*—whether by praying to death or by direct poisoning is not stated, but the superstition of the times made such rumours possible, and the arbitrary rule of the chiefs made them probable to credulous minds —*Kalaniopuu* resolved to abduct *Kamehameha* from the surveillance and grasp of *Alapai*. The legend leaves the guilt or innocence of *Alapai* an open question; and posterity possesses too few data to pronounce a definite verdict in the matter. On the one hand, the social conditions and customs of the times, as well as the personal precedents of *Alapainui*, would seem to support the charge. It was, no uncommon event in those days for a chief to disembarrass himself of an obnoxious and powerful vassal, against whom open force or other violence would be unadvisable, by the process of praying to death, "*Anaana*," or by secret poisoning, "*Akuahanai;*" and as late as thirty years ago, the belief was common that if a person died suddenly in the prime of life, without any known cause of death, he had either been prayed to death or poisoned by secret enemies; and the belief still lingers in many quarters where none would expect it, and divinations and counter-prayers are resorted to in place of blisters and aperients. It was known, moreover, that the father of *Keoua* had been killed in battle by *Alapainui*, when, after *Keawe's* death, both were contending for the sovereignty of Hawaii, and the fate that befell the father might, with some show of reason, be apprehended for the son. On the other hand, the personal character and conduct of *Alapainui* would go far towards his acquittal. He was always known, and in after years quoted, as a most affectionate parent and kinsman, and the solicitude and care with which he brought up the young chiefs *Kalaniopuu* and *Keoua*, and employed them about his person in the most confidential and important positions for so many years, would seem to indicate that he entertained no suspicion of them, and harboured no ill-will towards them. On the whole, we are inclined to deal gently with the memory of *Alapainui*, and are prone to believe that *Kalaniopuu* gave but too willing an ear to the advice of his Kahu, named *Puna*, and to the tales of those restless spirits to whom peace and good order had become irksome, and who, even in savage courts, indulge in intrigues for selfish ends and foment strife in hopes of change.

Whether *Kalaniopuu* really believed or affected to believe that his own life was threatened, he deemed it advisable to withdraw the young *Kamehameha* from the court of *Alapai*. He laid his plans accordingly, and going by land, accompanied by his young half-brother *Keawemauhili* and a few trusty followers, he dispatched a large war-canoe under command of *Puna* to meet him at an appointed place, in order to take his party on board, should they be pursued. *Kalaniopuu* arrived that night at Piopio, and found most of the prominent chiefs, then residing with the court at Hilo, assembled at the house of *Keoua* for the purpose of wailing over the corpse. *Kalaniopuu* attempted to bring away the young *Kamehameha*, but was opposed and frustrated in his design by the other chiefs present, and a fight ensued, from which *Kalaniopuu* escaped on board of his war-canoe.

The revolt of *Kalaniopuu* was no longer doubtful. Forces were gathered on both sides, and a civil war commenced. Several battles were fought—at Paieie near Puaaloa, at Kualoa, at Mokaulele, and at Mahinaakaka, at which latter place *Kalaniopuu* narrowly escaped being taken prisoner. After that *Kalaniopuu* retreated to Kau, where he was born, declared himself independent of *Alapainui* and sovereign (Moi) of the Puna and Kau districts as the heir of *Kalaninuiamamao*, to whom they appear to have been allotted by his grandfather *Keawe*.

For reasons that have not come down to our day, *Alapainui* made no further attempts to subdue his contumaceous kinsman and vassal, but remained for upwards of a year at Hilo, apparently unconcerned at the defection of one-third of his kingdom. He then removed to Waipio in Hamakua, the cherished residence of *Liloa* and the ancient Hawaii Mois. Having remained here for some time, he proceeded to Waimea and Kawaihae in Kohala. At this latter place he sickened, and died at Kikiakoi some time in the year 1754, having previously bequeathed his power and dignity as Moi of Hawaii to his son *Keaweopala*.

Alapainui, according to the custom among great chiefs, had several wives, the principal one among whom, however, was *Keaka*, the mother of *Keaweopala*. Another wife was *Kamakaimoku*, previously referred to. She was the mother of a daughter, *Manona*, who became the grandmother of *Kekuaokalani*, the cousin of *Liholiho Kamehameha II.*, and the defender of the ancient religion when the tabus were abolished. Another wife was *Kamaua*, with whom *Alapai* had two children, *Kauwaa*,[1] a daughter, and *Mahiua*, a son.

In the allotment of lands among the chiefs and members of the deceased Moi's family—which, since the time of *Keawenui-a-umi*, appears to have become a custom on the death of a Moi—*Keeaumoku*, surnamed *Papaiaaheahe*, a son of *Keawepoepoe*, who was a uterine brother of *Alapainui*, became dissatisfied with his allotment and retired to Kekaha, where he commenced open rebellion against *Keaweopala*. The latter promptly sent an armed *Keaweopala.* forced against him and drove him off from the land, and obliged him to seek refuge at sea on board of his canoes. In this extremity *Keeaumoku* fled to *Kalaniopuu* for succour and shelter. On learning the death of *Alapainui* and the disposition made of the government, *Kalaniopuu* had collected his forces and started from Kau to contest the sovereignty of Hawaii with *Keaweopala*. Arrived at Honomalino in South Kona, he there met the vanquished *Keeaumoku*, and, joining their forces and fleets, proceeded to the northward. *Keaweopala*, advised of the movements and designs of *Kalaniopuu*, hastened from Waimea, and, crossing the "Aamoku" and passing by the "Ahua-a-Umi," he descended in Kona and met *Kalaniopuu* between Keei and Honaunau. The battle that ensued is said to have continued for several days, owing partly to the ruggedness of the ground and the obstinate valour of the combatants, and the issue was for a long time uncertain. Finally *Kalaniopuu* won the day; *Keaweopala* was slain, and his adherents acknowledged the new Moi of Hawaii.

It is related that when the battle was at the hottest and

---

[1] *Kauwaa* married *Nahili*, and had two daughters : *Alapai*, who was married to the late *John Young Keoniana*, son of *John Young* and *Kaoanaeha*, and Premier during the reign of *Kamehameha III.*, and uncle to the present Queen Dowager *Emma R. Kaleleonalani.* The other daughter was *Kaulunae*, who married *Kanehiwa*, and was the mother of a son, *Lipoa*, and a daughter, *Julia Moemalie.*

the issue most doubtful, *Holoae*,[1] the Kahuna or priest of *Kalaniopuu*, informed him that the only means of obtaining victory was to kill *Kaakau*, the priest of *Keaweopala*, whose prayers and powers prolonged the contest. Acting on the advice, *Kaakau* was singled out in the battle by *Kalaniopuu's* soldiers and slain, after which the victory soon was won.

Keaweopala is known to have had two wives; one was *Keoua*, with whom he had a daughter, *Peleuli;* the other was *Kaukuhakuonana*,[2] with whom he had two sons, *Kanehiwa* and *Kuapuu*.

Kalaniopuu was now sole sovereign of Hawaii, and, at the usual redistribution of lands at his accession, apparently all were satisfied or none dared to resist. For several years afterwards he occupied himself diligently in reorganising the affairs of the state, augmenting the warlike resources of the island, building war-canoes, collecting arms, &c., and his own and the neighbouring islands enjoyed a season of rest from foreign and domestic strife and warfare.

Kalaniopuu. But *Kalaniopuu* was ambitious of fame in his island world by warlike exploits and by enlarging his domain with the acquisition of neighbouring territory. Possibly also he may have been moved by reasons of policy, such as finding occupation abroad for the young and restless chiefs with whom every district abounded. Suddenly, therefore, he concentrated his forces and war-canoes at Kohala, and, without previous rupture of peace or declaration of war, he invaded Maui, where *Kamehamehanui* then ruled as Moi, and made a descent in the Hana district. Little or no resistance was offered, and in a short time he

---

[1] *Holoae* was of the *Paao* race of Kahunas and descended from him. He was the great-grandfather of the late *Luahine*, who was the wife of *Kaoleioku*, the oldest son of *Kamehameha I.*, and grandmother of the present Hon. *Mrs. C. R. Bishop.*

[2] *Kanehiwa* married *Kaulunae*, who was the granddaughter of *Alapainui*, and mother of the late *Lipoa* and *Julia Moemalie*, both of Honolulu. *Kanepuu* was the grandfather of the late *Kamaipuupaa.*

possessed himself of the two valuable districts of Hana
and Kipahulu, as well as the celebrated fort on Kauwiki
Hill overlooking the harbour of Hana. The date of this
invasion is approximately, and probably correctly, fixed at
1759.

Kalaniopuu appointed *Puna*—the same who counselled
him to revolt against *Alapainui*—as governor over the
conquered districts ; and a number of Hawaii chiefs were
placed in various positions, and endowed with lands, both
in Hana and Kipahulu. Satisfied with the success of his
campaign, *Kalaniopuu* then returned to Hawaii.

But *Kamehamehanui*, though taken by surprise by
the invasion of East Maui by *Kalaniopuu*, was not a
man to yield to such a usurpation and affront without
an effort to recover the lost districts. Carefully and
thoroughly he made his preparations, collecting his forces
from Maui, and strengthening himself with a number
of auxiliaries drawn from the neighbouring islands of
Molokai and Lanai, under well-known and valiant chiefs.
Conspicuous among the former were *Kaohele*,[1] *Kaolohaka-
a-keawe, Awili, Kumukoa,* and *Kapooloku ;* among the
latter were *Namakeha, Kalaimanuia,* and *Kealiiaa.* With
these forces *Kamehamehanui* set out for Hana and laid
siege to the fort on Kauwiki. Several battles were
fought with the Hawaii army under *Puna*, especially at
Makaolehua and at Akiala, where the Maui forces were
victorious, and in which the valour of *Kaohelelani* is
greatly extolled. The fort of Kauwiki, however, with-
stood all attempts to take it, and, after a prolonged and
unsuccessful siege, *Kamehamehanui* withdrew his forces,
and left Hana in possession of *Kalaniopuu*, while *Puna*
remained as its governor and chief ; and it does not appear
that *Kamehamehanui* again attempted to drive the

[1] *Kaohelelani* was the brother of *Kawau*(k) and *Kaoenaia*(k), chiefs of Kalaupapa, Molokai. *Kaoenaia,* through his daughter *Kamai,* was the great-grandfather of the author's wife.

Hawaiians out of Hana. In the native legends this campaign is called the war of " Kapalipilo."

Suspension of hostilities, if not peace, between Maui and Hawaii obtained for several years after this abortive attempt to recapture the fort of Kauwiki. During this interval not many noteworthy events transpired, at least none are related, except the displacement of *Puna* as governor of Hana and commander of the important fort of Kauwiki, and the appointment of *Mahihelelima* in his place. This change was effected by a *ruse* practised upon *Puna* by *Mahihelelima*, but it was afterwards confirmed by *Kalaniopuu*.

Another event during this interval was the revolt and escape and subsequent adventures of *Keeaumoku*, the son of *Keawepoepoe*, the same who, on the death of *Alapainui*, had rebelled against *Keaweopala* and joined *Kalaniopuu*. The cause of his defection from the latter is not stated. Revolt and turbulence seem to have been his natural element until age cooled his temper, and the conquest of the group by *Kamehameha I.* deprived conspirators of the support and aid they formerly had found in the neighbouring islands. However, it happened *Keeaumoku* rose in revolt against *Kalaniopuu*, and intrenched himself at the fort of Pohakuomaneo, between Pololu and Honokane, in North Kohala. When informed of the revolt of *Keeaumoku*, *Kalaniopuu* crossed the mountains with an adequate force, took the fort by assault, extinguished the rebellion, but missed the arch-rebel; for *Keeaumoku* escaped over the Pali, reached the shore, and obtaining a canoe, was safely landed on Maui, where, on account of his mother, *Kumaiku*—of the Maui line of chiefs—he was hospitably received by *Kamehamehanui* and the great chiefs of that house.

After the death of *Kamehamehanui*, which happened about 1765, *Keeaumoku* took one of his widows for wife. This lady was *Namahana*, daughter of *Kekaulike* and his wife

Haalou, and consequently half-sister of the deceased king and of his brother and successor, *Kahekili*. The latter was greatly displeased with the match, possibly considering his brother's widows as his own special inheritance, and looking upon the intrusion of *Keeaumoku* as an act of rebellion and hostility towards himself.

At that time the large and fertile land of Waihee was in the possession of *Namahana*, and here she and her new husband took up their abode. They appear to have kept court in princely style, and thither gathered many of the gay and restless spirits of the time, besides her mother, *Haalou*, and her brothers, *Kekauhiwamoku* and *Kauhiwawaeono*. Several Molokai chiefs whom *Peleioholani*, the Oahu king, had despoiled of their lands and driven out of the island, had also found refuge and entertainment at *Namahana's* court in Waihee, among whom are mentioned by name *Kumukoa*, the son of *Keawe* of Hawaii, who at that time must have been considerably aged.

While this brilliant assembly were passing their time at Waihee, *Kahekili* had come over the mountain from Lahaina and was holding his court at Pihana and at Paukukalo in Wailuku, and the ill-will which the marriage of *Keeaumoku* and *Namahana* had engendered soon found an occasion to show itself.

Among the subordinate landholders in Waihee, occupying a subdivision of land called Kaapoko, was a warrior named *Kahanana*. For some reason, now unexplained, this *Kahanana* had frequently been neglected when the chief of Waihee distributed fish, after fortunate catches, among the subordinates and warriors living on the land. Incensed at what he considered a studied neglect and insult, *Kahanana* donned his feather cape—the *Ahuula*—and his helmet—the *Mahiole*—and went in the night to Nuikukahi in Waiehu and killed three men belonging to *Keeaumoku*. An *emeute* arose, sides were taken, and the *Kahanana* party being supported by *Kahekili*, a general fight ensued, in which *Keeaumoku* and the Waihee party maintained their ground for some days, but were eventually overmatched, beaten, and obliged to flee. This battle is known in the regions as the battle of "*Kalai-iliili.*"

The Waihee coterie of chiefs having thus been broken up, some fled over the Lanilili spur of the Eka mountains into the Kaanapali district. Among these were *Keeaumoku*, his wife *Namahana*, her mother *Haalou*, and her brothers *Kekuamanoha* and *Kauhiwawaeono*, and at Kaanapali they embarked for Molokai. But the hot anger of *Kahekili* pursued the fugitives. Invading Molokai, he engaged *Keeaumoku* and his Molokai allies in a sea-fight, was again victorious, and *Keeaumoku* fled to Hana, where *Mahihelelima*, the governor under *Kalaniopuu*, received him and his wife and entertained them at Kauwiki. The naval engagement just referred to is in the native legend called the battle of "*Kalauonakukui.*"

At Kauwiki *Keeaumoku* appears to have found a short repose in his turbulent career, at least he is not heard of again for some years. It is probable that he made his peace with *Kalaniopuu* and was permitted to remain at Hana, where the afterwards so famous *Kaahumanu*, wife of *Kamehameha I.*, was born in 1768.

Again several years pass by, of which the native legends make no mention, *Kalaniopuu* still holding portions of the Hana district on Maui and the great fort of Kauwiki; but about the year 1775 the war between Hawaii and Maui broke out again.

The Hawaii forces at Hana, apparently under the command of *Kalaniopuu* in person, had made an incursion or raid in the Kaupo district, which still acknowledged the rule of *Kahekili*. Taken by surprise and unprepared, the Kaupo people suffered great destruction of property, cruelty, and loss of life at the hands of the Hawaii soldiers; and the expedition is called in the legends the war of "*Kalaehohoa,*" from the fact that the captives were unmercifully beaten on their heads by the war-clubs of the Hawaii troops.

When *Kahekili* heard of this fresh irruption into his domain, he immediately sent two detachments of soldiers, under the command of *Kaneolaelae,* to the support and relief of the Kaupo people. A sanguinary battle ensued between the Hawaii and Maui forces near the point of land called "Kalaeokailio." *Kalaniopuu's* army was utterly routed and pursued to their fleet, which was lying under lee of the said point of land, and barely a remnant escaped on board and returned to Hana. After this severe repulse *Kalaniopuu* went back to Hawaii, determined to make preparations for a fresh invasion that would prove irresistible.

Among the warriors on the Hawaii side in this battle of "Kalaeakailio" the legends make honourable mention of the valour of *Kekuhaupio,* whose fame as a warrior chief stood second to none of his time, and of *Kamehameha,* afterwards so famous in history, and who on that occasion gallantly supported *Kekuhaupio* and rescued him from inevitable capture.

A whole year was consumed by *Kalaniopuu* in preparing for the next war with Maui. Six army corps or brigades were organised, and became known by the names of *I, Ahu, Mahi, Palena, Luahine,* and *Paia ;* the members of the royal family were formed into a life-guard, called *Keawe ;* and the *Alii-ai-alo*—the nobles who had the privilege of eating at the same table with the Moi—composed two regiments called *Alapa* and *Piipii.*

While thus preparing material resources, *Kalaniopuu* was not forgetful of his duties to the god whom he acknowledged and whose aid he besought. This god was *Kaili*—pronounced fully "*Ku-kaili-moku*"—who, from the days of *Liloa,* and probably before, appears to have been the special war-god of the Hawaii Mois. To ensure the favour of this god, he repaired and put in

good order the Heiaus called "*Ohiamukumuku*" at Kahaluu, and "*Keikepuipui*" at Kailua, in the Kona district, and the high-priest *Holoae* was commanded to
maintain religious services and exert all his knowledge
and power to accomplish the defeat and death of the
Maui sovereign.

Kahekili, the Maui king, was well informed of the
preparations of *Kalaniopuu*, and in order not to be out-
done by the latter in reference to the spiritual powers,
and there being apparently no high-priest on Maui at the
time of adequate celebrity and power to cope with the
Hawaii high-priest *Holoae*, he sent to Oahu and prevailed
upon *Kaleopuupuu*, the high-priest of *Peleioholani*—and
who after *Peleioholani's* death appears not to have been
employed in that capacity by his successors—to come to
Maui and take charge of the religious rites and magical
processes whereby to counteract the incantations and
powers of the Hawaii high-priest. This *Kaleopuupuu*
stood high in the Hawaiian priesthood, being a descendant of *Kaekae*, *Maliu*, and *Malea*, the foreign priests
whom *Paumakua* of Oahu is said to have brought with
him on his return from foreign voyages about seven
hundred years previously. Following his instructions,
Kahekili repaired and consecrated the Heiau called "*Ka-
luli*" at Puuohala on the north side of Wailuku, and was
greatly comforted by the assurances of *Kaleopuupuu* that
the Hawaii forces would be caught like fish in a net—
"*Ua komo ka ia i ka makaha ua puni i ka nae.*"

In 1776 *Kalaniopuu* embarked his forces and landed
them without resistance in the Honuaula district, from
Keonioio to Makena. Plunder and spoliation marked
his arrival, and the country people fled to the woods and
mountain ravines for shelter. Taking part of his forces
around by water, *Kalaniopuu* landed again at Kiheipukoa,
near the Kealia or salt marsh between Kalepolepo and
Maalaea. The landing being effected early in the day,
it was resolved to push forward at once, and "On to

Wailuku!" where *Kahekili* was residing, became the war-cry of the day. The detachment or regiment known as the *Alapa*, mustering eight hundred men, was selected for this hazardous expedition, and with high courage they started across the isthmus of Kamaomao, now known as the Waikapu common, determined, as the legend says, "to drink the waters of the Wailuku that day." This regiment was considered the bravest and best of *Kalaniopuu's* army, every man in its ranks being a member of "*la haute noblesse*" of Hawaii. They are said to have all been of equal stature and their spears of equal length; and the legend represents their appearance—with their feather cloaks reflecting the sunshine and the plumes of their helmets tossing in the wind—as a gorgeous and magnificent spectacle.

Little did this gallant troop apprehend the terrible fate that awaited them. Little did *Kalaniopuu* know the wily warrior with whom he was contending. Offering no resistance to the enemy while crossing the common, *Kahekili* distributed his forces in various directions on the Wailuku side of the common, and fell upon the Hawaii *corps d'armée* as it was entering among the sand-hills south-east of Kalua, near Wailuku. After one of the most sanguinary battles recorded in Hawaiian legends, and deeds of valour that await but another Tennyson, the gallant and devoted *Alapa* were literally annihilated; only two out of the eight hundred escaped alive to tell *Kalaniopuu* of this Hawaiian Balaclava, and the only prisoner brought alive to *Kahekili* was *Keawehano*, a chief of Hilo, and he died of his wounds before he could be sacrificed at the Heiau by the victors. This battle is called the "*Ahulau ka piipii i Kakanilua.*"

When, in the evening of that day, the news of the battle was brought to *Kalaniopuu* at Kiheipukoa, where he and the royal family and the main body of his army were encamped, consternation and sorrow filled his mind at the loss of his gallant eight hundred. A council of war was called in the night, at which the following chiefs are said to have assisted :—*Keawemauhili*, half-brother of *Kalaniopuu; Kalanimanookahoowaha*, a scion of the *Luahine* family of Kohala ;[1] *Keawe-a-Heulu*, of the great *I* family, and also called in the legend a scion of *Imakakaloa* of Puna ; *Nuuanu*, from Naalehu in Kau ; *Naeole*,[2] a scion of the *Wahilani* family in Kohala ; *Kanekoa*,[3] from Waimea ; *Nanuekaleiopu*, from Hamakua ; *Kameeuiamoku* and *Kamanawa*,[4] the twin children of *Keawepoepoe ; Kekuhaupio*, a relation and son-in-law of the high-priest *Holoae ;* besides the sons and relatives of *Kalaniopuu*.

In that council it was resolved to march the entire army on Wailuku the following day, and, by a bold attack, retrieve the fortunes of the previous day.

Kahekili had not been idle during the night. Distributing his own forces and the auxiliary Oahu troops, under the Oahu king, *Kahahana*,[5] among the sandhills, from Waikapu to Wailuku, which skirt that side of the common, and stationing a reserve force at the turn of the Waikapu stream, he awaited the approach of the enemy coming from the Kealia saltponds. Long and severe was the contest, but again the Hawaii army was beaten

---

[1] The *Luahine* family in Kohala, to which *Keaka*, the wife of *Alapainui*, belonged, is said to be descended from *Keakealanikane*, the grandson of *Keawe-Nui-a-Umi*.

[2] The same that stole *Kamehameha I.* away from his mother on the night of his birth.

[3] He was son of *Kalanikeeaumoku*, the son of *Keawe*, Moi of Hawaii. His mother was a lady called *Kailakanoa*.

[4] In more than one legend *Kameeiamoku* and *Kamanawa* are called the tabued twin children of *Kekaulike*, and half-brothers of *Kahekili;* but all the genealogies that I have had access to represent them as the sons of *Keawepoepoe* and *Kanoena ;* the former a son of *Kalanikauleleiaiwi*

and her Kauai husband *Lonoikahaupu ;* the latter a daughter of *Lonoanahulu*, of the great *Ehu* family. It is not easy to tell whether the legends or the genealogies are correct. The former frequently give the *chronique scandaleuse* of their time, either directly or by innuendo ; the latter are generally such as the parties themselves, or their descendants, wished to be understood as a fact, and so handed down to posterity.

[5] He was a relative of *Kahekili* on his mother's side, and had been elected Moi of Oahu by the Oahu chiefs after they had deposed *Kumahana*, the son of *Peleioholani*, about 1773.

back with fearful slaughter ; but, although victorious, the battle must have cost *Kahekili* dearly, for it is not mentioned that the pursuit of the fleeing remnant of *Kalaniopuu's* army was ever very close or long protracted.

In this extremity *Kalaniopuu* proposed to send his wife, *Kalola*, who was own sister to *Kahekili*,[1] as an ambassadress to solicit peace and personal safety. *Kalola*, however, refused to go, distrusting the temper of her victorious brother, and alleging to *Kalaniopuu* that she feared for her own life, inasmuch as this had been a war of devastation and conquest (" *Kaua hulia mahi*"), and not characterised by princely courtesy ; but in her turn she proposed that *Kalaniopuu's* son, *Kiwalao*, the nephew of *Kahekili* and the tabued heir of *Kalaniopuu*, should be sent with *Kameeiamoku* and *Kamanawa*, to soothe the temper of *Kahekili*, and obtain the most favourable terms possible.

The advice was acted on, and, dressed up with all the royal insignia of his rank, and accompanied by *Kameeiamoku* and *Kamanawa*, the former carrying the chief's *Ipu-kuha*, and the latter his *Kahili*, *Kiwalao* proceeded to Wailuku. The proclamation of his heralds and the insignia of his rank passed him safely through the ranks of the Maui soldiers, who, according to custom, prostrated themselves at the approach of so high a chief.

When it was reported to *Kahekili*, who was reposing at " Kalanihale," in Wailuku, that *Kiwalao* was approaching, he is said to have turned round on the mat, face upward ;[2] a sign of kindly intentions and good-humour.

On entering the house, *Kiwalao* went direct to where *Kahekili* was reposing, and sat down on his lap They saluted each other, and wailed according to custom. When the wailing was over, *Kameeiamoku* and *Kamanawa*,

[1] She was daughter of *Kekaulike* and *Kekuiapoiwanui*, the parents of *Kahekili*, *Kamehamehanui*, and a daughter named *Kuhooheiheipahu*.

[2] " Iluna ke alo." A contrary position, "Ilalo ke alo," would have been the certain death-warrant of *Kiwalao*.

according to the etiquette of the time, crawled up ("*Kokolo*") to *Kahekili* and kissed his hands. *Kiwalao* being too high a chief to commence the conversation, the negotiations were opened by *Kahekili*. The conditions of peace are not mentioned, but *Kalaniopuu* and *Kahekili* met afterwards, and a peace was concluded, whereupon *Kalaniopuu* returned to Hawaii.

The defeat and humiliation of *Kalaniopuu* in this last campaign rankled deep in his mind, and hardly a year had elapsed after his return to Hawaii before we find him afloat again with a large force, carrying war and desolation into *Kahekili's* dominions. His first descent on Maui was at Mokolau, in the Kaupo district, where the inhabitants were plundered and ill-treated On hearing of this new invasion, *Kahekili* sent troops to Kaupo, and apparently cleared the country of the invaders, for it is said that *Kalaniopuu* left Kaupo, and made his next descent on the island of Kahoolawe, and, not finding much booty there, steered for Lahaina, whither *Kahekili* and the Oahu auxiliaries hastened to oppose him. After some partial successes, *Kalaniopuu* attempted to take a fortified place called Kahili, between Kauaula and Kanaha, where the chiefs of Lahaina had taken refuge ; but failing in the assault, and being repulsed with considerable loss, he embarked his force and landed on Lanai.

During this campaign at Lahaina we first meet with the name of *Keaulumoku*,[1] the great bard and prophet, who at that time was following *Kahahana*, the Oahu king, whom he afterwards left and went to Hawaii, where he was received at the court of *Kalaniopuu*. Some time after the death of the latter, *Keaulumoku* composed the famous chant, " *Hau-i-Kalani*," describing the horrors of the civil war then desolating the island of Hawaii, and prophesying the success and glory of *Kamehameha I.*

Kalaniopuu ravaged the island of Lanai thoroughly, and

---

[1] *Keaulumoku* was the son of *Kauakahiakua*, a cousin of *Kekaulike*, king of Maui. His mother was a lady from Naohaku, Hamakua, Hawaii.

the Lanai chiefs, unable to oppose him, retreated to a fortified place called "Hookio," inland from Maunalei. But being short of provisions, and their water supply having been cut off, the fort was taken by *Kalaniopuu,* and the chiefs were killed. This Lanai expedition is remembered by the name of *Kamokuhi.*

From Lanai *Kalaniopuu* proceeded with his fleet and army up the Pailolo channel, between Molokai and Maui, touching at Honokohau, where provisions were obtained. Then, rounding Kahakuloa, he stood to the eastward, and landed at Hamakualoa, on Maui, where he plundered the country, and committed fearful barbarities on the people, until *Kahekili* came to their support with his forces, and, after several encounters, drove *Kalaniopuu* on board of his fleet. Foiled in Hamakualoa, *Kalaniopuu* made his next descent in the Koolau district, committing similar depredations and barbarities there. While there, he was joined by *Mahihelelima,* the Hawaii governor of the adjoining Hana district, with a select force of warriors, and being thus enabled to rally and hold his ground against *Kahekili,* he again attempted the invasion of Hamakualoa, where the war was protracted, with varying success, for several months.

It was during the early part of this campaign of 1778 that the English discovery ships "Resolution" and "Discovery," under command of Captain James Cook, arrived at these islands. The subject of his discovery, his communications with the natives, and his violent death, may as well be discussed in this place as in any other. They form an epoch in the history of the group, and their consequences, reacting on the destiny and development of this and other Polynesian groups, amount almost to a revolution, as unique as it is instructive, in the history of mankind. One hundred years have passed since that memorable event, and yet there linger a few persons on the various islands who were born before Cook arrived, and who have witnessed the stupendous changes that

have occurred since then; and the children and grandchildren of many of those who took a part in the scenes
then transacted, and who heard the tale of the arrival and
death of "Lono" from the lips of then living witnesses,
are still alive, or have left their memoirs of that time in
writing.

The objects of Captain Cook's voyage of discovery are
well known, and need not be repeated here. The question
has arisen, and been in some measure discussed—Whether
Captain Cook was aware of the existence of the Hawaiian
group from information received from Spanish authorities,
and looked for it on purpose to find or rediscover it, or
whether he was entirely ignorant of its existence, and thus
by merest accident discovered it?

There can be no doubt that in the early part of the
sixteenth century shipwrecked Spaniards arrived at the
Hawaiian Islands, as already stated on page 106, &c., and
I think that various evidences, set forth in the "North
Pacific Pilot," London, 1870, and in the document from
the Colonial Office in Spain, procured at the solicitation of
the Hawaiian Minister of Foreign Affairs in 1866—both
published in "The Friend," Honolulu, October 1873—
will satisfy the majority of those who take an interest in
the matter that the Hawaiian group was discovered in
1555 by Juan Gaetano, a Spaniard sailing from the coast
of New Spain to the Spice Islands.[1] And we will, in the
sequel, attempt to show that it is extremely probable that
other Spanish vessels besides that of Gaetano passed by
or through the Hawaiian Archipelago on their way to or
from Manilla.

But if the priority of the discovery, as a fact, must be
conceded to the Spaniards, yet the credit of the redis-
covery, as an act tending to enlarge the knowledge of
mankind, and extend the area of civilised and Christian

[1] See Appendix No. 3.

activity, must be awarded to Captain Cook. The Spaniards knew of the existence of the Hawaiian group, but they buried that knowledge in their logbooks and archives, and it was as barren of results to themselves as to others. Cook gave the world the benefit of his discovery, and in the fulness of time added another star to the family group of civilised peoples.

In attempting to reproduce a correct narrative of Captain Cook's discovery of, visit to, and intercourse with the Hawaiian Islands, I have taken due heed of what has been written on the subject by himself and by Captain King in their journal of " A Voyage to the Pacific Ocean," printed by order of the Lords Commissioners of the Admiralty, 1784, as well as of what has been written by others ; but as I am not writing a history of Captain Cook, but a history of the Hawaiian group, I have also consulted the Hawaiian reminiscences of that memorable event, as handed down to still living children or grand-children by those who figured more or less prominently at the lifting of the curtain in January 1778 on Kauai, and at the close of the drama in February 1779 on Hawaii. The one story in several instances supplements the other ; and in some cases where the two differ, and, from ignorance of the language and the people, Captains Cook and King were misled as to facts, the Hawaiian version gives a more natural, and consequently a more probably correct, account of the transaction.

On the 8th of December 1777, Captain Cook, with H.B.M. ships " Resolution" and " Discovery," left the island of Bolabola, Society group, bound to the north-west coast of America. Before leaving he had inquired of the natives if any land or islands known to them existed to the north or north-west, and was told that they knew of none.[1] Standing up through the south-east trades, he discovered Christmas Island, lat. 1° 58′ N., long. 157° 32′ W., on the 24th of December. Leaving that island

[1] Vol. ii. p. 180.

on the 2d January 1778, steering to the north, he discovered on the 18th January the island of Oahu, bearing north-east by east, and soon after saw the island of Kauai, bearing north. On the 19th January, at sunrise, Oahu bore east several leagues distant, and he therefore stood for the other island seen the day before, and not long after discovered a third island, Niihau, bearing west-north-west. When approaching the east side of Kauai several canoes came off, and a barter of bits of iron for hogs and vegetables commenced. Speaking of the appearance of the natives Cook says :[1]—" There was little difference in the casts of their colour, but a considerable variation in their features, some of their visages not being very unlike those of Europeans." Coasting along the south-east side of the island, he saw several villages, some near the sea, others more inland. Standing off and on during the night, Cook again approached the land on the 20th of January, when several canoes came off filled with people, some of whom ventured on board. The ships were now off Waimea Bay, and Cook sent three armed boats ashore to look for a watering-place, under command of Lieutenant Williamson. On his return the Lieutenant reported that he had found a good watering-place, but that, on attempting to land, he was so pressed upon by the natives, who had flocked to the beach, that he was obliged to fire,[2] by which one native was killed. Between three and four o'clock that afternoon the ships anchored in Waimea Bay, Kauai, and Captain Cook went ashore. I quote his remarks upon that occasion, as they will throw some light upon his subsequent conduct at Hawaii,—a conduct that has been the subject of no little animadversion. He says :[3]—" The very instant I leaped ashore the collected body of the natives fell flat upon their faces, and remained in that very humble posture till, by expressive signs, I prevailed upon them to rise. They then brought a great many small pigs, which they presented to me, with plantain

<hr>

[1] Vol. ii. p. 192.   [2] Ibid., p. 198.   [3] Ibid., p. 199.

trees, using much the same ceremonies that we had seen practised on such occasions at the Society and other islands ; and a long prayer being spoken by a single person, in which others of the assembly sometimes joined, I expressed my acceptance of their proffered friendship by giving them in return such presents as I had brought with me for that purpose."

On the 21st January, in the morning, the business of watering the ships began ; trade with the natives was established ; and everything having the appearance of friendliness and goodwill, Cook took a walk up the country, and returned on board. On the 22d January a southerly storm with rain set in ; and on the 23d, on endeavouring to change the anchorage of the " Resolution," which was rather too close inshore, the ship drifted off to sea ; and after cruising about from the 24th to the 29th, and being unable to regain the roadstead of Waimea, he steered for Niihau, and anchored off the west point of that island on the last-named day, having been joined by the " Discovery " on the 25th.

Cook says that when he ordered the boats ashore at Waimea to search for a watering-place, he gave orders [1] " not to suffer more than one man to go with him (the officer) out of the boats," and explains the motive of the order to be " that I might do everything in my power to prevent the importation of a fatal disease into this island, which I knew some of our men now laboured under, and which, unfortunately, had been already communicated by us to other islands in these seas. With the same view I ordered all female visitors to be excluded from the ships. . . . Many of them had come off in the canoes. They would as readily have favoured us with their company on board as the men; but I wished to prevent all con- nection which might, too probably, convey an irreparable injury to themselves, and, through their means, to the whole nation."

[1] Vol. ii. p. 195.

Giving Cook all credit for his good intentions, it is lamentable to reflect that his orders were so little heeded and so badly executed. The native accounts are positive and unanimous that the intercourse between the seamen of the ships and the native women, both ashore and on board, was notorious and unchecked. The native historians all say that on the night that Cook's ships anchored at Waimea, a grand council was held at the house of *Kamakahelei*, the highest chiefess on the island, and the actual hereditary sovereign of that part of Kauai, when some proposed to seize the ships by force and run them ashore for the sake of the plunder that would be obtained, while others of a more pacific or more timid mind proposed to propitiate the newcomers—whom, or rather whose captain, they in some confused manner connected with the old and distorted legend of Lono—with presents and with the charms of their women. The latter advice was acted on, and hogs, vegetables, kapa, and women were sent on board, and among the latter was *Kamakahelei's* own daughter, *Lelemahoalani;* and during the last generation of Hawaiians it was openly said, and never contradicted, that that night *Lelemahoalani* slept with *Lono* (Cook).

Native historians [1] are particularly bitter against the memory of Captain Cook on account of the introduction of the venereal disease in the group by the seamen of the ships under his command; and they argue, that had Cook himself shown greater continence, his orders referred to above would have been better obeyed. The resentment is natural, the argument cogent; but it is an *ex post facto* argument, which takes no notice of the times and the circumstances under which Cook and his seamen were placed, nor of the social condition, customs, and modes of thinking which at that time obtained among the Hawaiians. I am not called upon to defend the personal morality of Cook. Though superior to many

[1] D. Malo and S. M. Kamakau.

of his day as a naval commander and a discoverer in
unknown seas, yet he was probably no better than the
majority of men of his education, training, and pursuits
would have been under the same or similar circumstances;
nor were the simple sailors of a hundred years ago more
sensitive to moral teachings or more obedient to naval
discipline than are such men at the present time. On
the other hand, the Hawaiians of that time were not the
race of Nature's innocents which the school of Rousseau
loved to paint; their moral darkness, or rather their deep
ignorance of the precepts and principles which ought to
restrain and guide a Christian or a moral person, has so
often and so broadly been described by others, that I may
only allude to it here. Placed under particularly trying
circumstances, confronted with men whom they looked
upon as divine, or supernatural beings at least, the
Hawaiians freely gave what in their moral ethics there
was no prohibition to give; and the seamen—well, they
were mortal men with mortal passions, and they only
followed the famous saying inaugurated by the Buccaneers and become proverbial ever since, that "there
was no God on this side of Cape Horn."

The result, however, was death and indescribable misery
to the poor Hawaiians, and no wonder that the memory
of Captain Cook is not cherished among them.

When Cook says that he gave orders to "exclude the
women from on board the ships," and the native testimony asserts that numerous women, and the queen's own
daughter among them, passed one or more nights on
board, there is but one way to escape from the dilemma,
and that is to assume what was probably the fact, though
Cook does nowhere acknowledge it—namely, that his
orders were not properly carried into effect.

Cook remained at anchor off Niihau from the 29th
January to the 2d of February 1778, where, owing to
the unfavourable weather and the high surf, twenty of

his men, with an officer, were left ashore two nights, and were hospitably treated by the natives.

On February 1, Cook landed a ram-goat, two ewes, a boar, and a sow of English breed, and seeds of melons, pumpkins, and onions, which were given to a prominent native.

Cook does not mention that he met any superior chief while staying at Waimea, Kauai; and yet it is indisputable that *Kamakahelei* and her family were there.[1] But on Niihau he was told that the island owed allegiance to *Kaneoneo*, and that Kauai was ruled by several chiefs, notably by *Kaneoneo*,[2] *Kaeo*,[3] and *Terarotoa*.[4] After Cook left Kauai, however, and while the " Discovery " was still detained there, a high chief, before whom the natives prostrated themselves, came on board and was entertained by Captain Clerke.[5] This chief is said to have been " a young man accompanied by a young woman, supposed to be his wife," and his name as reported to Cook was *Tamahano*.[6]

[1] S. M. Kamakau, in his account, states that both *Kaeo* and *Kamakahelei* received Cook and exchanged presents with him on the day that he went ashore, but he does not mention that they visited the ships. Apparently Cook was ignorant of their exalted rank when he met them ashore.

[2] *Kaneoneo* was the son of *Kumahana*, king of Oahu, and grandson of the famous *Peleioholani*. He was one of the husbands of *Kamakahelei*.

[3] *Kaeo*, or, more correctly, *Kaeokulani*, was a son of *Kekaulike*, king of Maui, and his wife *Hoolau*, a great-granddaughter of *Lonoikamakahiki* of Hawaii on her father's side. *Kaeokulani* was another husband of *Kamakahelei*, and father of *Kaumualii*, the last independent king of Kauai.

[4] I have been unable to identify this name with any of the known chiefs of that time on Kauai. The singular manner in which Captain Cook and those around him apprehended the native names of persons and places, and reproduced them in writing, is sometimes sorely perplexing to Polynesian scholars.

[5] Cook's Voyages, vol. ii. p. 245.

[6] It is uncertain who this high chieftain might have been. *Kumahana*, the son of *Peleioholani*, to whom the name most probably corresponds, was doubtless then on Kauai, if alive, whither he had fled after being dethroned on Oahu by his chiefs and subjects in 1773; but he was not " a young man " at the time. If he had died in the interval between his deposition and 1778, it is possible that his son *Kaneoneo* might, according to frequent usage, have assumed his father's name, or presented himself under that name on board of the "Discovery." Or it might have been a younger son of *Kumahana*, bearing his father's name, of whom, however, native traditions are silent.

It is probable that Cook's estimate of the populousness of Kauai is too high. Judging from the section of the island that he saw, and taking the village of Waimea as a standard, he estimated sixty such villages on the island, with a total of 30,000 inhabitants.[1] The ancient native division of the island gives no account of so many villages as Cook supposed, yet it may safely be assumed that the island contained 20,000 people at that time. On the second visit to Kauai, Captain King estimates the population at 54,000; but his calculation is based on the assumption[2] that the whole coast-line of all the islands was as thickly inhabited as the bay of Kealakeakua on Hawaii. On Niihau Cook supposed, judging from the "thinly-scattered habitations of the natives,"[3] that there " were not more than five hundred people on the island;" but King, according to his rule of calculation, assumes the island to have had 10,000 inhabitants.[4] It is plain that Cook underrated Niihau as much as he overrated Kauai, and that King's rule of calculation was not borne out by fact. Yet there can be no doubt that all the islands at that time were vastly more populous than they ever have been since; and there exist no valid réasons for assuming a greater or more rapid depopulation between 1778 and 1832, when the first regular census taken gave an approximately correct enumeration of 130,000, than between the latter year and 1878, when the census gave only 44,088, exclusive of foreigners.

It has been presumed by several writers that Captain Cook was acquainted with the existence of the Hawaiian group from the chart captured on board of the Spanish galleon "Santissima Trinidad" by Commodore Anson in 1742, where a group of islands in the same latitude, but with somewhat varying longitude, were laid down; and that with him it was not a discovery, inasmuch as he merely found what he sought for.

[1] Vol. ii. p. 230. [2] Vol. iii. p. 128.
[3] Vol. iii. p. 218. [4] Vol. iii. p. 129.

That the Spanish navigators between Acapulco and Manilla, at least some of them, knew of the existence of the Hawaiian group, I think is no longer doubtful, and may yet be proven as an historical fact when Spanish archives in the Old and New World shall have been thoroughly ransacked.[1] The chart above referred to is *prima facie* evidence, and, as we shall see hereafter, Hawaiian tradition confirms the inference. But that Cook had any previous knowledge of such a group in such a place, or that he knew that it was known to the Spaniards, I consider hardly probable, or at all consistent with what he says on the very subject of the discovery of the group. On p. 251, vol. ii., he says: " Had the Sandwich Islands been discovered at an early period by the Spaniards, there is little doubt that they would have taken advantage of so excellent a situation, and have made use of Atooi " (Kauai), " or some other of the islands, as a refreshing place to the ships that sail annually from Acapulco for Manila. An acquaintance with the Sandwich Islands would have been equally favourable to our Buccaneers, who used sometimes to pass from the coast of America to the Ladrones with a stock of food and water scarcely sufficient to preserve life. . . .

" How happy would Lord Anson have been, and what hardships would have been avoided, if he had known that there was a group of islands half-way between America and Tinian, where all his wants could have been effectually supplied ! "

If these words mean anything at all, they convey the unavoidable inference that Cook had no previous knowledge of the existence of the group. To argue the contrary, as Mr. Jarves has done,[2] is to accuse Cook of a hypocrisy and disingenuousness that his works give no warrant for, and of which competent men who can appreciate the real traits of his character will acquit him.

[1] See Appendix No. 1, and p. 108.
[2] History of Hawaiian Islands, by J. J. Jarves, 4th ed., p. 50.

Let us now see how this unexpected meeting of Europeans and Polynesians affected the latter, what impressions they received, what accounts they gave of it.

It is reported by the native historians that during one of *Peleioholani's* (king of Oahu) maritime excursions—1740–70—a ship was seen off the Oahu channel by the crew of his famous war-canoe, but it was too far off to be boarded or spoken. If such was really the case, the impression of such a sight was confined to but a few persons, and was of too indefinite a nature to have been long retained, and was probably only revived as a reminiscence after Captain Cook's arrival. However that may be, the astonishment and excitement of the Hawaiians as Cook's vessels approached the coast of Kauai were thoroughly genuine and extravagant. David Malo, the Hawaiian historian, who heard the account of Cook's arrival from actual eye-witnesses, writes in his *Moolelo Hawaii* (Hawaiian History), printed in 1838, as follows:—

"It is at Waimea, on Kauai, that Lono first arrived. He arrived in the month of January, in the year of our Lord 1778. *Kaneoneo* and *Keawe* were the chiefs of Kauai at that time. He arrived in the night at Waimea, and when daylight came the natives ashore perceived this wonderful thing that had arrived, and they expressed their astonishment with great exclamations.

"One said to another, 'What is that great thing with branches?' Others said, 'It is a forest that has slid down into the sea,' and the gabble and noise was great.[1] Then the chiefs ordered some natives to go in a canoe and observe and examine well that wonderful thing. They went, and when they came to the ship they saw the iron that was attached to the outside of the ship, and they were greatly rejoiced at the quantity of iron.

---

[1] S. M. Kamakau, in his History, adds: "Others said it was an 'Auwa-alalua'* from Olohe, Mana, but the priest *Kuoho* said it was the Heiau (temple) of *Lono*, with the ladders of *Keolewa*, and the steps to the altars."

---

* "A large species of fish; an animal that sails in the sea like a canoe."—*Andrews' Hawaiian Dictionary.*

" Because the iron was known before that time from wood with iron (in or on it) that had formerly drifted ashore, but it was in small quantity, and here was plenty. And they entered on board, and they saw the people with white foreheads, bright eyes, loose garments, corner-shaped heads, and unintelligible speech.

" Then they thought that the people (on board) were all women, because their heads were so like the women's heads of that period. They observed the quantity of iron on board of the ship, and they were filled with wonder and delight.[1]

" Then they returned and told the chiefs what they had seen, and how great the quantity of iron. On hearing this, one of the warriors of the chief said, ' I will go and take forcible possession of this booty, for to plunder is my business and means of living.'

" The chiefs consented. Then this warrior went on board of the ship and took away some of the iron on board, and he was shot at and was killed. His name was *Kapupuu.* The canoes (around the ship) fled away and reported that *Kapupuu* had been killed by a ball from a squirt-gun.[2]

" And that same night guns were fired and rockets were thrown up. They (the natives) thought it was a god, and they called his name *Lonomakua,* and they thought there would be war.[3]

" Then a chiefess named *Kamakahelei,* mother of

[1] Kamakau (S. M.) mentions that the party sent consisted of *Kaneokahoowaha, Kuohu* the priest, and *Kiikiki,* another chief ; that when they came on board they saluted Cook by prostrating themselves and with prayer, and that they were kindly received.

[2] Hawaiian *Waiki.* Judge Andrews, Hawaiian Dictionary, gives the following explanation :—" 4. The ball, anciently made of stone, and projected from a squirt-gun. ' Hai mai ua make o *Kapupuu* i ka *Waiki,*' he said that *Kapupuu* was killed by the *Waiki,* i.e., the wad or ball of the gun." S. M. Kamakau adds that the unfortunate *Kapupuu* was a retainer of *Kaeo,* and that when the people were urging the chief to avenge the death of *Kapupuu,* the priest *Kuohu* dissuaded them from so perilous and reckless an adventure.

[3] Kamakau relates that *Kuohu,* the priest, had his doubts whether the newcomers were gods or mortal men,

Kaumualii, said, ' Let us not fight against our god ; let us please him that he may be favourable to us.' Then *Kamakahelei* gave her own daughter as a woman to *Lono ; Lelemahoalani* was her name ; she was older sister of *Kaumualii*. And *Lono* slept with that woman, and the Kauai women prostituted themselves to the foreigners for iron."

The news of Cook's arrival, and all the wonders connected therewith, spread rapidly over the entire group, and here, as elsewhere, the reports were swelled by repetition. Kauai natives brought the news to Oahu, and a Hawaii native, whose name has been preserved as *Moho*, and who at the time was living on Oahu, brought the intelligence with all its embellishments to Maui, and made his report to *Kalaniopuu*, who was then at Hana.

It will thus be seen that before Captain Cook returned from the north-west coast of America, in the fall of that year, his fame had preceded him throughout the group,[1] and the people were fully prepared to receive him as an impersonation of *Lono*, one of the great gods of the Hawaiian trinity, and render him the homage and worship due to so great and mysterious a visitant, until his long

and that having tried to ascertain by means of the sacred cup (*Ka ipu Aumakua*), he came to the conclusion that " they were not gods but *Haole* (foreigners), from the country whence *Kaekae* and *Kukanaloa* * came ;" but the young people and the majority looked upon Cook as the god *Lono*.

[1] After Cooke's departure *Kaeo* sent *Kaneokahoowaha* and *Kaukapua* to Oahu to acquaint King *Kahahana* of the arrival of the foreigners, and all the wonders connected therewith. After hearing the wonderful tale, *Kaopuhuluhulu*, the high-priest of *Kahahana*, replied : " Those people are foreigners (*Haole*) from Hiikua, from Melemele, from Uliuli, from Keokeo. They are surely the people that will come and dwell in this land " (*O na Kanaka na e noho aku ka aina*). Others said : " Those are the people of whom *Kekiopilo*, the prophet of *Kupihea*, spoke when he said, ' the foreigners should come here—white people— and as for their dogs, people should ride upon them ; and they should bring dogs with very long ears.' " Others thought they were the " Haole" referred to in the chant of *Kualii*. (S. M. Kamakau's account of Cook's visit.)

---

* *Kaekae* and *Maliu* were the two white priests said to have been brought from a foreign country by *Paumakua*, vide p. 25 ; and *Kukanaloa* was the native name of the white man shipwrecked at Keei, Kona, Hawaii, *vide* p. 106.

séjour at Kealakeakua Bay and his ill-advised projects destroyed the illusion and caused his death.

On February 2, 1778, Captain Cook left the island of Niihau to prosecute the objects of his voyage, connected with the exploration of Behrings Straits and the North-West Passage. When the inclemency of the weather and the approach of winter precluded farther researches in the north, Cook returned with a light heart to the sunny isles that he discovered at the commencement of that year. On the 26th of November the island of Maui was seen well to the westward, and later in the day the island of Molokai. Cook was now off the Hamakua coast, and in the morning of the 27th the isthmus of Kamaomao was visible. The ships were lying off and on, and considerable trading was done with the natives, whom Cook found were advised of his visit to Kauai in the early part of the year; and, as indubitable proof of that fact, he states with regret that he observed that they had already been infected with the disease which his crew communicated to the Kauai women. In beating to windward, Cook found himself, on the 30th of November, off the north-east end of Maui. Here more canoes came off trading, and *Kalaniopuu* came off on board. After *Kalaniopuu* left the ship some six or eight natives remained, " who chose to remain on board," and whose double sailing-canoe, having arrived to attend them, was towed astern all night. That evening Cook discovered the island of Hawaii, and next morning his visitors left him and returned to Maui. Cook crossed the Hawaii channel, and hove-to off the Kohala coast on the evening of December 1st.

During the whole of the month of December Cook kept beating round the east side of Hawaii, frequently standing inshore and trading with the natives. On the 5th of January 1779, Cook rounded the south cape of Hawaii, and on the 17th of that month he anchored in the bay of

Kealakeakua, on the south-west side of the island, in the south Kona district.

The Hawaiian accounts are somewhat more detailed, by stating that it was off the village of Wailua, in the Koolau district, that the Hawaiian chiefs came on board of Cook's ship and remained there that night. Although *Kalaniopuu* was at Wailua at that time, yet no Hawaiian account mentions that he went on board personally;[1] but they all concur that it was *Kamehameha*, afterwards king of Hawaii, who went on board and passed the night in Cook's ship; and they state, moreover, that when the ships stood off to sea for the night and *Kamehameha* did not return, a great wailing was set up ashore by *Kalaniopuu* and his retinue, thinking that *Kamehameha* had been abducted by the ship and was lost; and their joy was proportionately great when he returned the next day.[2]

The native accounts farther remark that the first place on Hawaii off which Cook stopped to trade after leaving Maui was near the village of Kukuipahu, in the district of North Kohala; that crowds of people went off to see the vessels and the wonders that they contained; that when the natives saw the sailors eating water-melons,—this fruit being unknown to them,—they fearfully exclaimed, " These men are gods indeed; see them eating human flesh " (the meat of the melon), "and the fire burns in their mouths " (pipes or cigars).

As Cook proceeded up the west side of Hawaii, along

[1] It will be seen farther on that Captain King says that, when they had arrived at Kealakeakua, he recognised *Kalaniopuu* as one of those Hawaiian chiefs that had come on board off the east end of Maui. S. M. Kamakua states that *Kalaimamahu*, the brother of *Kamehameha* and maternal grandfather of the late king *Lunalilo*, was one of those who stayed on board that night.

[2] The native account that *Kalaniopuu* sent *Kepaalani* with a smart canoe and six picked men to hunt up the ships on the ocean and recover and bring back *Kamehameha* and his company, is possibly true in the main, but confused as to time and detail. Cook expressly states that after *Kalaniopuu* left, six or eight of his company remained on board, and that " a double sailing-canoe came soon after to attend upon them, which we towed astern all night." That probably was the canoe which *Kalaniopuu* sent off under *Kepaalani* to bring *Kamehameha* back.

the Kona coast, the populousness of the country and the abundance of provisions surprised and delighted him. This is what he says in his journal, as on the 16th of January he approached the bay of Kealakeakua :—

"At daybreak on the 16th, seeing the appearance of a bay, I sent Mr. Bligh, with a boat from each ship, to examine it, being at this time three leagues off. Canoes now began to arrive from all parts; so that before ten o'clock there were not fewer than a thousand about the two ships, most of them crowded with people, and well laden with hogs and other productions of the island. We had the most satisfying proof of their friendly intentions; for we did not see a single person who had with him a weapon of any sort, Trade and curiosity alone had brought them off. Among such numbers as we had at times on board, it is no wonder that some should betray a thievish disposition. One of our visitors took out of the ship a boat's rudder. He was discovered, but too late to recover it. I thought this a good opportunity to show these people the use of firearms; and two or three musquets, and as many four-pounders, were fired over the canoe which carried off the rudder. As it was not intended that any of the shot should take effect, the surrounding multitude of natives seemed rather more surprised than frightened."

After anchoring and mooring his ships on January 17th, Cook's journal continues :—"The ships continued to be much crowded with natives, and were surrounded by a multitude of canoes. I had nowhere in the course of my voyages seen so numerous a body of people assembled at one place. For besides those who had come off to us in canoes, all the shore of the bay was covered with spectators, and many hundreds were swimming round the ships like shoals of fish. We could not but be struck with the singularity of this scene; and perhaps there were few on board who now lamented our having failed in our endeavours to find a northern passage homeward last summer.

To this disappointment we owed our having it in our power to revisit the Sandwich Islands, and to enrich our voyage with a discovery which, though the last, seemed in many respects to be the most important that had hitherto been made by Europeans throughout the extent of the Pacific Ocean."

After Cook's ships had anchored, two chiefs, named *Palea* and *Kanina,* came on board, and the former informed him that *Kalaniopuu,* the king of Hawaii, was absent on Maui, but would be back in a few days, and he and *Kanina* appear to have made themselves serviceable in keeping order among the natives and preventing the ships from being overcrowded. Another prominent man was also introduced to Cook by *Palea,* whose name was *Koa,* and was apparently the highest officiating priest of the place in the absence of the high-priest who accompanied *Kalaniopuu.*[1] Of this interview Captain King says:[2]—"Being led into the cabin, he approached Captain Cook with great veneration, and threw over his shoulders a piece of red cloth, which he had brought along with him. Then stepping a few paces back, he made an offering of a small pig which he held in his hand, while he pronounced a discourse that lasted for a considerable time. This ceremony was frequently repeated during our stay at Owhyhee, and appeared to us, from many circumstances, to be a sort of religious adoration. Their idols we found always arrayed in red cloth in the same manner as was done to Captain Cook, and a small pig was their usual offering to the *Eatooas.*"[3]

That same afternoon Captain Cook landed and was received by *Koa, Palea,* and a number of priests, who conducted him to the Heiau, just north of the Napoopoo

---

[1] There is no doubt that *Holoae* was the recognised high-priest of *Kalaniopuu;* where he was, however, at the time of Cook's arrival at Kealakeakua, is not easy to say. Native accounts assert that *Pailili* or *Pailiki,* the son of *Holoae,* was with *Kalaniopuu* on Maui, and officiating priest on that expedition.

[2] Vol. ii. p. 5.

[3] The divinities.

village and at the foot of the Pali.[1] Here the grand ceremony of acknowledging Cook as an incarnation of *Lono,* to be worshiped as such, and his installation, so to say, in the Hawaiian Pantheon took place. The scene is so vividly described by Captain King, that I need not apologise for its repetition here. Captain King says :[2]—

"Before I proceed to relate the adoration that was paid to Captain Cook, and the peculiar ceremonies with which he was received on this fatal island, it will be necessary to describe the *Morai,* situated, as I have already mentioned, at the south side of the beach at *Kakooa* (Kealakeakua). It was a square solid pile of stones, about forty yards long, twenty broad, and fourteen in height.[3] The top was flat and well paved, and surrounded by a wooden rail, on which were fixed the skulls of the captives sacrificed on the death of their chiefs. In the centre of the area stood a ruinous old building of wood, connected with the rail on each side by a stone wall, which divided the whole space into two parts. On the side next the country were five poles, upward of twenty feet high, supporting an irregular kind of scaffold; on the opposite side toward the sea, stood two small houses with a covered communication.

"We were conducted by Koah to the top of this pile by an easy ascent leading from the beach to the north-west corner of the area. At the entrance we saw two large wooden images, with features violently distorted, and a long piece of carved wood of a conical form inverted, rising from the top of their heads; the rest was without form, and wrapped round with red cloth. We were here met by a tall young man with a long beard, who presented Captain Cook to the images, and after

---

[1] The name of this Heiau is *Hikiau.* It was sacred to *Lono,* and its ruins may still be seen. By a not uncommon *esprit de corps,* its priests were the firmest and most constant believers in Captain Cook's identity with *Lono.*

[2] Vol. iii. p. 6.

[3] It was one of the ancient Heiaus, of a truncated pyramidal form, that obtained before the southern migratory period.—*The Author.*

chanting a kind of hymn, in which he was joined by Koah, they led us to that end of the *Morai* where the five poles were fixed. At the foot of them were twelve images ranged in a semicircular form, and before the middle figure stood a high stand or table, exactly resembling the *Whatta* of Otaheiti, on which lay a putrid hog, and under it pieces of sugar-cane, cocoa-nuts, bread-fruit, plantains, and sweet potatoes. Koah having placed the Captain under the stand, took down the hog and held it toward him ; and after having a second time addressed him in a long speech, pronounced with much vehemence and rapidity, he let it fall on the ground and led him to the scaffolding, which they began to climb together not without great risk of falling. At this time we saw coming in solemn procession, at the entrance of the top of the *Morai*, ten men carrying a live hog and a large piece of red cloth. Being advanced a few paces, they stopped and prostrated themselves ; and Kaireekeea, the young man above mentioned, went to them, and receiving the cloth, carried it to Koah, who wrapped it round the Captain, and afterwards offered him the hog, which was brought by Kaireekeea with the same ceremony.

" Whilst Captain Cook was aloft in this awkward situation, swathed round with red cloth, and with difficulty keeping his hold amongst the pieces of rotten scaffolding, Kaireekeea and Koah began their office, chanting sometimes in concert and sometimes alternately. This lasted a considerable time ; at length Koah let the hog drop, when he and the Captain descended together. He then led him to the images before mentioned, and having said something to each in a sneering tone, snapping his fingers at them as he passed, he brought him to that in the centre, which, from its being covered with red cloth, appeared to be in greater estimation than the rest. Before this figure he prostrated himself and kissed it, desiring Captain Cook to do the same, who suffered himself to be directed by Koah throughout the whole of this ceremony.

" We were now led back to the other division of the *Morai*, where there was a space, ten or twelve feet square, sunk about three feet below the level of the area. Into this we descended, and Captain Cook was seated between two wooden idols, Koah supporting one of his arms, whilst I was desired to support the other. At this time arrived a second procession of natives, carrying a baked hog and a pudding, some bread-fruit, cocoa-nuts, and other vegetables. When they approached us, Kaireekeea put himself at their head, and presenting the pig to Captain Cook in the usual manner, began the same kind of chant as before, his companions making regular responses. We observed that after every response their parts became gradually shorter, till, toward the close, Kaireekeea's consisted of only two or three words, which the rest answered by the word *Orono*.

" When this offering was concluded, which lasted a quarter of an hour, the natives sat down fronting us, and began to cut up the baked hog, to peel the vegetables and break the cocoa-nuts; whilst others employed themselves in brewing the *Awa*, which is done by chewing it in the same manner as at the Friendly Islands. Kaireekeea then took part of the kernel of a cocoa-nut, which he chewed, and wrapping it in a piece of cloth, rubbed with it the Captain's face, head, hands, arms, and shoulders. The *Awa* was then handed round, and after we had tasted it, Koah and Pareea began to pull the flesh of the hog in pieces, and to put it into our mouths. I had no great objection to being fed by Pareea, who was very cleanly in his person, but Captain Cook, who was served by Koah, recollecting the putrid hog, could not swallow a morsel; and his reluctance, as may be supposed, was not diminished when the old man, according to his own mode of civility, had chewed it for him.

" When this last ceremony was finished, which Captain Cook put an end to as soon as he decently could, we quitted the *Morai*, after distributing amongst the people some pieces of iron and other trifles, with which they seemed highly gratified. The men with wands conducted us to the boats, repeating the same words as before. The people again retired, and the few that remained prostrated themselves as we passed along the shore. We immediately went on board, our minds full of what we had seen, and extremely well satisfied with the good dispositions of our new friends. The meanings of the various ceremonies with which we had been received, and which, on account of their novelty and singularity, have been related at length, can only be the subject of conjectures, and those uncertain and partial; they were, however, without doubt, expressive of high respect on the part of the natives; and, so far as related to the person of Captain Cook, they seemed approaching to adoration."

In another place[1] Captain King, relating Captain Cook's visit to the habitations of the priests in the neighbourhood of the observatory, says :—

" On his arrival at the beach, he was conducted to a sacred building called *Harre-no-Orono,* or the house of *Orono,* and seated before the entrance, at the foot of a wooden idol, of the same kind with those on the *Morai.* I was here again made to support one of his arms, and after wrapping him in red cloth, Kaireekeea, accompanied by twelve priests, made an offering of a pig with the usual solemnities. The pig was then strangled, and a fire being kindled, it was thrown into the embers; and after the hair was singed off, it was again presented, with a repetition of the chanting, in the manner before described. The dead pig was then held for a short time under the Captain's nose, after which it was laid, with a cocoa-nut, at his feet, and the performers sat down. The *awa* was then brewed and handed round, a fat hog, ready dressed, was brought in, and we were fed as before.

" During the rest of the time that we remained in the bay, whenever Captain Cook came on shore he was

[1] Pp. 13-15.

attended by one of those priests, who went before him, giving notice that the *Orono* had landed, and ordering the people to prostrate themselves. The same person also constantly accompanied him on the water, standing in the bow of the boat with a wand in his hand, and giving notice of his approach to the natives, who were in canoes, on which they immediately left off paddling, and lay down on their faces till he had passed. Whenever he stopped at the observatory, Kaireekeea and his brothers immediately made their appearance with hogs, cocoa-nuts, bread-fruit, &c., and presented them with the usual solemnities. It was on these occasions that some of the inferior chiefs frequently requested to be permitted to make an offering to the *Orono*. When this was granted, they presented the hog themselves, generally with evident marks of fear on their countenances, whilst Kaireekeea and the priests chanted their accustomed hymns.[1]

"The civilities of this society[2] were not, however, con-

[1] One of the formulated prayers or addresses with which the priests and others generally accosted Captain Cook in his character of Lono has been preserved by Kamakua, and I insert it here:—"Ou mau Kino e Lono i ka lani. He ao loa, he ao poko, he ao kiei, he ao halo, he ao hoopu-a i ka lani, mai Uliuli, mai Melemele, mai Kahiki, mai Ulunui, mai Haehae, mai Omaokuululu, mai Hakalauai, mai ka aina o Lono i wahi aku ai i ka lewa nuu, i ka lewa lani, i ka papa ku, i ka papa kukui a Leka—O Lalohana,—O Olepuu-kahonua. E Ku, E Lono, E Kane, E Kanaloa, E ke Akua mai ka Apapalani o ka Apapanuu, mai Kahiki-ku, a Kahiki-moe, eia ka mohai, eia ka alana; E ola i ke Alii, E ola i na pulapula, a kau a kau i ke ao malamalama ia lana honua. Amama, ua noa!" Which may be translated as follows:—"O Lono in heaven! you of the many shapes (or beings). The long cloud, the short cloud, the cloud just peeping (over the horizon), the wide-spreading cloud, the contracted cloud in the heaven, (coming) from' Uliuli, from Melemele, from Kahiki, from Ulunui, from Hakalauai, from the country of Lono situated in the upper regions, in the high heavens, in proper order, in the famous order of Leka. O Lalohana, O Olepuu-kahonua; Eh Ku, Eh Lono, Eh Kane, Eh Kanaloa, Eh the god from Apapalani of Apapanuu, from Kahiki east, from Kahiki west, here is the sacrifice, here is the offering. Preserve the chief, preserve the worshippers, and establish the day of light on the floating earth! Amen.[*]

[2] The priests.

[*] The phrase, "*Amama, ua noa,*" invariably used at the conclusion of every Hawaiian heathen prayer, corresponds, in so far, to the Christian Amen. Literally it means "it is offered, the tabu is taken off," or the ceremony is ended.

fined to mere ceremony and parade. Our party on shore received from them every day a constant supply of hogs and vegetables, more than sufficient for our subsistence, and several canoes loaded with provisions were sent to the ships with the same punctuality. No return was ever demanded, or even hinted at in the most distant manner. Their presents were made with a regularity more like the discharge of a religious duty than the effect of mere liberality; and when we inquired at whose charge all this munificence was displayed, we were told it was at the expense of a great man called Kaoo, the chief of the priests, and grandfather to Kaireekeea, who was at that time absent attending the king of the island."

After these detailed accounts of the reception of Cook by the chiefs, priests, and common people, there can be no doubt that, so far as the latter were concerned, they looked upon him as a god, an "*Akua*,"[1] possessed of hitherto unknown and terrible powers of destruction, and of an inexhaustible mine of that metal which they so highly coveted, accompanied by a crew of wonderful beings, "*Kupueu*," of different colour, speech, and customs than their own, who had come from another and unknown world, "*Mai ka lewa mai.*" Coming to them from over the sea, and apparently having the thunder and the lightning at his command, no wonder that the natives regarded Captain Cook as an avatar of the great *Lono-noho-ik a-wai* of their religious creed, whose attributes may be found described in the chant of the deluge (see vol. i. pp. 93, 94), and their adoration was as natural as it was spontaneous, and their gifts "more like the discharge of a religious duty," as Captain King expresses it. But that

[1] It should be borne in mind that to the heathen Hawaiian the word *Akua* did not convey the same lofty idea as the word God or Deity does to the Christian. To the Hawaiians the word *Akua* expressed the idea of any supernatural being, the object of fear or of worship. This term was also, as Judge Andrews says in his Hawaiian Dictionary, "applied to artificial objects, the nature and properties of which Hawaiians did not understand, as the movement of a watch, a compass, the self-striking of a clock, &c." For etymology of the word *Akua*, see Appendix, No. 4.

Captain Cook should have permitted himself to foster and keep up that delusion into which the natives had naturally fallen, by complacently receiving and assisting at the adoration which he must have perceived and known was only intended for the Divine Being, however gross the native conception of that Being might have been, that is the great blot which some of Cook's critics, native and foreign, Malo, Dibble, and Jarves, have thrown upon his character, and, penetrating the designs of Providence, they have not failed to consider his violent death as an act of Divine punishment.

Can nothing be said for Captain Cook against this terrible charge of self-deification?

That intelligent men, writing long after the event, when the religious customs and modes of thought of the natives were well understood and their intentions in the matter were well known, would not have lent themselves to "perform a part in this heathen farce," as Jarves calls it, is perfectly intelligible; but that, before giving their verdict, they should not have been able to place themselves in the position of Cook, who was ignorant of those customs and modes of thought, and naturally enough construed their intentions as those of goodwill, respect, and friendship, is a lamentable defect in a critic, the more so when the object of his criticism is dead and cannot reply to the charge, and has left no materials for his friends from which to argue what his own construction of the affair might have been. To Captain King, who seems to have been not only a kinder man but also a gentleman of finer susceptibilities than Captain Cook, these ceremonies "seemed approaching to adoration," though he had no doubt that on the part of the natives they were "expressive of high respect;" and so little did even he perceive the blasphemous act of self-deification in what transpired, that he actually took an active part in the performance, not exactly understanding "the meaning of the various ceremonies," but certainly not apprehending that a damaging judgment would be passed upon Captain Cook or himself for so doing.

If we now look back to p. 161, and see what Cook himself says of his reception on Kauai, we find that he had been the recipient of "much the same ceremonies on such occasions at the Society and other islands." To him, then, this prostration of bodies, offerings of pigs, chanting of hymns, &c., of which he understood nothing, were no new things, for he had seen them on Kauai and elsewhere, and, though details might vary, they were substantially "much the same," and to him they were apparently only significant of respect and friendship.

"The apology of expediency," which Jarves [1] says has been offered, has then no room in the argument. It was never offered by Cook or King, and its admission would imply a consciousness of the infraction of a moral duty in that respect which neither Cook nor King were ever conscious of or ever admitted. Captain Cook committed several errors in his intercourse with the natives, and their consequences proved fatal to him; but I think that a candid posterity, judging him as his contemporaries would have judged him, will acquit him of a wilful assumption of divine honours or of a conscious participation in his own deification.

The native accounts relate what Captain Cook apparently was not aware of, viz., that when the ships arrived at Kealakeakua, the bay was under a tabu, the festival days connected with the ancient celebration of the new year not having as yet expired. But as his fame had preceded him throughout the group, and Cook himself was looked upon as a god (an *Akua*) and his ships as temples (*Heiau*), the priests and chiefs who governed in the bay in the absence of *Kalaniopuu* proclaimed an exception to the tabu in the matter of the ships of the newcomers—a lucky thought, a well-timed compromise to gratify their curiosity and soothe their consciences; for most assuredly

[1] History of the Hawaii Islands, p. 54.

without some such arrangement not a single canoe would
have dared to ripple the quiet waters of the bay.

The business of recruiting the ships, caulking their sides,
erecting an observatory ashore, salting pork for ships' stores,
mending sails, &c., was now proceeded with, and every
assistance the natives possibly could give was unhesitat-
ingly and liberally given.

On the 24th January *Kalaniopuu* returned from Maui,
and one of his first acts was to put a tabu on the bay, no
canoes being allowed to leave the beach. All that day no
vegetables were brought on board as usual. After a week
of feasting and plenty, a day of fasting caused considerable
disappointment and irritation among the ships' companies.
As a specimen of the inconsiderate and overbearing manner in which the foreigners returned the unbounded
liberality and kindness of the natives when their wants
and desires were in the least crossed, the following remarks
of Captain King may illustrate. After mentioning the
fact of the tabu having been laid on the bay, he says [1]—
" The next morning, therefore, they (the ships' crews) endeavoured, both by threats and promises, to induce the
natives to come alongside; and as some of them were at
last venturing to put off, a chief was observed attempting
to drive them away. A musquet was immediately fired
over his head to make him desist, which had the desired
effect, and refreshments were soon after purchased as usual.
In the afternoon Tereeoboo" (*Kalaniopuu*) " arrived, and
visited the ships in a private manner, attended only by
one canoe, in which were his wife and children. He
stayed on board till near ten o'clock, when he returned to
the village of Kowrowa" (Kaawaloa).

On the 26th January *Kalaniopuu* made a formal state
visit to the ships, and I again quote from Captain King :—

" About noon, the king, in a large canoe, attended by
two others, set out from the village, and paddled toward
the ships in great state. Their appearance was grand and

magnificent. In the first canoe was Tereeoboo and his chiefs, dressed in their rich feathered cloaks and helmets, and armed with long spears and daggers; in the second came the venerable Kaoo,[1] the chief of the priests, and his brethren, with their idols displayed on red cloth. These idols were busts of a gigantic size, made of wickerwork, and curiously covered with small feathers of various colours, wrought in the same manner with their cloaks. Their eyes were made of large pearl-oysters, with a black nut fixed in the centre; their mouths were set with a double row of the fangs of dogs, and, together with the rest of their features, were strangely distorted. The third canoe was filled with hogs and various sorts of vegetables. As they went along, the priests in the centre canoe sung their hymns with great solemnity; and after paddling round the ships, instead of going on board, as was expected, they made toward the shore at the beach where we were stationed.

"As soon as I saw them approaching, I ordered out our little guard to receive the king; and Captain Cook, perceiving that he was going on shore, followed him, and arrived nearly at the same time. We conducted them into the tent, where they had scarcely been seated, when the king rose up, and in a very graceful manner threw over the Captain's shoulders the cloak he himself wore, put a feathered helmet upon his head, and a curious fan into his hand. He also spread at his feet five or six other cloaks, all exceedingly beautiful and of the greatest value. His attendants then brought four very large hogs, with sugar-canes, cocoa-nuts, and bread-fruit; and this part of the ceremony was concluded by the king's exchanging names with Captain Cook, which amongst all the islanders

[1] As the native testimony is concurrent and clear that *Holoae* was the high-priest of *Kalaniopuu*, at least during the latter years of his reign, and attended him in his expeditions to Maui in 1776-78, it is possible that *Kaoo* might have been another name or sobriquet of *Holoae*, given to the foreigners instead of the ordinary and well-known *Holoae.* Such transpositions and changes of names in the same person were and are of frequent occurrence.

of the Pacific Ocean is esteemed the strongest pledge of friendship. A procession of priests, with a venerable old personage at their head, now appeared, followed by a long train of men leading large hogs, and others carrying plantains, sweet potatoes, &c. By the looks and gestures of Kaireekeea, I immediately knew the old man to be the chief of the priests before mentioned, on whose bounty we had so long subsisted. He held a piece of red cloth in his hands, which he wrapped round Captain Cook's shoulders, and afterward presented him with a small pig in the usual form. A seat was then made for him next to the king, after which Kaireekeea and his followers began their ceremonies, Kaoo and the chiefs joining in the responses.

"I was surprised to see, in the person of this king, the same infirm and emaciated old man that came on board the 'Resolution' when we were off the north-east side of the island of Mowee ; and we soon discovered amongst his attendants most of the persons who at that time had remained with us all night. Of this number were the two younger sons of the king,[1] the eldest of whom was sixteen years of age, and his nephew, Maiha-maiha,[2] whom at first we had some difficulty in recollecting, his hair being plastered over with a dirty brown paste and powder, which was no mean heightening to the most savage face I ever beheld.

"As soon as the formalities of the meeting were over, Captain Cook carried Tereeoboo, and as many chiefs as the pinnace could hold, on board the 'Resolution.' They were received with every mark of respect that could be shown them ; and Captain Cook, in return for the feathered cloak, put a linen shirt on the king, and girt his own hanger round him. The ancient Kaoo and about half a dozen more old chiefs remained on shore, and took up their abode at the priests' houses. During all this time not a canoe was seen in the bay, and the natives

---

[1] *Keoua Kuahuula* and *Keoua Peeale,* sons of *Kalaniopuu* and *Kanekapolei.*
[2] Kamehameha.

either kept within their huts or lay prostrate on the
ground. Before the king left the 'Resolution,' Captain
Cook obtained leave for the natives to come and trade
with the ships as usual; but the women, for what reason
we could not learn,[1] still continued under the effects of
the tabu; that is, were forbidden to stir from home or
to have any communication with us."

When Captain Clarke of the "Discovery" paid his visit
to Kalaniopuu on shore,[2] he was received with the same
formalities as were observed with Captain Cook, and on
his coming away, though the visit was quite unexpected,
he received a present of thirty large hogs, and as much
fruit and roots as his crew could consume in a week.[3]

When the scientific members of the voyage started for
an excursion into the interior of the island, we are told
"that it afforded Kaoo a fresh opportunity of showing
his attention and generosity. For as soon as he was
informed of their departure, he sent a large supply of
provisions after them, together with orders that the inhabitants of the country through which they were to pass
should give them every assistance in their power. And
to complete the delicacy and disinterestedness of his conduct, even the people he employed could not be prevailed
on to accept the smallest present."[4]

Again, the day before their departure from the bay,
Kalaniopuu gave them another large present of hogs and

[1] The reason was not far to search.
While the fame of Cook had spread
throughout the group, the disease connected with his arrival at Kauai had
also spread; and when *Kalaniopuu*,
on his return from Maui, found the
women received by hundreds at a
time on board the ships, he took the
only course left him, though, alas!
too late to restrict the evil. It is
somewhat remarkable that on his
arrival at Hawaii, neither Cook nor
King make the slightest mention of
having taken any similar precautions
against the spreading of the disease,

which he says took on Kauai. And
when it was left to the sovereign of
the island to protect his people as
best he could, his act, instead of
awakening reflection and suggesting
the cause, became a subject of wonder. Neither Cook nor King seem to
have felt the quiet rebuke implied
by the tabu being laid on the women.

[2] When at Kaawaloa, *Kalaniopuu*
dwelt at Awili in *Keaweaheulu's* place
on Hanamua.

[3] Vol. iii. p. 22.

[4] Ibid.

vegetables. Captain King says, "We were astonished at the value and magnitude of this present, which far exceeded everything of the kind we had seen, either at the Friendly or Society Islands." [1]

And how did Captain Cook requite this boundless hospitality, that never once made default during his long stay of seventeen days in Kealakeakua Bay, these magnificent presents of immense value, this delicate and spontaneous attention to his every want, this friendship of the chiefs and priests, this friendliness of the common people? By imposing on their good nature to the utmost limit of its ability to respond to the greedy and constant calls of their new friends; by shooting at one of the king's officers for endeavouring to enforce a law of the land, an edict of his sovereign that happened to be unpalatable to the newcomers, and caused them some temporary inconvenience after a week's profusion and unbridled license; by a liberal exhibition of his force and the meanest display of his bounty; by giving the king a linen shirt and a cutlass in return for feather cloaks and helmets, which, irrespective of their value as insignia of the highest nobility in the land, were worth singly at least from five to ten thousand dollars, at present price of the feathers, not counting the cost of manufacturing; by a reckless disregard of the proprieties of ordinary intercourse, even between civilised and savage man, and a wanton insult to what he reasonably may have supposed to have been the religious sentiments of his hosts. [2]

[1] Vol. iii. p. 29.

[2] Captain Cook being in want of fuel for the ships, sent Captain King to "treat with the priests for the purchase of the rail that surrounded the top of the Morai." King says (vol. iii. p. 25), "I had at first some doubt about the decency of this proposal, and was apprehensive that even the bare mention of it might be considered by them as a piece of shocking impiety. In this, however, I found myself mistaken. Not the slightest surprise was expressed at the application, and the wood was readily given, even without stipulating for anything in return." But when the sailors carried off, not only the railing of the temple, but also the idols of the gods within it, even the large-hearted patience of Kaoo gave up, and he meekly requested that the central idol at least might be restored. Captain King failed to perceive that

It is much to be regretted that no acts of kindness, benevolence, or sympathy, or any endeavours to ameliorate the material or mental condition of his generous hosts, have been recorded to relieve the dark, harsh, greedy, and imperious traits of Captain Cook's character, which his stay at Hawaii indelibly impressed on the memory of the natives. To them he was a god or the incarnation of a god, no doubt, but a god to be feared, not loved, and from whose further visits they devoutly prayed to be delivered. To use a common expression, he "wore out his welcome," a fact of which Captain King apparently became sensible when he wrote as follows :—

"Tereeoboo and his chiefs had for some days past been very inquisitive about the time of our departure. This circumstance had excited in me a great curiosity to know what opinion this people had formed of us, and what were their ideas respecting the cause and object of our voyage. I took some pains to satisfy myself on these points, but could never learn anything further than that they imagined we came from some country where provisions had failed, and that our visit to them was merely for the purpose of filling our bellies. Indeed, the meagre appearance of some of our crew, the hearty appetites with which we sat down to their fresh provisions, and our great anxiety to purchase and carry off as much as we were able, led them naturally enough to such a conclusion. To these may be added a circumstance which puzzled them exceedingly, our having no women with us, together with our quiet conduct and unwarlike appearance. It

the concession of the priests was that of a devotee to his saint. The priests would not sell their religious emblems and belongings for "thirty pieces of silver" or any remuneration, but they were willing to offer up the entire Heiau, and themselves on the top of it, as a holocaust to *Lono*, if he had requested it. So long as Cook was regarded as a god in their eyes, they could not refuse him. And though they exhibited no resentment at the request, the want of delicacy and consideration on the part of Captain Cook is none the less glaring. After his death, and when the illusion of godship had subsided, his spoliation of the very Heiau in which he had been deified, was not one of the least of the grievances which native annalists laid up against him.

was ridiculous enough to see them stroking the sides and
patting the bellies of the sailors (who were certainly
much improved in the sleekness of their looks during our
short stay in the island), and telling them, partly by signs
and partly by words, that it was time for them to go, but
if they would come again the next bread-fruit season, they
should be better able to supply their wants. We had
now been sixteen days in the bay, and if our enormous
consumption of hogs and vegetables be considered, it need
not be wondered that they should wish to see us take our
leave. It is very probable, however, that Tereeoboo had
no other view in his inquiries at present than a desire to
make sufficient preparation for dismissing us with presents suitable to the respect and kindness with which
he had received us. For, on our telling him that we
should leave the island on the next day but one, we
observed that a sort of proclamation was immediately
made through the villages, to require the people to bring
in their hogs and vegetables for the king to present to
the *Orono* on his departure."

On the 4th of February 1779, the ships being ready,
Cook left Kealakeakua Bay to visit and explore the leeward side of the group. When abreast of Kawaihae Bay,
on February 6th, which Captain King writes " Too-yah-
yah," he says that they saw "to the north-east several
fine streams of water," [1] and a boat was sent ashore to
look for an anchorage, but could not find any suitable
watering-place.

On the 8th of February the ships encountered a gale,

[1] Captain Vancouver, if I remember correctly, also speaks of streams
of running water in the neighbourhood of Kawaihae. I am not aware
of any stream now coming down to
the seashore, unless in extraordinary
heavy freshets ; and as no extraordinary southerly storm occurred
while the ships were lying at Kealakeakua, those streams that Cook saw
must have been an ordinary feature
of the landscape. It is possible that
since that time unrecorded earthquakes and the terribly wasteful
destruction of the forests in the
interior may have diverted and dried
up the streams that fertilised the
lower slopes of the Kohala mountains
and gladdened the sight of transient
navigators.

during which the fishes of the fore masthead gave way, and it became necessary to seek a port where to repair the damage. After some consideration it was resolved to return to Kealakeakua, and on the 11th February the ships anchored again in nearly their former position.

On this occasion their reception was not of that boisterous jubilant kind as on their former visit, an ominous silence reigned along the shore, and not a canoe came off to the ships. A boat sent ashore to inquire the reason, soon returned and informed Captain Cook that *Kalaniopuu* was absent and had left the bay under tabu. However, the injured mast was sent ashore, carpenters and sailmakers set to work, the observatory erected anew on the ground formerly occupied on the south side of the bay. The priests still remained friendly, and, for the protection of the workmen and their tools, tabued the place where they were at work.

There can be no doubt that during the absence of the ships reflection had sobered the judgment of the natives, and measurably cooled their enthusiasm. When the excitement of the novelty had subsided, it was found that the visit of *Lono* and his crews had been a tremendous drain on their alimentary resources, for which their only equivalents were some scraps of iron, a few hatchets and knives. But another, and perhaps a principal, reason of their waning friendliness is probably correctly expressed by the native historian, D. Malo, when he says, "The long and amorous intercourse of the foreigners with the women, and the great liking which some of the women had taken to the foreigners, was the reason why the men became opposed to *Lono* and his whole crew of foreigners." Another fact tended not a little to weaken the dread with which the natives had at first beheld the foreigners— the death from sickness and funeral on shore of one of the seamen. However firm their opinion might have been about Cook and his being a god—the *Lono* of their ancient creed—yet it was evident that *Lono's* companions, however wonderful in other respects, were mortals like themselves, that could be reached by sickness and subdued by death. From such or similar mingled motives the conduct of the natives had become, if not actually hostile, yet troublesome and defiant. The return of the ships was not viewed with pleasure, and the ill-will of the natives, and their readiness to measure themselves with the foreigners in actual combat, did not wait long for an opportunity to manifest itself.

On the 12th of February *Kalaniopuu* returned to the bay, the tabu was taken off, and he visited Captain Cook on board. It cannot now be positively known whether *Kalaniopuu* personally shared in the unfriendly and jealous feeling entertained by his subordinate chiefs and the common people. If he did, he knew how to dissemble ; but it is due to the memory of *Kalaniopuu* to state that no act of his has been recorded that would indicate that he was not as loyal and liberal on the second visit of Cook to the bay as on the first. The priests also remained friendly to Cook, to his officers and men, although their friendship was badly requited.

In the afternoon of the 13th February a watering-party belonging to the " Discovery " was interrupted and impeded by some of the chiefs, who had driven away the natives engaged in assisting the sailors to roll the casks to the shore. When informed of this, Captain King immediately went to the watering-place. On seeing him approach, the natives threw away the stones with which they had armed themselves. After remonstrating with the chiefs, they drove away the crowd that had collected at the prospect of an affray, and the watering-party were no more molested.

On the events which followed this first attempt of the natives to resist and defy the foreigners there are three independent sources of information. First, Captain King's continuation of Captain Cook's journal of the " Voyage to the Pacific Ocean," vol. iii. ; second, Ledyard's Life, by Sparks ; and, third, the native reminiscences as recorded by D. Malo, S. Dibble, and S. M. Kamakau. The main facts are the same with all these authorities, though each one supplies details that are omitted or unknown to the others. Captain King received his information, where he was not personally present, from Lieutenant Philips and others who accompanied Cook ashore on that ill-fated 14th of February. Ledyard professes to have been one of the company who went ashore with Cook, and was an eye-witness to the whole affray. Malo, Dibble, and Kamakau obtained their information from some of the high chiefs who were present at the time and formed the " Ai-alo" (court circle) of *Kalaniopuu.* There are a few discrepancies between King's and Ledyard's accounts, but they are not very material, and may be owing to want of correct information on the one part, and to exaggeration and a confused memory on the other, whose memoirs were only written years after the event.

Among these various versions of the same melancholy event and the causes that led to it, I prefer to follow the compilation of the native authorities as prepared by Rev. Sheldon Dibble in his " History of the Sandwich Islands," printed at Lahainaluna, 1843, as the least inflated and probably most correct account that can now be obtained. Mr. Dibble says :—

" Some men of Captain Cook used violence to the canoe of a certain young chief whose name was *Palea.* The chief making resistance, was knocked down by one of the white men with a paddle.

" Soon after, *Palea*[1] stole a boat from Captain Cook's

[1] This was the same *Palea* who from the first had been the constant, kind, and obliging friend of Captain Cook and all the foreigners, and who, only the day before Cook's death, had saved the crew of the pinnace of the " Resolution " from being stoned to death by the natives, exasperated at the brutal and insolent manner in which *Palea* had been treated by an officer of the "Discovery." It was during the night after the above fracas, the night of the 13th February, that the cutter of the "Discovery" was stolen from her mooring, as King himself admits, " by Palea's people, very probably in revenge for the blow that had been given him," and not by *Palea* himself. The boat had been taken to Onouli, a couple of miles higher up the coast, and there broken to pieces.

ship. The theft may be imputed to revenge, or to a desire
to obtain the iron fastenings of the boat.

"Captain Cook commanded *Kalaniopuu*, the king of the
island, to make search for the boat and restore it. The
king could not restore it, for the natives had already
broken it in pieces to obtain the nails, which were to them
the articles of the greatest value.

"Captain Cook came on shore with armed men to take
the king on board, and to keep him there as security till
the boat should be restored.

"In the meantime was acted the consummate folly and
outrageous tyranny of placing a blockade upon a heathen
bay, which the natives could not possibly be supposed
either to understand or appreciate. The large cutter and
two boats from the 'Discovery' had orders to proceed to
the mouth of the bay, form at equal distances across, and
prevent any communication by water from any other part
of the island to the towns within the bay, or from within
to those without.

"A canoe came from an adjoining district, bound within
the bay. In the canoe were two chiefs of some rank,
Kekuhaupio and *Kalimu*.[1] The canoe was fired upon from
one of the boats, and *Kalimu* was killed. *Kekuhaupio*
made the greatest speed till he reached the place of the
king, where Captain Cook also was, and communicated
the intelligence of the death of the chief. The attendants
of the king were enraged, and showed signs of hostility;
but were restrained by the thought that Captain Cook was
a god.[2] At that instant a warrior, with a spear in his
hand, approached Captain Cook, and was heard to say
that the boats in the harbour had killed his brother, and

[1] *Kekuhaupio* was the great warrior chief under *Kalaniopuu* who had instructed *Kamehameha* in all the martial exercises of the time. He was the son-in-law of the high-priest *Holoae*, and his daughter *Kailipakalua* was the great-grandmother of the present Hon. Mrs. Pauahi Bishop. *Kalimu* was the brother of *Palea*, but I have been unable to trace their pedigree.

[2] King mentions that when *Kalaniopuu* manifested a willingness to go on board the "Resolution" with Captain Cook, and his two younger sons were already in the pinnace, his

he would be revenged. Captain Cook, from his enraged appearance and that of the multitude, was suspicious of him, and fired upon him with his pistol. Then followed a scene of confusion, and in the midst of it Captain Cook being hit with a stone, and perceiving the man who threw it, shot him dead. He also struck a certain chief with his sword whose name was *Kalaimanokahoowaha.*[1] The chief instinctively seized Captain Cook with a strong hand, designing merely to hold him, and not to take his life, for he supposed him to be a god, and that he could not die. Captain Cook struggled to free himself from the grasp, and as he was about to fall uttered a groan. The people immediately exclaimed, ' He groans—he is not a god,' and instantly slew him. Such was the melancholy death of Captain Cook.

" Immediately the men in the boat commenced a deliberate fire upon the crowd. They had refrained in a measure before for fear of killing their captain. Many of the natives were killed. In vain did the ignorant natives hold up their frail leaf-mats to ward off the bullets. They seemed to imagine that it was the fire from the guns that was destructive, for they not only shielded themselves with mats, but took constant care to keep them wet. Soon round-shot from one of the ships was fired into the middle of the crowd, and both the thunder of the cannon and the effects of the shot operated so powerfully that it produced a precipitate retreat from the shore to the mountains.

" The body of Captain Cook was carried into the interior of the island, the bones secured according to their custom, and the flesh burnt in the fire. The heart, liver, &c., of

wife, whom King calls Kanee-Kab-areea, came along, and " with tears and entreaties besought him not to go on board." The lady's name was *Kanekapolei*, referred to in a previous note. S. M. Kamakau states that the lady was *Kalola*, another of *Kalaniopuu's* wives; but it will be

seen hereafter that *Kalola* and her son *Kiwalao* were probably on Maui at this time.

[1] He was also known by the name of Kanaina, and from him the late Charles Kanaina, father of the late King Luaalilo, received his name.

Captain Cook were stolen and eaten by some hungry children, who mistook them in the night for the inwards of a dog. The names of the children were *Kupa, Mohoole,* and *Kaiwikokoole.* These men are now all dead. The last of the number died two years since at the station of Lahaina. Some of the bones of Captain Cook were sent on board his ship, in compliance with the urgent demands of the officers, and some were kept by the priests as objects of worship." [1]

The other side of the bay, where the carpenters and sailmakers were at work, and where the observatory was erected, and where Captain King was in charge, shared also in the confusion, strife, and bloodshed which had been enacted at Kaawaloa.[2] Protected by *Kaoo* and the priests, the injured mast, the instruments at the observatory, and the ships' artisans, returned on board unhurt. Negotiations were entered into for the recovery of the bodies or bones of Captain Cook and the four marines that had been killed in the affray at Kaawaloa, and the ships, finding their situation precarious, concluded to procure a supply of water and leave the bay. The watering, however, was not suffered to proceed unmolested. The throwing of stones by the natives was at first responded to by the musquets of the foreigners, by the guns from the ships, and finally by burning the village of Napoopoo,[3] in which conflagration the houses of the friendly and faithful priests were destroyed.

"On the evening of the 18th February," Captain King writes, " a chief called Eappo,[4] who had seldom visited us,

---

[1] Or, as I have heard native authorities suggest, as objects of revenge, for the purpose of making fish-hooks or arrow-heads of them.

[2] King reports that he learned from some of the priests that seventeen natives were killed in the action at Kaawaloa, where Cook fell, of whom five were chiefs, and that eight natives were killed at the observatory at Napoopoo, three of whom were of the highest rank. Of the merely wounded no account was made.

[3] A cocoa-nut tree is still standing near the landing-place at Napoopoo whose trunk was pierced through and through by one of the cannon-balls fired on this occasion. The hole made by the ball has never closed up. A melancholy souvenir of *Lono's* visit.

[4] I am unable to ascertain the proper name of this chief. Captain King's orthography must be wrong.

but whom we knew to be a man of the very first consequence, came with presents from Tereeoboo to sue for peace. These presents were received, and he was dismissed with the same answer which had before been given, that until the remains of Captain Cook should be restored, no peace would be granted. We learned from this person that the flesh of all the bodies of our people, together with the bones of the trunks, had been burnt; that the limb bones of the marines had been divided among the inferior chiefs, and that those of Captain Cook had been disposed of in the following manner :—The head to a great chief called Kahoo-opeou,[1] the hair to Maia-maia, and the legs, thighs, and arms to Tereeoboo."

The fact that *Kamehameha* was a party to the division of these sad relics of Captain Cook is of itself no proof that he was directly or indirectly a leader or a prominent actor in the fatal affray at Kaawaloa. But the careful historian will not fail to note what Captains Portlock and Dixon, who were the first foreigners that arrived at Hawaii after the death of Captain Cook, and who had been with Cook on his last disastrous voyage, say of *Kamehameha ;* that he declined to visit their ships when anchored in Kealakeakua Bay, from apprehension that they had come to avenge the death of Captain Cook, in regard to which Portlock expressly says,[2] that *"Kamehameha* took an active part in the unfortunate affray which terminated in the much-lamented death of Captain Cook." And again, in the "Voyage of John Meares," who visited the islands the next year after Captain Portlock, we are told that *Kamehameha* took no common pains to persuade Captain Douglas that *Tereeoboo* was poisoned

[1] I am equally unable to give the correct name of this chief, unless, which is probable from his known position as *Kalaniopuu's* generalissimo, it was *Kekuhaupio* above referred to. "Maia-maia," who got the hair, is evidently *Kamehameha.* Jarves, in his "History of the Ha-

waii Islands," mentions that "Liho-liho" (the son of Kamehameha I.) is said to have carried a portion of them (the bones of Cook) to England, and to have presented one of the sad relics to the widow of Cook.

[2] Voyage Round the World, by Portlock, 1786, p. 61.

for having encouraged the natives to the murder of Captain Cook.[1] What grounds Portlock had for the assertion that he makes are not stated. He may have spoken of his own personal knowledge, having attended Cook on his last visit to these islands, or he may have expressed what was the current opinion at the time. What motive *Kamehameha* might have had in endeavouring to impose upon Captain Douglas by the story of *Kalaniopuu* having been poisoned by the revolted chiefs for murdering Captain Cook can only be surmised from concurrent circumstances. Certain it is, if Meares' representation of the conversations between *Kamehameha* and Captain Douglas is correct, that *Kamehameha* knowingly told Captain Douglas three distinct untruths in thus imposing upon him. We know now, from native annals and from native contemporary eye-witnesses, that *Kalaniopuu* was at first a willing companion of Cook, then a passive, and lastly a frightened spectator of the affray going on around him, and took no active part in the final tragedy. We know that the chiefs did not revolt from him during the remainder of his life for this or any other cause; and we know that he did not die from poison administered by the revolted chiefs, who threatened worse outrage if he refused to submit, but that he died three years after Cook, of old age and debility. It is impossible to believe that *Kamehameha* was ignorant of these facts, and it is but fair to infer that his motive, in thus misrepresenting things, was to screen himself from the odium and reprisals which he anticipated would follow an act in which he had been a prominent if not a chief actor. Neither Captain Cook nor Captain King mention the presence of *Kiwalao*, the son and heir-presumptive of *Kalaniopuu*, and native historians are equally silent as to his whereabouts at the time of Cook's death. In his absence, therefore, *Kamehameha* was the next highest chief of the blood-royal, and might naturally be supposed to have

[1] Voyage of John Meares, 1787, 1788, 1789, London, 1790, p. 374.

resented and forcibly resisted the attempted abduction of his aged uncle, and to have taken an active part in the affray which ensued. The persistent efforts of Captain Cook to bring *Kalaniopuu* on board of his ship, and his unprovoked firing upon the canoes in the bay, would have been enough to fire the blood of civilised men into resistance, much more that of a semi-barbarous chief; and if *Kamehameha* " took an active part in the unfortunate affray," as Portlock says, the impartial historian will not blame him.

On the 20th and 21st of February, " Eappo and the king's son " brought what remained of the bones of Captain Cook on board of the " Resolution," and Eappo having been dismissed with a request to tabu the bay, the bones were committed to the deep with military honours; and on the 22d of February, in the evening, the ships left Kealakeakua Bay for the last time. " The natives, at the time," Captain King says, " were collected on the shore in great numbers, and as we passed along, received our last farewells with every mark of affection and good-will."

On the 24th February, being off the south side of Maui, in the channel between Kahoolawe and Lanai, canoes from Maui came alongside to sell provisions, and Captain King learned from them that they had already heard of the transactions at Kealakeakua and the death of Captain Cook.

Going to the southward of Lanai, and rounding the east and north points of Oahu, the ships anchored off the mouth of the Waialua river on the 27th February. The two captains and Captain King landed, and, he says, " we found but few of the natives, and those mostly women ; the men, they told us, were gone to Morotoi to fight[1]

---

[1] The " Tahy-terree" of Captain King was the well-known *Kahekili*, king of Maui. The report of Waialua, or Oahu men, warring against *Kahekili* on Molokai is hardly correct. There is no doubt that Molokai was in a distracted condition at the time, and individual free lances from Oahu were probably engaged on the sides of contending chiefs ; but in 1779 *Kahahana*, the Oahu king, had but lately returned from Maui, where he

Tahy-terree, but that their chief, Perreeoranee,[1] who had stayed behind, would certainly visit us as soon as he heard of our arrival."

On the 1st of March, the ships not finding watering facilities at Waialua, and having crossed the channel on the 28th, anchored in their former places off Waimea, Kauai. Of their welcome there Captain King writes :— " We had no sooner anchored in our old stations than several canoes came alongside of us, but we could observe that they did not welcome us with the same cordiality in their manner and satisfaction in their countenances as when we were here before. As soon as they got on board, one of the men began to tell us that we had left a disorder amongst their women, of which several persons of both sexes had died. As there was not the slightest appearance of that disorder amongst them on our first arrival, I am afraid it is not to be denied that we were the authors of this irreparable mischief."

On the first day of their stay at Waimea the watering-party experienced much trouble and annoyance from the natives, who were apparently left to themselves in the absence of their chiefs, and who demanded a hatchet as the price for each cask of water that was filled, and who strove in different ways to obtain possession of the musquets of the marines. When the party were getting into the boats to return on board, the natives commenced throwing stones and made a rush for the boats. Two musquets were fired at them, and they dispersed, leaving one fellow wounded on the beach. The next day, however, no further trouble was experienced, some of the chiefs having apparently returned, and the watering-place being tabued by the erection of small white flags around it.

had assisted *Kahekili* in his wars against *Kalaniopuu* of Hawaii, and the rupture between *Kahekili* and *Kahahana* did not occur till sometime afterward, in 1780–81.

[1] "Perreeoranee," properly *Peleioho-* *lani.* He, and the only one of that name who was king of Oahu, died about the year 1770. The one that Captain King refers to must have been a namesake and an inferior chief in the Waialua district.

• Several chiefs having come off on board on the 3d of
March, Captain King learned that contentions and wars
had occurred between the two high chiefs *Kaneoneo* and
Keawe[1] in regard to the goats which Captain Cook had
left at Niihau, and that during the period of dispute the
goats had been killed.

The mother and sister of *Keawe,* and also *Kaneoneo,*
visited the ships, making presents to Captain Clarke.

On the 8th of March the ships left Kauai and anchored
at their former station at Niihau, and on the 15th of
March took their final departure for the north.

———————

Thus ended the episode of *Lono* (Captain Cook), but its
influence on the Hawaiian people was lasting and will
long be remembered. He came as a god, and, in the
untutored minds of the natives, was worshipped as such ;
but his death dispelled the illusion ; and by those whom
he might have so largely benefited he is only remembered
for the quantity of iron that for the first time was so
abundantly scattered over the country, and for the introduction of a previously unknown and terrible disease.[2]
As education and intelligence are spreading, however,
among the natives, they will gradually learn to appreciate
the benefits that have followed and will continue to follow
in the wake of his first discovery. The reproaches that
have been levelled at his memory will gradually fade, as
men learn to judge others according to the standard of the
times and the exceptional circumstances under which they
lived and had to act ; and while time will eradicate the
evils attributed to Cook's arrival, time will also bring into
greater prominence the advantages and blessings, the light
and the knowledge, to which his discovery opened the

———

[1] I have referred to *Kaneoneo* before in note to page 164. *Keawe* was
another grandson of *Peleioholani* of Oahu.

[2] S. M. Kamakau states that fleas and mosquitoes were unknown in the
Hawaiian group until the arrival of Cook's ships.

portals, and enable future historians, be they native or foreign, to draw a truer, more just, and more generous balance. In contemplating what the Hawaiians were one hundred years ago and what they are this day, no candid person can fail to kindly remember the man who first tore the veil of isolation that for centuries had shrouded the Hawaiians in deeper and deeper growing darkness, who brought them in relation with the civilised world, and who pointed the way for others to bring them that knowledge which is power and that light which is life.

After Captain Cook's death and the final departure of the two ships, *Kalaniopuu* dwelt some time in the Kona district, about Kahaluu and Keauhou, diverting himself with Hula performances, in which it is said that he frequently took an active part, notwithstanding his advanced age. Scarcity of food, after a while, obliged *Kalaniopuu* to remove his court into the Kohala district, where his headquarters were fixed at Kapaau. Here the same extravagant, *laissez-faire*, eat and be merry policy continued that had been commenced at Kona, and much grumbling and discontent began to manifest itself among the resident chiefs and the cultivators of the land, the " Makaainana." *Imakakaloa*, a great chief in the Puna district, and *Nuuanupaahu*, a chief of Naalehu in the Kau district, became the heads and rallying-points of the discontented. The former resided on his lands in Puna, and openly resisted the orders of *Kalaniopuu* and his extravagant demands for contributions of all kinds of property ; the latter was in attendance with the court of *Kalaniopuu* in Kohala, but was strongly suspected of favouring the growing discontent.

One day, when the chiefs were amusing themselves with surf-swimming off Kauhola, in the neighbourhood of Halaula, *Nuuanupaahu* was attacked by an enormous shark. He perceived his danger too late, and the shark bit off one of his hands. Nothing daunted, *Nuuanupaahu* sprang to his feet, and standing upright on the surf-board, shot through the surf and landed safely. But from loss of blood and exhaustion he died a few days after at Pololu, and the court of *Kalaniopuu* was thus relieved from further anxiety in that quarter.

It appears from the native accounts that at this time *Kiwalao*, the son of *Kalaniopuu*, and his mother, *Kalola*, were absent on Maui, on a visit to her brother *Kahekili*. Messengers were sent to recall them to Hawaii, and in the meanwhile the court moved from Kohala to the Waipio valley in Hamakua district. When *Kiwalao* arrived, a grand council of the highest chiefs was convened, at which, with the approval of the chiefs present, *Kalaniopuu* proclaimed *Kiwalao* as his heir and successor in the government and the supervision of the tabus and the "palaoa pae," and he intrusted the care of his particular war-god, *Kukailimoku*, to his nephew *Kamehameha*, who was, however, to be subordinate to *Kiwalao*. The Heiau of Moaula, in Waipio, was then put in repair and consecrated to the service of the war-god aforesaid.

Having thus arranged his worldly and spiritual affairs to his satisfaction, *Kalaniopuu* started with his chiefs and warriors for Hilo, in order to subdue the rebel chief of Puna. In Hilo *Kalaniopuu* consecrated the Heiau called Kanowa, in Puueo, to the service of his war-god; then took up his abode at Ohele, in Waiakea, and then the war with *Imakakoloa* commenced. The rebel chieftain fought long and bravely, but was finally overpowered and beaten. For upwards of a year he eluded capture, being secreted by the country-people of Puna. In the meanwhile *Kalaniopuu* moved from Hilo to the Kau district, stopping first at Punaluu, then at Waiohinu, then at Kamaoa, where he built the Heiau of Pakini in expectation of the capture of *Imakakaloa*. Finally, exasperated at the delay, and the refuge given to the rebel chief by the Puna people,

Kalaniopuu sent *Puhili,* one of his Kahus, to ravage the Puna district with fire, *i.e.*, to burn every village and hamlet until *Imakakoloa* should be found or the people surrender him. Commencing with the land of Apua, it was literally laid in ashes. It is said that through some accident one of *Imakakoloa's* own nurses became the means of betraying his hiding-place. He was found, captured, and brought to *Kalaniopuu* in Kamaoa, Kau.

Imakakoloa is represented to have been a young man of stately aspect, and with hair on his head so long as to have reached to his heels. That he had secured the affection of his people is shown by the war he waged and the shelter he found among them when the war was over, and he was hunted as an outlaw by *Kalaniopuu's* warriors and servants.

When *Imakakoloa* was to be sacrificed at the Heiau of Pakini, the performance of the ceremony devolved on *Kiwalao,* as representing his father. The routine of the sacrifice required that the presiding chief should first offer up the pigs prepared for the occasion, then bananas, fruit, &c., and lastly, the captive chief. But while *Kiwalao* was in the act of offering up the pigs and fruit, *Kamehameha* catches hold of the slain chief and offers him up at the same time, and then dismisses the assembly.

The native authorities intimate that *Kamehameha* was instigated to this act of insubordination by some chiefs who, in fomenting strife and jealousy between the two cousins, saw an opportunity of profit to themselves. As no names of such Hawaiian Achitophels are given in the native accounts, it may possibly be but a surmise of *Kamehameha's* contemporaries, who in that way sought to remove the blame from his shoulders. The more probable motive would be irritation and a sense of slight at being superseded, as it were, by *Kiwalao* in the performance of the sacrifices to that particular god which *Kalaniopuu* had officially and solemnly intrusted to his care at Waipio. While, therefore, native chroniclers do not go deep enough in search of motives to an act that doubtless coloured the subsequent intercourse of the cousins, and left its sting in both their breasts, the resentment felt by *Kamehameha* at what he considered an intrusion upon his prerogative may very likely have been fanned into flame by evil counsellors.

This daring act of *Kamehameha* created an immense excitement in the court circle of *Kalaniopuu* and among the chiefs generally, and not a few looked upon it as an act of rebellion. When *Kalaniopuu* was informed of the transaction, he called *Kamehameha* privately to his side, and told him that the sentiment of the chiefs about the court was so bitter and hostile to him that it would be difficult to answer for his safety, and advised him kindly to leave the court and go to Kohala for a season, but to be careful to attend to the observances due to his god *Kukailimoku.*

Kamehameha˙ took his uncle's advice, and in company with his wife *Kalola*,[1] his brother *Kalaimamahu*,[2] and the god *Kaili*, he left Kau, and passing through Hilo, went to Halawa, his patrimonial estate in Kohala, where he remained till the death of *Kalaniopuu.*

From Kamaoa *Kalaniopuu* moved down to Kaalualu and Paiahaa, and from there to Kalae, where he attempted to dig a well in order to obtain good water, but failed to reach it. In his anger and disappointment he killed the soothsayer who had endeavoured to dissuade him from so fruitless an attempt.

Intending to go to Kona once more, *Kalaniopuu* left the seashore of Kalae and went up to Kailikii, in Waioa-

---

[1] *Kalola* was the daughter of *Kumukoa*, who was the son of *Keaweikeka-hialiikamoku*, the king of Hawaii, and his wife *Kane-a-Lae*. *Kalola* afterwards had *Kekuamanoha*, a younger brother of *Kahekili* of Maui, for husband, and became the mother of the valiant and faithful *Manono*, the wife of *Kekuaokalani*, a nephew of *Kamehameha.*

[2] *Kalaimamahu* was the son of *Keouakalanikupuapaikalani* and *Kamakaeheukuli*, who was a daughter of *Haae*, of the famous *Mahi* family in Kohala, and his wife *Kalelemauli-okalani*. *Kalaimamahu* was the father of the late *Kekauluohi*, who was mother of the late King *Lunalilo.*

hukini, where he sickened and died some time in the month of January 1782.[1] Of course his exact age cannot be ascertained, but he was very old, and probably upwards of eighty years old when he died.

It has been often asserted that *Kalaniopuu* was the son of *Peleioholani*, and that his mother, *Kamakaimoku*, was pregnant with him when *Kalaninuiamamao* brought her to Hawaii as his wife from Oahu, where her mother and brothers were living at Waikele, in the Ewa district; and it is said that his mother called him *Ka-lei-opuu*, after the ivory ornament with braids of human hair worn as a necklace by the Oahu chiefs, which name the Hawaii chiefs and nurses (Kahu) perverted to *Kalaniopuu*. The truth or error of this assertion was apparently an open question in *Kalaniopuu's* own lifetime, and will probably ever remain so.

During the last years of *Kalaniopuu's* life, *Kahekili*, the Maui king, invaded the Hana district of Maui, which since 1759 had been an appanage of the Hawaii kingdom. Successful this time, *Kahekili* reduced the celebrated fort on the hill of Kauwiki and reannexed the Hana district to the Maui dominion. The particulars will be given when treating of *Kahekili's* reign among the Maui sovereigns.

Kalaniopuu had at different times of his life six wives; their names were—

(1.) *Kalola*, the great tabu chiefess of Maui, daughter of *Kekaulike* and his wife *Kekuiapoiwanui*. With her he had but one child, *Kiwalao*, who succeeded him as king of Hawaii.

(2.) *Kalaiwahineuli*, the daughter of *Heulu* and his wife *Kahikiokalani*, and thus a cousin on his mother's side. With her he had a son, *Kalaipaihala*, great-grandfather of the present queen-dowager, *Emma Kaleleonalani*.

(3.) *Kamakolunuiokalani*, with whose pedigree I am not acquainted. With her he had a daughter, *Pualinui*, who became the mother of the late *Luluhiwalani* of Lahaina.

---

[1] Jarves in his history says that *Kalaniopuu* died in April 1782. I know not Jarves' authority.

(4.) *Mulehu*, of a Kau chief family. With her he had a daughter, *Manoua* or *Manowa*, who became the grandmother of the late *Asa Kaeo*, and great-grandmother of the present *Peter Kaeo Kekuaokalani.* With another husband, named *Kalaniwahikapaa*,[1] *Mulehu* became the grandmother of the late *A. Paki*, and great-grandmother of the present Mrs. *Pauahi Bishop.*

(5.) *Kanekapolei* is claimed by some to have been the daughter of *Kauakahiakua*, of the Maui royal family, and his wife *Umiaemoku;* by others she is said to have been of the Kau race of chiefs. With her he had two sons, *Keoua Kuahuula* and *Keoua Peeale.* The former contested the supremacy of Hawaii with *Kamehameha* after the death of *Kiwalao;* the latter made no name for himself in history.

(6.) *Kekuohi* or *Kekupuohi*, with whose pedigree I am not acquainted, and who had no children with *Kalaniopuu.*

MAUI.

After *Piilani's* death (p. 87), his oldest son, *Lono-a-Pii*, followed him as the Moi of Maui. His character has been severely handled by succeeding generations and the legends they handed down. He is represented as unamiable, surly, avaricious—unpardonable faults in a Hawaiian chieftain. His niggardliness and abuse of his younger brother, *Kiha-a-Piilani*, drove the latter into exile and brought about his own downfall and death, as already narrated on page 98.

Lono-a-Pii's wives were—*Kealana-a-waauli*, a great granddaughter of *Kahakuokane*, the sovereign of Kauai, and grandson of *Manokalanipo.* With her he had a daughter called *Kaakaupea*, who became the wife of her uncle *Nihokela*, and mother of *Piilaniwahine*, the wife of *Kamalalawalu.* *Lonoapii* had another daughter named *Moihala*, from whom descended *Kapuleiolaa*, one of the

Lono-a-Pii.

---

[1] Son of *Kumukoa-a-Keawe* and *Kaulahoa* (w).

wives of *Kanaloauoo* and ancestress of *Sarai Hiwauli*, wife of the late Hon. *John Ii.*

There is a legend, or rather a version, of the war which *Umi-a-Liloa* undertook against *Lono-a-Pii* on behalf of his brother *Kihapiilani*, which states that when *Umi* arrived with his fleet at Hana, he was informed that *Lono-a-Pii* had died, and that a son of his named *Kalanikupua* reigned in his stead, and had charge of the fort of Kauwiki at Hana; that *Umi* was disposed to spare the young man and allow him to remain on the throne of his father, but *Piikea*, *Umi's* wife, strongly opposed such clemency, and persuaded her husband to prosecute the war and place *Kihapiilani* as Moi of Maui. I know not the source of this version, but finding it among the legends of this period, and it being the only one which mentions a son of *Lono-a-Pii*, I refer to it under reserve.

Kihapiilani.   *Kihapiilani*, who thus forcibly succeeded his brother as Moi of Maui, had been brought up by his mother's relatives at the court of *Kukaniloko* of Oahu, and only when arrived at man's estate returned to his father on Maui. Having, as before related, through the assistance of his brother-in-law *Umi* obtained the sovereignty, he devoted himself to the improvement of his island. He kept peace and order in the country, encouraged agriculture, and improved and caused to be paved the difficult and often dangerous roads over the Palis of Kaupo, Hana, and Koolau—a stupendous work for those times, the remains of which may still be seen in many places, and are pointed out as the " Kipapa" of *Kihapiilani.* His reign was eminently peaceful and prosperous, and his name has been reverently and affectionately handed down to posterity.

Kihapiilani had two wives—(1.) *Kumaka*, who was of the Hana chief families, and a sister of *Kahuakole*, a chief at Kawaipapa, in Hana. With her he had a son named *Kamalalawalu*, who succeeded him as Moi of Maui. (2.) *Koleamoku*, who was daughter of *Hoolae*, the Hana chief at Kauwiki, referred to on page 99. With her he had a son called *Kauhiokalani*, from whom the Kaupo chief families of *Koo* and *Kaiuli* descended.

Kamalalawalu followed his father as Moi of Maui. He enjoyed a long and prosperous reign until its close, when his sun set in blood and disaster, as already narrated on page 123, &c. His reputation stood deservedly high among his contemporaries and with posterity for good management of his resources, just government of his people, and a liberal and magnificent court according to the ideas of those times, and in recognition of all which his name was associated with that of his island, and Maui has ever since been known in song and saga as *Maui-a-Kama.* His sumptuous entertainments of the two Hawaii kings, *Keawenui-a-Umi* and his son *Lonoikamakahiki*, are dilated upon in the legends; and Maui probably never stood higher, politically, among the sister kingdoms of the group than during the life of *Kamalalawalu.* *Kamalala-walu.*

There are no wars mentioned in the legends as having been undertaken by *Kamalalawalu* except the one against *Lonoikamakahiki* of Hawaii, in which *Kamalalawalu* lost his life, and in which the old king's obstinacy was the cause of the disaster that befell his army and himself. But from certain allusions in the legends the inference may with great probability be drawn that the chiefs of Lanai became subject or tributary to Maui during this reign; but whether through war or negotiation is not apparent.

Kamalalawalu had only one recognised wife, *Piilani-wahine.* She was the daughter of his cousin *Kaakaupea*, who was the daughter of *Lono-a-Pii*, and who in the family chants was also known by the name of *Kamaikawekiuloloa.* With this wife he had six children, four boys and two girls, named respectively *Kauhi-a-kama*, *Umikalakaua*, *Kalakauaehu-a-kama*, *Pai-kalakaua*, *Piilanikapo*, and *Kaunoho.* The first succeeded him as Moi of Maui; the third, through his children *Kawaumahana*, *Kihamahana*, and *Moihala*, became widely connected with the aristocracy of the other islands, and progenitor of several still living families. Of the other four children of *Kamalalawalu* little is known.

Kauhi-a-kama followed his father on the throne of Maui. It is related of him that when *Kamalalawalu* was meditating and preparing for the invasion and war on Hawaii, he sent *Kauhi* on a secret mission to explore and report upon the condition, resources, and populousness of the Kohala and Kona districts; and that *Kauhi* performed his mission so carelessly or ignorantly, that, on his return to Maui, he led the old king to believe that those districts were but thinly peopled and totally unprepared to resist an invasion; and that this incorrect report from his own son confirmed *Kamalalawalu* in his project of invasion. It is further related that after the disastrous battle at Hokuula, where *Kamalalawalu* and the best part of his army perished, *Kauhi* escaped to Kawaihae, where he hid himself among the rocks for two days until discovered by *Hinau*, who assisted him and procured a canoe, in which they crossed over to Maui.

Returned to his own island, *Kauhi* assumed the government left vacant by the death of his father, and gratefully remembered the services of *Hinau* by heaping wealth and distinction upon him, until, in an evil hour, *Hinau* was enticed to return to Hawaii on a visit, was caught by the orders of *Lonoikamakahiki*, slain, and sacrificed at the Heiau.

Of the subsequent career of *Kauhi* not much is said in the legends. It appears, however, that at the close of his reign he headed an expedition to Oahu; that having landed at Waikiki, he was met by the Oahu chiefs, and was defeated and slain, his body exposed at the Heiau of Apuakehau, and that great indignities were committed with his bones. And it is further said that the memory of this great outrage instigated his descendant, *Kahekili*, to the fearful massacre of the Oahu chiefs, when, after the battle at Niuhelewai, he had defeated the Oahu king, *Kahahana*, and conquered the island.

Kauhiakama, like his father, had but one recognised wife, *Kapukini*. She was the daughter of *Makakaualii*, the grandson of *Keliiokaloa*, of the Hawaii reigning family, and sister to the celebrated *Iwikauikaua*. Their only known son was *Kalanikaumakaowakea*, who followed his father as Moi of Maui. Peace and its attendant blessings obtained on Maui during his reign ; and not a cloud abroad or at home gave rise to an item in the legend or the chants referring to his name among the Mois of Maui. *Kalani-kaumaka-owakea.*

Kalanikaumakaowakea had two wives—(1.) *Kanea-kauhi*, or, as she was also called, *Kaneakalau*. With her he had a son, *Lonohonuakini*, who succeeded him as Moi, and a daughter, *Piilaniwahine*, who became the wife of *Ahu-a-I*, of the great *I* family on Hawaii, and mother of *Lonomaaikanaka*, the wife of *Keaweikekahialiiokamoku* and mother of *Kalaninuiamamao*. (2.) *Makakuwahine*, a daughter of *Kanelaaukahi* and his wife *Kamaka*, of the *Keaunui-a-Maweke-Laakona* family. With her he had a son named *Umi-a-Liloa*, from whose three children, *Papai-kaniau*, *Kuimiheua*, and *Uluehu*, a number of prominent chief families descended. *Kalanikaumakaowakea* had another son called *Kauloaiwi*, but whether with the first or second wife, or with some other, is not very clearly ascertained.

Lonohonuakini ascended the throne of Maui under the flattering auspices of peace and prosperity bequeathed by his father, and, with singular good fortune, succeeded in maintaining the same peaceful and orderly condition during his own reign also. Though the yearly feasts and the monthly sacrifices were performed as usual, though bards gathered to the chieftain's court to chant the deeds of his ancestors and extol the wealth and glory of his own reign, yet the smooth and placid stream of this and the preceding reigns left no ripple on the traditional record, and considering the convulsed condition of the neighbouring islands, this absolute silence is their noblest epitaph. *Lonohonua-kini.*

Lonohonuakini's wife was *Kalanikauanakinilani*, with

whom he had the following children :—*Kaulahea*, a son, who succeeded his father in the government; *Lonomakaihonua*, who was grandfather to the celebrated bard *Keaulumoku ; Kalaniomaiheuila*, mother of *Kalanikahimakeialii*, the wife of *Kualii* of Oahu, and, through her daughter *Kaionuilalahai*, grandmother of *Kahahana*, the last independent king of Oahu, of the Oahu race of chiefs, who lost his life and his kingdom in the war with Maui in 1783.

Kaulahea. *Kaulahea* continued the same peaceful policy as his father and grandfather had pursued, and Maui deservedly rose to be considered as a model state among its sister kingdoms of the group. It is probable, however, that during this period were sown the seeds of disintegration which in the next two reigns destroyed the independence and autonomy of the island of Molokai, whose chiefs in their internal divisions and quarrels began to seek outside support, some from Maui, some from Oahu.

But no prospect of foreign conquests, however tempting, induced *Kaulahea* to forsake the peaceful path of his fathers, and no domestic troubles with his feudal chiefs distracted his attention or impoverished his resources.

Kaulahea had two wives — (1.) *Kalanikauleleiaiwi*, daughter of *Keakealani*, the sovereign queen of Hawaii, and half-sister of *Keawekekahialiiokamoku*, already referred to on page 128. With her he had a daughter named *Kekuiapoiwanui*, also known in the chants by the names of *Kalanikauhihiwakama* and *Wanakapu.*[1] (2.) *Papaikaniau*, also known as *Lonoikaniau*, the daughter of his

[1] I am aware that certain genealogists contend that *Kekuiapoiwanui* was the daughter of *Keawe* and *Kalanikauleleiaiwi;* that she was born at Olowalu or Ukumehame while her said parents were on a visit to Maui; that *Kaulahea*, the Moi of Maui, and then living at Wailuku, hearing of the event, sent to *Keawe* and asked that the new-born child be given to him to be brought up as a wife for his son *Kekaulike,* and that *Keawe* and his wife complied with the request. I know not how old that assertion may be ; but I am certain that neither David Malo, who was instructed by *Ulumeheihei Hoapilikane,* nor S. M. Kamakau, who was particularly well informed in the Maui genealogies, so understood it or so expressed it. It was a matter of frequent occurrence in those days

uncle, *Umi-a-Liloa*. With her he had a son named *Kekau-like*, also known by the name of *Kalaninuikuihonoikamoku*, who succeeded him as Moi of Maui.[1]

Kekaulike's reign over Maui continued for a long time *Kekaulike.* on the same peaceful and prosperous footing as that of his predecessors; but towards the close of his life, after the death of *Keawe* of Hawaii, the civil war then raging on Hawaii presented too tempting an opportunity for invasion, possibly conquest, or at least unresisted plunder, and *Kekau-like* assembling his fleet and his warriors, started on the expedition recorded on page 133. It was a raid on a grand scale, that brought no laurels to *Kekaulike's* brow, and did not materially cripple the resources of Hawaii.

We know that *Kekaulike* died the year that *Kamehameha I.* was born, 1736–40, probably nearer the former year, and thus we have here a starting-point for computing the generations of chiefs on Maui.

When *Kekaulike* was on his death-bed, while being brought from Mokulau in Kaupo—where he landed on his return from the raid on Hawaii—to Wailuku, he appointed his son *Kamehamehanui* as his successor, thus breaking the rule of primogeniture which generally was observed on such occasions. But this deviation from a common rule was probably based upon the consideration that not only was *Kamehamehanui* an *Alii Niaupio*, being the son of *Kekuiapoiwanui*, but also that the said mother was of higher rank than *Kahawalu*, the mother of *Kekaulike's* first-born son, *Kauhiaimokuakama*.

Kekaulike enjoyed the company of several wives, and was blessed with a numerous progeny. We know who

that high chiefesses visited the other islands and contracted alliances according to their own liking, and as long as they liked. They were as much at liberty to have more than one husband as the high chiefs were to have more than one wife, and the whole life of *Kalanikauleleiaiwi* shows that she availed herself of her privileges in that respect.

[1] It is said by some genealogists that *Kaulahea* had another son named *Kanaluihoae*, who was the father of *Numakeha*, of whom more hereafter; but I am inclined to follow those who represent *Kanaluihoae* as the son of *Uluehu*, a brother of *Papaikaniau*, the wife of *Kaulahea*, and his cousin. *Kanaluihoae's* mother was *Kulani-kauhialiiohaloa*.

was his first wife, but the order in which the others were obtained is not certain. They probably were contemporary with each other, or nearly so.

The wives and children of *Kekaulike* were—

(1.) *Kahawalu*, from the Kaupo or Hana chief families. With her he had but one son, the aforesaid *Kauhiaimokua-kama*, whose ambition and whose fate is mentioned on page 140–42. Of this *Kauhi's* descendants, the most prominent in Hawaiian history was his daughter's [1] son, *Kalai-moku*, famous in the latter part of the wars of *Kamehameha I.*, and as prime minister of the kingdom after *Kame-hameha's* death. That branch of the family is now extinct; but from another daughter [2] of *Kauhi*, who became one of the wives of *Keaumokupapaia*, there still survives a grandson in the valley of Pelekunu, on Molokai.

(2.) *Kekuiapoiawanui*, who was his half-sister, as before stated. With her he had the following children :—*Kame-hamehanui*, a son who succeeded his father as Moi of Maui. *Kalola*, a daughter, who became the wife of *Kalaniopuu*, the king of Hawaii, and bore to him his son and successor, *Kiwalao*. She was also at one time the wife of *Keouakalanikupua*, *Kamehameha I.'s* father, and with him had a daughter, *Kekuiapoiwa Liliha*, who became the mother of *Keopuolani*, the queen of *Kamehameha I.* *Kalola* was also the mother of a girl, *Kalanikauikikilo-kalaniakua*, who in those days was one of the highest tabu chiefs, on whom the sun was not permitted to shine, and who, unless with extraordinary precautions, only

---

[1] *Kamakahukilani.* She was of the Kaupo *Koo* family. Her mother's name was *Luukia.* She married *Keku-amanoha*, one of *Kekaulike's* sons with *Haalou*, and thus became the mother of *Kalaimoku*, mentioned above; of his brother *Poki*, whose turbulent career met a tragical close on a sandalwood expedition to the New Hebrides in 1829; and of a daughter, *Kahaku-haakoi*, who became the mother of *Kahalaia*, the first governor of Kauai

after *Kaumualii's* death, and of *Kea-hikuni Kekauonohi*, a granddaughter of *Kamehameha I.*

[2] *Kalolawahilani.* With *Keaumo-kupapaia* she had a son, *Keakakilohi*, who, with *Kamahanakapu*—a daughter of *Kawelookalani* and his wife *Naonoaina*, the former a brother of *Kamehameha I.*, the latter a granddaughter of *Kaiakea* of Molokai—begat a son, *Kalaniopuu*, the person referred to above.

moved about when the sun was so low as not to throw its beams upon her head. There was another daughter of *Kekaulike* and *Kekuiapoiwanui* on the genealogy, named *Kuhoohiehiepahu*, but she is not further referred to, and probably died young. The youngest scion of this union was a son, *Kahekili*, who succeeded his brother *Kamehamehanui* as Moi, and was the last independent king of Maui.

(3.) *Kane-a-Lae*, daughter of *Lae*, one of the independent chiefs of the eastern part of Molokai. She had previously been one of the wives of *Keawe* of Hawaii. With her he had a daughter named *Luahiwa*, who became one of the wives of his son *Kahekili*.

(4.) *Hoolau*, daughter of *Kawelo-aila*, a grandson of *Lonoikamakahiki* of Hawaii, and of *Kauakahiheleikaiwi*.[1] With her he had two sons and one daughter—*Kekauhiwamoku*, from whom descended *Keouawahine*, the grandmother of her Highness *Ruth Keelikolani; Kaeokulani*, who married *Kamakahelei*, sovereign of Kauai, and became father of *Kaumualii*, the last independent sovereign of that island, and grandfather of the present queen, *Kapiolani*, and her sisters ; and *Manuhaaipo*, who was the mother of *Kailinaoa* and grandmother of *Ahu Kai Kaukualii.*

(5.) *Haalou*, daughter of *Haae*, the son of *Kauaua-a-Mahi* and brother of *Alapainui* of Hawaii, and of *Kalelemauliokalani*, daughter of *Kaaloapii*, a chief from Kau, and of *Kaneikaheilani*, said to have been a daughter or granddaughter of *Kawelo-a-Mahunalii*, who in his day was the Moi of Kauai. With her *Kekaulike* had one son and two daughters—(1.) *Kekuamanoha*, previously referred to ; (2.) *Namahana-i-Kaleleokalani*, who was first the wife of her half-brother *Kamehamehanui*, with whom she had two sons, *Pelioholani* and *Kuakini*, who both died young ; afterwards she became the wife of *Keeaumokupapaiahiahi*, the son of *Keawepoepoe* of Hawaii, with whom she had three daughters (*Kaahumanu, Kaheiheimalie*, and

[1] Of the Kauai aristocracy.

Kekuaipiia) and two sons (*Kecaumokuopio*, known by the English name of George Cox, and *Kuakini*, also known as John Adams); (3.) *Kekuapoi-ula*, said to have been the most beautiful woman of her time, and who became the wife of *Kahahana*, the king of Oahu.

Kamohomoho, a high chief on Maui in the time of *Kahekili*, is said to have been a son of *Kekaulike*, but his mother's name has not been handed down.

amehame-
inui. *Kamehamehanui* followed his father *Kekaulike* as Moi of Maui. I have on previous pages described his relations with *Alapainui* of Hawaii, and his troubles and civil war with his half-brother, *Kauhiaimokuakama*. After this nothing transpired to interrupt the peace and tranquillity of Maui until the abrupt invasion by *Kalaniopuu* of Hawaii, about the year 1759, when the districts of Hana and Kipahulu were wrenched from the crown of Maui and became subject to Hawaii. It is probable that, although *Kamehamehanui* failed in retaking the fort of Kauwiki, Hana, yet to some extent he curtailed the possessions of Hawaii outside of Kauwiki, more especially on the Koolau side.

It should be mentioned that in his younger days, when quite a lad, *Kamehamehanui* was brought up at Moanui, Molokai, in the family of his nurse and "Kahu," *Palemo*, of whom several descendants still survive.

Kamehamehanui resided most of his time at Wailuku, and there he died about the year 1765. He had two wives—his half-sister, *Namahana*, with whom he had two children, *Pelioholani* and *Kuakini*, who both died young; and *Kekukamano*, whose lineage is unknown to me, and with whom he had three sons, *Kalaniulumoku*, *Kalani-helemailuna*, and *Peapea*, all apparently of tender age at the time of his death. Of the two first, several scions still survive; the line of the last, I believe, is extinct, *Peapea* himself having been killed in 1794 by the explosion of a barrel of gunpowder at the fort of Kauwiki, Hana.

When *Kamehamehanui* died, the government of Maui

devolved by force of circumstances upon his brother *Kahekili*, the youngest son of *Kekaulike* and *Kekuia-* *poiwanui*, and the highest chief in the absence of his sister *Kalola*, the wife of *Kalaniopuu*.

Kahekili is said, by those who knew him in mature life and later age, to have been of a stern, resolute, and reserved temper, living much by himself and avoiding crowds. He gave freely, as became a chief, but was annoyed at the boisterous *éclat* which his largesses elicited. He was laborious and persistent, cold, calculating, and cruel. Successful in all his enterprises during a long life, yet its close was clouded by reverses, and he presented the singular instance of a monarch who conquered another kingdom but was not able to keep his own. In an age when tattooing was declining as a custom, he made himself conspicuous by having one side of his body from head to foot so closely tattooed as to appear almost black, while the other side bore the natural colour of the skin. In a state of society where a number of wives was looked upon as an indispensable portion of a chief's establishment, *Kahekili* contented himself with only two wives. Being a younger son, with no prospect or expectation of ascending the throne until nearly fifty years old, he had lived as a private nobleman, a dutiful son, and a loyal brother during the two preceding reigns. But after the death of *Kamehamehanui's* children with *Namahana*, *Kahekili* was the highest chief on Maui, and as such assumed the government at his brother's death by common consent as of right.

I have mentioned on foregoing pages (149–57) the domestic trouble of *Kahekili* with *Keeaumoku-papaia*, the new husband of his sister *Namahana*, and his wars with *Kalaniopuu*, the Moi of Hawaii, up to the fall of the year 1778, and the arrival of the discovery ships under command of Captain Cook.

In 1781 *Kahekili*, hearing of the weakness and approaching end of *Kalaniopuu*, prepared his forces to recover the districts of East Maui, which for so long a time had been under the rule of the Hawaii king. *Mahihelelima* was still Governor of Hana, and with him were a number of Hawaii chiefs of high renown and lineage,[1] *Kalokuoka-maile, Naeole, Malualani, Kaloku,* and others. *Kahekili* divided his forces in two divisions, and marched on Hana by Koolau and by Kaupo. The fort on Kauwiki was invested, and the siege continued for many months. The Hawaii chiefs were well provisioned, and the fort held out stoutly until *Kahekili* was advised to cut off the water supply of the fort by damming and diverting the springs in the neighbourhood. The measure succeeded, and the garrison, making desperate sorties beyond their lines to procure water, were slain in numbers and finally surrendered, expecting no mercy and obtaining none. *Mahihelelima* and *Naeole* made good their escape to Hawaii,[2] but the larger number of Hawaii chiefs and soldiers were slain and their corpses burnt at Kuawalu and at Honuaula. This war is called in the native legends the war of *Kaumupikao.*

Thus the famous fort of Kauwiki fell again into the power of the Maui king, but its prestige was gone, and we never hear of it again as a point of strategical importance.

According to the political economy of those days, *Kahekili* fell back from the devastated neighbourhood of Kauwiki to the large plain of Makaliihanau, above Muolea, in Hana district, and employed himself, his

---

[1] *Kalokuokamaile* was the son of *Keouakalanikupuapaikalani,* and half-brother of *Kamehameha I.;* his mother was *Kulanilehua,* also called *Kahiki-kala,* said to have been a grand-daughter of *Mopua* of Molokai. *Kalokuokamaile,* through his daughter *Kaohelelani,* became the grandfather of the late *Laanui,* and great-grand-father of the present Mrs. *Elizabeth Kaaniau Pratt.*

Naeole was the same Kohala chief who abducted *Kamehameha I.* on the night that he was born.

Malualani was the son of *Kekau-like,* the granddaughter of *Keawe* of Hawaii, and her husband, *Kepoo-mahoe.* He was grandfather of the late *Kalaipaihala* of Lahaina. *Malualani's* sister, *Kalaikauleleiaiwi II.,* was the great-grandmother of the present queen, *Kapiolani.*

Who the last-mentioned *Kaloku* was I am unable to determine.

[2] It is said by some that *Malualani* also escaped to Hawaii, and was afterwards killed in an affray at Makapala, Kohala.

chiefs, and his soldiers in planting a food-crop for the coming year. The surrender of Kauwiki may be dated as of the early part of 1782, about the time of *Kalaniopuu's* death.

In order to understand the political relations between *Kahekili* and *Kahahana*, the king of Oàhu, and the causes of the war between them, it is necessary to go back to the year 1773, when *Kumahana*, the son of *Peleioholani*, was deposed by the chiefs and Makaainana of Oahu. Though *Kumahana* had grown-up children at the time, yet the Oahu nobles passed them by in selecting a successor to the throne, and fixed their eyes on young *Kahahana*, the son of *Elani*, one of the powerful Ewa chiefs of the *Maweke Lakona* line, and on his mother's side closely related to *Kahekili* and the Maui royal family. *Kahahana* had from boyhood been brought up at the court of *Kahekili*, who looked upon his cousin's child almost as a son of his own. What share, if any, indirectly, that *Kahekili* may have had in the election of *Kahahana*, is not known; but when the tidings arrived from Oahu announcing the result to *Kahekili*, he appears at first not to have been overmuch pleased with it. The Oahu chiefs had deputed *Kekela-okalani*, a high chiefess, a cousin to *Kahahana's* mother and also to *Kahekili*, to proceed to Wailuku, Maui, and announce the election and solicit his approval. After some feigned or real demurrer, *Kahekili* consented to *Kahahana* going to Oahu, but refused to let his wife *Kekuapoi-ula* go with him, lest the Oahu chiefs should ill-treat her. Eventually, however, he consented, but demanded as a price of his consent that the land of Kualoa in Koolaupoko district should be ceded to him, and also the "Palaoa-pae" (the whalebone and ivory) cast on the Oahu shores by the sea.

Hampered with these demands of the crafty *Kahekili*, *Kahahana* started with his wife and company for Oahu, and landed at Kahaloa in Waikiki. He was enthusiastically received, installed as Moi of Oahu, and great were the rejoicings on the occasion.

Shortly after his installation, *Kahahana* called a great council of the Oahu chiefs and the high-priest *Kaopulupulu*, and laid before them the demands of *Kahekili* regarding the land of Kualoa and the "Palaoa-pae." At first the council was divided, and some thought it was but a fair return for the kindness and protection shown *Kahahana* from his youth by *Kahekili;* but the high-priest was strongly opposed to such a measure, and argued that it was a virtual surrender of the sovereignty and independence of Oahu. Kualoa being one of the most sacred places on the island, where stood the sacred drums of *Kapahuula* and *Kaahu-ulapunawai*, and also the sacred hill of Kauakahi-a-Kahoowaha; and the surrender of the "Palaoa-pae" would be a disrespect to the gods; in fact, if *Kahekili's* demands were complied with, the power of war and of sacrifice would rest with the Maui king and not with *Kahahana*. He represented strongly, moreover, that if *Kahahana* had obtained the kingdom by conquest, he might do as he liked, but having been chosen by the Oahu chiefs, it would be wrong in him to cede to another the national emblems of sovereignty and independence. *Kahahana* and all the chiefs admitted the force of *Kaopulupulu's* arguments, and submitted to his advice not to comply with the demands of *Kahekili*.

Kahekili was far too good a politician to display his resentment at this refusal of his demands, knowing well that he could not have the slightest prospects of enforcing them by war so long as the Oahu chiefs were united in their policy, and that policy was guided by the sage and experienced high-priest *Kaopulupulu*. He dissembled, therefore, and kept up friendly relations with *Kahahana*, but secretly turned his attention to destroy the influence of *Kaopulupulu* in the affairs of Oahu, and create distrust and enmity between him and *Kahahana*. In this object he is said to have been heartily advised and assisted by his own high-priest, *Kaleopuupuu*, the younger brother of

Kaopulupulu, and who envied the latter the riches and consideration which his wisdom and skill had obtained for him. Moreover, the warlike preparations of his brother-in-law, the Hawaii king *Kalaniopuu,* cautioned him against precipitating a rupture with so powerful an ally as the Oahu king; and *Kahekili* was but too glad to obtain the assistance of *Kahahana* and his chiefs in the war with *Kalaniopuu,* 1777–78, *Kahahana's* forces arriving from Molokai just in time to share the sanguinary battle on the Waikapu common,[1] related on page 153, and the subsequent events of that war.

After the return of *Kalaniopuu* to Hawaii in January 1779, *Kahahana* went over to Molokai to consecrate the Heiau called Kupukapuakea at Wailau, and to build or repair the large taro patch at Kainalu known as Paikahawai. Here he was joined by *Kahekili,* who was cordially welcomed and royally entertained. On seeing the fruitfulness and prosperity of the Molokai lands, *Kahekili* longed to possess some of them, and bluntly asked *Kahahana* to give him the land of Halawa. *Kahahana* promptly acceded to the request, not being moved by the same considerations regarding the Molokai lands as those of Oahu, Molokai having been conquered and subjected as an appanage or tributary to the Oahu crown by *Peleioholani.* At this meeting, while discussing *Kahahana's* previous refusal to give *Kahekili* the Kualoa land and the "Palaoa-pae" on Oahu, *Kahekili* expressed his surprise at the opposition of *Kaopulupulu,* assuring *Kahahana* that the high-priest had offered the government and • throne of Oahu to him (*Kahekili*), but that out of affection for his nephew he had refused; and he intimated strongly that *Kaopulupulu* was a traitor to *Kahahana.*

The poisoned arrow hit its mark, and *Kahahana* returned to Oahu filled with mistrust and suspicion of his faithful

[1] They arrived on the evening of the day that the famous "Alapa" regiment of *Kalaniopuu* was annihi- lated by *Kahekili,* and joined in the next day's general battle.

high-priest. A coolness arose between them. *Kahahana* withdrew his confidence from, and slighted the advice of, the high-priest, who retired from the court to his own estate in Waialua and Waimea, and caused himself and all his people and retainers to be tatooed on the knee, as a sign that the chief had turned a deaf ear to his advice. It is said that during this period of estrangement *Kahahana* became burdensome to the people, capricious and heedless, and in a great measure alienated their good-will. It is said, moreover, that he caused to be dug up dead men's bones to make arrow-points of wherewith to shoot rats— a favourite pastime of the chiefs ; and that he even rifled the tombs of the chiefs in order to make Kahili handles of their bones, thus outraging the public sentiment of the nation. That *Kahahana* was imprudent and rash, and perhaps exacting, there is no doubt; and that conquered chieftains' bones were the legitimate trophies of the victors is equally true ; but that *Kahahana* would have violated the tombs of the dead—an act even in those days of the greatest moral baseness—is hardly credible, and is probably an after exaggeration, either by the disaffected priestly faction or by the victorious *Kahekili* plotters.

While such was the condition on Oahu, *Kahekili* reconquered the district of Hana, as already related, and, hearing of the death of *Kalaniopuu* and the subsequent contentions on Hawaii, he felt secure in that direction, and seriously turned his attention to the acquisition of Oahu. He first sent some war-canoes and a detachment of soldiers under command of a warrior chief named *Kahahawai*[1] to the assistance of *Keawemauhili*, the then inde-

[1] It is related by S. M. Kamakau, that when *Kahekili* heard of the defeat and death of *Kiwalao*, and that *Kamehameha* had assumed the sovereignty of the Kona, Kohala, and Hamakua districts on Hawaii, he then sent *Alapai-maloiki* and *Kaulunae*, two sons of *Kumaaiku* (w) and half-brothers of *Keeaumoku-papaiahiahi*, to ask *Kamehameha* to assist him with some double canoes in his projected war against *Kahahana*, and that *Kamehameha* had refused, replying that when he had subdued the chiefs of Hilo and Kau he then would consider *Kahekili's* request ; and that when *Keawemauhili*, the chief of Hilo, heard of this refusal, he hastened to send some double canoes and other costly presents to

pendent chief of Hilo, in his contest with *Kamehameha*.[1] He next sent his most trusted servant *Kauhi* to *Kahahana* on Oahu, with instructions to inform *Kahahana* in the strictest confidence that *Kaopulupulu* had again offered him the kingdom of Oahu, but that his regard for *Kahahana* would not allow him to accept it, and exhorting *Kahahana* to be on his guard against the machinations of the high-priest. Credulous as weak, *Kahahana* believed the falsehoods sent him by *Kahekili*, and, without confiding his purpose to any one, he resolved on the death of *Kaopulupulu*. Preparations were ordered to be made for a tour of the island of Oahu, for the purpose of consecrating Heiaus and offering sacrifices. When the king arrived at Waianae he sent for the high-priest, who was then residing on his lands at Waimea and Pupukea, in the Koolau district, to come to see him. It is said that *Kaopulupulu* was fully aware of the ulterior objects of the king, and was well convinced that the message boded him no good ; yet, faithful to his duties as a priest and loyal to the last, he started with his son *Kahulupue* to obey the summons of the king. Arrived at Waianae, *Kahulupue* was set upon by the king's servants, and, while escaping from them, was drowned at Malae.[2] *Kaopulupulu* was killed at Puuloa, in Ewa.

Thus foolishly and cruelly *Kahahana* had played into

Kahekili; and that this was the reason why *Kahekili* sent *Kahahawai* and some soldiers to assist *Keawemauhili* against *Kamehameha*.

[1] *Kahahawai* was from Waihee, Maui. He was a special friend of *Kahekili* (an "Aikane"), and was the father of *Keaholawaia* and *Haia*.

[2] The legend relates that when *Kaopulupulu* saw his son set upon and pursued by *Kahahana's* retainers, he called out to him, "*I nui ke aho a moe i ke kai ! No ke kai ka hoi ua aina.*" This was one of those oracular utterances in which Hawaiian priests and prophets were as adept as any of

their brethren in other lands. Its literal meaning is—"It is far better to sleep in the sea ; for from the sea comes life or the means of living." Those who heard it and reported it found the fulfilment of the prophecy when *Kahekili*, coming over the sea from Maui, conquered Oahu and caused *Kahahana* to be slain. Others sought the fulfilment in the conquest of the group by *Kamehameha* coming from Hawaii ; others found it in the arrival of the foreigners, coming over the ocean with new ideas, knowledge, and arts.

the hand of *Kahekili*, who, with his high-priest *Kaleo-puupuu*, had for a long time been plotting the death of *Kahahana's* ablest and wisest counsellor.

Though executions *de par le roi* of obnoxious persons for political reasons were not uncommon in those days throughout the group, and by the proud and turbulent nobility generally looked upon more as a matter of personal ill-luck to the victim than as a public injustice, yet this double execution, in the necessity of which few people except the credulous *Kahahana* believed, greatly alienated the feelings of both chiefs and commoners from him, and weakened his influence and resources to withstand the coming storm.

The death of *Kaopulupulu* took place in the latter part of 1782 or beginning of 1783.

As soon as *Kahekili* heard that *Kaopulupulu* was dead, he considered the main obstacle to his acquisition of the island of Oahu to be removed, and prepared for an invasion. He recalled the auxiliary troops under *Kahahawai* which he had sent to the assistance of *Keawemauhili* in Hilo, and assembled his forces at Lahaina. Touching at Molokai on his way, he landed at Waikiki, Oahu. Among his chiefs and warriors of note on this expedition are mentioned *Kekuamanoha, Kaiana, Namakeha, Kalaikoa, Kamohomoho, Nahiolea, Hueu, Kauhikoakoa, Kahue, Kalani-nuiiulumoku, Peapea, Manono-Kauakapekulani, Kalaniku-pule, Koalaukane.*[1] Besides his own armament, he had

[1] *Kekuamanoha* was a son of *Ke-kaulike*, king of Maui, and his wife, Haalou. He was thus a half-brother to *Kahekili*. His son was the celebrated *Kalaimoku*, prime minister during the regency of *Kaahumanu*. His other son was *Boki*, at one time governor of Oahu.

Kaiana, also called *Keawe-Kaiana-a-Ahuula*, was the son of *Ahuula-a-Keawe*, who claimed *Keawe* of Hawaii as his father and *Kaolohaka-a-Keawe* as his brother. *Kaiana's* mother was the famous *Kaupekamoku*, a grand-daughter of *Ahia* (w) of the *I* family

of Hilo, Hawaii. This was the same *Kaiana* who went to China in 1787 with Captain Meares, returned to Hawaii, and was finally killed in the battle of Nuuana, 1796. His cousin, *Kaiana Ukupe*, the son of *Kaolohaka*, was father of the late *Kaikioewa*, governor of Kauai.

Namakeha was son of the above-mentioned *Kaupekamoku* and *Kana-luihoae*, a brother or cousin of *Ke-kaulike* of Maui. In after-life *Nama-keha* rebelled against *Kamehameha I.*, and was slain in battle, 1796.

Nahiolea was another son of the

several double canoes furnished him by *Keawemauhili* of Hilo, and by *Keouakuahuula* of Kau.

Kahahana was at *Kawananakoa*, in the upper part of Nuuanu valley, when the news came of *Kahekili's* landing at Waikiki, and hastily summoning his warriors, he prepared as best he could to meet so sudden an emergency. As an episode of this war the following legend has been preserved and may prove interesting:—When the news of the invasion spread to Ewa and Waialua, eight famous warriors from those places, whose names the legend has retained, concerted an expedition on their own account to win distinction for their bravery and inflict what damage they could on *Kahekili's* forces. It was a chivalrous undertaking, a forlorn hope, and wholly unauthorised by *Kahahana*, but fully within the spirit of the time for personal valour, audacity, and total disregard of consequences. The names of those heroes were *Pupuka,*[1] *Makaioulu, Puakea, Pinau, Kalaeone, Pahua, Kauhi,* and

same above-mentioned *Kaupekamoku* and *Kuimiheua II.*, a cousin of *Kekaulike* of Maui. *Nahiolea* was father of the late *M. Kekuanaoa*, governor of Oahu, and father of their late majesties *Kamehameha IV.* and *V.*, and of her Highness *Ruth Keelikolani.*

Kamohomoho is always called a brother of *Kahekili* in the native accounts, but I have been unable to learn who his mother was.

Kauhikoakoa was a son of *Kauhiaimokuakama,* the elder brother of *Kahekili*, who rebelled against his brother, *Kamehamehanui*, and was drowned after the battle near Lahaina. *Kauhikoakoa's* mother was *Luukia,* of the Kaupo *Koo* family of chiefs.

Kalaninuiulumoku was the son of *Kamehamehanui* of Maui, and *Kekumano* (w), and thus a brother of *Kalanihelemailuna,* the grandfather of the present Hon. Mrs. *Pauahi Bishop.*

Peapea was another son of *Kamehamehanui* of Maui. He was subse-

quently killed at Hana by the explosion of a keg of gunpowder.

Manonokauakapekulani, also called *Kahekilinuiahunu,* was the son of *Kahekili* of Maui and *Luahiwa,* a daughter of *Kekaulike* of Maui and *Kane-a-Lae* (w).

Kalanikupule, son and successor of *Kahekili* of Maui. His mother was *Kauwahine.*

Koalaukane, another son of *Kahekili* and *Kauwahine.*

Kalaikoa, Hueu, and *Kahu,* unknown to me.

[1] *Pupuka,* an Oahu chief of considerable importance, was father of *Inaina,* the wife of *Nahiolea,* and mother of *Kekuanaoa,* late governor of Oahu.

Tradition is silent on the descent and connections of the other heroes of this band. They and theirs were probably all exterminated, and not being maritally connected with the victorious side, no scions were left to chant their names.

Kapukoa. Starting direct from Apuakehau in Waikiki, where *Kahekili's* army was encamped and organising preparatory to a march inland to fight *Kahahana*, the eight Oahu warriors boldly charged a large contingent of several hundred men of the Maui troops collected at the Heiau. In a twinkling they were surrounded by overwhelming numbers, and a fight commenced to which Hawaiian legends record no parallel. Using their long spears and javelins with marvellous skill and dexterity, and killing a prodigious number of their enemies, the eight champions broke through the circle of spears that surrounded them. But *Makaioulu,* though a good fighter was a bad runner, on account of his short bow-legs, and he was overtaken by *Kauhikoakoa,* a Maui chief. *Makaioulu* was soon tripped up, secured, and bound by *Kauhikoakoa,* who, swinging the captive up on his own shoulders, started off with him for the camp to have him sacrificed as the first victim of the war. This affair took place on the bank of the Punaluu taro patch, near the cocoa-nut grove of Kuakuaaka. *Makaioulu,* thus hoisted on the back of his captor, caught sight of his friend *Pupuka,* and called out to him to throw his spear straight at the navel of his stomach. In hopes of shortening the present and prospective tortures of his friend, and knowing well what his fate would be if brought alive into the enemy's camp, *Pupuka* did as he was bidden, and with an unerring aim. But *Makaioulu,* seeing the spear coming, threw himself with a violent effort on one side, and the spear went through the back of *Kauhikoakoa.* Seeing their leader fall, the Maui soldiers desisted from farther pursuit, and the eight champions escaped.

In the beginning of 1783—some say it was in the month of January—*Kahekili,* dividing his forces in three columns, marched from Waikiki by Puowaina, Pauoa, and Kapena, and gave battle to *Kahahana* near the small stream of Kaheiki. *Kahahana's* army was thoroughly routed, and he and his wife *Kekua-poi-ula* fled to the mountains. It is related that in this battle *Kauwahine,* the wife of *Kahekili,* fought valiantly at his side.

Oahu and Molokai now became the conquest of *Kahekili,* and savagely he used his victory.

For upwards of two years or more *Kahahana* and his wife and his friend *Alapai*[1] wandered over the mountains of Oahu, secretly aided, fed, and clothed by the country people, who commiserated the misfortunes of their late king. Finally, weary of such a life, and hearing that *Kekuamanoha,* the uterine brother of his wife *Kekuapoiula,* was residing at Waikele in Ewa, he sent her to negotiate with her brother for their safety. Dissembling his real intentions, *Kekuamanoha* received his sister kindly and spoke her fairly, but having found out the hiding-place of *Kahahana,* he sent messengers to *Kahekili* at Waikiki informing him of the fact. *Kahekili* immediately returned peremptory orders to slay *Kahahana* and *Alapai,* and he sent a double canoe down to Ewa to bring their corpses up to Waikiki. This order was faithfully executed by *Kekuamanoha;* and it is said that the mournful chant which still exists in the Hawaiian anthology of a bygone age under the name of "*Kahahana*" was composed and chanted by his widow as the canoe was disappearing with her husband's corpse down the Ewa lagoon on its way to Waikiki.

The cruel treachery practised on *Kahahana* and his sad fate, joined to the overbearing behaviour and rapacity of the invaders, created a revulsion of feeling in the Oahu chiefs, which culminated in a wide-spread conspiracy against *Kahekili* and the Maui chiefs who were distributed over the several districts of Oahu. *Kahekili* himself and a number of chiefs were at that time living at Kailua ; *Manonokauakapekulani, Kaiana, Namakeha, Nahiolea, Kalaniulumoku,* and others, were quartered at Kaneohe and Heeia ; *Kalanikupule, Koalaukane,* and *Kekuamanoha* were at Ewa, and *Hueu* was at Waialua.

The Oahu leaders of the conspiracy were *Elani,* the

---

[1] I have been unable to learn who this *Alapai* was, and of what family.

father of *Kahahana, Pupuka,* and *Makaioulu,* above referred to, *Konamanu, Kalakioonui,* and a number of others. The plan was to kill the Maui chiefs on one and the same night in the different districts. *Elani* and his band were to kill the chiefs residing at Ewa; *Makaioulu* and *Pupuka* were to kill *Kahekili* and the chiefs at Kailua; *Konamanu* and *Kalaikioonui* were to despatch *Hueu* at Waialua. By some means the conspiracy became known to *Kalanikupule,* who hastened to inform his father, *Kahekili,* and the Maui chiefs at Kaneohe in time to defeat the object of the conspirators; but, through some cause now unknown, the messenger sent to advise *Hueu,* generally known as *Kiko-Hueu,* failed to arrive in time, and *Hueu* and all his retainers then living at Kaowakawaka, in Kawailoa, of the Waialua district, were killed. The conspiracy was known as the " *Waipio Kimopo* " (the Waipio assassination), having originated in Waipio, Ewa.

Fearfully did *Kahekili* avenge the death of *Hueu* on the revolted Oahu chiefs. Gathering his forces together, he overran the districts of Kona and Ewa, and a war of extermination ensued. Men, women, and children were killed without discrimination and without mercy. The streams of Makaho and Niuhelewai in Kona, and that of Hoaiai in Ewa, are said to have been literally choked with the corpses of the slain. The native Oahu aristocracy were almost entirely extirpated. It is related that one of the Maui chiefs, named *Kalaikoa,* caused the bones of the slain to be scraped and cleaned, and that the quantity collected was so great that he built a house for himself, the walls of which were laid up entirely of the skeletons of the slain. The skulls of *Elani, Konamanu,* and *Kalakioonui* adorned the portals of this horrible house. The house was called "Kauwalua," and was situated at Lapakea in Moanalua, as one passes by the old upper road to Ewa. The site is still pointed out, but the bones have received burial.

The rebellion of the Oahu chiefs appears to have had

its supporters even among the chiefs and followers of *Kahekili*. *Kalaniulumoku*, the son of *Kamehamehanui* and nephew of *Kahekili*, took the part of the Oahu chiefs, and was supported by *Kaiana, Namakeha, Nahiolea,* and *Kaneoneo*,[1] the grandson of *Peleioholani*. Their struggle was unsuccessful, and only added to the long list of the illustrious slain. *Kalaniulumoku* was driven over the Pali of Olomana and killed; *Kaneoneo* was killed at Maunakapu, as one descends to Moanalua; *Kaiana, Nahiolea,* and *Namakeha* escaped to Kauai. A number of chiefesses of the highest rank—"Kapumoe"—were killed, mutilated, or otherwise severely afflicted. *Kekelaokalani*, the cousin of *Kahahana's* mother and of *Kahekili*, made her escape to Kauai. As an instance of deep affection, of bitterness of feeling, and of supreme hope of return and revenge at some future day, it is said that she took with her when she fled some of the Oahu soil from Apuakehau, Kahaloa, Waiaula, and Kupalaha at Waikiki, and deposited it at Hulaia, Kaulana, and Kane on Kauai.

The events above narrated bring us down to the early part of 1785.

While *Kahekili* was carrying on the war on Oahu and suppressing the revolt of the Oahu chiefs, a serious disturbance on Maui had occurred which gave him much uneasiness. It appears that he had given the charge of his herds of hogs that were running in the Kula district and on the slopes of Haleakala to a petty chief named *Kukeawe*. This gentleman, not satisfied with whatever he could embezzle from his master's herds, made raids upon the farmers and country people of Kula, Honuaula, Kahikinui, and even as far as Kaupo, robbing them of their

[1] In 1779 we have seen that *Kaneoneo* was on Kauai. He had been contending with his cousin *Keawe* for the supremacy of Niihau and the possession of the goats left there by Captain Cook, and he had been worsted in the contest. What brought him to Oahu, and what part he played there during those troublous times, is not well known. After the overthrow and death of *Kahahana* he probably returned to Oahu in the hope that the chapter of accidents might prepare a way for him to recover the throne that his father had lost.

hogs, under pretext that they belonged to *Kahekili.* Indignant at this tyranny and oppression, the country people rose in arms and a civil war commenced. *Kukeawe* called the military forces left by *Kahekili* at Wailuku to his assistance; a series of battles were fought, and finally *Kukeawe* was killed at Kamaole-i-kai, near Palauea, and the revolted farmers remained masters of the situation.

When *Kahekili* was informed of this disturbance and its upshot, he appointed his eldest son and heir-apparent, *Kalanikupule*, as regent of Maui, and sent him back there at once with a number of chiefs to restore order and to pacify the people, while he himself preferred to remain on Oahu to ensure its subjection and to reorganise that newly conquered kingdom.

Kalanikupule departed for Maui, accompanied by his aunt, *Kalola*, the widow of *Kalaniopuu*, and by her new husband, *Kaopuiki*; by her daughters, *Kekuiapoiwa Liliha*, widow of *Kiwalao*, and *Kalanikauikikilo*; and by her granddaughter, *Keopuolani*. His brother *Koalaukane*, and his uncle *Kamohomoho*, and a noted warrior chief named *Kapakahili*, were also sent off as his aids and counsellors. *Kalanikupule's* personal popularity, his affable manners, and the supreme authority vested in him, soon tranquillised the revolted country people, who had only risen in defence of their own property against the unauthorised oppression of *Kukeawe*, and peace and order was again established on Maui.

While the events above narrated were transpiring on Oahu and on Maui, *Kamehameha I.* had fought and won the battle of Mokuohai, in which *Kiwalao*, the son and successor of *Kalaniopuu*, was slain, had assumed the sovereignty of the districts of Kona, Kohala, and Hamakua, on Hawaii, and was carrying on desultory war with *Keawemauhili* and *Keouakuahuula*, the independent chiefs of Hilo and Kau, with varying and not very marked success. Towards the close of the year 1785 or beginning of 1786, during a truce between the contending chiefs on Hawaii, *Kamehameha I.*, probably considering the defenceless condition of Maui on account of the absence of most of the prominent chiefs with *Kahekili* on Oahu, and deeming the opportunity favourable, fitted out an expedition under command of his younger brother, *Kalanimalokuloku-i-kapookalani,* to retake the districts of Hana and Kipahulu which had been reconquered by *Kahekili* during the last year of *Kalaniopuu's* life. The expedition landed successfully, and soon took possession of the coveted districts. Contrary to all previous practice, *Malokuloku* scrupulously caused to be respected the private property of the country people and farmers, and thereby not only secured the good-will of the inhabitants towards the Hawaii invaders, but earned for himself the sobriquet of *Keliimaikai* (the good chief), by which he was ever after known.

As soon as *Kalanikupule* received tidings of this invasion, he immediately sent *Kamohomoho* with what forces he could muster to drive the invaders out of Maui. The hostile armies met on the Kipahulu side of the Lelekea gulch, and the battle waged with great fierceness. After hard fighting the Hawaii troops were driven back as far as Maulili, in Kipahulu, where they were joined by a reinforcement under *Kahanaumaikai*, and the battle continued. But victory rested with the Maui troops, and what were not killed of the Hawaii expedition fled back to Kohala. *Keliimaikai* narrowly escaped with his life, and would have been captured but for his timely rescue by his Kahu, *Mulihele,* who hid him until nightfall, when, by the assistance of the country people, whom his kind treatment had conciliated, he obtained a passage over to Hawaii; and it was remarked of *Kamehameha*, as an instance of his love for this younger brother, that he was more rejoiced at his safe return than grieved at the loss of the expedition.

It was in this year, 1786, that the first vessels after the death of Captain Cook visited the Hawaiian Islands.

The "King George" and "Queen Charlotte," from London, commanded by Captains Portlock and Dixon, touched at Kealakeakua Bay on the 26th of May; but finding the natives troublesome, and no chief of apparently sufficient authority to keep them in order, they left on the 27th, touched off the east point of Oahu on 1st June, anchored at Waialae Bay on 3d June, discovered Waikiki Bay as a preferable anchoring ground,[1] and touched at Waimea, Kauai, on the 13th June. In the fall of that year those ships returned to the islands, again visiting Hawaii, Maui, Oahu, and Kauai, for the purposes of trade. Having anchored off Waikiki,[2] *Kahekili* came on board, and during their stay treated them hospitably and kindly.[3] In December of that year, while at Kauai, they met with *Kaeo*, the principal chief, and *Kaiana*,[4] who appears to have found a refuge there from the dire vengeance which *Kahekili* had executed upon the Oahu chiefs and their sympathisers.

On the 28th May 1786, La Perouse, commanding the French exploring expedition, anchored near Lahaina on Maui. He was favourably received, but did not meet with *Kahekili*, who was then on Oahu.

In August 1787, Captain Meares in the ship "Nootka"

---

[1] Portlock says that he found the country "populous and well cultivated."

[2] On December 1, 1786, Portlock describes *Kahekili* as "an exceedingly stout, well-made man, about fifty years old, and appears to be sensible, well disposed, and much esteemed by his subjects." He says further, that at that time *Kahekili* drank no awa, nor would he touch any spirits or wines that were offered him on board.

[3] Jarves, quoting from Portlock's "Voyage Round the World," says that "an old priest who came frequently on board informed Captain Portlock that there was a plot brewing to cut off both vessels. As no other evidence of such a design transpired, it was either a false report, or effectually checked by the vigilance constantly displayed by the crews, and dread of firearms, the effect of which the king, at his request, had been shown." The native accounts make no mention of any such plot.

[4] Jarves, *loc. cit.*, calls *Kaiana* a brother of *Kaeo*. *Kaiana's* mother, *Kaupekamoku*, was a daughter of *Kukaniauaula*, of whom I have no direct genealogy, but whom I have reason to believe was the same as *Papaikaniau*, the wife of the Maui king *Kaulahea*, and grandmother of Kaeo. Hence the high rank which *Kaupekamoku* enjoyed among her contemporaries; and hence *Kaiana* was a cousin of *Kaeo*.

arrived at the islands in company with the "Iphigenia," Captain Douglas. While at Kauai, *Kaiana* embarked with Captain Meares for a voyage to Canton, and was returned the following year in the "Iphigenia;" but *Kaeo* having become inimical to him in his absence, he proceeded in the ship to Hawaii, where at *Kamehameha's* request he landed with his foreign acquired property, including guns, powder, &c., in January 1789. His high aristocratic connections, his well-known personal bravery, his at the time large, miscellaneous, and valuable property, and the fact of his having visited "Kahiki," those foreign lands of which the legends told and of which *Kualii* sang, procured for him a distinction at the court of *Kamehameha*, that in the end turned his head with vanity and ambition and caused his ruin.

At this period a' number of vessels, following in the tracks of those just mentioned, chiefly occupied in the fur trade on the north-west coast of America, visited the islands for refreshments and for trade, touching regularly on their passage to and from China, bartering arms and ammunition with the different chieftains, and not a few runaway seamen from those vessels became scattered over the islands.[1]

Among those trading vessels was the American snow "Eleanor," Captain Metcalf, accompanied by her tender, a small schooner called the "Fair America," under command of the son of Captain Metcalf. The vessels had been trading off the coasts of Hawaii during the winter months of 1789, and, leaving the tender off Hawaii, the larger vessel went over to Maui and anchored off Honuaula in the month of February 1790, and trading was com-

[1] It became quite fashionable for every chief of note to have one or more of these runaway foreigners in his employ. They were not always the best specimens of their class, but they made themselves serviceable as interpreters and factors in trading with the foreign ships; and their skill and adroitness in managing fire-arms, and in many other things hitherto unknown to the Hawaiians, made them valuable to the chiefs, who aided them to run away from their ships, or even kidnapped them if other means failed, as will be seen hereafter.

menced with the natives. The native accounts state that the captain was an irritable and harsh man, and liberal in his use of the rope's-end on trifling provocations; yet trade was continued and his ill-usage submitted to for the gain the common people thought they obtained in the barter of their commodities for those that the foreigner brought them.

Kalola, the widow of *Kalaniopuu,* with her new husband, *Kaopuiki,* and her family, were at this time living at the village of Olowalu, some fifteen miles from where Metcalf's vessel was anchored. Hearing of the arrival of the trading ship at Honuaula, *Kaopuiki* got ready a number of hogs and other produce, and started for Honuaula to trade for musquets, ammunition, and such other articles. It is not known that *Kaopuiki* received any bad usage from Captain Metcalf, although others did; but noticing that the ship's boat was left towing astern during the night, *Kaopuiki* formed the design of getting the boat into his possession. The following night the plan was carried into effect, the boat was cut adrift from the vessel, the watchman, who had fallen asleep in her, was killed, the boat towed ashore and broken up for the sake of the iron fastenings, and *Kaopuiki* and his men returned to Olowalu.

When the loss of the boat and the death of the seaman were ascertained in the morning, Captain Metcalf fired on the people ashore, and took two prisoners, from one of whom belonging to Olowalu it is thought that he received information as to who the party was that had stolen his boat. In a day or two the vessel left her anchorage at Honuaulu and came-to off Olowalu. The following day *Kalola* put on a tabu in connection with some festival or commemoration relating to her own family; the tabu to be binding on all for three days, no canoes to leave the shore, and the being burned alive was the penalty of disobedience. This tabu was called "*Mauumae.*" On the fourth day the tabu was taken off, and the native canoes crowded to the vessel for the purposes of trade. Canoes from the imme-

diate neighbourhood of Olowalu and Ukumehame, from
Lahaina, Kaanapali, and from Lanai, came, in good faith
and suspecting no harm, to exchange their produce for the
coveted articles of the white man's trade.

But Captain Metcalf meditated a terrible revenge for
the loss of his boat and the death of his seaman.[1] As the
canoes collected around the ship, he ordered the guns and
small arms to be loaded, and the unsuspicious natives were
ordered to keep their canoes off the waists of the ship, and
when any strayed either under the bows or the stern, they
were pelted with stones or other missiles until they
rejoined the fleet of canoes lying off either broadside of
the ship waiting for the trade to commence. When all

[1] Jarves in his History, page 69, mentions that "the bones of the murdered seaman and the remains of the boat, for which a reward was offered, had been delivered up ; and the natives supposing the anger of the captain appeased by the attack he had already made, innocently asked for the promised reward. This he said they should have." This circumstance is not referred to in the native accounts, which merely state that when the boat had been towed a long distance from the ship the sleeping sailor woke up and began to cry out for help ; but the ship was then too far off to hear him, and that then, to stop his cries, he was killed and thrown overboard from the boat. No mention of any reward is made, or of the recovery of the bones of the seaman and the remnants of the boat, though such may have been the case. The tragedy enacted at Olowalu was horrible enough without the spice of such accursed perfidy ; yet, if Mr. Young—who was on board of the "Eleanor" at the time, and subsequently resided and died on the islands—had so reported it, it undoubtedly was so. In Vancouver's Voyage, vol. ii., page 136, edition 1798, Vancouver says that "Young stated that on a reward being offered for the boat and the man, Mr. Metcalf was informed that the former was broken to pieces and the latter had been killed. The bones of the man were then demanded, which, with the stem and the stern-post of the boat, were carried on board the snow in about three days." On demanding their reward, "Mr. Metcalf replied they should have it, and immediately ordered all the guns to be loaded and fired among the canoes." But Mr. Young was dead some years before Mr. Jarves arrived, and as Mr. Dibble, who knew Mr. Young well in his lifetime, says nothing in his History of the islands of the recovery of the remains or of the promised reward, on which the native narrative is equally silent, I am inclined to think that either Young's memory was somewhat confused, or that Vancouver misunderstood Young. The dead seaman thrown overboard in the middle of Maalaea Bay would probably have been food for sharks before it drifted ashore ; and as the boat was taken and broken up at Olowalu, and no communication had with the ship until the day of the massacre, I think the story of the recovery and the reward as *prima facie* doubtful.

was ready, Captain Metcalf mounted on the rail and gave orders to open the ports of the ship, that had hitherto been closed. The guns of the ship, loaded with small shot and grapnel, and the musketry of the sailors, were fired in the crowd of canoes lying within easy range on both sides. The carnage was immense. Over a hundred natives were killed outright, and several hundred more or less seriously wounded. The confusion, the wailing, the rush to escape, was indescribable.[1]

After this cruel and wanton vengeance on an innocent and unsuspecting multitude—for the main trespasser, *Keopuiki,* was not among the slain, and does not appear to have been afloat that day—Captain Metcalf lifted his anchor and proceeded to Hawaii to join his tender, the " Fair American."

It was probably in the morning of the 17th March 1790 that the tender was captured off Kaupulehu, in North Kona, by *Kameeiamoku,*[2] a great chief and supporter of *Kamehameha,* and all the crew killed, including Metcalf's son, excepting the mate, Isaac Davis, whose life, from some sudden impulse of compassion, was spared.[3]

---

[1] "The bodies of the slain were dragged for with fish-hooks" (after the vessel had sailed), "and collected in a heap on the beach, where their brains flowed out of their skulls."—*Moolelo Hawaii,* by D. Malo.

[2] Grandson of *Kalanikauleleiaiwi,* wife of *Keawe* of Hawaii. Having gone on board of Metcalf's ship one day, he was, for some reason not recorded, beaten with a rope's-end. Smarting under the indignity offered to him, he vowed to avenge himself on the first foreign vessel that fell in his power. Not long after, the unfortunate tender came in his way. Her crew consisted of only five men and the captain. Fitting out his canoes, *Kameeiamoku* went off to the sloop, taking with him a number of retainers, seven of whom are mentioned by name, and four other chiefs, his relatives—*Kalaukoa, Manukoa, Kanuha,* and *Keakaokalani*—and a quantity of trade as a pretext for boarding. At a given signal the crew were attacked, young Metcalf thrown overboard and drowned, and the rest of the crew killed except Isaac Davis.

Vancouver relates (p. 137, vol. ii.), that on the 22d March *Kamehameha I.* and Young set out for where the schooner was, that he severely reprimanded *Kameeiamoku* for his breach of hospitality and inhumanity, and ordered the schooner to be delivered up to him in order to be restored to the owner. *Kamehameha I.* also took the wounded Davis under his special care and as a companion to Young.

[3] See Vancouver for particulars, vol. ii. p. 139, ed. 1798.

The vessel was hauled ashore, the booty of guns, ammunition, articles of trade, and the wounded prisoner, Davis, were afterwards taken to *Kamehameha,* then stopping at Kealakeakua, where Metcalf's ship, the "Eleanor," was lying. On the same day a party of seamen from the "Eleanor," with the boatswain, John Young, had been ashore. Young, who had wandered inland and been separated from his shipmates, found his return to the beach barred by orders of *Kamehameha,* who, having obtained a quantity of arms and ammunition, was anxious of having a foreigner in his employ who knew how to use them and keep them in order. When the boat's crew returned to the ship, John Young was missing. Captain Metcalf remained two days off the bay, firing guns and awaiting Young's return; but *Kamehameha* having received intelligence of the capture of the tender by *Kameeiamoku,* and having heard of the massacre at Olowalu, would not permit a canoe to leave the beach or go alongside the ship, lest Metcalf should retaliate as he had done on Maui.

The two captive foreigners, Young and Davis, finding their lives secure and themselves treated with deference and kindness, were soon reconciled to their lot, accepted service under *Kamehameha,* and contributed greatly by their valour and skill to the conquests that he won, and by their counsel and tact to the consolidation of those conquests.

It is not clearly stated by native authorities in what manner the feud between *Kamehameha* and *Keawemauhili* of Hilo had been composed. Certain it is that during the summer of this year (1790), *Kamehameha,* assuming the style of "Moi" of Hawaii, sent to *Keawemauhili* of Hilo and *Keoua-Kuahuula* of Kau to furnish him with canoes and troops for a contemplated invasion of Maui. *Keawemauhili* complied with the summons of *Kamehameha,* and sent a large force of men and canoes under command of his own sons *Keaweokahikiona, Eleele* or *Elelule, Koakanu,* and his nephew *Kalaipaihala. Keoua-Kuahuula* positively refused to obey the summons, acknowledging no feudal obligations to *Kamehameha*, and deeming the projected war with Maui as unwise and unprovoked.

Having collected his forces in Kohala, *Kamehameha* crossed the Hawaii channel, making his descent in Hana, and, as the natives say, his canoes covered the beach from Hamoa to Kawaipapa.

When *Kalanikupule* heard of the landing of *Kamehameha* at Hana, and that he was marching with his force through the Koolau district, he sent *Kapakahili* with the best troops he had through the Hamakua districts to meet and resist the progress of the invader.

Of the campaign in Hamakualoa some mementoes are still pointed out. The fortified position at Puukoae on Hanawana, which was attacked and taken by *Kamehameha*, who had brought his fleet round from Hana. The hill is known as "Kapuai-o-Kamehameha," to the west of the Halehaku stream, where he encamped for the night after taking Puukoae. Here his war-god *Kukailimoku* was paraded around the camp, to ascertain by the usual auguries—the more or less erect position of the feathers, &c.—the issue of the campaign; and the answers being favourable, *Kamehameha* engaged *Kapakahili* in battle the following morning. For some time the result was uncertain, but reinforcements having come up to *Kamehameha*, the Maui forces were routed, and fled as far as Kokomo, where a final stand was made. Fighting desperately, and with hardly a hope of retrieving the fortune of the day, *Kapakahili* encountered *Kamehameha* on the field, and one of those single combats ensued in which the fate of an empire depends on the personal prowess of one or the other of the combatants. *Kapakahili* was killed, the Maui men fled and dispersed, and the road to Wailuku lay open to *Kamehameha*.

After this victory *Kamehameha* moved his fleet to Kahului, and hauled up his canoes from there to Hopukoa without opposition. After two days of preparation he marched on to Wailuku, where *Kalanikupule* awaited him with such forces as he had been able to collect. This battle was one of the hardest contested on Hawaiian record. We have no detailed account of the disposition of the forces on either side; we only know that the battle commenced at Wailuku and thence spread up the Iao valley, the Maui army defending valiantly every foot of the ground, but being continually driven farther and farther up the valley, *Kamehameha's* superiority in the number of guns, and the skilful management of the same under the charge of Young and Davis, telling fearfully upon the number of his foes, and finally procuring him the victory. The author has conversed with people who were present at the battle and escaped with their lives, and they all tell that before the battle commenced the women and children, and the aged who could move, were sent up on the mountain-sides of the valley, where they could look down upon the combatants below. They speak of the carnage as frightful, the din and uproar, the shouts of defiance among the fighters, the wailing of the women on the crests of the valley, as something to curdle the blood or madden the brain of the beholder. The Maui troops were completely annihilated, and it is said that the corpses of the slain were so many as to choke up the waters of the stream of Iao, and that hence one of the names of this battle was "Kepaniwai" (the damming of the waters).

Kalanikupule, his brother *Koalaukani, Kamohomoho,* and some other chiefs escaped over the mountain and made their way to Oahu. *Kalaniakua, Kekuiapoiwa Liliha,* and her daughter *Keopuolani,* crossed over to Olowalu, where they joined their mother, *Kalola,* and after a hurried preparation they all left for Molokai, and took up their residence with *Kekuelikenui* at Kalamaula.

It does not appear that *Kamehameha* took any active steps at this time to secure the conquest of Maui by leaving garrisons or organising the government. The island was completely conquered, its fighting force destroyed, its land wasted, and its chiefs seeking refuge on Oahu and Molokai. It is probable that his intention was to follow up his victory by an invasion of Oahu, where *Kahekili* still ruled with unbroken force. But deeming it an object of sound policy to come to some terms with *Kalola*, and, if possible, get her daughters and granddaughter in his possession, he sent a messenger named *Kikane* ahead to Molokai to request of *Kalola* that she would not go to Oahu, but go back with him to Hawaii, where she and her daughters would be provided for as became their high rank. He then re-embarked his forces, and leaving Kahului, sailed to Kaunakakai, on Molokai, deeming it prudent also to secure the adhesion of its chiefs before proceeding to Oahu.

When *Kamehameha* arrived at Kaunakakai he was informed that *Kalola* was very sick and not expected to live long. He at once went over to Kalamaula and had an interview with her, renewing his request that she should confide her daughters and granddaughter to his care and protection. To which *Kalola* is said to have replied, " When I am dead, my daughters and granddaughter shall be yours." Not long after this *Kalola* died and was mourned with the customary rites attending the death of so high a chiefess. The custom of " Moepuu "[1] was observed, so was tattooing and other practices. Even *Kamehameha* had some of his teeth knocked out in token of sorrow. When the mourning season was ended *Kalola's* bones were deposited in Konahele, and *Kamehameha* took charge of her daughters and granddaughter, not only as a legacy from the mother, but as a seal of reconciliation between himself and the older branch of the *Keawe* dynasty, the representatives of *Kiwalao*.

When the funeral rites were finished and the tabus taken off, and the creed and customs of the time permitted business to be attended to, *Kamehameha* dispatched two

[1] See vol. i. p. 108.

messengers to Oahu. One was *Kikane*, above referred to, the other was *Haalou*, the mother of *Namahana*, and grandmother of *Kamehameha's* wife, *Kaahumanu*. The mission of *Kikane* was to *Kahekili;* that of *Haalou* was originally intended for Kauai, to seek some renowned soothsayer, for which that island was famous, and obtain his opinion as to the best way in which to obtain the supremacy of Hawaii for *Kamehameha*.

Kikane presented himself before *Kahekili* at Waikiki, and in the name of *Kamehameha* offered him two Maika-stones, "Ulu-maika," one black and the other white. *Kahekili* looked at them and said, "This one (the white) represents agriculture, fishing, husbandry, and the prosperity of the government; that one (the black), is a symbol of war. Does *Kamehameha* want to go to war with Oahu?" On *Kikane* replying that such was *Kamehameha's* intention, and that he had been sent as a herald to arrange with *Kahekili* in a courteous and chiefly manner about the place of landing and the field of battle, *Kahekili*, after some consideration of the various plans proposed by *Kikane*, replied, "Go, tell *Kamehameha* to return to Hawaii, and when he learns that the black kapa covers the body of *Kahekili* and the sacrificial rites have been performed at his funeral,[1] then Hawaii shall be the Maika-stone that will sweep the course from here to Tahiti; let him then come and possess the country." *Kikane* then presented one more request from *Kamehameha*, which was for the gods *Olopue* and *Kalaipahoa*.[2]

[1] "*A kau ka puaa i ka nuku*," lit., "when the hog has been placed at his nose." This was one of the sacrificial observances on the demise of high chiefs, and is used as a trope to indicate the entire funeral ceremony. The offering of hogs in sacrifice on the death of a person, especially a chief, was a mark of respect similar to that offered to the idols of the gods ; and the savour of the baked animal was supposed to refresh and comfort the spirit of the defunct, still hovering about its mortal remains.

[2] *Olopue* or *Ololupe* was a god who conducted the spirits of chiefs to their final abode after death, and assisted them on the journey. This god was greatly feared by the warrior chiefs of olden times.

Kalaipahoa. This god was made of the wood of the Nioi tree, in which his spirit or essence was supposed to reside. It was an exceedingly poison-

Kahekili gave him a chip of the *Kalaipahoa*, but the *Olopue* was in charge of the high-priest *Kaopuhuluhulu*, and *Kikane* did not obtain it for his master.

Haalou's mission was more successful. Arrived at Oahu, she was spared the further journey to Kauai by finding the object of her search at Kamoku in Waikiki. His name was *Kapoukahi*. He was a Kauai man, and related to *Haalou's* grandmother *Kaneikaheilani*. Hence he received her overtures kindly, and in reply to her inquiries, instructed her to tell *Kamehameha* to build a large Heiau for his god at Puukohola, adjoining the old Heiau of Mailekini near Kawaihae, Hawaii; that done, he would be supreme over Hawaii without more loss of life.

Having accomplished their errands, *Kikane* and *Haalou* returned to *Kamehameha* on Molokai.

While these events transpired on Maui and Molokai, *Kamehameha's* power on Hawaii was seriously threatened. When *Keouakuahuula* heard of the assistance in men and canoes which *Keawemauhili* of Hilo had furnished to *Kamehameha* on his expedition to Maui, he was greatly irritated, and considered it as a breach of the agreement between them to jointly oppose *Kamehameha's* pretensions to sovereignty. To punish, therefore, his former ally, *Keoua* invaded Hilo. A battle was fought at Alae in Hilo-paliku, in which *Keawemauhili* was killed, and *Keoua* added the district of Hilo to his own possessions of Puna and Kau. Elated with his victory, he entered *Kamehameha's* estates, overran Hamakua, destroying valuable fish ponds and taro patches at Waipio, and plundering the inhabitants. From Waipio he crossed over to Waimea in Kohala, committing similar ravages and barbarities.

---

ous wood, said to have been found only on Mounaloa, Molokai, though I have heard it said that it was also found on Lanai. That species of the Nioi is now extinct. The least particle of the wood inserted in the food or drink was sure to kill the consumer. It is said to have been discovered by *Kaiakea* of Molokai, at least its uses, or rather abuses, were greatly in vogue in the latter part of his generation.

When the news of these transactions by *Keoua* reached *Kamehameha* at Kaunakakai, he was deeply moved at the death of his uncle *Keawemauhili,* and at the ravages and cruelties committed on his people and possessions by *Keoua.* All thoughts of invading Oahu, even of securing Maui, were given up, for a season at least, for the one imperious necessity of hastening back to Hawaii to protect his own estates and to punish the audacious *Keoua.* Gathering his army and his fleet together, *Kamehameha* evacuated Maui and Molokai, and returned to Hawaii.

This brings us to the latter months of the year 1790, for it is known that the eruption of Kilauea, which destroyed a portion of *Keoua's* army on its return to Kau, took place in November 1790.

The abrupt departure of *Kamehameha* and his fleet from Molokai and his return to Hawaii took a great weight off the mind of *Kahekili,* and plans of vengeance, if not of aggrandisement, occupied his thoughts and brightened his vision in the immediate future. He was doubtless encouraged by *Kaeokulani,* who by this time had obtained the supremacy of Kauai, and who urged upon his aged brother the golden opportunity of *Kamehameha's* difficulties with *Keoua-kuahuula* to avenge the defeat of *Kalanikupule* on Maui, and to deal a crushing blow to the growing power of *Kamehameha.* Negotiations and preparations having been perfected between the Kauai and Oahu sovereigns during the winter months of 1790–91, *Kaeokulani* left Kauai with a well-equipped fleet of war canoes, accompanied by his nephew *Peapea,*[1] his military commanders *Kiikiki* and *Kaiawa,* his foreign gunner Mare Amara,[2] and a number of ferocious trained dogs, and arrived at Oahu in the spring of 1791.

---

[1] *Peapea* was a son of *Kamehameha-nui,* already referred to.

[2] Who this man was and in what ship he arrived at the islands, I am unable to say. His first name was "Mare," Hawaiianised, but the second name, "Amara," is but the Hawaiian corruption of the English "Armourer." The man was probably the gunner or blacksmith of some of the foreign vessels trading at the islands.

Kahekili appointed his son *Kalanikupule* as regent of Oahu during his absence, and the combined fleets of *Kahekili* and *Kaeokulani* started for the Windward Islands. Making a short stay at Kaunakakai, Molokai, the fleet passed to the windward side of Maui, and landed for a while at Waihee and Waiehu. It would appear from subsequent facts as if some convention or stipulation had been agreed upon between *Kahekili* and *Kaeokulani*, in virtue whereof *Kahekili* had transferred, either provisionally or permanently, the sovereign authority over Maui to *Kaeo*. Certain it is that the latter on his arrival, commenced to divide up the island, apportioning the various districts among the Kauai chiefs and warriors. This proceeding gave great umbrage to the sons of *Kahekili* and to the ancient Maui chiefs, and came near breaking up the entire expedition of the two kings. A quarrel and an *émeute* arose on this subject at Paukukalo, near Waiehu, between the Kauai and Maui chiefs, in which *Koalaukani*, one of the sons of *Kahekili*, greatly distinguished himself for his bravery against a vastly superior number of Kauai warriors.

In some way not now particularly remembered, this misadventure was smoothed over without more serious results, and the two fleets left Waiehu, *Kaeokulani* going round by the Koolau side to Hana to recruit, and *Kahekili* going farther on to Mokulau in Kaupo, for the same purpose. It is reported that while at Hana, *Kaeokulani* ascended the famous hill of Kauwiki, and, in a spirit of bravado, threw his spear up into the air, exclaiming, " It is said of old that the sky comes down close to Hana, but I find it quite high, for I have thrown my spear, ' Kamoolehua,' and it did not pierce the sky, and I doubt if it will hit *Kamehameha;* but hearken, O Kauai ! you chiefs, warriors, and relations, be strong and be valiant, and we shall drink the water of Waipio and eat the taro of Kunaka."

Leaving Hana, the fleet of *Kaeokulani* sailed direct for

Waipio, Hawaii, where he landed his troops and ravaged the valley thoroughly. The acts of spoliation and barbarity committed on this occasion were the common occurrence of war in those days, and would not of themselves have stained the memory of *Kaeokulani* in the native estimation; but his disregard and desecration of the ancient tabu places, the tearing up and overturning the sacred pavement of *Liloa*, the burning of the sacred pepper-tree supports of the ancient palace of the Hawaiian kings, said to have been built by *Kahoukapu*, and his general demolition and destruction of all the sacred and valued mementoes of ancient times, in which that valley was so rich,—these and similar acts were regarded as unpardonable acts of vandalism, for which the insulted gods and "Aumakuas" would in due time exact a condign and fearful punishment.

While these outrages of the Hawaiian public sentiment were perpetrated by *Kaeokulani* in Waipio, the *Kahekili* division of the fleet, leaving Mokulau, had landed at Halawa in the Kohala district of Hawaii, and after various desultory and unimportant skirmishes with the troops of *Kamehameha*, proceeded to join *Kaeokulani* at Waipio.

Kamehameha was in the Kona district when he received the tidings of the invasion of *Kahekili* and *Kaeokulani*. His preparations to repel the invasion were not long in being perfected. Collecting a large fleet of double canoes, many of which were filled with small cannon obtained from traders, and with the sloop which *Kameeiamoku* had captured from the ship "Eleanor" the preceding year,[1] he

---

[1] So the native account collected by S. M. Kamakau says; but Vancouver, in vol. ii. p. 165, says that in March 1793 the sloop was lying in a creek about four miles from Kealakeakua, where she had been hauled up, and was fast decaying for want of necessary repairs. The impression is obtained from Vancouver's recital of what Young and Davis told him that the vessel had not been used since she was captured. But Vancouver does nowhere state that Young and Davis had told him of their accompanying *Kamehameha* in his campaigns, while at the same time he expressly states that for a long time after their capture they invariably accompanied *Kamehameha* wherever he went. The silence of Vancouver is, therefore, no denial of the correctness of the native account.

started for Waipio, placing John Young and Isaac Davis in command of his artillery. Not far from Waipio, near the Pali Hulaana of Waimanu, the hostile fleets met, and the first naval battle was fought in Hawaiian waters in which modern gunnery formed a conspicuous element of strength on both sides. No particulars of this battle have been handed down; no chief of any prominence lost his life in this engagement. It is said, however, to have been sanguinary, and many lives and not a few canoes on either side were lost of whom Hawaiian fame had made no note ; but the artillery of *Kamehameha* seems to have been too heavy or too well served for his foes, as he remained master of the situation; and *Kahekili* and *Kaeokulani* returned to Hana in Maui with their shattered fleet, and with no farther thoughts of invading Hawaii, fortunate if they might be able to defend Maui from the retaliatory invasion by *Kamehameha*, which they certainly expected, and which they are known to have strained all their resources to frustrate.

This sea-fight off Waipio is remembered by the natives under the name of "*Ke-pu-waha-ula-ula*" and also of "*Kawai.*" It occurred in 1791, before the death of *Keoua Kuahuula*.

Some time after this, *Peapea Makawalu*, the nephew of *Kahekili* and *Kaeo*, was fatally wounded by the explosion of a keg of gunpowder on the hill of Kauwiki. He was removed to Honokohau in the Kaanapali district, where he shortly afterwards died from his wounds.[1]

Kahekili and *Kaeo* remained on Maui during the winter of 1791 and during the whole of the year 1792. It was during this latter year that Captain Vancouver, commanding H.B.S.S. "Discovery" and "Chatham," arrived at these islands. Touching at Kealakeakua Bay on Hawaii on 3d

---

[1] Vancouver in his "Voyage of Discovery," vol. iii., says that in March 1794 he heard from the natives of Maui that *Peapea*, whom he calls by his other name *Namahana*, had only a short time before been killed by an explosion of gunpowder.

March, he inquired after *Kalaniopuu*, and learned that he was dead. *Kamehameha* being absent,[1] Vancouver, passing by Maui without stopping, proceeded to Oahu and anchored off Waikiki on 7th March. There he learnt that *Kahekili* and *Kaeo* were absent on Molokai or Maui making preparations to repel an expected invasion by *Kamehameha*, and no person of distinction appearing, he left Oahu on the 8th and anchored at Waimea, Kauai, on the 9th, and left there for the north-west coast of America on the 14th of the same month.

The political situation of the islands of this group at this period may be concisely stated in this way. On Hawaii *Kamehameha* and *Keoua Kuahuula* were still contending for the sovereignty of the island, though *Keoua's* strength was gradually being exhausted. The great Heiau of Puukohola had been built, yet *Keoua* stubbornly defended himself, and his subjection by war seemed as distant as ever. By false representations and promises of safety he was induced during the fall of this year or early in 1792 to go to Kawaihae to confer with *Kamehameha*, and on his arrival was treacherously killed and sacrificed at the Heiau. On Maui, Molokai, and Oahu, *Kahekili* was still the recognised actual sovereign, but owing to his great age and feeble health the regency of Oahu and Molokai was intrusted to his son *Kalanikupule;* and his brother *Kaeokulani* remained with him on Maui to administer the affairs of that island, while the government of Kauai and the guardianship of *Kaeokulani's* son, *Kaumualii,* the legitimate Moi of Kauai, was intrusted to a high chief named *Nakaikuaana.*[2]

As Oahu had virtually lost its autonomy on the overthrow and death of *Kahahana*, the events connected with

[1] On 5th March Vancouver stopped off Kawaihae, where he saw *Keeaumoku,* and gave him some goats, seeds, &c.

[2] Such is his name in the native accounts. Vancouver calls him always by the name of *Enemo*, and says that his other name was *Wakea;* and it is said that he was a brother of *Kaahumanu*, one of *Kamehameha's* wives. The real name and the lineage of this chief are unknown to me.

its history may properly be referred to under the reigns of the Maui kings.

Vancouver's visit to Oahu in March 1792 left no special recollections in the native mind but the to them singular and inexplicable fact that these two foreign vessels positively refused to barter guns, ammunition, and arms for hogs, potatoes, or refreshments of any kind that might be offered. The foreign traders who had visited the islands since their discovery by Captain Cook had so recklessly pandered to the lust of the native chieftains to possess fire-arms and ammunition, used only for their own destruction, that they could not appreciate the humane motive of Vancouver in his refusal, and his reception, though civil and without any untoward accidents, was proportionately cool.

On the 7th of May 1792 the English national ship "Dædalus," acting as a storeship for Vancouver's expedition, and under command of Lieutenant Hergest, arrived off the north coast of Oahu, and standing in for the land, came-to off the mouth of the Waimea stream, in the Koolauloa district. While lying off and on in this roadstead a party was sent ashore on the 11th to procure fresh water, accompanied by Lieutenant Hergest and Mr. Gooch, the astronomer.

The result of this watering-party was unfortunate, and another tragedy was enacted, which, although entirely unprovoked by the foreigners, has not received a moiety of the sympathy and comments from the civilised world which have shed such a halo over the memory of Cook as a martyr to science. Lieutenant Hergest and Mr. Gooch were foully murdered by the natives of Waimea, on set purpose, for the sake of plunder. By his own harsh and injudicious conduct Captain Cook drove the natives of Kealakeakua into open resistance, and fell ingloriously in an affray of his own seeking. In thus expressing myself, I only give utterance, as an historian, to what I know to be the native national sentiment on the subject. The Hawaiians never felt that they were in the wrong, or admitted that they were to blame for the death of Captain Cook, but they freely admit that they were solely to blame for the deaths of Lieutenant Hergest and Mr. Gooch, and they acquiesced then in, and appreciate now, the justice of Vancouver's proceedings in that regard the following year.

By comparing the native narratives of this transaction at Waimea with that of Vancouver and other foreign writers, I think the following will contain briefly the substantial facts of the case.

After the repulse of *Kahekili* and *Kaeokulani* in the naval engagement called "Kepuwahaulaula," off the Pali Hulaana, on the Hamakua coast of Hawaii, the inferiority of firearms on the losing side had become disastrously manifest, and a desire to obtain a more abundant supply became the dominant passion of the chiefs who had shared and lost in the above-mentioned campaign. Whether *Kahekili* or *Kaeo* ordered or countenanced any violent measures against foreign vessels or their crews for the purpose of obtaining arms is doubtful, and has never been charged against them by the foreigners nor admitted by the natives.[1] But it is tolerably clear that *Kalanikupule*, *Kahekili's* viceroi on Oahu, had instructed his chiefs and military officers, or at least that they so understood his instructions, that although he was not willing to compromise himself by allowing violent measures or treatment of foreign vessels or their crews at the principal trading port at Waikiki, where he himself resided, yet violent measures, if successful in obtaining guns, side-arms, and ammunition—peaceful barter failing—from any vessels that might touch at the out-of-way districts of the island, would not only not be punished, but would be looked upon and rewarded as a service rendered to the state or the sovereign.

---

[1] Vancouver distinctly exculpates *Kahekili* and *Kaeo* from any complicity, direct or indirect, in this sad affair.

When, therefore, *Koi*[1]—a military chief who had shared in the late campaign against Hawaii, and was now stationed in the neighbourhood of Waimea—observed the arrival of the "Dædalus" and the landing of the watering-party, he laid his plans to obtain some of the coveted articles.

The watering-party, finding the water near the mouth of the stream rather brackish, rolled their casks some distance farther up, where the water was thoroughly fresh. Having filled their casks, the seamen were rolling them to the sea, assisted or impeded, as the case might be, by the natives that were crowding around them. In this general scramble a dispute arose between the seamen and the natives, a melee ensued, in which a Portuguese sailor was killed,[2] and the rest of the sailors escaped on board of their boats that were laying off the mouth of the river. Meanwhile Lieutenant Hergest and Mr. Gooch had been enticed away from the watering-party by *Koi* and his men, under pretext of selling them some fine hogs and vegetables, when suddenly they were attacked with stones,[3] knocked down, and killed. The boats with the watering-party on board fired on the natives on the beach. The "Dædalus," seeing the boats firing, brought her broadside to bear on the scene and fired for some time up the valley, but apparently no great damage was done to the natives. That evening the "Dædalus" stood off to sea, and proceeded to join the Vancouver expedition on the north-west coast of America.[4]

[1] *Koi* was an important personage among the courtiers of *Kahekili.* He was also a priest of the *Kaleopuu-puu* family, and to him belonged the Heiau and the grounds at Kapokea, in Waihee, Maui.

[2] The native accounts make no mention of killing the Portuguese sailor. They state that the sailors, seeing the natives surrounding and stoning Lieutenant Hergest and Mr. Gooch, deserted their water-casks

that they were rolling to the sea, and ran speedily to the boats and commenced firing on the natives.

[3] *Kapaleaiuku* and *Kuania* were the two men of *Koi's* following who commenced throwing stones at the two officers.

[4] The account given by Captain Vancouver, vol. ii. p. 96, as he received it from Mr. New, the master of the "Dædalus," is as follows :—

"In the morning of the 7th of May

THE POLYNESIAN RACE. 249

The guns, pistols, side-arms, &c., of the killed foreigners
were secured by *Koi*, their bodies taken to Mokuleia, in
the Waialua district, where they were dissected and the
bones kept for future use ; and in due time *Koi* presented
himself at Waikiki before *Kalanikupule* with the spoils
which he had obtained, and, as the native legend says,
Kalanikupule was greatly rejoiced at the acquisition to
his armoury.

In the spring of 1793 Vancouver returned from the
coast of America to the Hawaiian group, and anchored
off Kawaihae, Hawaii, on 13th February. Having been
kindly and liberally entertained by *Kamehameha* and the
Hawaii chiefs, to whom he had brought some cattle from
California, and having fully discussed, and, as he thought,
satisfactorily arranged a plan for the pacification of the

the 'Dædalus' arrived in that bay
where the 'Resolution' and 'Discovery' had anchored in 1779, but
Mr. Hergest declined anchoring there,
as he considered the inhabitants of
that neighbourhood to be the most
savage and deceitful of any amongst
those islands. For this reason he lay
to, and purchased from the natives
some hogs, vegetables, and a few
gourds of water. In the evening he
stood off shore, and desired that the
inhabitants would bring a farther
supply of water and refreshments
the next morning; but it falling
calm, and the current setting the
ship to the westward, it was near
noon on the 11th before they regained
the shore, when Mr. Hergest receded
from his former wise determination,
and, unhappily for himself and those
who fell with him, ordered the ship
to be anchored. The cutter was
hoisted out and veered astern for
the better convenience of purchasing
water from the natives, but before
three casks were filled, which was
soon done, he ordered the cutter
alongside, the full casks to be taken
out and replaced by empty ones ; and

then, accompanied as usual by Mr.
Gooch, he went on shore, and another
boat was hoisted out for the purpose
of obtaining water, while those on
board continued making purchases
until near dusk. At this time the
cutter returned with only five persons instead of the eight who had
gone on shore in her, from whom was
learned the distressing intelligence
that Mr. Hergest and Mr. Gooch, and
two of the boat's crew, having landed
unarmed with two of the water-casks
to fill, their defenceless situation was
perceived by the natives, who immediately attacked them, killed one of
the people, and carried off the commander and the astronomer. The
other, being a very stout active man,
made his escape through a great
number of these savages, fled to the
boat, and with two others landed
again with two muskets, and with the
intention to rescue their officers and
to recover the body of their messmate.
They soon perceived that both Mr.
Hergest and Mr. Gooch were yet
alive amongst a vast concourse of the
inhabitants, who were stripping them
and forcing them up the hills behind

islands, Vancouver left Kealakeakua on 8th March, and touching at Kawaihae on the 9th, anchored in Maalaea Bay, Maui, on the 11th, having the previous evening, while to the eastward of Molokini, fallen in with a canoe purporting to have been sent by *Kahekili* to inquire who he was and what his intentions. Vancouver returned a satisfactory answer, and despatched the chief in command of the canoe with a suitable present for *Kahekili*.

About noon of the 11th *Kamohomoho* arrived at Maalaea and informed Vancouver that he had been sent by *Kahekili* to pilot the ship to Lahaina. That same evening the " Discovery " and the " Chatham " anchored off Lahaina.

Vancouver's description of Lahaina, as it was in 1793, may interest the Hawaiian reader. He says:[1]

" The village of Raheina is of some extent towards the

the village; they endeavoured to get near the multitude, but were so assailed by stones from the crowd, who had now gained the surrounding hills, that they were under the painful necessity of retiring; and as night was fast approaching, they thought it most advisable to return on board, that more effectual means might be resorted to on this unfortunate occasion.

" Mr. New immediately assembled all the officers, to consult with them what was best to be done. It was agreed to stand off and on with the ship during the night, and in the morning to send the cutter, well manned and armed, on shore, and if possible to recover their unfortunate commander and shipmates. An old chief belonging to Attowai, who had been on board since the ' Dædalus ' entered the bay, and had been promised by Mr. Hergest a passage to his native island, went also in the boat to assist as interpreter, and went towards the natives, of whom he demanded the absent gentlemen, on which he was informed they were both killed the preceding night. Having delivered this message, he

was sent back to demand their bodies, but was told in reply that they had both been cut in pieces and divided among seven different chiefs; at least it was so understood by those in the boat from the language and signs which the chief made use of.

"After this conversation the savages came in great numbers towards the seaside and threw stones at the party in the boat, who fired several times, and at length obliged them to retire. Finding their errand to be completely fruitless, the boat returned on board, in which the old chief re-embarked, and the vessel bore away to land him, agreeably to a former promise, at Attowai; but when they were about five or six leagues to leeward of Woahoo, about five in the evening, the old chief made a sudden spring overboard and swam from the ship, which was instantly brought to; but on finding that he still continued to swim from them, without the least inclination of returning on board, they filled their sails, and having then no business at Attowai, they made the best of their way towards Nootka, agreeably to my directions."

[1] Vol. ii. p. 176.

north-west part of the roadstead. It seemed to be plea-
santly situated on a space of low or rather gently elevated
land, in the midst of a grove of bread-fruit, cocoa-nut, and
other trees. To the eastward the country seemed nearly
barren and uncultivated, and the shores were bounded by
a reef, on which the surf seemed to break with so much
force as to preclude any landing with our boats. In the
village the houses seemed to be numerous and to be well
inhabited. A few of the natives visited the ships ; these
brought but little with them, and most of them were in
very small miserable canoes. These circumstances strongly
indicated their poverty, and proved what had been frequently asserted at Owhyhee, that Mowee and its neighbouring islands were reduced to great indigence by the
wars in which for many years they had been engaged."

While on Hawaii, Vancouver had been told that three
of the murderers of Lieutenant Hergest of the " Dædalus "
had been put to death by the orders of *Kahekili ;* but he
was also told there that those murders were premeditated [1]
by them (*Kahekili* and *Kaeo*), and committed by their
express orders, for the sole purpose of revenging a difference
that had happened between them and Mr. Ingraham.[2]
He was assured, however, by *Kamohomoho* and *Kahekili*
that such was not the case ; that not only had no such
orders been issued by *Kahekili* or *Kaeo*, nor had any chief
been connected with the murder of the " Dædalus' " people,
but that it had been perpetrated by a lawless gang living
on that side of Oahu ; and that as soon as they (*Kahekili*
and *Kaeo*) became acquainted with the sad event, they
had immediately sent orders to Oahu to arrest and put to
death those who were guilty of the murder, and that in
consequence three of the most prominent of the gang had
been executed, three or four others equally guilty having
escaped to the mountains and eluded pursuit for a long
time. As Vancouver insisted that those men should also
be caught and punished by their own chiefs as a warning

[1] Vol. ii. p. 177.   [2] Of the " Hope," a North-West trader.

to others, it was arranged that *Kamohomoho* should accompany him to Oahu in order to see *Kahekili's* orders to that effect duly executed.

During his stay on Hawaii, Vancouver had taken great pains to impress upon *Kamehameha* and his chiefs the necessity, propriety, and mutual advantages of the island chiefs living in peace and harmony with one another, instead of impoverishing each other by continual wars and the destruction of people and property. Though the Hawaii chiefs were rather reluctant to accede to this new peace policy, they finally agreed that if Vancouver could induce *Kahekili* and *Kaeo*—whom they greatly distrusted— to enter honestly and fairly into such an arrangement, they would be content with Hawaii for themselves, and leave Maui and the leeward islands to *Kahekili* and *Kaeo.* Acting upon this understanding, Vancouver lost no time, after his arrival at Lahaina, to lay before *Kahekili* and the Maui chiefs there assembled the propositions of *Kamehameha* and the Hawaii chiefs, backed by his own serious recommendations. *Kahekili* and the chiefs listened attentively, admitted the great benefit that would accrue to their country from a period of peace and rest, but that they knew *Kamehameha* too well to place any reliance upon his promises to keep the peace. He was ambitious of fame, they said, and greedy of possessions. Their jealousy and mistrust of *Kamehameha* was apparently deep rooted and not easily overcome. After a lengthy discussion the meeting was adjourned till the following day, when *Kaeo*, who was now on Molokai, would have returned. On the 13th March, *Kaeo* being present, the subject was resumed, and it was proposed that Vancouver should return to Hawaii with *Kaeo* on board as ambassador from *Kahekili*, and that then and there, under the eyes of Vancouver, the treaty of peace should be negotiated and concluded. With this Vancouver stated his inability to comply, on account of the limited time at his disposition ; but he proposed to send a letter to John Young, asking

him to notify *Kamehameha* that *Kahekili* and the Maui
chiefs were willing to enter into a treaty of peace on the
conditions agreed upon between *Kamehameha* and Vancouver, and that a prominent chief should be sent with
this letter, assuring them that on receipt of said letter
Kamehameha would assemble his chiefs and ratify the
peace thus concluded, adding that if *Kamehameha* should
refuse, he, Vancouver, would withdraw his friendship and
favour from him and his island. To this proposition
Kahekili, Kaeo, and the other chiefs agreed, and a high
chief, whom Vancouver calls *Martier,*[1] was appointed to
carry the letter to Hawaii and conclude the negotiations.
The great good-will and disinterested endeavours of Vancouver to establish a peace between the Hawaii and Maui
sovereigns unfortunately came to nothing. Though the
native historians make no mention of this transaction,
either in the life of *Kamehameha* or that of *Kahekili,* yet
we gather from what Vancouver says, on his return that
winter to the islands, that the Maui chiefs appear to have
performed their part of the plan proposed by Vancouver.
He then learned[2] that a small party had arrived from
Maui on the west coast of Hawaii, but had been driven
away by the inhabitants. Several versions of the affair
were told to Vancouver, and this is what he says :—

"Immediately on my arrival here I inquired if my
letter from Mowee had been received, and received an
answer in the negative. But I was given to understand
that a small party from that island had arrived on the
western side of Owhyhee, whose object was suspected to
be that of seizing some of the inhabitants there for the
purpose of taking them away and of sacrificing them in
their religious rites at Mowee; and some reports went
so far as to assert that this diabolical object had been
effected. On farther inquiry, however, this fact appeared

---

[1] Who this chief may have been I
am unable to tell. The name as
Vancouver gives it bears no resemblance to any known chief's name
of that time. The English of that
day made sad havoc of Polynesian
names.
[2] Vol. iii. p. 49.

to be by no means established, as it was positively insisted on by some, and by others as positively denied. One circumstance, however, both parties agreed in—that of the people from Mowee having been under the necessity of making a hasty retreat. I could not understand that any chief was in the neighbourhood of the place where they had landed ; and *Tamaahmaah* himself, either from a conviction that they had been unfairly dealt with, or that I should disapprove of the suspicious narrow policy that had influenced the conduct of his people on this occasion, was unwilling to allow that he had been made duly acquainted with their arrival, and was always desirous of avoiding the subject in conversation.

" After many attempts to fix his attention, I at length explained to him what was the result of my negotiation with the chiefs at Mowee ; and he then seemed to concur in opinion with me, that the party from Mowee who had landed on the western side of Owhyhee, could be no other than the embassy charged with my letter and invested with powers to negotiate for a general pacification."

Although Vancouver's kindly disposition accepts the foregoing explanation, and appears loath to charge the failure of the Maui embassy to *Kamehameha* or his chief counsellors, yet to those acquainted with the character of the people and the spirit of that time, the desire to please and the fear to offend those whom they looked upon as present friends and possible auxiliaries in their dreams of conquest, their power of equivoques and peculiarity of expressing them, to such the hesitating "*pelapaha*," [1] with which *Kamehameha* seemed to concur in opinion with Vancouver, joined to his " unwillingness to allow that he had been made duly acquainted," &c., and "desire of avoiding the subject in conversation," would be good if indirect proofs of his knowledge of and collusion with those who forcibly repelled and frustrated the Maui embassy. It is doing *Kamehameha* no injustice, and it is no

[1] " Perhaps so."

detraction from his other great qualities, to say that he was not equal to the large-hearted philanthropy of Vancouver. And so ended the last and best-laid scheme of peacemaking between these jealous and embittered foes, and henceforth the conquest of the leeward islands was but a question of time and of favourable opportunity in the not distant future.

To Hawaiian readers it may be interesting to know the description that Vancouver gives of *Kahekili* and *Kaeo*. The former especially had filled so prominent a part in Hawaiian politics for the last thirty years. Speaking of the first meeting with *Kahekili*, Vancouver says: [1]—

" On Wednesday afternoon, 13th March 1793, we were honoured with the presence of *Titeeree*, who I was given to understand was considered as the king of all the islands to leeward of Owhyhee, and that from him *Taio* derived his authority. There seemed, however, nothing in his character or appearance to denote so high a station, nor was his arrival attended by any accumulation in the number of the natives on the shores or in the canoes about the vessels. He came boldly alongside, but entered the ship with a sort of partial confidence, accompanied by several chiefs who constantly attended him. His age, I suppose, must have exceeded sixty. He was greatly debilitated and emaciated, and from the colour of his skin I judged his feebleness to have been brought on by an excessive use of the ava. His faltering voice bespoke the decline of life, and his countenance, though furrowed by his years and irregularities, still preserved marks of his having been in his juvenile days a man of cheerful and pleasing manners, with a considerable degree of sensibility, which the iron hand of time had not entirely obliterated."

Of *Kaeokulani* Vancouver says, referring to the circumstance of *Kaeo* reminding him of a lock of his hair that he had given *Kaeo* when visiting the islands in 1778, on

[1] Vol. ii. p. 182.

board of the "Resolution" with Captain Cook, and which
exchange of friendship's tokens Vancouver seems to have
forgotten :—

"The circumstance of the hair having before been frequently mentioned to me, had made me endeavour to
recall the person of this former friend to my remembrance,
and on recollection, I suspected that *Taio* must have been
a young chief, at that time about eighteen years of age,
who had made me several presents, and who had given
me many other instances of his friendly attention. But
to my great surprise, on his entering the cabin, I beheld
him far advanced in years, seemingly about fifty, and
though evidently a much younger man than *Titeeree*, yet
nearly reduced to the same state of debility. If he were
really the person I had considered him to have been, I
must have been much mistaken with respect to his age
on our former acquaintance, or the intemperate use of
that pernicious intoxicating plant, the ava, which he took
in great quantities, assisted by the toils of long and
fatiguing wars, had combined to bring upon him a pre-
mature old age. Notwithstanding these appearances of
the decline of life, his countenance was animated with
great quickness and sensibility, and his behaviour was
affable and courteous. His inquiries were of the most
sagacious nature respecting matters of useful information.
The shrewdness of his understanding, his thirst to acquire
and wish to communicate useful, interesting, or entertain-
ing knowledge, sufficiently indicated a very active mind,
and did not fail to impress us with a very favourable
opinion of his general character."

On the 18th March Vancouver left Lahaina with *Kamohomoho* on board. After examining the southern and
western shores of Molokai, he anchored off Waikiki, Oahu,
on the 20th March 1793.

The main object of Vancouver's visit to Waikiki was
to see that the remaining murderers of the officers and
man of the "Dædalus" were apprehended and punished.

Kamohomoho, who had accompanied Vancouver as high commissioner from *Kahekili* to attend to this business, secured the apprehension of three natives, who were brought on board the " Discovery " for trial. A native —whom Vancouver calls *Tohoobooarto,* who had been a voyage to China with some of the foreign traders, who spoke a little English, and who said he had visited the " Dædalus " in Waimea Bay, and went ashore in the same boat as Lieutenant Hergest after dissuading him from landing—was the principal witness who identified the prisoners to *Kamohomoho*, by whose orders they were apprehended. A Mr. Dobson, who had been midshipman of the " Dædalus " on the occasion, identified one of the prisoners as having been very turbulent and insolent on board of the " Dædalus " before Lieutenant Hergest went ashore, and who immediately followed him thither, and whom the crew of the " Dædalus," after the occurrence, accused of having been the ringleader or principal actor in the murders committed on shore. Adding to this the general belief of the chiefs present that the prisoners were concerned in and guilty of the crime they stood accused of—an opinion confirmed by *Kalanikupule* himself, who, however, pleaded sickness as an excuse for not attending the trial—Vancouver considered himself justified in sanctioning their conviction and punishment. The three prisoners denied their guilt, and stoutly asserted their ignorance of the whole occurrence. " This very assertion," Vancouver thinks, " amounted almost to self-conviction, as it is not easy to believe that the execution of their comrades by *Titeeree's* orders for the same offence with which they had been charged had not come to their knowledge, or that it could have escaped their recollection." [1]

On the 22d March the prisoners were placed in a double canoe alongside of the " Discovery," and, in sight of the shore and of numbers afloat in their canoes, were

[1] Vol. ii. p. 209.

publicly executed, a chief, whom Vancouver calls *Tennavee*, shooting each one of them with a pistol.

It is very probable that the three first natives who were punished with death by the order of *Kahekili* for the murder of the "Dædalus" people were more or less concerned in the affair, and that when *Kahekili* learned from the foreigners residing with him that such an outrage on an English national vessel would surely, sooner or later, meet with condign punishment and prove highly injurious to himself, he then ordered the execution of the three first offenders as an expiation, and to put himself right on the record, as it were. And it is equally probable—their protestations to the contrary notwithstanding—that the three last offenders, who were executed in the presence of Vancouver, were also implicated in the murder. But we have the positive declaration of S. M. Kamakau, who in after-life conversed with one of the parties participating in the murder, that *Koi*, the head and instigator of the whole affair, and his immediate subordinates, were neither apprehended, punished, nor even molested, and that the parties executed were criminals of other offences, who, their lives having been forfeited under the laws and customs of the country, were imposed upon Vancouver as the guilty parties in the "Dædalus" affair.

On the 23d March, *Kalanikupule*, the son of *Kahekili* and the viceroy on Oahu, visited Vancouver, who thus describes him :—" *Trytooboory* appeared to be about thirty-three years of age ; his countenance was fallen and reduced, his emaciated frame was in a most debilitated condition, and he was so totally deprived of the use of his legs, that he was under the necessity of being carried about like an infant; to these infirmities was added a considerable degree of fever, probably increased by the hurry and fatigue of his visit."

On the 24th March Vancouver left Waikiki, and after inspecting the Puuloa inlet to the Ewa lagoon, proceeded

to Kauai. In mid-channel he fell in with a fleet of
canoes on their way from Kauai to Maui, carrying dis-
patches and a number of prisoners to *Kaeo*, informing
him of a revolt that had occurred on Kauai against the
authority of *Enemo*, his regent there, and of its suppression. At the head of this fleet was a single canoe that
attracted Vancouver's attention. It was made from an
American pine-tree that had drifted ashore on Kauai; it
was the largest single canoe that he had seen, being sixty-
one and a half feet long. It carried, as trophies of the
suppression of the revolt, the leg-bones, with some of the
flesh adhering, of two chiefs that had been engaged in it
and been killed. The other canoes carried a number of
prisoners, several of whom, Vancouver says, " were his
(*Kaeo's*) nearest relations; one in particular was his half-
sister, who had also been his wife or mistress, and had
borne him some children."

Arrived off Waialua, Kauai, Vancouver was kindly
received by *Kaumualii* and the chiefs there present, and
proceeding to Waimea, he landed and provided for two
Hawaiian girls from Niihau, whom an English trader had
carried off the preceding year to the north-west coast of
America, where Vancouver found them, and kindly gave
them a passage home.

On his return from the American coast in the spring of
1794, Vancouver visited Hawaii first. Leaving that island
on March 3d and proceeding westward, he spoke some
canoes off Hamakuapoko, Maui, who told him that *Kahekili* was on Oahu, and that *Kaeo* was on Molokai at that
time.

Of the occurrences on the leeward group of the islands
under the sway of *Kahekili* and *Kaeo* from March 1793
to March 1794, our only information comes from Vancouver's valuable account of his voyage. We there learn
that shortly before his arrival—either latter part 1793
or in the early part of 1794, while he was at Hawaii—
Enemo's conduct as regent under *Kaeo* on Kauai had

become so suspicious and apparently disloyal, that *Kahc-kili*, advised of the fact, and acting for his brother *Kaeo*, who was absent on Maui or Molokai, sent an embassy to Kauai to investigate the matter. Vancouver intimates that the "renegade white men" in *Enemo's* employ had instigated him to his disloyal conduct, and that they killed the greater pórtion of *Kahekili's* messengers. In this critical situation *Kahekili*, notwithstanding his advanced age, acted with his usual promptitude and decision. Obtaining a passage for himself and his following on board of the English ship "Butterworth," Captain Brown, he proceeded to Kauai and summoned *Enemo* to justify himself. Either overawed by the presence of *Kahekili*, or conscious of his own innocence, *Enemo* met *Kahekili* in conference, a compromise of existing difficulties was effected, and *Enemo* was retained as regent of Kauai.

From the native accounts it does appear that, after the above trouble on Kauai, *Kahekili* visited Maui once more, and returning to Oahu in the month of "Ikiiki" (June), died in the month of "Kaaona" (July) 1794 at Ulukou, Waikiki. His age is not accurately known, but as by all native accounts he was the reputed, if not the legitimate and acknowledged, father of *Kamehameha I.*, he could not well have been less than eighty years old, and was probably some years older. The same authorities state that *Kameeiamoku* and his twin-brother *Kamanawa* secretly took *Kahekili's* body away and hid it in one of the caves at Kaloko in North Kona, Hawaii. If this fact is truly accredited to those two Hawaiian chieftains, and, although happening in comparatively modern times, I have never heard or seen it disputed, it will, in consideration of the ancient customs, go far to justify the current opinion of that time, shared alike by chiefs and commoners, that *Kameeiamoku* and *Kamanawa* were the children of *Kekau-like* of Maui, and thus half-brothers of *Kahekili*. This relationship receives farther confirmation from the native legends when they relate that, on learning the birth of

Kamehameha, Kahekili sent these two sons of his father *Kekaulike*[1] to Hawaii to be and act as "Kahus"[2] to *Kamehameha*. In no other way can the otherwise singular fact be explained that two of *Kamehameha's* oldest and most prominent and trusted councillor chiefs, during a time of what may be called suspended hostilities, should have repaired from Hawaii to Oahu for the purpose of securing and safely hiding (Huna-kele) the bones of *Kamehameha's* political rival; nor the otherwise equally inexplicable fact that they should have been permitted by *Kalanikupule, Kahekili's* son and successor, to carry their design into effect. Under the social system of the old *régime*, and of time-hallowed custom, *Kamehameha* would have had no power to prevent those chiefs from executing their pious errand, and *Kalanikupule* would have had no motive to mistrust their honesty when resigning to them his father's remains ; and a breach of trust on their part would have consigned them to an infamy of which Hawaiian history had no precedent, and so deep, that the Hawaiian language would not have had a word detestable enough wherewith to express it.

Kahekili had two wives :—(1.) *Kauwahine*, of the Kaupo *Koo* and *Kaiuli* chief families. Her children were— *Kalanikupule* and *Koalaukani*, already referred to, and two daughters, *Kailikauoha* and *Kalola ;* the former became the wife of *Ulumeheihei Hoopilikane* (son of *Kameeiamoku*) and mother of *Liliha*, the princely and popular wife of governor *Boki* of Oahu after the death of *Kamehameha I. ;* of the latter daughter, *Kalola*, nothing is known with certainty. (2.) *Luahiwa*, daughter of *Kekaulike* and his Molokai wife *Kane-a-Lae*, and thus a half-sister to *Kahekili*. With her *Kahekili* had a son, *Kahekilinuiahunu*, also frequently called *Manonokauakapekulani*, who married

---

[1] Though every Hawaiian genealogy in my possession invariably states that *Kameeiamoku* and *Kamanawa* were the twin children of *Keawepoepoe* and his wife *Kanoena*, yet all the older legends which refer to these two chiefs call them the sons of *Kekaulike*. "Na keiki kapu a *Kekaulike*."

[2] "Guardians, attendants."

his cousin *Kailinaoa,* the daughter of *Manuhaaipo,* one of the sons of *Kekaulike* and *Hoolau.*

Although *Kalanikupule,* at his father's death, was recognised as the Moi of Maui and its dependencies, Lanai, Molokai, and Oahu, yet the previous arrangement between *Kahekili* and *Kaeokulani* remained in force for some time, the latter governing Maui and the adjacent islands, while *Kalanikupule* ruled over Oahu.

Towards the close of the year 1794 *Kaeo* became very desirous of revisiting Kauai and placing affairs there on a better footing. Embarking with his chiefs and his soldiers, he left Maui and stopped a while on Molokai to collect tribute and take in supplies.

It is not stated in the native accounts whether any jealousy or ill-feeling had arisen between *Kaeo* and *Kalanikupule,* nor, if so, what may have been the occasion of it. Certain it is that when *Kalanikupule* was informed that *Kaeo* was coming with a great force on his way to Kauai, he assembled his chiefs and fighting men in Waimanalo, Koolaupoko district, in readiness to repel *Kaeo* should he attempt a landing. Not aware of the hostile reception that awaited him, *Kaeo,* after leaving Molokai, steered for Kukui in Kalapueo, Waimanalo, but when arriving there he was repulsed by the Oahu forces, and a skirmishing fight was kept up for two days, during which time *Kaeo's* fleet kept at sea off the coast, exchanging shots with the forces ashore, with apparently no great losses on either side, except that the commander of the Oahu troops was shot by *Kaeo's* foreign gunner, Mare Amara, near a little brook named Muliwaiolena.

By this time *Kalanikupule* had crossed the mountain and arrived on the scene of action. What influences had operated a change in his mind is not known, but he stopped farther hostile proceedings, permitted *Kaeo* and his followers to land, and invited him to a conference at Kalapawai, in Kailua. What took place at this meeting is not known, but to all appearance friendship and good-

will were restored between uncle and nephew, and *Kaeo*
remained some time the guest of *Kalanikupule.*

Still anxious to proceed to Kauai, and unwilliug to tax
the hospitality of his nephew too far, *Kaeo* refitted his
fleet and re-embarked his men. Leaving Kailua and
proceeding by easy stages, he touched at Wailua and at
Waianae before intending to cross the channel to Kauai.
Stopping a few days at Waianae, a defection sprang up
among his troops and was surely and rapidly spreading,
and is said to have been fomented by *Kaiawa* and other
chiefs. On the eve of departure for Kauai, *Kaeo* was
informed of the conspiracy and of its magnitude, and that
the conspirators had resolved to throw him overboard on
the passage to Kauai. The motives of this sudden conspiracy have not transpired. No oppressive or tyrannical
act had been committed by *Kaeo*, who, on the contrary,
had always been very popular with his subjects. On the
other hand, subsequent events go far to show that it was
hardly possible that *Kalanikupule* had tampered with
the fealty of *Kaeo's* chiefs during their *séjour* at Kailua,
or they would have saved themselves at the battle of
Kukiiahu.

In this great emergency *Kaeo* showed himself equal to
the occasion. Only a bold stroke could extricate him
from the threatening peril. There would be no possible
chance to cope with the conspirators if once they were
embarked and afloat on the ocean. Could he divert the
rebellion he was unable to suppress? Yes; one course
was open, and only one. He might save his life and gain
a kingdom, or at least fall in battle as became a brave
man, instead of being thrown overboard like a dog. The
expression he made use of on this occasion, when com-
municating his resolution to his intimate friends, has been
preserved and recorded : " *E aho hoi ka make ana i ke
kaua, he nui na moepu* "—" It is better to die in battle ;
many will be the companions in death." Next morning
the departure for Kauai was countermanded, the canoes

were ordered to be dismantled and hauled up ashore, and the troops were ordered to prepare for a march on Waikiki and war with *Kalanikupule*.

Kaeo had judged his men correctly. The prospect of battle and renown, the hope of booty and new lands in the fertile valleys of Oahu, brought them back to their allegiance like a charm, and the cloud of revolt fled afar from the camp.

When this new order was proclaimed, the tidings of *Kaeo's* altered designs flew fast and far. A number of people from Wailua and Waianae flocked to his banner, and *Kalanikupule* hurried forward what forces he could collect at the moment to stop the advance of *Kaeo*.

In the month of November 1794 *Kaeo* broke up his camp at Waianae and marched on Ewa. At a place named Punahawele he encountered the troops of *Kalanikupule*, who had received an auxiliary force of armed seamen from the English vessels "Jackal" and "Prince Leboo," under command of Captain Brown, who shortly previous had been the first to enter the harbour of Honolulu, known to the natives by the name of Kou. In this first battle *Kaeo* was victorious. Some of *Kalanikupule's* hired foreigners were shot by *Kaeo's* gunner, Mare Amara, and the native troops were routed. Desultory fighting continued for several days afterwards, in all of which fortune still adhered to the arms of *Kaeo*, who slowly but steadily advanced through the Ewa district.

Worsted but not disheartened, *Kalanikupule* collected his scattered forces between Kalauao and Aiea, in Ewa, determined to dispute by another pitched battle the progress of *Kaeo*. The native chroniclers have noted the disposition of *Kalanikupule's* forces. His brother *Koalaukani* occupied with the right wing the raised main road from Kalauao to Aiea; his uncle *Kamohomoho* with the left wing occupied the shingly beach at Malei; and *Kalanikupule* himself, with his chiefs, occupied the middle of Aiea, while Captain Brown with his armed boats occupied a commanding position off the shore. We know not how *Kaeo* had marshalled his forces. He was probably advancing through the cultivated fields below and beyond the ravine of Kalauao. The battle took place on the 12th December 1794. It was a long and sanguinary conflict, and occupied nearly the whole of that day, The furious onset of *Koalaukani* descending from the upland where he was posted is said to have broken the main column of *Kaeo's* army, and decided the fortune of the day. *Kaeo* personally is said to have displayed prodigies of valour, but was finally compelled to flee, and with six of his companions in arms sought shelter in a small ravine near the shore of Aiea. His yellow feather cloak, the " Ahuula," betrayed his presence and his rank to the men stationed in the boats off shore, who fired at him and his party while the pursuers rushed upon them from above ; and thus, with his face to the foe, like a lion at bay, died *Kaeokulani*, a perfect type of the personal daring, the martial skill, and the princely qualities that formed the *bcau ideal* of a Hawaiian chieftain and the admiration of his contemporaries. The native historian Kamakau says that *Kaeo's* wives and several prominent chiefs were also killed in this battle, which received by the natives the name of "the battle of Kukiiahu." We are not told who those wives of *Kaeo* were. *Kamakahelei*, the Kauai princess and mother of his son *Kaumualii*, was certainly not among the number.

Towards evening of the day of the battle the corpses of the slain were collected and piled up in heaps near the shore at Paaiau. As an instance of an extraordinary escape, it is related that a woman named *Kahulunui-kaaumoku*, a daughter of *Kuohu*, the high-priest of Kauai, was among the number that were killed where *Kaeo* fell. To all outward appearance the woman was dead, and as such picked up and thrown on the pile of corpses. Life still lingered, however, though the woman was unconscious. During the early part of the night an owl, or some other carrion bird, hovering over the pile of corpses, alighted on the woman's head and attempted to pick out her eye. The blow of the bird's beak and the smart of the torn eyelid brought her back to consciousness and a sense of her situation. Watching her opportunity when the sentinel's back was turned, she cautiously slipped off from the ghastly company, and crawling on the ground, reached the waters of the bay. She then swam to the farther side of Aiea, where she landed, and then went to the upper part of Halawa valley. Here she found a cave in which she hid herself, fully expecting to die from her wounds and exhaustion before morning. Morning came, but the woman was still alive; and one of her Kahus, going up to the mountain, passed by her cave, recognised her, and preserving her secret, brought her food and ointment. Two days after the battle *Kalanikupule* proclaimed an amnesty, and forbade any farther pursuit and slaughter of those who might have escaped the battle. *Kahulunuikaaumoku* recovered from her wounds; in after years she embraced Christianity, and died as late as 1834.

Beside the "Jackal" and "Prince Leboo" there was lying in Honolulu harbour at this time an American sloop, the "Lady Washington," Captain Kendrick. When Captain Brown and his sailors returned to Honolulu from the battle of Kukiiahu, he caused a salute to be fired in honour of the victory. A wad from one of the guns entered the cabin of the "Lady Washington" and killed Captain Kendrick, who was at dinner at the time. Captain Kendrick was buried ashore, and the natives looked upon the funeral ceremony as one of sorcery to procure the death of Captain Brown. The son of Captain Kendrick requested *Kalanikupule* to take good care of his father's grave; but that very night the grave was opened and robbed by the natives, as alleged, for the purpose of obtaining the winding-sheet. Shortly afterwards the "Lady Washington" left for China.

The native accounts state that when Captain Brown engaged to assist *Kalanikupule* in his war with *Kaeo*, *Kalanikupule* had promised to pay him 400 hogs for his services. After the return from the war it appears that Captain Brown insisted upon some additional conditions, to which *Kalanikupule* and his chiefs strongly objected, and at which they were much annoyed, and plans, said to have been suggested by *Kamohomoho*, began to be entertained of cutting off the two vessels, should a favourable opportunity offer. The difficulty about the payment seems to have been amicably arranged, and Captain Brown acquiesced in the terms of the original agreement. Accordingly *Kalanikupule* commenced sending off the hogs in great numbers. Being short of salt wherewith to cure the pork, Captain Brown applied to *Kalanikupule*, who told him to send to the salt-ponds at Kaihikapu and help himself to as much as he wanted. The boats of the two vessels were sent off accordingly, and it happening to be high water on the reef at Keehi, they arrived at Kaihikapu without inconvenience, and loaded up with salt. In returning, however, the tide at Keehi was at low water, and the boats grounded.

In the meanwhile Captain Brown, who had now been a long time in the harbour, and considered himself on the most friendly and intimate terms with the Oahu chiefs, and suspecting no treachery, had invited *Kalanikupule* and a number of others on board of his vessels, it being New Year's day 1795. *Kalanikupule, Kamohomoho,* and a number of other chiefs and men of lesser note, repaired on board and were feasted and entertained by the two captains. When the visitors perceived that the ships' boats had grounded on the reef at Keehi and the crews were unable to return to the vessels, a general and preconcerted attack was made on the few foreigners that remained on board. Captains Brown and Gardner were killed and most of the seamen on board, while at the same time an overwhelming party was sent off to kill the boats' crews, and take possession of the boats. The greater number of the crews were killed, but a few were spared to assist in navigating the vessels.

In possession of these two vessels, with all their stores of arms and ammunition, *Kalanikupule* became so elated, that, in a council with his chiefs, it was resolved to start forthwith to Hawaii and to conquer that kingdom from *Kamehameha*. The account of the subsequent proceedings are differently narrated by Dibble, Jarves, and by Kamakau; but although the two latter agree best together, I prefer to follow Dibble's account as probably the most correct as regards the facts, though he is wrong in the year that he assigns to them.

After describing the capture of the vessels, Mr. Dibble says:—"The ship's deck was soon crowded with soldiers and set sail under the management principally of a a few foreigners. When they were fairly out of the harbour off Waikiki, the foreigners began to cover the rigging with oil that was extremely offensive, which so increased the sea-sickness of the king and his soldiers as to be insupportable, and they insisted upon returning into the harbour. On setting sail the second time, *Kamohomoho* advised that the foreigners should go in canoes, and natives only on board ship. *Kalanikupule* replied in English, "No." The soldiers therefore set sail in a fleet of canoes, and the foreigners with *Kalanikupule*, with all the guns, muskets, ammunition, and other means of warfare, and a few attendants perhaps, on board the ship. The foreigners, instead of sailing for Hawaii, stood directly out into the open ocean, sent *Kalanikupule* ashore at Waikiki, and took a final leave of the islands. It is said they touched at Hawaii and delivered the arms and ammunition to *Kamehameha*."

Kamakau's account differs somewhat in details, but it is substantially the same as to the results—the failure of *Kalanikupule* to hold the vessels he had captured and carry out the plans he had formed, and the success of the surviving seamen in escaping with their ships.

Before proceeding farther with the closing events of the

Hawaiian autonymous states under the old *régime,* it is proper to take up the Oahu line of kings from the time of *Kukaniloko* to the death of *Kahahana,* which closed the autonomy of that island.

OAHU.

Kalaimanuia followed her mother, *Kukaniloko,* as Moi of Oahu. No foreign or domestic wars appear to have troubled her reign, and little is known of her history. She was born at Kukaniloko, that famous birthplace of Hawaiian royalty, and resided most of her time at Kalauao, in the Ewa district, where the foundations of her houses are still pointed out at Kukiiahu and at Paaiau. To her is attributed the building of the great fishponds of Kapaakea, Opu, and Paaiau. Her husband was *Lupe Kapukeahomakalii,* a son of *Kalanuili* (k) and *Naluehiloikeahomakalii* (w), and he is highly spoken of in the legends as a wise and kind man, who frequently accompanied his royal spouse on the customary circuits of inspection of the island, and assisted her in the government and administration of justice.

An instance of *Lupekapu's* mildness of disposition has been preserved in the legends. Once a native stole a hog from the chief. When the theft was found out, *Lupekapu* goes to the house of the thief and asks, " Did you steal my hog ? " The native answered trembling, " Yes." *Lupekapu* then ordered the thief to prepare an oven and bake the hog. When that was done, he was told to sit down and eat. The thief fell to with a light heart, but on attempting to rise, when his natural appetite was satisfied, he was sternly told to continue eating until he was told to desist. When nearly suffocated with food, the poor wretch was told to get up, and *Lupekapu* told him, " Next time that you steal your neighbour's hogs, the law of the land that *Mailekukahi* established will punish you, viz., you will be sacrificed as a malefactor,

Kalaima-
nuia.

and your bones will be scraped to make fish-hooks and arrow-heads of."

Kalaimanuia and *Lupekapu* had four children, three sons and one daughter. The first were *Ku-a-Manuia*, *Kaihikapu-a-Manuia*, and *Hao*; the latter was *Kekela*. According to ancient custom the sons were given over to their several Kahus or guardians, chiefs of high rank and generally related to the parents, to be by them brought up and educated. Thus *Ku-a-M.* was brought up at Waikiki, *Kaihikapu-a-M.* at Waimanalo, Koolaupoko, and *Hao* at Waikele, Ewa; but the daughter, *Kekela*, was brought up with her parents.

Before her death *Kalaimanuia* made the following dispositions of the government and the land. She appointed her eldest son, *Ku-a-M.*, to succeed her as Moi of Oahu, and she gave him the Kona and Koolaupoko districts for his maintenance. To *Kaihikapu-a-M.* she confided the charge of the tabus, the religious culte, and her family gods, "Kukalani" and "Kuhooneenuu;" and for his maintenance she gave him the lands of Kalauao, Aiea, Halawa, and Moanalua. To *Hao* she gave the districts of Ewa and Waianae, subject in authority, however, to his elder brother. And to her daughter, *Kekela*, she gave the districts of Waialua and Koolauloa.

Ku-a-Manuia is spoken of in the legends as an exceedingly greedy and ambitious king, who endeavoured to wrest the lands from his brothers that had been given to them by their mother; and by his niggardliness he incurred the ill-will of the priests and the country-people, and became very unpopular. This manner of bickering and disputes with his brothers continued for about six years, when finally *Ku-a-M.* resolved on an armed attack on his brother, *Kaihikapu-a-M.*, who was at the time building the two fishponds at Keehi known as Kaihikapu and Lelepaua. *Kaihikapu-a-M.* defended himself against this sudden attack; the country-people and his brother *Hao* hurried up to his assistance, and a general battle was fought between Lelepaua and Kapuaikaula, in which *Ku-a-M.* was slain. Not long ago a memorial stone was still pointed out on that field as marking the place where *Ku-a-M.* fell.

The legends have not preserved the names of *Ku-a-Manuia's* wives or children.

Kahikapu-a-Manuia followed his brother as Moi of Oahu. Tradition has preserved his memory as a pious and worthy chief, who built new Heiaus, repaired the old, and encouraged devotion and religious exercises. During one of the circuits of the island which the Moi occasionally made to inspect the condition of the country, to administer justice, and to dedicate or repair Heiaus, he visited his brother *Hao*, who lived at Waikele, Ewa, and, as the legend says, was surprised and disturbed in his mind at the wealth of all kinds and the number of vassals and retainers, both chiefs and commoners, that followed the banner of his opulent brother.

Apprehensive that a chief with so abundant material resources might any day rise in revolt and assert his independence, *Kaihikapu-a-M.* returned to Waikiki and took counsel with his high-priest, *Luamea.* The priest advised him that open force would not prevail against *Hao*, but that he might be overcome by stratagem and surprise. The native legend makes a kind of Trojan horse of an enormous shark that had been caught off Waikiki by *Kaihikapu-a-M.*, and which was sent as a present to *Hao*, from which, while *Hao* was occupied in dedicating it to the gods, armed men issued and slew *Hao*, his priest, and attendant chiefs, who, occupied with the sacrifice, were unarmed and unprepared.

I am inclined to believe that the embellishments of the legends, as in many other cases, are of a much later time, and that the actual fact of the matter was the sending of a valuable present, the bearers of which surprised *Hao* at the Heiau and killed him there.

Hao's son *Napulanahu-mahiki* escaped from the assassins

Kaihikapu-a-Manuia.

and fled to Waianae, where he maintained himself against *Kaihikapu-a-M.* until the death of the latter. By marrying his aunt *Kekela, Napulanahu* came into possession also of the Waialua and Koolauloa districts, and the island was thus divided into two independent sections, which continued until *Kakuhihewa's* reign.

Kaihikapu-a-Manuia's wife was *Kaunui-a-Kanehoalani,* a daughter of *Kanehoalani,* who was a grandson of *Lo Lale* (k) and *Keleanohoanaapiapi* (w), referred to on previous pages. *Kaunui's* mother was *Kualoakalailai* of the *Kalehenui* branch of the *Maweke* line, but whose pedigree I am not in possession of. With this wife *Kaihikapu-a-M.* had a son named *Kakuhihewa,* who succeeded him as Moi. If *Kaihikapu-a-M.* had other wives or other children, the legends are silent on the subject.

uhihewa. As *Kakuhihewa* was not only one of the great kings of Oahu, but also celebrated throughout the group for all the princely qualities that formed the *beau ideal* of a highborn chief in those days, the legends relating to him are somewhat fuller, or have been retained better, than those of many of his contemporaries or successors.

Kakuhihewa was born at Kukaniloko, in the sleeping-place consecrated by the tabu of *Liloe.* From thence he was taken to Hoolonopahu by his grandfather *Kanehoalani.* Forty-eight chiefs of highest rank, conspicuous among whom were *Makokau, Ihukolo, Kaaumakua, Pakapakakuana,* were present at the ceremony of cutting the navel-string of the new-born chief, and the two sacred drums, named "Opuku" and "Hawea," announced the august event to the multitude. Several Kahus were duly appointed to watch over and bring up the heir-apparent, whose childhood was principally passed between Waipio, Waiawa, and Manana in the Ewa district.

During his youth *Kakuhihewa* was instructed in all the sciences and accomplishments known among his people, and such as became a chieftain of his rank and expectations. Spear exercise of the various kinds, single-stick,

stone-throwing, the use of the sling and the javelin, and
the knowledge of martial tactics, were taught him by a
number of masters, whose names the legend has preserved,
and whose skill is said to have been so great that they
could hit the smallest bird or insect at long distances.
The use of the bow and arrow was taught him by the
famous *Mailele.* The bow was never used in war, but
was a fashionable weapon to shoot rats and mice with.
There being no beasts of prey or wild animals on the
islands, the rats were the only *fera natura* that offered
the sports of the chase to the chiefs and their followers,
with whom it seems to have been a fascinating amuse-
ment, and heavy bets were frequently put upon this or
that archer's skill. The arrows were generally tipped
with the sharpened bones of birds or of human beings.

When *Kakuhihewa* succeeded his father in the dignity
of Moi of Oahu, his first care was to reunite the divided
empire of the island. Instead of continuing the war with
his cousin *Napulanahumahiki,* he made peace with him,
and married his daughter *Kaea-a-Kalona,* generally known
in the genealogies by the name of *Kahaiaonuiakauailana,*
with whom the three districts of Waianae, Waialua, and
Koolauloa again fell under the sway of the legitimate Moi
of Oahu; and during the balance of his long reign, no
war or rebellion distracted the country or diminished his
power.

The legends speak in glowing terms of the prosperity,
the splendour, and the glory of *Kakuhihewa's* reign. Mild
yet efficient in his government, peace prevailed all over the
island, agriculture and fishing furnished abundant food for
the inhabitants; industry throve and was remunerated, population and wealth increased amazingly, and the cheerful,
liberal, and pleasure-loving temper of *Kakuhihewa* attracted
to his court the bravest and wisest, as well as the brilliant
and frivolous, among the aristocracy of the other islands.
Brave, gay, and luxurious, versed in all the lore of the
ancients of his land, a practical statesman, yet passion-

ately fond of the pleasures of the day, wealthy, honoured, and obeyed, *Kakuhihewa* made his court the Paris of the group, and the noblest epitaph to his memory is the sobriquet bestowed on his island by the common and spontaneous consensus of posterity—"*Oahu-a-Kakuhihewa.*"

Kakuhihewa's principal royal residences were at Ewa, Waikiki, and Kailua. On the latter land, at a place called Alele, he built a magnificent mansion, according to the ideas of those times. It was named Pamoa,[1] and is said to have been 240 feet long and 90 feet broad. To those who remember the large houses of even inferior chiefs in the latter years of the old *régime*, ere the feudal power was completely broken, the above dimensions, as given in the legend, will not appear extravagant, and were probably correct.

Kakuhihewa had three wives, some legends say four. (1.) *Kaea-a-Kalona* or *Kahaiaonuiakauailana*, the daughter of *Napulanahumahiki*, above referred to, and *Kekela*, the daughter of *Kalaimaneia*. With her he had two sons and one daughter—*Kaihikapu-a-Kakuhihewa*, *Kanekapu-a-Kakuhihewa*, and *Makakaialiilani*. (2.) *Kaakaualani*, the daughter of *Laninui-a-Kaihupee* and his wife *Kauhiiliula-a-Piilani*; the former a descendant of the *Kalehenui-a-Maweke* branch, the latter a daughter of *Piilani*, king of Maui. With her he had a son named *Kauakahinui-a-Kakuhihewa*. (3.) *Koaekea*, whose pedigree I am not in possession of, and with whom he had a son named *Kalehunapaikua*. The fourth wife mentioned by some legends, though not by all, was *Kahamaluihi*, a daughter of *Kaioe*—a descendant of the *Kumuhonua-a-Mulielealii* branch of the *Maweke* line—and *Kawelo-Ehu*, of the Kauai branch descending from *Ahukini-a-Laa*. She is said to have become afterwards the wife of *Kanekapu-a-Kakuhihewa*.

Kanekapu-a-Kakuhihewa.

When *Kakuhihewa* died, the office and dignity of Moi of Oahu descended to his oldest son, *Kanekapu-a-Kakuhihewa*, in whose family it remained for five generations

[1] Some legends give the name as Kamooa.

afterwards. In other respects the island appears to have been divided between the three oldest brothers.

No legends remain of the life of *Kanekapu-a-Kakuhi-hewa.* The brothers agreed well together; no dissensions seem to have troubled their lives, and peace and abundance blessed the land. Occasional allusions in the legends of other chiefs would seem to indicate, however, that the gay ·temper and sumptuous style of living, which had made *Kakuhihewa* so famous among his contemporaries, were in a great measure shared by his son *Kaihikapu-a-Kakuhi-hewa,* whose brilliant *entourage* continued the lustre of his father's court.

Kanekapu-a-Kakuhihewa's wives were : (1.) *Kalua,* with whose name some confusion appears to have been made by the genealogies. On some she is said to have been one of the daughters of *Hoohila*—a daughter of *Kalaniuli* (k) and *Kaulala* (w)—and her husband *Kealohi-Kikaupea,* and thus a sister to *Kaioe,* the mother of *Kahamaluihi,* above referred to; but as *Hoohila* was a half-sister of *Kakuhi-hewa's* grandfather *Lupekapukeahomakalii,* and is referred to in the legends of *Kakuhihewa* as an old lady in his days, it is hardly probable that any of her daughters could have been the mate of *Kakuhihewa's* son. That she was descended from *Hoohila,* and in the Meles and legends is known as *Kalua-a-Hoohila,* there is no doubt, and I think it therefore more reasonable to assume that she was a granddaughter or great-granddaughter of *Hoohila.* The only child that *Kanekapu-a-Kakuhihewa* had with this wife was a son, *Kahoowahaokalani.* (2.) *Kahamaluihi,* just mentioned above, with whom he had no children.

Kaihikapu-a-Kakuhihewa, though acknowledging his brother *Kanekapu-a-Kakuhihewa* as the Moi of Oahu, kept his gay and brilliant court sometimes at Ewa, some-times at Waikiki. We know but little of the history of his life. The Meles and legends merely allude to certain events known to have transpired during his time as if they were too well known in the community at the time those accounts in verse or prose were composed to require farther details. Thus there can be no doubt that it was during his time that *Kauhi-a-Kama*, the Moi of Maui, started an armed expedition to Oahu, landed at Waikiki, and met a violent death there at the hands of the Oahu chiefs; but we know not the cause of the quarrel or the invasion, nor if *Kaihikapu-a-Kakuhihewa* was personally present at Waikiki and shared in the battle and took part in the outrage committed on *Kauhi-a-Kama's* body at the Heiau of Apuakehau. We know that the great civil war between *Kawelo-a-Maihunalii* and his cousin or near relative, *Aikanaka*, on Kauai, occurred during this period, and that *Kawelo-a-Maihunalii*—whose wife belonged to the *Kalona* family of Oahu, and who had obtained lands in Ewa on the slope ascending to the Kolekole pass of the Waianae mountains—was assisted with men, arms, and canoes by *Kaihikapu-a-Kakuhihewa* during the war; but we learn nothing from those legends that throws any light on the contentions which distracted the island of Kauai between the time of *Kahakumakalina* and that of *Kawelomahamahaia*.

Kaihikapu-a-Kakuhihewa's wife was *Ipuwai-a-Hoalani*, a daughter of *Hoalani* and *Kaua Kamakaohua;* the former a brother to *Kakuhihewa's* wife, *Kaakaualani*, the latter a daughter of *Kamakaohua*, a chief in Kohala, Hawaii, to whom belonged the Heiau of Muleiula, on the land of Kahei. With this wife *Kaihikapu-a-K.* had a daughter named *Kauakahikuaanaauakane*, who married *Iwikaui-kaua*, referred to on p. 126, and thus became the grandmother of the famous *Kalanikauleleiaiwi*, the wife of *Keaweikekahialiiokamoku*, king of Hawaii.

Of *Kauakahinui-a-K.* I have found no mention in the legends, except that he was the ancestor of *Papaikaniau*, one of the wives of *Kaulahea*, Moi of Maui, and of her brothers *Kuimiheua* and *Uluehu*, from whom several distinguished families descended.

Of *Kalehunapaikua*, the fourth son of *Kakuhihewa*,

nothing is known but the fact, which the genealogists carefully kept from oblivion, that from him descended the celebrated *Kaupekamoku* and her three warrior sons, *Nahiolea, Namakeha,* and *Kaiana-a-Ahaula.*

Kahoowahaokalani appears to have been recognised as Moi of Oahu after his father, *Kanekapu-a-K.* His life and reign have furnished no theme for bards or *raconteurs,* from which the historian infers that peace and prosperity were uninterrupted. *Kahoowaha's* wife was *Kawelolau-huki,* whose pedigree is not clearly stated, but who was undoubtedly either a daughter or a niece of *Kaweloma-hamahaia* of Kauai. Their son was

Kauakahi-a-Kahoowaha, who followed his father as Moi of Oahu. On the subject of his life the legends are as barren as on that of his father, with one exception. It is stated that *Kauakahi-a-K.* sent an ambassador named *Kualona-ehu* to the court of *Kawelomakualua* and his sister-wife, *Kaawihiokalani* on Kauai, who are said to have been the first to establish the dreaded " Kapu wela o na Lii," the " Kapu-moe," which compelled all persons, on penalty of death, to prostrate themselves before a high chief, or when he was passing. On the return of the ambassador the tabu which he had witnessed on Kauai was introduced and proclaimed on Oahu by *Kauakahi-a-K.,* and it is intimated that his grand-aunt, *Kahama-luihi,* was still alive at that time, and actively contributed to the introduction of the above tabu. From Oahu this tabu is said to have been introduced on Maui in the reign of *Kekaulike.*

The expression of the legend would seem to convey the impression that *Kawelomakualua* and his wife were the first to institute the " Kapu-moe " in the Hawaiian group. Such impression, I believe, would be incorrect, in view of the fact that the " Kapu-moe "—prostration before chiefs —was a well-known institution in all, or nearly all, the principal groups of Polynesia before they were visited by Europeans in the eighteenth century. Like many other

Kahoowa-haokalani

Kauakahi-a-Kahoowaha.

common customs with that race, it may have slumbered or been discontinued on the Hawaiian group for many generations, and probably the Kauai chieftains were the first to revive its practical application, and hence were said to have been the first to establish it.

Kauakahi-a-Kahoowaha's wife was *Mahulua.* She was doubtless of a rank corresponding to his own, but I have found no allusion to her pedigree in the legends or genealogies now extant. Their first-born, and perhaps their only son, was *Kualii.* If they had other children, their names have been eclipsed and forgotten in the superior renown of *Kualii.*

Kualii.

Kualii succeeded his father as Moi of Oahu, but by that time it would appear that the title had become more nominal than real, and that the Ewa and Waialua chiefs ruled their portions of the island with but little regard for the suzerainty of the Moi, who, since the time of *Kanekapua-Kakuhihewa,* resided chiefly on their patrimonial estates in the Koolaupoko district.

Kualii was born at Kalapawai, on the land of Kailua, Koolaupoko district. The ceremony of cutting the navel-string was performed at the Heiau of Alala, and thither, for that occasion, were brought the sacred drums of Opuku and Hawea. During his youth *Kualii* was brought up sometimes at Kailua, at other times at Kualoa. One of the special tabus attached to Kualoa, whenever the chief resided there, was that all canoes, when passing by the land of Kualoa, on arriving at Makawai, should lower their masts and keep them down until they had passed the sea off Kualoa and got into that of Kaaawa. I note the tabu and the custom, but I am not certain of the underlying motive. It may have been a religious observance on account of the sacred character of the "Pali o Kualoa," or a conventional mode of deference to the high chief residing there. It was strictly observed, however, and woe to the infractor of the tabu.

So far as known to me, only one legend of the life and

acts of *Kualii* has been reduced to writing and preserved. There doubtless were at one time several other legends regarding a king so widely known, so thoroughly feared, and so intimately connected with the highest families on Maui, Molokai, and Kauai as was *Kualii*, and as was his hardly less illustrious son, *Peleioholani.* But the political destruction of the house of *Kualii* by *Kahekili* of Maui, the spoliation of the territorial resources of its scions by the successful conquerors, and perhaps in no inconsiderable degree the· idea set afloat by both the Maui and Hawaii victors that the *Kualiis* were a doomed race, all these co-operative causes first rendered the recital of such legends treasonable, next unfashionable, and lastly forgotten. As a singular good fortune, however, amidst the destruction of so much ancient lore that doubtless clustered round the names of *Kualii* and *Peleioholani*, several copies of the celebrated Mele or chant of *Kualii* have been preserved and reduced to writing; and Polynesian students are under great obligation to Mr. Curtis J. Lyons for his English translation of the same.[1]

The above legend of *Kualii*, to which I have referred, appears to be rather a compilation of previous existing legends than an original one, and its compilation was probably as late as the latter part of the reign of *Kamehameha I.*, when upwards of a century had elapsed since the death of *Kualii*, and time had covered the original historical data with its ivy of fable and myth. Subjecting this legend, however, to the same critical examination with which I have treated other legends; allowing for the exaggerations and embellishments incident to and

[1] This remarkable chant will be found in Appendix, marked 5. In the accompanying translation into English I have differed in several places from that of Mr. Lyons—for the better or for the worse, let the Hawaiian scholar determine. I have had the advantage of comparing four versions of this celebrated chant— one collected on Hawaii, one on Oahu, one given by S. M. Kamakau to my collector, S. N. Hakuole, and lastly, the one furnished by Kamakau to Judge Andrews and Mr. Lyons—and I feel thus tolerably sure that the text I have followed is as nearly correct as such things can be when handed down by oral tradition only.

unavoidable in a legend that is told by professional *raconteurs* to admiring audiences, and is orally handed down for several generations; and having compared it with other legends treating of *Kualii's* contemporaries, and with the Mele just referred to,[1] I have been able to arrive at the following data as probably historical facts:—

Kualii's first attempt to bring the Oahu chiefs to their proper status as feudatories of the Moi of Oahu was directed against the chief of the Kona district. The legend gives the name of the principal chief in Kona as *Lonoikaika*, but I doubt the correctness of the name. The occasion of the collision was this:—In the valley of Waolani, a side valley from the great Nuuanu, stood one of the sacred Heiaus called Kawaluna, which only the highest chief of the island was entitled to consecrate at the annual sacrifice. As Moi of Oahu the undoubted right to perform the ceremony was with *Kualii*, and he resolved to assert his prerogative and try conclusions with the Kona chiefs, who were preparing to resist what they considered an assumption of authority by the Koolaupoko chief. Crossing the mountain by the Nuuanu and Kalihi passes, *Kualii* assembled his men on the ridge of Keanakamano, overlooking the Waolani valley, descended to the Heiau, performed the customary ceremony on such occasions, and at the conclusion fought and routed the Kona forces that had ascended the valley to resist and prevent him. The Kona chiefs submitted themselves, and *Kualii* returned to Kailua.

We next hear of *Kualii* making an expedition to Kauai for the purpose of procuring suitable wood from which to manufacture spears for his soldiers. Succeeding in this, and fully prepared, *Kualii* turned his attention to·the Ewa and Waialua chiefs and their subjection to his authority.

---

[1] Of that Mele or chant, however, there is no doubt as to its age. It was evidently composed during the lifetime of *Kualii*, who must have died some time previous to 1730.

The hostile forces met on the land of Kalena and the plain of Heleauau, not far from Lihue, where *Kualii* was victorious. The Ewa chiefs, however, made another effort to retrieve their fortunes, and fought a second battle with *Kualii* at Malamanui and Paupauwela, in which they were thoroughly worsted, and the authority of *Kualii* as Moi of Oahu finally secured and acknowledged.

Having thus subdued the great district chiefs of Oahu, it is related, and the Mele confirms the fact, that *Kualii* started with a well-equipped fleet to make war on Hawaii, but what in reality was only a well-organised raid on the coast of Hilo — kind of expedition not at all uncommon in those days, and undertaken as much for the purpose of keeping his warriors and fleet in practice and acquiring renown for himself, as with a view of obtaining territorial additions to his kingdom. As this expedition took place in the earlier part of *Kualii's* life and reign, it probably occurred while *Keakealaniwahine* was still the Moi of Hawaii, and before the accession of her son *Keawe.* Landing at Laupahoehoe, the subordinate chief there hastily assembled what force he could command to repel the invader. The name of this chief is given as *Haalilo,* but as this is the only time and the only legend that mentions him, I am unable to connect his name with any of the great Hawaii families. In the battle that ensued this *Haalio* was defeated, and *Kualii* having secured such plunder as usually fell to the victors on such excursions, was preparing to make his next descent on the Puna district, when news came to him from Oahu that the Ewa and Waianae chiefs had revolted again. Hastily returning to Oahu, he met the hostile chiefs at Waianae, and after a severe contest, routed them effectually with great slaughter near the watercourse of Kalapo and below Eleu.

Having again crushed rebellion at home, it is said in the legend that Kualii made a second voyage to the Hilo district, but what he did or how he succeeded is not stated. On his return from Hilo, however, while recruiting his force at Kaanapali, Maui, he was met by a deputation from the Kona chiefs of Molokai, invoking his assistance against the Koolau chiefs of that island, who had encroached upon the fishing-grounds of the former. The deputation consisted of a chief named *Paepae* and a chiefess named *Kapolei*, the daughter of *Keopuolono*. According to their request, *Kualii* crossed over to Molokai and landed at Kaunakakai, where the Kona chiefs were assembled. After agreeing upon their operations, their forces and *Kualii's* fleet rendezvoused at Moomomi on Kaluakoi, and from there made their descent on Kalaupapa, where the Koolau chiefs had collected. A well-contested battle was fought, the Koolau chiefs were beaten, and having satisfactorily settled the territorial disputes of the Molokai chiefs, *Kualii* returned to Oahu.

The legend refers to an expedition that *Kualii* made to Lanai, but the incidents related are so full of anachronisms, as to render the whole account unreliable. That *Kualii* made an armed excursion to Lanai is quite probable, and in accordance with the spirit and customs of his age, but that the excursion was made as related in the legend is highly improbable.

But what neither legend nor Mele refers to, however, is *Kualii's* connection with the Kauai chiefs and his influence there. And yet it is incontestable, that during his own lifetime he had established his son *Peleioholani* as Moi over at least the Kona section of Kauai. Had this connection been the result of war and conquest, it is hardly probable that the legend and the Mele would have both been silent about it. It arose then, probably, from a matrimonial connection of himself as well as of his said son *Peleioholani* with Kauai chiefesses, heiresses of the Kona districts. Of *Kualii's* wives only one is known by name, viz., *Kalanikahimakeialii*, a Maui chiefess, whose mother was *Kalaniomaiheuila*, a daughter of *Lonohonuakini*, king of Maui. Other legends speak of the large family of *Kualii*, but without mentioning his wives or their descents. It may fairly be assumed, therefore, that his relations with Kauai originated from such a cause.

Kualii is said to have lived to an extremely old age, and to have possessed unusual strength and vigour to the last. It is related that when *Kualii* was upwards of ninety years old, *Peleioholani* arrived one time from Kauai on a visit to his father on Oahu. Without endorsing the details of the legend, it suffices to say that a quarrel arose between father and son, that the latter assaulted the former, and a scuffle ensued, in which the old man, getting the grip of the "lua"[1] on his son, handled him so severely that, when released from the paternal grasp, he started at once for Kauai, and never revisited Oahu until after his father's death.

Kailua, in Koolaupoko, seems to have been the favourite residence of *Kualii*, and there he died at a very advanced age. Shortly before his death he called his trustiest Kahu and friend to his side and strictly enjoined upon him the duty of hiding his bones after death, so that mortal man should never get access to them or be able to desecrate them. When *Kualii* was dead, and the body, according to custom, had been dissected and the flesh burned, the Kahu carefully wrapped the bones up in a bundle and started off, as everybody thought, to hide them in some cave or sink them in the ocean. Instead of which, he repaired to a lonely spot and there pounded up the bones of the dead king into the finest kind of powder. Secreting this about his person, the Kahu returned to court and ordered a grand feast to be holden in commemoration of the deceased. Immense preparations were made, and the chiefs from far and near were invited to attend. The night before the feast the Kahu quietly and unobserved mixed the powdered bones of the dead king in the Poi prepared for the morn-

[1] The "lua" in ancient wrestling-matches was a grip or a position in which the one who had that advan- tage could easily, if he chose, break the back of the other.

ing's feast. At the close of the meal the following day
the Kahu was asked by the chiefs present if he had faithfully executed the wishes of the late king regarding his
bones. With conscious pride at his successful device,
the Kahu pointed to the stomachs of the assembled company and replied that he had hidden his master's bones in
a hundred living tombs. The legend does not say how
the guests liked their repast, but the Kahu was greatly
applauded.

As before stated, the name of only one of *Kualii's* wives
has come down to present times. *Kalanikahimakeialii* was
the daughter of *Kaulahea*, king of Maui, and his sister
Kalaniomaiheuila, and thus a chiefess of the highest rank,
an *Alii Pio*. Three children were born from this union, two
sons, *Kapiohookalani* and *Peleioholani*, and one daughter,
Kukuiaimakalani.

This is perhaps the proper place to refer to the celebrated
Mele or chant of *Kualii*.[1] It is one of the longest known
chants in the Hawaiian anthology, comprising 563 lines
according to some versions, and 612 according to others;
the difference being more in the manner of transcribing
than in the actual matter of the two versions. This Mele,
which is referred to and quoted in the legend, is said to
have been composed by *Kapaahulani* and his brother
Kamakaaulani, and chanted by the former within hearing
of the two armies previous to the battle of Keahumoa
against the rebellious Ewa chiefs. It bears all the internal
evidences, in language, construction, and imagery, of having
been composed at the time it purports to be, and was widely
known among the *élite* and the priesthood at the time of
Captain Cook's arrival. There is in some versions of this
chant an addition of some 200 lines, but their genuineness has been called in question, and I think justly so.
They are probably of later origin than the time of *Kualii*.
It is to the first and undoubted portion of this chant that

[1] See Appendix No. V.

I wish to call the attention, for in it occur the following lines—

> " *O Kahiki, moku kai a loa,*
> *Aina o Olopana i noho ai !*
> *Iloko ka moku, i waho ka la ;*
> *O ke aloalo o ka la, ka moku, ke hiki mai.*
> $\quad$ *Ane ua ike oe ?*
> $\qquad$ *Ua ike.*
> *Ua ike hoi aú ia Kahiki.*
> *He moku leo pahaohao wale Kahiki.*
> *No Kahiki kanaka i pii a luna*
> *A ka iwi kuamoo o ka lani ;*
> *A luna, keehi iho,*
> *Nana iho ia lalo.*
> *Aole o Kahiki kanaka ;*
> *Hookahi o Kahiki kanaka,—he haole ;*
> *Me ia la he Akua,*
> *Me aú la he kanaka ;*
> $\quad$ *He kanaka no,*
> *Pai kau, a ke kanaka hookahi e hiki.*
> *Hala aku la o Kukahi la o Kulua,*
> *O Kukahi ka po, o Kulua ke ao,*
> *O hakihana ka ai,*
> *Kanikani ai a manu—a !*
> *Hoolono mai manu o lanakila !*
> *Malie, ia wai lanakila ?*
> $\qquad$ *Ia ku no.*"

Which may be rendered in English—

> O Kahiki, land of the far-reaching ocean,
> Land where Olopana dwelt !
> Within is the land, outside is the sun ;
> Indistinct is the sun and the land when approaching.
> $\quad$ Perhaps you have seen it ?
> $\qquad$ I have seen it.
> I have surely seen Kahiki.
> A land with a strange language is Kahiki.
> The men of Kahiki have ascended up
> The backbone of heaven ;
> And up there they trample indeed,
> And look down on below.
> Kanakas (men of our race) are not in Kahiki.
> One kind of men is in Kahiki—the Haole (white man).
> $\quad$ He is like a god ;
> $\quad$ I am like a man ;
> $\qquad$ A man indeed,

Wandering about, and the only man whó got there.
Passed is the day of Kukahi and the day of Kulua,
The night of Kukahi and the day of Kulua.
By morsels was the food ;
Picking the food with a noise like a bird !
Listen, bird of victory !
Hush ! with whom the victory ?
With Ku indeed.

The above verses, from 137 to 161 of the chant, following the two versions which I possess, throw a singular and
unexpected light on the knowledge, mode of thoughts, and
relation to the outer world possessed by the Hawaiians of
two hundred years ago.   From these we learn that *Kualii*
had visited " Kahiki," that foreign, mysterious land where
the white man (" Haole ") dwelt, with his proud manners
and his strange language, a land shrouded in mists and
fogs, and reached only after a long voyage, when provisions fell short, and from which he successfully escaped
or returned to his island home.

Knowing that in the Hawaiian language " Kahiki " is a
general term, designating any and all foreign lands outside
of the Hawaiian group—those inhabited by cognate races
as well as by alien—the natural queries arise—Which was
the Kahiki that *Kualii* visited ? how did he get there,
and how return ?

Although the chant says that it was the land where
Olopana formerly dwelt, and thus seems to indicate that
it was the Tahiti of the Georgian group in the South
Pacific, yet the farther designation instantly dispels that
idea when it speaks of a country where the sun and the
land are seen indistinctly, as if shrouded in fogs and
appearing to elude or dodge (" aloalo ") the view of the
approaching mariner ; when it speaks of a people with a
strange language (" leo pahaohao ")—an expression that
could never have been used by an Hawaiian when referring to the kindred dialects of his race ;—and finally,
when it expressly states that the people of that Kahiki
(foreign land) were not of the same race as the narrator,

but were white men (" Haole "), aliens in race as well as in language.

While the chant thus enunciates with startling precision the fact that in the middle part of the seventeenth century, or thereabout, *Kualii* had actually visited a land where white men lived, yet it gives us hardly any light whereby to determine in which direction the land was situated or by what people it was inhabited, nor yet as to the question how *Kualii* was brought there and returned. In answer to all these questions the historian can only offer a more or less probable conjecture.

From the middle to the close of the seventeenth century, the time when *Kualii* flourished, the only lands bordering on the Pacific that were held by the white man, the Haole, were the western coast of America, the Ladrone Islands, and different places in the Philippine Islands. Between those places the regular trade was carried on by the Spanish galleons. I have endeavoured to show[1] that there can be little doubt that the Hawaiian group was discovered by Gaetano, a Spanish navigator, as early as 1555, and that this discovery was probably utilised by other Spanish galleons from time to time, though no written evidence of that fact has yet been found. To judge from the long discontinuance of native Hawaiian voyages to foreign lands—a discontinuance dating back to the time of *Laa-mai-kahili*, or some fourteen generations—and the consequent loss of nautical knowledge, it is hardly credible that *Kualii* started for Kahiki in his own Hawaiian canoes. But it is probable —and the only way to account for the fact vouched for by the chant—that some Spanish galleons, passing by the islands, had picked up *Kualii* and his company while fishing off the Oahu coast, carried them to Acapulco, and brought them back on the return trip. I am inclined to prefer the voyage to Acapulco or the American coast, in place of Manilla, from the fact that

[1] See p. 109, and Appendix No. III.

the chant describes the country as having "the land within
and the sun outside "—

"*Iloko ka moku, iwaho ka la*,"—

which is a peculiarly Hawaiian expression, and, though
not much used at present, may have been more prevalent
in olden times, indicating that the land was to the eastward of the voyager. One may hear to this day among
the native population such geographical terms as "*Kohala-iloko, Hamakua-iloko*," expressing Eastern Kohala on
Hawaii and Eastern Kamakua on Maui, in distinction from
"*Kohala i waho*," Western Kohala, &c. Moreover, the
word "*Aloalo*," which I have rendered as "indistinct,"
from its identity with the Tahitian "*Aroaro*," "indistinct,
dark, mysterious," would seem to apply with greater force
to the high mountain land back of the American coast,
shrouded in clouds or fogs, than it would to the neighbourhood of Manilla.

I have thus offered my conjecture, based partly, it is
true, upon an assumption of probable incidents in the
Spanish galleon trade, and also upon what I consider the
correct exegesis of the native text in the chant referred
to. The assumption may never be proven by the evidence
of Spanish log-books, the exegesis may partly or wholly
be controverted by some more able scholar than I claim
to be; but while the chant itself remains an undisputed
heirloom from the period and the chief whose acts it
describes, the voyage of *Kualii* to that foreign land, where
the white man dwelt with his strange and alien language,
must be accepted as an historical fact, and as such I have
referred to it here.

When *Kualii* died he was followed as Moi of Oahu by
his son *Kapiohookalani*, and his other son, *Peleioholani*,
succeeded him as sovereign over that portion of Kauai
which in some now forgotten manner had come under the
sway of *Kualii*.

Of the unfortunate campaign which *Kapiohookalani*

*Kapiohoo-
kalani.*

undertook against Molokai in order to reduce its chiefs to subjection, and in which he lost his life, mention has been made on page 137, &c.

The legends are silent as to who was *Kapiohookalani's* wife, but his son's name was *Kanahaokalani,* who was but a child when his father died, and who appears to have only survived him about one year, for in the war between *Alapainui* of Hawaii and *Kauhiaimokuakama,* the revolted brother of *Kamehamehanui* of Maui, we find that *Peleioholani* had succeeded his nephew as Moi of Oahu, and had gone with his fleet and warriors to Maui to assist *Kauhi* against *Alapainui. Vide* page 140, &c.

On his return from this expedition to Maui *Peleioholani* *Peleioholani.* visited the windward side of Molokai, and is said to have brought the Koolau chiefs to acknowledge him as their sovereign, though their subjection was neither very thorough nor very lasting. This must have been about the year 1738.

There is no special legend now extant that treats of *Peleioholani's* life and acts ; but all Hawaiian legends that refer to him even incidentally speak of him as a most celebrated warrior king of his time, and as one of the highest tabu chiefs in the group. Yet, with the exception of his campaigns against *Alapainui* on Oahu and on Maui, I find no mention of any wars with the greater islands which he undertook after that and in which he distinguished himself, unless his several expeditions to keep the Molokai chiefs in subjection form the basis for his renown and for the terror that he inspired.

About the year 1764 or 1765, for some reasons not now known, the Molokai chiefs killed *Keelanihonuaiakama,* a daughter of *Peleioholani,* and on that occasion he took such a signal vengeance upon them that the island remained quiet in the possession of the Oahu sovereigns until the downfall of *Kahahana.* In this crusade and last military expedition of *Peleioholani* the revolted Molokai chiefs, mostly from the Koolau and Manae sides of the island, were either killed and burned or driven out of the island to seek refuge at the courts of Maui and Hawaii. The *Kaiakea* family alone appears not to have been disturbed in their possessions or persons by the irate monarch, and their exemption was probably owing to the fact that *Kaiakea's* wife, *Kalanipo*, was *Peleioholani's* own niece, being the daughter of his sister *Kukuiaimakalani*.

About the year 1770 *Peleioholani* died on Oahu at an advanced age. He is reported as having had two wives: —(1.) *Halakii*, of whose pedigree I have found no mention in the legends of the time, but who most probably belonged to the Kauai aristocracy. The children with this wife, whose names have been remembered, were a son, *Kumahana*, and a daughter, *Keelanihonuaiakama;* [1] (2.) *Lonokahikini*, of whose ancestry and kindred no mention is made. It is said that with this wife he had two children, a son *Keeumoku*, of whom nothing further is known, and a daughter *Kapueo*, who is said to have lived to an advanced age.

Kumahana

Kumahana followed his father as Moi of Oahu. He appears to have been an indolent, penurious, unlovable chief, and for these or other reasons incurred the illwill and estranged the loyalty of chiefs, priests, and commoners to such a degree that, after enduring his rule for three years, he was formally deposed from his office as Moi by the chiefs of Oahu in council assembled. So thoroughly had he succeeded, during his short incumbency of office, to make himself disliked, that, in an age so peculiarly prone to factions, not a voice was heard nor a spear was raised in his defence. It was one of those few bloodless revolutions that leave no stain on the pages of history. There was no anger to appease, no vengeance to exact, it was simply a political act for prudential reasons. His deposition atoned for his incompetency, and he and his family were freely allowed to depart for Kauai, where they found refuge among their kindred in Waimea. I

---

[1] It will be seen in the next section on Kauai, that probably *Kaapuwai*, the wife of *Kaumeheiwa* of Kauai, was also a daughter of *Peleioholani*.

have not learned who was his wife, and the only son of his to whom history refers was *Kaneoneo*, who married *Kamakahelei*, the sovereign chiefess of Kauai, and who was killed in a fruitless attempt to recover the kingdom of Oahu by joining the insurgent chiefs under *Kahekili's* iron rule, as narrated on page 265.

Kahahana was elected by the Oahu chiefs to succeed *Kumahana* as Moi of Oahu. His election, his reign, and his tragical end have already been narrated on page 225, and with his downfall Oahu ceased to be an independent state, and became a tributary to the Maui kings, with whose history it thenceforth became associated. Kahahana.

KAUAI.

The last portion of the ancient history of Kauai, from the time of *Kahakumakapaweo* until the close of the eighteenth century, is the most unsatisfactory to whoever undertakes to reduce the national legends, traditions, and chants to some degree of historical form and sequence. The legends are disconnected and the genealogies are few. The indigenous Kauai folklore of this period was singularly obscured and thrust in the background by that of Oahu during the ascendancy of *Kualii* and of *Peleioholani*, and by that of Maui during the time of *Kaeokulani*. When, subsequently to this period, after the death of *Kamehameha*, *Kaumualii*, the last independent king of Kauai, removed to Honolulu and became the spouse of *Kaahumanu*, most of his nobles followed him thither, and Kauai folklore suffered a further eclipse. That the ruling families of Kauai were the highest tabu chiefs in the group is evident from the avidity with which chiefs and chiefesses of the other islands sought alliance with them. They were always considered as the purest of the " blue blood " of the Hawaiian aristocracy; and even at this day, when feudalism has vanished and the ancient chants in honour of deceased ancestors are either silent or chanted in secret, it is no small honour and object of pride to a family to be able to trace its descent from *Kahakumakapaweo* through one or the other of his grandsons, *Kahakumakalina* or *Ilihiwalani*. But of the exploits and transactions of most of the chiefs who ruled over Kauai during this period, there is little preserved to tell.

Kalanikukuma. *Kalanikukuma* followed his father *Kahakumakapaweo* as Moi of Kauai. No legend attaches to his name. His wife was *Kapoleikauila*, but whence descended is now not known. He is known to have had two sons, *Kahakumakalina* and *Ilihiwalani*, or, as he is called on some genealogies, *Ilimealani*. The latter married *Kamili*, a sister of *Kaulala* of the Oahu *Maweke-Elepuukahonua* line, and from him descended *Lonoikahaupu*, the great-grandfather of *Kaumualii*.

Kahakumakalina. Of *Kahakumakalina* as little is known as of his father except the genealogical trees which lead up to him. It has been stated before that *Akahiilikapu*, one of *Umi-a-Liloa's* daughters, of Hawaii, went to Kauai and became the wife of *Kahakumakalina*, with whom she had two children, a son named *Keliiohiohi*, who was father of the well-known *Akahikameenoa*, one of the wives of *I* of Hilo, and of a daughter *Koihalauwailaua* or popularly *Koihalawai*, who became the wife of *Keawenui-a-Umi* of Hawaii. After *Akahiilikapu* returned to Hawaii, *Kahakumakalina* took another wife, whose name on the genealogies is *Kahakumaia*, but whose parentage is not given. With her he had a son *Kamakapu*, who succeeded him as Moi of Kauai.

Kamakapu. Of *Kamakapu* nothing further has been remembered than that his wife's name was *Pawahine*, and that their son was *Kawelomahamahaia*.

Kawelomahamahaia. Both the legends and the family chants refer to *Kawelomahamahaia* as one of the great kings of Kauai under whom the country prospered, peace prevailed, and population and wealth increased. His wife was *Kapohinaokalani*, but of what family is not known. They had several children, and the names of the following have been preserved :—*Kawelomakualua, Kaweloikiakoo, Kooakapoko,* sons, and *Kaawihiokalani* and *Malaiakalani,* daughters.[1] *Kawelomakualua* followed his father as Moi, the prin- *Kawelomakualua* cipal royal residence being at Wailua. He is mentioned in the legends with almost equal veneration to that of his father. His wife was his sister *Kaawihiokalani,* and she bore him two sons, twin brothers, *Kawelo-aikanaka* and *Kawleo-a-peekoa.*

I have been unable to learn, and the legends that have been preserved throw no light upon, the origin of the *Kealohi* family, which about this time had become prominent on the Kauai legends, the first of the name, *Kealohikanakamaikai,* having married *Kaneiahaka,* a granddaughter of *Ilihiwalani,* the brother of *Kahakumakalina.* From the tenor of the legends I infer that the older branch of *Kahakumakalina* were the titular sovereigns of Kauai, while the younger branch of *Ilihiwalani* were the "Alii-Aimoku" of Waimea and the south-western section of the island. The children of *Kealohikanakamaikai* and *Kaneiahaka* were *Kealohi-a-peekoa, Kealohikikaupea, Kauakahilau,* sons, and *Kapulauki,* a daughter. The first son obtained a lordship of Waianae on Oahu, and became connected with the powerful Ewa chiefs. The second sought his fortune among the Koolau chiefs on Oahu, and seems to have been connected with the *Kanekapu-a-Kakuihewa* family, for I find his name mentioned as a relative in the *Kualii* legends. The third son apparently remained on Kauai, and eventually married his niece *Kuluina,* and became the father of *Lonoikahaupu.* The daughter *Kapulauki*—with whom the fief of Waimea and perhaps the whole Kona side of Kauai, as descended from *Ilihiwalani,*

---

[1] It is nowhere clearly stated, but the course of events and the tenor of the legends make it extremely credible, that *Keawelomahamahaia* had another daughter, named *Kawelolauhuki,* who became the wife of *Kahoowahaokalani,* the son of *Kanekapu-a-Kakuihuoa* and Moi of Oahu, and grandmother of *Kualii.* As the legends are silent, I can find no other reasonable way to explain the interest which *Kualii* acquired on Kauai after the close of the civil war between *Kaweloaikanaka* and *Kawelo-a-Maihunalii.*

appears to have remained—became the wife of *Kainaaila*, a son of *Kaihikapumahana* and grandson of *Lonoikama-kahiki* of Hawaii, and their child was a daughter *Kuluina*.

When *Kawelomakualua* died he was followed by his son *Kaweloaikanaka* as Moi of Kauai. *Kawelo-a-Maihunalii*, a cousin of the former, and a son of *Malaiakalani* and of *Maihunalii*, whose pedigree I have been unable to collect, for some reason not clearly stated in the legends became obnoxious to *Kaweloaikanaka* and was driven out of the island. The *Kawelo-a-Maihunalii* legends certainly state that he found a refuge with *Kaihikapu-a-Kakuhihewa* in Ewa, Oahu, and was given a land bordering on the Kole-kole Pass in the Waianae mountains; but unless *Kaihi-kapu-a-Kakuhihewa* had survived to an unprecedentedly old age, he must have been dead before this time, and the succour given to *Kawelo* must have come from *Kaihikapu's* sons or descendants. Certain it is, however, that *Kawelo* not only received the land on Oahu referred to for his maintenance, but in due time obtained both men and canoes to invade Kauai and make war on *Kaweloaikanaka*. The legends and chants referring to this war are lengthy, confused as to sequence of events, and so overloaded with the marvellous and fabulous, that very little reliance can be placed upon the details which they set forth. The result, however, is historically certain and vouched for by numerous other legends from the other islands, and that was the overthrow and death of *Kaweloaikanaka* and the transfer of the supremacy of Kauai to *Kawelo-a-Maihu-nalii*, or, as he is also called in some legends, *Kawelolei-makua*. How long he reigned is not known, but it is said that when he became old he was killed by having been thrown over a cliff by some rebellious subjects; but who they or their leader were, or what the occasion of the revolt, is not remembered. *Kawelo-a-Maihunalii's* wife was *Kanewahineikiaoha*, a daughter of *Kalonaikahailaau*, of the Koolau chief families on Oahu. They are known to have had a daughter, *Kaneikaheilani*, who became the

Kaweloai-kanaka.

Kawelo-a-Maihunalii.

wife of *Kaaloapii*, a Kau chief from Hawaii, and grandmother to *Haalou*, one of the wives of *Kekaulike* of Maui,
and to *Kamakaeheukuli*, one of the wives of *Kameeiamoku*,
a Hawaii chieftain and grandson of *Lonoikahaupu*.

What became of *Kaweloaikanaka's* family after his death
is not known. His wife's name was *Naki*, but of what
lineage is equally unknown at the present time. The
probability is that he left no sons to avenge his death or
reclaim the dignity of Moi after the death of *Kawelo-a-
Maihunalii*. His twin brother, *Kawelo-a-Peekoa*, so far as
I have been able to ascertain, is not heard of in the legends
after the death of his brother, and appears to have had
but one child, a daughter, named after her uncle, *Kau-a-
Kaweloaikanaka*, and who married a Molokai chief named
Kanehoalani, a grandson of *Kalanipehu* of that island, and
grandfather to the, in later times, well-known *Kaiakea*.

No legends that I have seen state how it happened, but
they all concur in representing *Kualii* of Oahu as the next *Kualii.*
chief over the windward side of Kauai after the death of
Kawelo-a-Maihunalii. The historical probability is that
Kualii reclaimed the succession to that portion of the
island, as well as the sovereignty, in the name of his
grandmother, *Kawelolauhuki*, one of the daughters of
Kawelomahamahaia. The legends of *Kualii* never speak
of Kauai as a conquered country, and the presumption is
that he came into possession by inheritance, as understood
in those days.

The *Ilihiwalani* branch of the Kauai royal family does
not appear to have been disturbed or evicted from its
possessions in the Kona part of the island by the usurpation of *Kawelo-a-Maihunalii*, for we find that *Kauakahilau*
and his wife *Kuluina* remained at Waimea, and that their
territory descended to their son, *Lonoikahaupu*.

From this time forward, to the arrival of Captain Cook
in 1778, a mist has fallen over the history of Kauai, its
legends and traditions, through which are but indistinctly
seen the outlines of some of her prominent men. *Kualii*

is called the Moi of Kauai, but, except on occasional visits, does not seem to have resided there, preferring Oahu and his paternal estates. But when he grew old he placed his son, *Peleioholani*, as his viceroy over Kauai, and the latter resided there for many years; yet of his administration and exploits while thus governing Kauai not a whisper has come down to break the silence brooding over Kauai history. And when, after the death of his brother *Kapiiohookalani*, he removed to Oahu, nothing seems to have transpired on Kauai worthy of note in Hawaiian annals, or, if so, it was obscured and forgotten in the course of the stirring events that followed close upon this historical calm and convulsed the islands from one end to the other.

Lonoika-haupu.

Of *Lonoikahaupu-Kauokalani*, the representative of the *Ilihiwalani* family and contemporary with *Kualii*, we should probably have known as little as we do of *Kualii* and *Peleioholani* in their relation to Kauai, were it not for the visit which he made to Hawaii, which brought his name in upon the legends and genealogies of that island.

Following the custom of the times, *Lonoikahaupu* set out from Kauai with a suitable retinue of men and canoes, as became so high a chief, to visit the islands of the group, partly for the exercise and practice in navigation, an indispensable part of a chief's education, and partly for the pleasures and amusements that might be anticipated at the courts of the different chieftains where the voyager might sojourn. Whether *Lonoikahaupu* stopped on Oahu or Maui, or, if so, what befell him there, is not known; but on arriving at Hawaii he found that the court of *Keaweikekahialiiokamoku*, the Moi of Hawaii, was at the time residing in Kau. Repairing thither, he was hospitably received, and his entertainment was correspondingly cordial, as well as sumptuous. The gay and volatile *Kalanikauleleiaiwi*, the imperious and high-born wife of *Keawe*, the Moi, became enamoured of the young Kauai chief, and after a while he was duly recognised as one of her husbands. From this union was born a son called

Keawepoepoe, who became the father of those eminent Hawaii chiefs, *Keeaumokupapaiahiahi, Kameeiamoku,* and *Kamanawa,* who placed *Kamehameha I.* on the throne of Hawaii. How long *Lonoikahaupu* remained on Hawaii has not been stated, but after a time he returned to Kauai and took for a wife there a lady known by the name of *Kamuokaumeheiwa,* but from what family she was descended has not been remembered. With this lady *Lonoikahaupu* had a son, *Kaumeheiwa,* who married *Kaa-* *Kaume-* *puwai,* of whose pedigree we have no positive information. *heiwa.* Their daughter was the well-known *Kamakahelei,* who appears to have been the sovereign or Moi of Kauai when Captain Cook arrived. How this change of dynasty from the older to the younger branch had been effected there are no legends existing to tell and no chants to intimate. The only solution of this historical problem will be to admit what was probably the fact, though the legends concerning it have been lost or forgotten, namely, that *Kaapuwai,* the wife of *Kaumeheiwa,* was the daughter of *Peleioholani,* on whom the possessions of that house on Kauai and the sovereignty of the island had been bestowed either before or at the death of *Peleioholani,* and thus, by her marriage with *Kaumeheiwa,* united the dignity and possessions of the two royal branches descending from *Manokalanipo* upon her daughter *Kamakahelei.*

We know that *Kumahana,* the son of *Peleioholani,* suc- *Kamaka-* ceeded him as Moi of Oahu about 1770, and that after *helei.* three years' reign he was deposed by the chiefs and commoners of that island, and that he was permitted to return with his family to Kauai, where probably he still held lands from which to maintain himself. But it has never been asserted on his behalf, and I have nowhere seen it intimated, that *Kumahana* ever was, or was considered to be, the Moi of Kauai as his father was, or his grandfather *Kualii* before him. A farther confirmation of the above proposition may be advanced from the well-known fact that *Kamakahelei's* first husband was *Kaneoneo,* the son of

Kumahana, with whom she had two daughters, *Lelema-hoalani*, referred to on page 169, and *Kapuaamohu*, who became one of the wives of *Kaumualii*, and grandmother of the present Queen *Kapiolani*. It is stated in some genealogies that *Kahulunuiaaumoku* was also a sister of *Kaumualii*, but whether she was a daughter of *Kamaka-helei* with either of her two husbands, or was the daughter of *Kaeokulani* with another wife, I have been unable to ascertain. When Captain Cook arrived at Kauai in January 1778, the native legends state that *Kaumeheiwa* and *Kaapuwai* were still alive, and that *Kamakahelei* had obtained a second husband in the celebrated *Kaeokulani*, a younger brother of *Kahekili*, the Moi of Maui.

All that we know with any certainty from that time on to the close of this period, has already been related under the section of Maui. With *Kaeokulani Kamakahelei* had a son named *Kaumualii*, whom Captain Vancouver intimates as having been about fourteen years old in 1792, but who was probably two or three years older.

Kamakahelei's first husband, *Kaneoneo*, died during the rebellion on Oahu against *Kahekili* about 1785–6; her second husband, *Kaeokulani*, died on Oahu in 1794, but the time of her own death has not been remembered, but it probably occurred shortly after that of *Kaeo*.

Kaumualii.   At his mother's death *Kaumualii* became the sovereign of Kauai, and, though young in years, appears from all descriptions to have been a prince of remarkable talents and a most amiable temper.

Though the cession of Kauai by *Kaumualii* to *Kamehameha I.* did not occur till 1810, yet as for convenience sake I have preferred to close the ancient Hawaiian history with the battle of Nuuanu in 1795, a year after the accession of *Kaumualii* to the throne of Kauai, I leave the modern history of that island, as well as of the entire group, to some future writer.

HAWAII.

By referring to page 154 of this volume, it will be seen that at the great council of chiefs held by *Kalaniopuu* some time in 1780, at Waipio, the succession as Moi of Hawaii was conferred and confirmed on his son, *Kiwalao*, and that, while no territorial increase was given to *Kamehameha*, the particular war-god—" Ku-Kaili-moku "—of the aged king was bestowed on him as a special heirloom, and its service and attention, and the maintenance of its Heiaus dedicated to that god, were enjoined upon him. It is known, and not contradicted, that during *Kalaniopuu's* lifetime all that remained to *Kamehameha* of his patrimonial estates was a not very extensive portion in the north Kohala district, of which Halawa may be considered the centre, and which was his favourite residence. Dibble, followed by Jarves, in their histories of these islands, state that before his death *Kalaniopuu* divided the island of Hawaii between *Kiwalao* and *Kamehameha*, giving the former the districts of Hilo, Puna, and Kau, and to the latter the districts of Kona, Kohala, and Hamakua, *Kamehameha*, however, being subordinate to, and acknowledging, the authority of *Kiwalao* as Moi of Hawaii. Dibble doubtless had his information from some of the chiefs in the train or in the interest of the *Kamehamehas;* but if we carefully look into the social condition of that period, the precedents that governed the distribution of land, and the political status of the prominent chiefs who took an active part in subsequent events, I think it will be found that the claims set up for a division of the island by *Kalaniopuu* between *Kiwalao* and *Kamehameha* is hardly correct in the strict and political sense that the apologists of *Kamehameha* advance it. Such a division is not mentioned by David Malo, by S. M. Kamakau, nor by the writer of the "Life of Kapiolani"[1]—gentlemen who

Kiwalao.

---

[1] See the "Eleele," a newspaper printed in Honolulu in 1845.

were contemporary with Mr. Dibble, and had access to the same and many other sources of information.

It had been the custom since the days of *Keawenui-a-Umi*, on the death of a Moi and the accession of a new one, to distribute and redivide the lands of the island between the chiefs and favourites of the new monarch. This division was generally made in a grand council of chiefs, and those who were dissatisfied had either to submit or take their chances of a revolt if their means and connections made it judicious to attempt it. Certain lands, however, appear to have become hereditary in certain families, and whatever changes and divisions took place elsewhere, these estates never went out of the family to whom they were originally granted. Such were the lands of Kekaha in North Kona, the property of the *Kameeiamoku* family since the days of *Umi-a-Liloa;* such the lands of Kapalilua in South Kona, the property of *Keeaumoku;* such the Halawa portion of the Kohala district, the patrimony of the *Mahi* family and, through his mother, of *Kamehameha;* and some other such estates in other parts. All other lands were subject to change in this grand council of division, unless their previous owners were of the court party or too powerful to be needlessly interfered with.

In this periodical distribution and redistribution of the lands of the islands, regard was generally had to the advantages of the country and the wants and convenience of the chiefs who shared in the division. Thus the chiefs on the windward sides of the island, Kohala-iloko, Hamakua, Hilo, Puna, always coveted the lands on the leeward side, the Kona districts, on account of its mild climate and its rich fishing-grounds; while the Kona chiefs coveted the lands in the windward districts on account of their streams of running water, their numerous taro lands, and abundant food. To accommodate, adjust, and conciliate these ever-clashing claims was the great business of state on the accession of a new monarch.

Had *Kalaniopuu* before his death made such a division of the districts as Dibble intimates, *Kiwalao* would have had no more right to divide the lands in Kona, Kohala, and Hamakua between his chiefs than *Kamehameha* would have had to divide the Hilo, Puna, and Kau lands between his chiefs. Though *Kamehameha* would have acknowledged *Kiwalao* as Moi of Hawaii, and owed him fealty as such against foreign foes or internal rebellion, yet within his own districts he would have been practically independent. Moreover, the district of Hilo was not in the power of *Kalaniopuu* to give to either *Kiwalao* or *Kamehameha*, for it was an hereditary fief in the *I* family, had been such from the time of *Keawenui-a-Umi*, had never been conquered since then by any of the reigning Moi, and was now held by *Keawemauhili* for his wife *Ululani*, the daughter of *Mokulani* and great-granddaughter of *I*. In the other districts of the island the ancient hereditary lordships ("Alii-ai-moku") had been gradually extinguished by conquests. *Alapainui*, the hereditary lord of Kohala, conquered Kona and the greater part of Hamakua from *Kalanikeeaumoku*, and constituted himself Alii-ai-moku over those districts. His son *Keaweopala* inherited those districts from his father, still leaving Hilo, Puna, and Kau districts under separate independent Alii-ai-moku. When *Kalaniopuu*, the independent Alii-ai-moku of Kau, overthrew *Keaweopala*, he conquered and invested himself with the lordships of Kona, Kohala, and Hamakua, and when afterwards he subdued and slew *Imakakaloa* of Puna, that district also became the apanage of the reigning Moi.

At the time of *Kalaniopuu's* death *Kamehameha* held possession of his ancestral home in Halawa, Kohala district. He also held possession of the Waipio valley in Hamakua, probably under gift from *Kalaniopuu*. And it is very likely that, like many other chiefs on the windward side of the island, he also held some land or lands in the Kona district, probably Kailua, though I have been unable to find any specific evidence of that fact. The sequence of this narrative gives, however, a plausibility to that assumption.

The pretended division of the island in equal parts between *Kiwalao* and *Kamehameha* I hold, therefore, to be a fiction of later years, when *Kamehameha's* power had been long established, and when bards and heralds, in shouting his praise, found it incumbent to represent him as the injured and unjustifiably attacked party in the contest with *Kiwalao*. But a hundred years have cooled the partisanship and the bitter hatreds of those days, and the impartial historian can now give a different judgment without, therefore, impugning the remarkably great qualities which distinguished *Kamehameha* above his rivals.

I hope I have made it plain that the lands which *Kamehameha* held in Hamakua and Kona were not his in his own right, but were what would now be called crownlands, in the gift of the sovereign, and revokable at his pleasure; and that on a particular occasion, like the accession of a new Moi, they might be retained in the hands of previous holders, or be lawfully given to others.

When the period of mourning the death of *Kalaniopuu* had expired, about the month of July 1782, *Kiwalao*, his uncle and chief counsellor, *Keawemauhili*, and the principal chiefs in attendance on the court, prepared themselves to bring the bones of *Kalaniopuu* to Kona, to be deposited, according to his last wish, with those of his ancestors in the "*Hale o Keawe*," that famous sanctuary or city of refuge (Puu-honua) on the land of Honaunau in South Kona. Of this grand ceremonial procession the Kona chiefs had been duly informed; but mistrusting the haughty and grasping temper of *Keawemauhili*, who appeared to have obtained complete influence over *Kiwalao*, and apprehensive lest, in the coming division of the lands, their possessions, which they held under *Kalaniopuu*, would be greatly shorn or entirely lost, they became restless, and anxiously looked round for a leader to meet the coming storm. The leading spirits of this growing conspiracy were *Keeaumoku* of Kapalilua, *Keawe-a-Heulu* of Kaawaloa, *Kameeiamoku* of Kaupulehu in Kekaha, *Kamanawa* of Kiholo, and *Kekuhaupio* of Keei, the veteran warrior chief, the hero of many battles, and the military instructor of *Kamehameha.*

Considering *Kamehameha,* on account of his high birth, his martial prowess, and of his being the heir to the redoubtable war-god of *Kalaniopuu,* as the most suitable person for their purposes, *Kekuhaupio* started off for Kohala, where *Kamehameha* had quietly remained since his quasi-disgrace at *Kalaniopuu's* court, narrated on page 203, cultivating and improving his lands, building canoes, and other peaceful pursuits.

When *Kekuhaupio* arrived with his canoes at Kapania in Halawa, he found *Kamehameha* and his brother *Kalai-mamahu* and their wives bathing in the sea and enjoying the sport of surf-swimming. When *Kamehameha* recognised *Kekuhaupio* on the canoe he repaired to his house, followed by the latter, who, after the customary salutations, entered upon the business that had brought him there. Gently reproaching *Kamehameha* for wasting his time in what he considered as unprofitable pursuits and in pleasures while the times were so unsettled, he represented that the only pursuit worthy of so great a chief would be the practice of war, and striving to obtain possession of the kingdom. He then informed him that *Kiwalao* was going to deposit the bones of *Kalaniopuu* at Honaunau, and intimated that if *Kiwalao* acted handsomely on the occasion (namely, the forthcoming division of the lands), all would be well, and quiet would prevail; but if not, then the country would belong to the strongest —" *aia ka aina ma ka ikaika.*"

To this proposition *Kamehameha* assented, and is said to have answered, "Your words are good; let us go to Kona at once, lest the king should already have arrived with the corpse. Let us pay our respects to the corpse, and we may then perchance learn the unkind disposition of the king"—*o i ia mai auanei e ke alii i ka lokoino.*

Collecting his followers *Kamehameha* set out without delay, in company with *Kekuhaupio*, for Kaupulehu in Kekaha, and stopped with *Kameeiamoku.*

When all was ready for the funeral procession, *Kiwalao* on his double canoe, with the corpse of the deceased king lying in state on board of another double canoe, and accompanied by his chiefs and retainers and a numerous party of well-armed men, set sail for Honaunau. The first day they came to Honomalino in Kona, and stopped there. The next day, when off Honokua, *Keeaumoku* came down from Kapalilua and went on board of the funeral canoe to see the corpse. After the wailing was over, *Keeaumoku* inquired whither they were going? One of the guardsmen, *Kaihikioi* by name, in attendance on the corpse, answered off-hand and apparently without forethought, "to Kailua." As the Kona chiefs had been informed that the corpse was to be deposited in the " Hale-a-Keawe " at Honaunau, this answer confirmed *Keeaumoku* in his opinion that *Kiwalao* and his chiefs had an intention to occupy the whole of Kona. Returning ashore, he started off that very night for Kekaha, where he knew that *Kamehameha* had arrived, and where he found *Kameeiamoku, Kamanawa, Kekuhaupio,* and a number of other chiefs in council, and informed them that *Kiwalao* with the corpse of his father had arrived at Honaunau. On the advice of *Kekuhaupio*, the assembled chiefs set out forthwith to take up their quarters at Kaawaloa, Napoopoo, and Keei, the ground about Hauiki being considered a good battlefield, should occasion so require.

There is no proof that *Kiwalao* intended to take the bones of his father any farther than the " Hale-a-Keawe," and the reply of the guardsman to *Keeaumoku* was probably a wanton and boastful expression, the man knowing or suspecting that in the coming division the landed possessions of the opulent Kona chiefs would be considerably curtailed. It has been said by those from whom D. Malo and Dibble obtained their information of this eventful journey, that it was the accident of a heavy rainstorm that obliged *Kiwalao* to stop at Honaunau, or he would have hurried on to Kailua. That information bears the impress of having come from the same quarter that was misled by the guardsman's insolent taunt to *Keeaumoku*. For not only did *Kiwalao* put in at Honaunau, as previously notified, and deposited his father's bones in the "Hale-a-Keawe" with all the ceremonies due on so solemn occasion, but remained there several days and commenced the business of dividing the lands.

When *Kiwalao* heard that *Kamehameha* had arrived at Kaawaloa, he went there and called on him, and was received with all the observances due to his high rank. After the wailing and salutations were over, *Kiwalao* addressed *Kamehameha*, saying, "Where are you? It is possible that we two must die. Here is our father (their uncle *Keawemauhili*) pushing us to fight. Perhaps only we two may be the ones that shall be slain. What misery for both of us!" *Kamehameha* answered evasively, "To-morrow we will come and visit the corpse of the king." After this interview *Kiwalao* returned to Honaunau.

The next day *Kamehameha* went to Honaunau and attended on the corpse of *Kalaniopuu*, when the ceremonial wailing over the dead was repeated. That part performed, *Kiwalao* ascended a platform outside the "Hale-a-Keawe" and addressed the assembled chiefs and commoners. He told them that in his last will *Kalaniopuu* had only remembered *Kamehameha* and himself. That the bequest to the former was the wargod *Kukailimoku*, and such lands as had been given him by *Kalaniopuu*; and that to himself (*Kiwalao*) was bequeathed the government of Hawaii and the position and dignity of Moi.

When the Kona chiefs heard this publication of the last will of *Kalaniopuu*, they were greatly dissatisfied, saying,

"Strange, very strange! Why not have divided the country, three districts to one and three to the other? that would have been equal. Now we will be impoverished, while the Hilo and Kau chiefs will be enriched, for the king is of their party. War would be better, decidedly better!" E aho ke kaua.

It is said that *Kamehameha* was rather reluctant to go to war. It was urged upon him, however, by the great Kona chiefs who feared for their possessions, but who, while preparing for the worst, were apparently loath to take the first step in rebellion, and prudently waited for the chapter of accidents to furnish a suitable pretext. They had not long to wait before the mad rashness of *Keouakuahuula* brought on a crisis.

As *Kamehameha* and the Kona chiefs were returning from Honaunau, after hearing the royal proclamation, *Kekuhaupio* invited *Kamehameha* to stop with him at Keei, and in the evening go back to Honaunau and visit *Kiwalao* at his own residence. *Kamehameha* assented, and at nightfall he and *Kekuhaupio* were paddled over to Honaunau. When they entered the house occupied by *Kiwalao*, preparations were in process for an Awa-party. The scene that ensued is thus related by a native historian :—" On seeing the awa roots passed round to be chewed, *Kekuhaupio* says to the king, ' Pass some awa to this one (*Kamehameha*) to chew.' The king replied, ' What occasion is there for him to chew it ? ' *Kekuhaupio* answered, ' It was so ordered by both of your fathers, that the son of the one should be the man of the other,[1] should either of them ascend the throne.' The awa was passed to *Kamehameha*, who chewed and prepared it, and handed the first bowl to the king. Instead of drinking it himself, however (*Kiwalao*), passed it to a special favourite sitting near him. As this chief was lifting the bowl to his mouth

---

[1] "*Kanaka.*" When used in this sense it means the principal business-man of a chief, the next in authority, a subject, but the highest subject in the land. Thus even in modern times the expression remained, and *Kalaimoku* was invariably called the "Kanaka" of *Kaahumanu* during her regency.

to drink, *Kekuhaupio* indignantly struck the bowl out of his hand, and addressed the king, saying, 'You are in fault, O king! Your brother has not prepared the awa bowl for such people but for yourself alone,' and pushing *Kamehameha* out of the house, he said, 'Let us go on board of our canoes and return to Keei.'"

This breach of etiquette or studied insult to *Kamehameha* was to his aged counsellor a sure indication of the king's unfriendly disposition towards his cousin; but it is possible that this conclusion was not altogether just toward *Kiwalao*. The want of etiquette was not, probably, premeditated by him. It was an unfortunate and unguarded oversight on his part, and the ceremony of the court was perhaps relaxed or forgotten in the convivial meeting of the evening. We have but few means left to estimate correctly the character of *Kiwalao*, but what there is seems to indicate that he was a good-natured, pleasure-loving monarch, who would rather have been on good than on bad terms with his cousin; but he was lacking in resolution, and indolently preferred to be led by his imperious uncle than to exercise his own judgment in State matters.

Some days afterwards the great business of dividing the lands of the kingdom was taken in hand. It does not appear that *Kamehameha* or any of the great Kona chiefs were present. It is reported that *Kiwalao* intimated a wish that some more lands should be given to *Kamehameha*, but that he was rudely interrupted by *Keawemauhili*, who told him that such was not the will of the late king, who had bequeathed to *Kamehameha* his wargod and such lands as he held at that time, adding, "You are the king; I am next under you, and the other chiefs are under us. Such was the will of your father." *Keawemauhili*, it appears, did not fail to remember himself in the division, and the chiefs and followers of his party were the most favoured. Towards the close of the session *Keoua Kuahuula* came to his brother, the king, asking for the gift of several lands, all of which he was told had already been disposed of by *Keawemauhili*. Among those lands was the valley of Waipio, in Hamakua, which had been given to *Kamehameha* by *Kalaniopuu*. Disgusted and chagrined, *Keoua* exclaimed, "Am I to have no share in this new division?" To which *Kiwalao* mildly replied, "You are no worse off than I am in this division. We will have to be content with the lands we held before."

Infuriated and disappointed, *Keoua Kuahuula* went to his own place, called his chiefs, kahus, warriors, and retainers together and ordered them to don their feather mantles and helmets and their ivory clasps, and, fully armed, to follow him. They proceeded at once to Keomo, a place south-east from Keei, and commenced cutting down cocoa-nut trees. This was in olden time tantamount to a declaration of war, or that the party so doing defied the lord on whose land the trees stood. From there he proceeded to the shore at Keei, where he fell in with some chiefs and other people who were bathing. With these a quarrel was soon picked; a fight ensued, in which some natives were killed by *Keoua*, and the corpses were taken to Honaunau to be offered in sacrifice by *Kiwalao*, which he did.

The slain people belonged to *Kamehameha*.

The crisis had come, and the pretext for the rising of the Kona chiefs.

The native historians are rather minute on some details connected with these events, while they touch but lightly on other matters that to us would appear of greater importance. But in carefully comparing the various now existing sources of information, it appears that a kind of skirmishing fight was kept up for two or three days, and that, although the fight originally commenced between *Keoua Kuahuula* and *Kamehameha*, without the command or sanction of *Kiwalao*, yet he was gradually drawn into it in support of his brother as against *Kamehameha*. The contest now had become one between *Kiwalao* and the *Kamehameha* faction, and the chiefs ranged themselves on either side. With *Kamehameha* stood *Keeaumoku, Keawe-*

a-Heulu,[1] *Kameeiamoku, Kamanawa, Kekuhaupio,* and some chiefs from Kohala, besides his brothers, *Kalaimamahu, Kawelookalani,* and *Kalanimalokuloku.*[2] With *Kiwalao* came the Hilo, Puna, and Kau chiefs, beside some notable defections from the *Kamehameha* party, especially *Kanekoa*[3] and *Kahai,* and some other chiefs of lesser note.

This mustering of forces on both sides, from day to day, eventually brought on a set battle. On a morning in July 1782, the chiefs of the *Kamehameha* party started for the battlefield, but *Kamehameha* himself was detained at Kealakeakua by *Holoae,* the old high-priest, and his daughter, *Pine,*[4] who were in the act of performing the auguries incumbent on the occasion. At the same time *Kiwalao* marched with his troops from Honaunau, and at Hauiki in Keei he met *Keeaumoku* with the opposing party, and the battle began. At first success leaned to the king's side; the rebel chiefs were driven back, a number of soldiers were slain and brought to *Kiwalao* to be sacrificed to his god, and expectation arose that the royal party would be victorious.

About this time *Kamehameha* arrived on the field, and the equilibrium of the battle was in a measure restored. While the fight was progressing, *Keeaumoku* got entangled with his spear in the rocky ground and fell. Immediately

[1] His father was *Heulu,* a great-grandson in direct descent from *I,* and on his mother's side a grandson of the famous *Mahiololi* of Kohala. His wife was at one time *Ululani,* also a descendant of *I,* and hereditary chiefess of the Hilo district. Their children were *Naihe,* a son who died childless, and *Keohohiwa,* a daughter, of whom the present royal family are the great-grandchildren. For reasons now unknown, but perfectly in consonance with the customs of that age, *Ululani* left *Keawe-a-Heulu* and became the wife of *Keawemauhili,* with whom she had several children. She

outlived both her husbands, and died towards the close of the century.
[2] Otherwise known as *Keliimaikai.*
[3] *Kanekoa* was a son of *Kalanikeeaumoku* and his wife *Kailakauoa,* and thus a paternal uncle of *Kamehameha.* Both he and his brother *Kahai* went over to the *Keawemauhili* party during this crisis. The present queen *Kapiolani,* on her father's side, is the great-grand-daughter of *Kanekoa.*
[4] She was the wife of *Kekuhaupio* above mentioned, and ancestress to present Hon. Mrs. *Pauahi Bishop.*

Kahai[1] and *Nuhi*[2] rushed upon him and stabbed him with their daggers, while *Kini* struck him in the back with his spear, exclaiming as he did so, " The spear has pierced the yellow-backed crab."[3] *Kiwalao* seeing *Keeaumoku* falling called out to the soldiers, " Be careful of the ivory neck-ornament, lest it be soiled with the blood." On hearing these words *Keeaumoku* knew that no quarter would be given, and expected every moment to be the last. His half-brother *Kamanawa*, however, had also seen him fall, and instantly despatched a division of his men to succour him, or at least bring his corpse off. Hurrying up to the spot they drove away the assailants of *Keeaumoku*, and one of the troop, *Keakuawahine* by name, armed with a sling, threw a stone that struck *Kiwalao* on the temple of his head and stunned him as he fell. When *Keeaumoku* saw *Kiwalao* falling he crawled up to him, and with an instrument garnished with shark's teeth cut his throat.

After *Kiwalao's* death the rout of his party became general. *Keoua Kuahuula* fled to the shore, where his canoes had been ordered to wait. Hastily embarking, he sailed back to Kau, where he was acknowledged as Moi and successor to his brother *Kiwalao*. A number of chiefs and warriors fled to the mountain and ultimately found their way through the forests to Hilo and Kau. A large number were taken prisoners, among whom was *Keawemauhili*.

This first battle of *Kamehameha* for the empire of the group has been called the battle of " Mokuohai."

When *Keawemauhili* was captured he was led to Napoo-poo and confined in a building at Waipiele, under the guard of *Kanuha*, there to await the pleasure of *Keeaumoku* as to the time when he was to be offered in sacrifice.

---

[1] The other uncle of *Kamehameha* referred to in note to previous page ; brother of *Kanekoa.*

[2] *Nuhi* was a chief from Waimea Hawaii, father of *Laanui,* and grand-father of the present Mrs. *Elizabeth Kaaniau Pratt.*

[3] " *Ku aku la ka laau i ka aama kua lenalena,*" referring to *Keeaumoku's* surname, *papai-ahiahi,* " the evening crab."

Kanuha and some of the other chiefs, either touched by compassion or awed by the high rank of the prisoner—he being one of the highest tabu chiefs and an " Alii Niaupio " for two consecutive generations—managed during the night to let him escape ; and, making good use of his opportunity, *Keawemauhili* crossed the mountain, and, after making a detour by Paauhau, in Hamakua, arrived safely in Hilo and proclaimed his independence of both *Kamehameha* and *Keoua Kuahuula.*

The result of the battle of Mokuohai was virtually to rend the island of Hawaii into three independent and hostile factions. The district of Kona, Kohala, and portions of Hamakua acknowledged *Kamehameha* as their sovereign. The remaining portion of Hamakua, the district of Hilo, and a part of Puna, remained true to and acknowledged *Keawemauhili* as their Moi ; while the lower part of Puna and the district of Kau, the patrimonial estate of *Kiwalao,* ungrudgingly and cheerfully supported *Keoua Kuahuula* against the mounting ambition of *Kamehameha.*

In order to properly understand the political relations and rival pretensions of these three chiefs, and to disillusion oneself from certain impressions obtained from those who in the earlier days wove the history of *Kamehameha* into legend and song, or from those who in after years kept up the illusion from force of habit or from interested motives, it may be well to " take stock," as it were, of the political capital with which each one supported his claim to supremacy.

Keawemauhili was undoubtedly the highest chief in rank, according to Hawaiian heraldry, of the three. He was the son of *Kalaninuiamamao* and *Kekaulikeikawe-kiuokalani,* the latter being the half-sister of the former and daughter of *Kauhiokaka,* one of *Keaweikekahialiio-kamoku's* daughters. Hence he was also called *Keawe-Wililua.* As " Aliiaimoku," or provincial chief of the populous district of Hilo and its late accretions in Hamakua and Puna, he was also the most powerful and opulent chief on Hawaii. He had always been loyal and faithful to his brother *Kalaniopuu* during his reign; and when at his death *Kiwalao* succeeded, he naturally was looked upon as the first prince of the blood, the Doyen of the Hawaiian aristocracy, and as such became the prime counsellor and executive minister under his nephew *Kiwalao*. When *Kiwalao* was killed in the battle of Mokuohai by the revolted Kona and Kohala chiefs, there was actually no chief living on Hawaii of sufficient rank and influence whom *Keawemauhili* would acknowledge as his superior, or to whom he could rightfully transfer his allegiance, except to *Kiwalao's* daughter, *Keopuolani*, who was then but an infant, and had fled with her mother and grandmother to *Kahekili* on Maui. The power and resources of *Kamehameha*, though successful in the late battle, were yet of too untried and unconsolidated a nature to impress themselves on *Keawemauhili* as a political necessity that must be submitted to without a struggle. Moreover, he looked upon *Kamehameha* and the chiefs associated with him as rebels against *Kiwalao* and himself. Under those circumstances *Keawemauhili* could not do otherwise than take the stand he did, and oppose the pretensions of *Kamehameha* with all his might.

Keoua Kuahuula, the half-brother of *Kiwalao*, while acknowledging the superior rank of his uncle *Keawemauhili*, shared fully in his opinions as to the status and claims of *Kamehameha*, whom they both looked upon as a rebel and usurper. At the death of his brother the lordship of Kau, provisionally at least, descended to him as the next heir of his father, and he was acknowledged as such by the Kau chiefs, as well as by the other members of his family, notably by his brothers *Kaoleioku*[1] and

[1] The mother of *Kaoleioku*, as well as of the two *Keouas*, was *Kaneka-polei*, one of the wives of *Kalaniopuu*. It was bruited, however, at the time of his birth that *Kamehameha* was his real father, and in after life the latter so acknowledged it. At this time, however, *Kaoleioku* adhered to the

Keoua Peeale. He was young, adventurous, and ambitious. He might hold his fief under his niece *Keopuolani*, but under *Kamehameha* never. In conjunction with his uncle *Keawemauhili* he deemed himself a match for *Kamehameha*, and thus personal enmity and political considerations urged him to assert the independence of his possessions and a war *à l'outrance* with *Kamehameha*. Of the bitterness of feeling that grew up between these two it is hardly possible now to form an adequate conception. Crimination and recrimination were bandied about between the rival courts and their adherents, and a period of intense excitement ensued, during which the characters of the rival chiefs were outrageously smirched by their respective opponents. From *Keoua's* point of view he would have been a traitor and coward had he yielded to *Kamehameha*, and so the strife went on for many a year to come.

In writing the history of this period thus much is due in justice to *Keawemauhili* and *Keoua Kuahuula*. It has been too much the habit of former writers to consider the battle of Mokuohai as an accident between two equally and legally constituted monarchs, and the opposition of *Keawemauhili* and *Keoua* as a selfish and wilful refusal to submit to lawful authority.

The last, but not least, prominent figure in the triangular fight that distracted Hawaii for upward of nine years was *Kamehameha*. His birth and lineage have already been related. His father, *Keoua Kalanikupua*, was the uterine brother of *Kalaniopuu*, and grandson of *Keawe* of Hawaii. His mother, *Kekuiapoiwa II.*, was a granddaughter of the same *Keawe* and, through her father *Haae*, a scion of the great *Mahi* family in Kohala. His rank was consequently high, among the very highest, and had *Kalaniopuu* had no son to succeed him as Moi of Hawaii, there can be

party and shared the fortunes of his brother *Keoua* until the death of the latter. *Kaoleioku* died in 1816, and, through his daughters *Pauahi* and *Konia*, became the grandfather of Her Highness *Ruth Keilikolani* and of Hon. Mrs. *Bernice Pauahi Bishop.*

hardly any doubt that the claims of *Kamehameha* by blood and rank would have prevailed over any other claimant in any convocation of chiefs to whom the subject might have been submitted. His patrimonial possessions, which he shared with his brothers *Kalaimamahu* and *Keliimaikai*, were small when compared with his rivals, and would never have justified or enabled him to compete for the throne of Hawaii, notwithstanding his high lineage; but his personal character, his well-known talents, and often-tried ability had brought him a host of powerful friends and created a confidence in him as a leader, when the interests of those friends were threatened by the intolerable greed of *Keawemauhili*, the fiery ambition of *Keoua Kuahuula*, and the weak and irresolute character of the actual sovereign. At this period *Kamehameha* was past the meridian of life, being some years over forty, and, after his retirement from the court of *Kalaniopuu*, appears to have found pleasure and occupation in his own family and in the cultivation of his lands; and it is not now known, and has never been alleged, that in any way he mixed in the intrigues or shared in the apprehensions which agitated the court and alarmed the country after the death of *Kalaniopuu*. It is certain, moreover, that it was the great Kona chiefs who sought him out—not he them —when their personal fears for their own possessions made them contemplate and counsel revolt as an escape from the unfair division of the lands which they apprehended under the new regime. It was their urgent solicitations, and the prospect of a crown which they held out, that moved *Kamehameha* from his quiet retreat in Kohala. The compact was that he should lead and they should aid, and the guerdon, which they reserved to themselves and their children, was the enjoyment and enlargement of their possessions and a participation in the administration of the government. And faithfully did *Kamehameha* perform his part till the day of his death. These chiefs were *Keeaumokupapaiahiahi*, *Kameeiamoku*, his brother

Kamanawa, and *Keawe-a-Heulu.* The three first were grandsons of the famous *Kalanikauleleiaiwi,* the wife of *Keawe* of Hawaii; the fourth was the most prominent male representative of the proud and powerful *I* family; and each one of these could on occasion have mustered some thousands of spears to battle. That these chiefs at that time, and for years afterwards, were looked upon by the commonalty, and looked upon themselves, as something more than the mere counsellors of *Kamehameha*—in short, as his partners in the conquest of the kingdom—is an historical fact that it is well not to forget; openly and tacitly during his and their lifetime *Kamehameha* acknowledged his indebtedness to them, and on sundry occasions, even after his power was confirmed, he bore and forbore with their crotchets and delinquencies where another monarch would have punished. This political relation between *Kamehameha* and those chiefs will go far to explain the fact why, failing heirs to the throne in the *Kamehameha* family, the national sentiment at the election of the present king went back to the head of one of those families who, in the war of Mokuohai, brought *Kamehameha* to the front of affairs; who placed the crown on his head that in those uncertain times might have dropped on one of their own; and who remained faithful and loyal to their choice in an age when intrigues, defection, and treason were the order of the day, and the rebel of one island or district was sure to find sympathy and assistance from the king of another.

When *Kahekili,* the king of Maui, learned the result of the battle of Mokuohai, and that *Kamehameha* ruled over the entire leeward side of the island of Hawaii, he sent the message to him asking for assistance in his contemplated invasion of Oahu, as related on page 220, note 1. Instead of returning to *Kahekili* the messengers were persuaded to remain on Hawaii, took service under *Kamehameha,* and were rewarded with lands.

Neither of the three independent chiefs of Hawaii was in a hurry to renew the war which all felt must end in

Kamehameha.

the extermination of two of the three. Warlike preparations resounded on every side; fashioning spears and daggers, building of war canoes, and enlisting men. How long this armed suspense, for it can hardly be called a truce, might have continued there is no knowing, but accident made it the duty of *Kamehameha* to be the first aggressor.

Kanekoa, one of the uncles of *Kamehameha*—who, it will be remembered, previous to the battle of Mokuohai, had gone over to the party of *Kiwalao* along with his brother *Kahai*, and after the battle had found refuge and protection with *Keawemauhili* at Hilo—for reasons not now remembered, revolted from *Keawemauhili* and took up arms to defend his real or pretended rights. The result was that he was defeated, and with his brother fled to Kau, where *Keoua* received him hospitably and gave him lands to live on. After a while—how long cannot be specified in months—difficulties arose between *Kanekoa* and *Keoua*, and the former raised troops and made war on the latter. *Keoua* immediately went in pursuit of the ungrateful rebel, and falling in with him between Olaa in Hilo and the crater of Kilauea in Kau, at a place not otherwise designated, fought a battle with him in which he was defeated and killed. When *Kanekoa* fell, his younger brother, *Kahai*, seeing safety in no other direction, fled to Kona, where *Kamehameha* was at the time residing, and presented himself before his nephew with all the signs of extreme grief and abject submission. Moved to compassion at the death of one uncle and the destitute condition of the other, and remembering the youthful days he had passed under the roof of *Kanekoa* at Waimea, he resolved to avenge his death and commence at once the long-deferred contest with *Keawemauhili* and *Keoua*.

After consulting with his counsellors and completing his preparations by sea and land, *Kamehameha* moved his forces to Kawaihae. The passage of the war canoes was endangered by stormy weather, and the army, marching over the mountain, suffered from cold and severe rains, so that the expedition was remembered by the name of " Kamaino." At Kawaihae the plan of the campaign was agreed upon in the council of *Kamehameha.* The fleet of war canoes under command of *Keeaumoku* was to attack and harass the Hilo coast, while the main army under command of *Kamehameha* marched inland, towards the crater of Kilauea, with the intention of preventing the junction of *Keoua's* and *Keawemauhili's* forces, and of fighting them in detail should no junction have been effected. Arriving at Kilauea, *Kamehameha* learned that *Keoua* with the Kau army was encamped at a place above Ohaikea in Kapapala, some twenty miles distant over a difficult country. A council of war was held, and it was considered more prudent to act in conjunction with their own fleet, which by this time ought to be off the Hilo coast. Orders were therefore given to descend to Hilo and give battle to *Keawemauhili* first.

On descending the mountain from the neighbourhood of Kilauea, *Kamehameha's* army debouched at a place called Puaaloa, just outside of the Panaewa woods, some three or four miles east of Hilo Bay. Here the Hilo army, reinforced by the Maui auxiliaries under *Kahahawai,* met the invaders and a severely-contested battle ensued, in which a number of lives were lost on both sides. *Kahahawai* and his lieutenant, *Kahuewa,* are said to have performed prodigies of valour. *Kamehameha's* brother, *Kalanimalokuloku,* narrowly escaped with his life. The Kona and Kohala forces were utterly routed, *Kamehameha* himself obliged to flee, and his defeat would have been decisive and fatal to himself and his chiefs had they not been able to save themselves on board of the fleet under *Keeaumoku,* that was hovering near the shore and received the fugitives. It is related that in his flight *Kamehameha* was pursued by a soldier from the opposite ranks named *Moo,* who tauntingly called out to him, " O Lord ! do not be in a hurry; it is only me" (*E Kalani E! e akahele paha ka holo, owau wale no*).

When *Kamehameha* had saved all that he could on board of his fleet, he sat sail for Laupahoehoe in North Hilo, where he landed and established his headquarters.

This second war of *Kamehameha* has been called "Kauaawa"—the bitter war—on account of its reverses.

A short time after his debarkation at Laupahoehoe *Kamehameha* started one day with his own war canoe and its crew alone, without making his object known to his counsellors, and unaccompanied by any of them. Steering for the Puna coast, he ran in upon the reef at a place called Papai in Keaau. A number of fishermen with their wives and children were out fishing on the reef, and, as they were about returning ashore, *Kamehameha* rushed upon them with the object of slaying or capturing as many he could, they being the subjects of *Keawemauhili*. The greater number of these people saved themselves by flight, but two men were hemmed off and they engaged in fight with *Kamehameha*. During the scuffle *Kamehameha's* foot slipped into a crevice of the coral reef, and, while thus entangled, he was struck some severe blows on the head with the fisherman's paddle. Luckily for *Kamehameha* the fisherman was encumbered with a child on his back, and ignorant of the real name and character of his antagonist. Extricating himself with a violent effort, *Kamehameha* reached his canoe and returned to Laupahoehoe.

This excursion is by native historians called "Kaleleike." It was one of those predatory expeditions and wild personal adventures characteristic of the times and the reckless daring of the chiefs.

In singular commemoration of his own narrow escape from death on the above occasion, for having wantonly attacked peaceable and unoffending people, *Kamehameha* in after life called one of his most stringent laws, punishing robbery and murder with death, by the name of *Mamalahoe*, the "splintered paddle."

The foregoing events must have occurred during the latter part of 1782 and early part of 1783, for it is well established that shortly after *Kamehameha's* raid on Keaau, and while he was still residing at Laupahoehoe, *Kahekili* of Maui sent *Akalele* to *Keawemauhili* to recall *Kahahawai* and the Maui auxiliaries in order to join *Kahekili* in his invasion of Oahu, which took place that year. Feeling perfectly secure as against any further attempts of *Kamehameha*, *Keawemauhili* readily released the Maui troops from his service, and both he and *Keoua* sent a number of war canoes to the assistance of *Kahekili*.

On his return passage from Hilo to Maui, *Kahahawai* stopped at Laupahoehoe and fearlessly presented himself before *Kamehameha*, who received his late enemy courteously and kindly.

Seeing no prospect of prosecuting the war to any advantage, *Kamehameha* shortly after this left Laupahoehoe and established his court at Halaula and at Hapuu, in Kohala, and seriously occupied himself with the reorganisation and improvement of his portion of the island. During his residence here, some time in the year 1784, *Kekuhaupio* died at Napoopoo, in Kona, having been accidentally but mortally wounded during a spear exercise. *Kekupaupio* enjoyed by the common consensus of all his contemporaries the reputation of having been the most accomplished warrior of his time, and as wise as he was brave. His death was a great loss to *Kamehameha* and his chiefs.

During the year 1785 *Kamehameha* again invaded the territories of Hilo. A protracted and desultory war was kept up with the combined Kau and Hilo forces; but no decisive results were obtained. In the absence of more definite information about this war, it is probable that *Kamehameha* was again repulsed, but that the Hilo and Kau chiefs were too weak to follow up their success by invading *Kamehameha's* territories.

At the close of the campaign *Kamehameha* returned to

Kohala and resided at Kauhola, in Halaula, where he turned his attention to agriculture, himself setting an example in work and industry. The war just referred to has been called the war of "Hapuu," and also the war of "Laupahoehoe-hope."

It was during this year of 1785 that *Kamehameha* took *Kaahumanu* to be one of his wives. This lady, who fills so prominent a place in modern Hawaiian history, after the death of *Kamehameha*, was the daughter of his counsellor, coadjutor, and most devoted friend, *Keeaumoku-papai-ahiahi;* her mother was *Namahana*, of the royal Maui family, and a half-sister to *Kahekili*. *Kaahumanu* was then about seventeen years old. Up to this period *Kamehameha* had had but two recognised wives. One was *Kalola*, referred to on page 201 ; the other was *Peleuli*. Her parents were *Kamanawa* and *Kekelaokalani*. The former a son of *Keawepoepoe* and grandson of *Kalani-kauleleiaiwi*, of the royal Hawaii family, and the latter a daughter of *Kauakahiakua* and *Kekuiapoiwa-Nui*, both of the royal Maui family. With this *Peleuli Kamehameha* had four children :—(1.) *Maheha Kapulikoliko*, a daughter, of whom nothing more is known ; (2.) *Kahoanoku Kinau*, a son, whose wife was *Kahakuhaakoi*, a daughter of *Kekuamanoha,* of the Maui royal family, with whom he had a daughter, *Keahikuni Kekauonohi*, who died in 1847 ; (3.) *Kaikookalani*, a son, whose wife was *Haaheo*, a niece of *Keawemauhili* by his sister *Akahi*, and who afterwards became the wife of *Kuakini*, one of the brothers of *Kaahumanu ;* (4.) *Kiliwehi*, a daughter, who became the wife of *Kamehamehakauokoa.*

Nothing worthy of notice appears to have transpired on Hawaii after the war of "Hapuu" until the following year (1786), when the expedition to Hana, Maui, was fitted out under command of *Kamehameha's* brother *Kala-nimalokuloku,* as already narrated on page 229, under the article of "Maui."

In 1786, as previously stated, the first foreign vessels

touched at the Hawaiian group after the death of Captain Cook. The discovery of the islands, with its brilliant opening and its tragical close, had been a nine years' wonder to the civilised world. The first impression of horror and affright had been softened by time, and cupidity growing stronger than fear, men thought more of the advantages that offered than the dangers that menaced.

In 1787-8-9 and 1790 a steadily increasing number of English, American, French, Spanish, and Portuguese vessels touched at the islands and traded with the people. Iron, pure and simple and in its various forms of utensils, guns, and ammunition brought fabulous prices, and other things in proportion. To the natives it was an era of wonder, delight, and incipient disease; to their chiefs it was an El Dorado of iron and destructive implements, and visions of conquest grew brighter as iron, and powder, and guns accumulated in the princely storerooms. The blood of the first discoverer had so rudely dispelled the illusion of the "Haole's" divinity that now the natives, not only not feared them as superior beings, but actually looked upon them as serviceable, though valuable, materials to promote their interests and to execute their commands. Not a few of the seamen belonging to the foreign ships that now dodged each other in the island ports and underbid each other in the island markets had deserted their vessels and taken service under this or that chief, and already the dawn of a new day had sent its grey streaks of morning across the dark sky of Hawaiian night. Men wondered no longer at the sight of a foreigner, and chiefs pondered deeply on themes of glory and conquest that would never have had a shadow of realisation but for the foreigners' arms and the foreigners' knowledge enlisted in their service.

It may well be supposed that *Kamehameha* neglected no opportunity of improving his circumstances and increasing his stores from the newborn commerce that courted his country. Ruling over the entire western half of Hawaii, with its splendid climate, its smooth sea, its regular sea-breeze, its commodious roadsteads, its dense population, and abundant food supply, there is no doubt that he and his chiefs took the lion's share of all the commerce that the foreign vessels brought to the group. Doubtless considerable trade was carried on with the windward districts, where *Keawemauhili* and *Keoua* ruled supreme, but for the reasons above stated the major part of such trade was distributed along the western coast, and whatever was of special value or use soon found its way to *Kamehameha's* warehouses.

For once at least commerce brought peace for a season. No wars have been recorded on the islands during this period. Chiefs and commoners were all too busy to raise supplies and other articles wherewith to barter for foreign commodities. If the hatchet was not actually buried, it was at least turned to a more productive use than the splitting of an enemy's head. Unfortunately the fires that mouldered were not quenched, and with increasing power and resources the old contentions burst out anew, and to *Kamehameha's* name attaches the odious and weighty responsibility of having set the island world ablaze again.

I have referred on page 222, note 1, and page 231 to *Kaiana-a-Ahuula*, his voyage to China along with Captain Mears in the ship " Nootka," and his return to the islands and debarkation on Hawaii in January 1789, where he was welcomed by *Kamehameha,* who looked upon his large and miscellaneous property of guns and ammunition, acquired while abroad, as a valuable aid in future enterprises.

The detention of John Young by *Kamehameha* and the narrow escape of Isaac Davis, two foreigners belonging to the American vessels " Eleanor " and " Fair American," have been already mentioned on pages 231 and 235 as occurring in March 1790. It must therefore have been during the middle, probably latter, months of that year that *Kamehameha* invaded Maui and fought the famous battle of Iao, which campaign is mentioned on page 237.

There is now no means of knowing at what time or in what manner *Keawemauhili* and *Kamehameha* came to a peaceable understanding, so much so as to induce the former to assist the latter with canoes, with men, and even with his own sons to command them in the campaign against Maui. That *Keawemauhili* did so assist *Kamehameha* is a well-known fact, and that *Keoua Kuahuula* did resent that assistance as a breach of the agreement between himself and *Keawemauhili* is equally well known. How he revenged himself by invading Hilo, by defeating and slaying *Keawemauhili* in the battle at Alae, ravaging the Hamakua district, and crossing over to Waimea, sent equal terror and devastation into the Kohala district, has already been mentioned on page 240, &c. The entire island lay open and defenceless before him, unless *Kaiana*, whom *Kamehameha* had left to guard the Kona district in his absence, could have made an effectual resistance. The news, however, had reached *Kamehameha* in time, and abandoning his conquests on Maui and Molokai, and his intended invasion of Oahu, he hurried back to Hawaii to defend his own dominions, to avenge the death of *Keawemauhili*, and to finally and definitely settle the question of superiority between himself and *Keoua.*

When *Kamehameha* landed at Kawaihae he learned that *Keoua* was at Waimea, and with the least possible delay he started to encounter his enemy. Whether *Keoua* had heard of the arrival of *Kamehameha* and wished to avoid him, or that he preferred some other battle-ground, it happened that when *Kamehameha* and his army had ascended to Waimea, *Keoua* had retreated to Paauhau, in the Hamakua district, where he awaited the arrival of *Kamehameha*. Here a battle was fought and obstinately contested on both sides. *Kamehameha* had one fieldpiece in action, known in the native account by the name of

"Lopaka," which appears to have greatly annoyed the *Keoua* party, until by a brilliant charge it was captured by *Kaiaiaiea*, one of *Keoua's* chiefs. Great carnage was committed on both sides, but the battle proved indecisive, and was renewed at Koapapa, not far distant, on the following day. Long and bitter was the strife of that day, but the powder falling short on the side of *Keoua*, he withdrew his forces and retreated to Hilo.

Though *Kamehameha* was victorious in the battle, and master of the field, yet his victory had cost him so dearly that he was unable to pursue the retreating foe, and, satisfied for the time with having driven *Keoua* out of his territory, he turned down to Waipio to recruit his losses.

Having reached Hilo, *Keoua*, considering that district now as part of his own possessions, stopped there awhile to divide the lands between his chiefs and soldiers; and having performed that act of suzerainty, he set out for his own home in Kau. It was on this return march that a great disaster befell a portion of his army while passing by the crater of Kilauea. The most graphic and correct account of that disaster is given by Dibble in his "History of the Sandwich Islands," page 65, and as it corresponds with the information that Kamakau received from a living witness to the event, I transcribe it here. Dibble says—

"His (*Keoua's*) path led by the great volcano of Kilauea. There they encamped. In the night a terrific eruption took place, throwing out flame, cinders, and even heavy stones to a great distance, and accompanied from above with intense lightning and heavy thunder. In the morning *Keoua* and his company were afraid to proceed, and spent the day in trying to appease the goddess of the volcano, whom they supposed they had offended the day before, by rolling stones into the crater. But on the second night and on the third night also there were similar eruptions. On the third day they ventured to proceed on their way, but had not advanced far before a more terrible and destructive eruption than any before took place; an account of which, taken from the lips of those who were part of the company and present in the scene, may not be an unwelcome digression."

"The army of *Keoua* set out on their way in three different companies. The company in advance had not proceeded far before the ground began to shake and rock beneath their feet, and it became quite impossible to stand. Soon a dense cloud of darkness was seen to rise out of the crater, and almost at the same instant the electrical effect upon the air was so great that the thunder began to roar in the heavens and the lightning to flash. It continued to ascend and spread abroad till the whole region was enveloped, and the light of day was entirely excluded. The darkness was the more terrific, being made visible by an awful glare from streams of red and blue light variously combined that issued from the pit below, and being lit up at intervals by the intense flashes of lightning from above. Soon followed an immense volume of sand and cinders, which were thrown in high heaven and came down in a destructive shower for many miles around. Some few persons of the forward company were burned to death by the sand and cinders, and others were seriously injured. All experienced a suffocating sensation upon the lungs, and hastened on with all possible speed.

"The rear body, which was nearest the volcano at the time of the eruption, seemed to suffer the least injury, and after the earthquake and shower of sand had passed over, hastened forward to escape the dangers which threatened them, and rejoicing in mutual congratulations that they had been preserved in the midst of such imminent peril. But what was their surprise and consternation when, on coming up with their comrades of the centre party, they discovered them all to have become corpses. Some were lying down and others were sitting upright, clasping with dying grasp their wives and children, and joining noses (their form of expressing affection) as in the act of taking a final leave. So much like life they looked that they at first supposed them merely at rest, and it was not until they had come up to them and handled them that they could detect their mistake. The whole party, including women and children, not one of them survived to relate the catastrophe that had befallen their comrades. The only living being they found was a solitary hog in company with one of the families which had been so suddenly bereft of life. In those perilous circumstances the surviving party did not even stay to bewail their fate, but leaving their deceased companions as they found them, hurried on and overtook the company in advance at the place of their encampment."

In the above disaster it is said that *Keoua* lost about 400 fighting men.

The war with *Keoua* was vigorously continued by *Kamehameha* during the year 1791. One army corps under command of *Keeaumoku,* to which John Young and Isaac Davis were attached, operated against Hilo, while another corps under *Kaiana-a-Ahaula* was sent against Kau. Though sorely pressed on both sides, yet *Keoua* bravely kept his ground during the spring and summer of that year, and no decisive advantages were gained by *Kamehameha* in any of the battles fought. The prolonged contest, however, began to tell upon the resources of *Keoua,* yet with consummate tact and bravery he showed a bold and ready front to every attack, from whatsoever quarter aimed.

No reminiscences of the operations against Hilo have survived, but of the campaign in Kau some notices have been collected by the native historians. Supported by a fleet of war canoes hovering about the South Cape (" Lae a Kalaeloa ") of Hawaii, *Kaiana* fought several engagements with *Keoua* at Paiahaa, at Kamaoa, and at Naohulelua, but they were what may be called drawn battles, *Kaiana* sometimes remaining ·master of the field, and sometimes being obliged to fall back on his flotilla for support. During one of the intermissions in this martial game *Keoua* suddenly changed his ground from Kau to Puna. *Kaiana* looked upon this move as a confession of weakness, followed *Keoua* into Puna, and with jubilant exultation anticipated an easy victory. At a place called Puuakoki the two forces met, and *Kaiana* was so severely handled by *Keoua* and by his generals, *Kaieiea* and *Uhai*, that he made a precipitate retreat out of Puna and returned with his men to Kona, reporting his ill success to *Kamehameha.*

Meanwhile the great Heiau on Puukohola, at Kawaihae, was approaching completion. It will be remembered (*vide* page 240) that when *Kamehameha* had sent *Haalou*, the grandmother of his wife *Kaahumanu*, to consult the wisest of the Kauai soothsayers, she brought back the advice of *Kapoukahi* to build a Heiau on Puukohola to the war-god *Kukailimoku*, and that that act would secure to *Kamehameha* the kingdom of Hawaii. Whether it was that *Kamehameha* preferred to try the efficiency of carnal weapons before having recourse to spiritual agencies, and believed more in his guns and his powder than in the prayers of his priests, certain it is that the building of the Heiau was but little advanced when *Kaiana* returned from Kau ; and as no victories have been reported from the army corps under *Keeaumoku* against Hilo, it is presumable that the campaign in that direction had been equally unsuccessful. After nine years of struggle between the two sections of the island, *Kamehameha* stood no nearer to the supremacy of Hawaii than he did on the day of Mokuohai. He was richer, no doubt, in men and arms and the means of destruction that commerce had brought him, but *Keoua* had also shared in the fruits of that commerce, and so their relative means were about the same as at the beginning of the contest.

Keoua had repulsed *Kamehameha* both from Kau and Hilo, but was probably too crippled by his victories to follow them up by invading Kona or Hamakua. *Kamehameha* had trusted to spear and gun, and, however successful in other directions and against other chiefs, they had proved powerless to subdue *Keoua ;* and so he bethought himself of the Kauai soothsayer's advice, and the construction of the Heiau on Puukohola was resumed with a vigour and zeal quickened, perhaps, by a consciousness of neglected duty. Relays of people were ordered from Kona, Kohala, and Hamakua to repair to Kawaihae to carry stones and assist at the building. Chiefs of the highest degree and common natives worked side by side, and *Kamehameha* himself set the example of carrying stones to the building. There was but one exception known, and that was *Kamehameha's* younger and favourite brother *Keliimaikai.* Tradition says that when all the chiefs set out to carry stones to the Heiau, *Keliimaikai* also took up a stone and started with the others. Seeing which, *Kamehameha* rushed up and, taking the stone from the other's shoulder, exclaimed, " Some one must observe the Tabu, be thou the one." He then ordered the stone that had been touched by *Keliimaikai* to be taken out to sea and sunk in deep water. To judge from the heathen ritual of that time and its stringent requisitions, the object of this exception doubtless was that some high chief of tabued rank should remain uncontaminated by the menial labour of carrying stones, so as to preside at the ordinary sacrifices and assist at the purification of the others, when the building should be completed.[1]

It is often difficult to bring the events of Hawaiian history into their proper chronological order. Regarding the war and the invasion of Hawaii, undertaken by the joint forces of *Kahekili* and *Kaeo,* related on page 242,

[1] The author a few years ago conversed with a centenarian Hawaiian at Kawaihaeuka who had assisted in carrying stones towards building this Heiau. His description of the thousands of people encamped on the neighbouring hillsides, and taking their turns at the work, of their organisation and feeding, their time of work and relaxation, the number of chiefs that attended, and who, as the old man said, caused the ground to tremble beneath their feet ; and the number of human victims that were required and duly offered for this or that portion of the building— this description was extremely interesting and impressive.

there is great difference between the Hawaiian authorities.
David Malo places the occurrence shortly after the death
of *Keoua*, but does not state the year; Jarvis places it
after the last departure of Vancouver, which took place in
1794; Dibble places it before the building of the Heiau
on Puukohola; and Kamakau places it before the death
of *Keoua.* The truth probably is this, that *Kahekili* and
Kaeo, learning the small progress which *Kamehameha* was
making in his war with *Keoua*, and believing him fully
occupied with all his men and means in its prosecution,
thought this a favourable opportunity to harass his provinces and retaliate his invasion of Maui the preceding
year, and, possibly also, as a diversion in favour of *Keoua.*
How, after ravaging Waipio and Kohala, they were beaten
in the sea-fight, known as "Kepuwahaula," has already
been narrated. Whether it took place before or after the
completion of the Heiau of Puukohola, it may now be
impossible to ascertain; but that it took place before the
death of *Keoua* there can be little doubt; and that the
defeat of *Kahekili* and *Kaeo* in some measure influenced
Keoua to enter into negotiations with *Kamehameha* seems
to be a probable inference. The same want of chronological precision characterises my historical predecessors
in regard to the time of *Keoua's* death. D. Malo,[1] without
stating any year, intimates that it happened before the
battle of "Kepuwahaula." Dibble[2] places the event
shortly after the eruption of Kilauea, referred to on page
324, which would bring it into the latter part of 1791
or beginning of 1792. Jarvis[3] says it occurred in 1793.
Kamakau says it occurred in 1791, after the completion of
the Puukohola Heiau. I believe Dibble and Kamakau
are nearest the truth. It certainly occurred after the
erection and consecration of Puukohola and before the
arrival of Vancouver in March 1792.

Dibble, Jarvis, and Kamakau all concur in stating that

[1] Moolelo Hawaii, page 105.   [2] History of Sandwich Islands, page 67.
[3] History of Hawaiian Islands, page 69.

Keoua was enticed by false promises to leave Kau and visit *Kamehameha* at Kawaihae, where he was murdered while in the act of landing. Dibble intimates that "the deed was not done at the order of *Kamehameha*." Jarvis says that *Keeaumoku* acted under "secret instructions," and scouts the idea of *Kamehameha* not being privy to the murder. Kamakau admits that it was done in the presence of *Kamehameha*, but leaves his reader to infer that it was an act of over-officiousness on the part of *Keeaumoku*, who slew *Keoua*. David Malo is silent on the subject. In critically examining the above sources of information, and from what appears to have been the general opinion of that generation of Hawaiians who were contemporary with the event, it is impossible to acquit *Kamehameha* of complicity in the cruel death of *Keoua*. It must have been planned in his council. It was executed by three of his highest chiefs and most trusted counsellors. The deed itself took place in his presence and within sound of his voice ; and there is no mention, tradition, or hint that he ever disapproved or regretted it, or in the slightest manner rebuked or punished those who treacherously enticed *Keoua* away, or him who actually stabbed him.

Before passing sentence, however, upon *Kamehameha* for what will always remain the darkest blot upon his otherwise fair name, the candid and impartial historian will not fail to take into consideration the political and social condition of the country and the principles of right and wrong that governed men's actions in that age. *Kamehameha* had contended with *Keoua* for the supremacy of Hawaii for more than nine years, and had failed to subdue him. Frequently routed, but never conquered, *Keoua* valiantly held his own, and on several occasions repelled the invaders of his territory. Each looked upon the other as an usurper, and the bitterest personal hatred had sprung up between them, heightened and envenomed, if possible, by the most outrageous vilifications with which each party branded he other. And in those days the putting away of an obnoxious person by secret means, be he chief or commoner, where open force had made default, was not a crime that the gods condemned or society criticised too severely. Moreover, even if the deed had been planned without the knowledge and done without the consent of *Kamehameha,* yet the very men who planned and executed it were also the very men who had raised *Kamehameha* on the throne, who had aided and supported him throughout this long contest, and who singly or jointly were too powerful to be safely rebuked or alienated for an act, whose very object was to remove his rival, to increase his power and render it for ever secure. Under these considerations, though the deed was none the less a cruel wrong and a foul murder, and posterity will so designate it, it is well to bear in mind that the actors in that deed, while undoubtedly the foremost men of their age, yet were men of that age and of no other, swayed by its modes of thought, following its modes of action. But *Kamehameha* and his victim have both mouldered in dust. Nearly a hundred years have folded their cooling wings over those burning hearts. The sceptre has passed from the family of the former, and not a scion remains of the latter to point a finger or call out for vengeance. Their disputes are settled, and history resumes its course.

In referring to the tragedy of *Keoua,* neither Dibble nor Jarvis gives any detail. I shall therefore follow Kamakau, whom I believe to be substantially correct, though somewhat verbose.

After the unsuccessful campaign of *Kaiana* against *Keoua,* and after the Heiau of Puukohola had been finished, but not yet consecrated, *Keaweaheulu* and *Kamanawa,* two of the four principal counsellors of *Kamehameha,* set out for Kahuku in Kau, where *Keoua* then held his court. *Keaweaheulu* and his party landed at Kailikii, and, passing over the upland of Keekeekai, arrived at *Keoua's* abode. On approaching the fence of the royal residence they prostrated themselves according to the etiquette of that time. Mutual recognitions were exchanged, and information given to *Keoua* of the arrival of *Kamehameha's* ambassadors. *Kaieiea*, the chief counsellor of *Keoua*, advised him to put the two chiefs to death, saying that "thus *Kamehameha* would lose two of his wisest and wiliest counsellors, and the supremacy of the island would easily pass to *Keoua*." Prompted by better feelings *Keoua* refused, remarking, "they are the brothers (near relatives) of my father, and they shall not die." They were accordingly admitted, and, crawling up according to custom, they embraced the feet of *Keoua* and wailed. When the wailing was over *Keoua* asked them what their errand was. They then said, "We have come to you, the son of our late lord and brother, to induce you to go with us to Kona to be united and reconciled with your younger brother (meaning *Kamehameha*), that you two may be the kings, and we, your parents, live under you. Let the war between you two come to an end." To which *Keoua* replied, "I am agreed; let us go to Kona."

The arrangements for the journey were soon made. Sending some of his party by land, *Keoua* himself embarked with the others in his double canoes. At Honomalino the overland party was picked up and they all proceeded to Kaawaloa, where they were the guests of *Keaweaheulu*, from Kaawaloa to Kailua, and from there to Luahinewai in Kekaha, which was the last stopping-place previous to Kawaihae. Here *Keoua* bathed and prepared himself for the possible events of the day; either a friendly reception by *Kamehameha*, or to die as became a chief of his rank and fortune. During the journey from Kau to this place *Kaieiea* had more than once endeavoured to obtain the consent of *Keoua* to kill *Keaweaheulu* and *Kamanawa* and to return to Kau, but *Keoua* had always and peremptorily refused.

There can be no doubt but that *Keoua* was well aware of the great risk he ran in thus trusting himself in the power of *Kamehameha.* His motives can only be guessed at. He may have felt a touch of the old chivalric spirit, and thought that his own life would be held as sacred as he had held the lives of *Kamehameha's* counsellors sacred. He may have been moved by the fatalism of the ancient creed, and, tired of the never-ending war and the unaccomplished objects of life, may have considered his course run and his time up, and that the only object worthy of consideration was how to die with the dignity and *éclat* becoming so great a chief. But men's motives are frequently of a mixed nature, seldom apprehended by themselves, and not always acknowledged. While *Keoua* fairly trusted the smooth speeches and large promises of *Keaweaheulu* and *Kamanawa,* yet with a singular contradiction of that trust he, on that fatal morning, prepared his own body for the sacrifice, selected out of his company those whom he wished to be his companions in death, his " Moe-pu," and caused all others to be put in a separate fleet of canoes to follow after him, under the charge of his half-brother, *Pauli Kaoleioku,* whose life he supposed *Kamehameha* would at all events spare, the young man being the natural son of *Kamehameha.*

Having deposited his feather cloaks and other valuables in *Keaweaheulu's* canoe, *Keoua* stepped on the platform of his own double canoe, followed by *Uhai,* his kahili-bearer, and by his ipu-bearer (whose name is not given). Twenty-four oarsmen propelled the canoe. When off Puako, the environs of Kawaihae burst upon his sight; the great and new Heiau of Puukohola; the fleet of war canoes, many of them mounted with guns, forming a semicircle in the bay, the crowds of chiefs and warriors upon the beach, and other war-like appearances. Observing this, *Keoua* said to *Keaweaheulu,* whose canoe was near his own, " It looks bad ashore, the clouds are flying unfavourably " (Ino uka, ke lele ino mai nei ke ao). To which *Keaweaheulu* replied, " By whom should the evil come on so pleasant a day ? " (Nawai hoi ka ino o ka la malie). *Keoua* merely repeated, "The clouds have an unfavourable flight."

When the canoes were close to the landing at Mailekini in Kawaihae, *Keeaumoku* surrounded *Keoua's* canoe with a number of men armed with spears, guns, and other weapons, and *Keaweaheulu's* canoe was separated from that of *Keoua*. Seeing *Kamehameha* on the beach, *Keoua* called out to him, "Here I am;" to which *Kamehameha* replied, "Rise, and come here that we may know each other." As *Keoua* was in the act of leaping ashore, *Keeaumoku* struck him with a spear. *Keoua* turned hastily and caught hold of the spear, endeavouring to wrench it out of the hands of *Keeaumoku*, but in vain, and falling down he expired. All the men in *Keoua's* own canoe, and in the canoes of his own immediate company, were killed, with two exceptions. One was *Kuakahela*, a priest of the Nahulu order, who succeeded in reaching the shore, and hastily entering the house of *Kekuiapoiwa*, and lifting up the edge of the mats, hid himself thereunder. *Kekuiapoiwa's* house being tabu, he was not pursued, and remained there until the proclamation was issued to cease slaying. The other saved one was *Laanui*, who had secretly left his canoe at Puako, before entering the bay of Kawaihae. All others but these two, of either high or low rank, that formed the escort of *Keoua*, were killed. And this cruel butchery, which must have required some time to execute, was done under the very eyes of *Kamehameha* himself, who never lifted his voice to stay the slaughter, until the second division of *Keoua's* escort, under the command of *Pauli Kaoleioku*, approached, then the word was given, and the lives of *Kaoleioku* and all his company were saved.[1]

The body of *Keoua* was taken to the Heiau of Puuko-

[1] One of the versions of this tragedy, current among the last generation of Hawaiians, was, that *Keliimaikai*, the younger brother of *Kamehameha*, interceded for the life of *Keoua*, but in vain, and that when the second division of *Keoua's* escort, in charge of *Kaoleioku*, arrived, *Keliimaikai* insisted that he also should be slain, saying to *Kamehameha*, "You have

hola and there sacrificed to *Kamehameha's* war-god *Ku-kailimoku.* It is not known whether *Keoua* had any children or what became of them. His wife's name was *Hiiakq,* but of what family I have been unable to ascertain.

Thus fell *Keoua;* and the districts ruled by him passed at once under the sceptre of *Kamehameha,* and once more the entire island of Hawaii bore fealty to one king alone. It was the first step in the consolidation of the group under one government, whereby civilisation could be made possible and permanent. Providence does not provide angels for the introduction of necessary reforms in human affairs. It works by the means at hand, and one age unavoidably leaves its imprint upon the next. Of *Kamehameha* and *Keoua,* the former was probably the better means for the end in view—the consolidation and civilisation of the group—but he left the marks of the age of heathenish darkness, in which he was reared, upon the work that he took in hand. We admire the edifice whose foundation he laid, but we note that one of its corner-stones is laid in blood.

After the death of *Keoua* it is not known how *Kamehameha* employed the spring months of 1792. It is fairly presumable, however, that he was visiting the newly-acquired districts of Hilo, Puna, and Kau, and incorporating them in the body politic of which he now was the sole head. Certain it is that when the English commander, Vancouver, approached the western coast of Hawaii in March 1792, *Kamehameha* was neither at Kealakeakua nor at Kawaihae. *Kaiana* was his lieutenant in the former place, and *Keeaumoku* at the latter. To *Keeaumoku* Vancouver gave some goats and fruit and garden seeds, and, being pressed for time, left for the

killed my *Hanai,** and I will now kill yours." To which *Kamehameha* replied, "He shall not die; he is the child of my youth;" and ordered his elder brother *Kalaimamahu* to proclaim a cessation of the slaughter.

* *Hanai* means a "foster-child."

Leeward Islands, and thence for the north-west coast of America.

On the 13th of February 1793, Vancouver returned from the coast of America and anchored at Kawaihae, where *Keeaumoku* was still dwelling. Mutual civilities were exchanged, and on the 19th Vancouver landed a bull and cow, the first of its kind, on these islands, intended as a present to *Kamehameha*, who had not yet arrived at the bay. Vancouver had some difficulty in landing the animals, but having satisfied the greediness of *Kamehameha's* brother, *Kalaimamahu*, the latter furnished a large double canoe, on which the animals were safely landed.[1]

On February 21st the ships were visited by *Kamehameha*, who had arrived at the bay, by his wife *Kaahumanu*,[2] by John Young, and a number of chiefs. It was the first time since the night off Maui, in November 1778,[3] that *Kamehameha* and Vancouver had met, and the surprise and pleasure was mutual, and a sincere friendship sprang up between those two.

On February 22d, Vancouver with his ships, and *Kamehameha* with his court, went to Kealakeakua. Here Vancouver landed five cows, two ewes, and one ram, as a present for *Kamehameha*, and exacted of him a promise that they should be tabued for ten years. Right royally did *Kamehameha* requite Vancouver's beneficent present. On his very first visit on board ninety of the largest-sized

---

[1] In vol. ii. p. 120, Vancouver says that on the 20th February 1793, *Kamehameha's* eldest son, about nine years old, came on board. Vancouver does not give the lad's name. It may have been *Kahoanoku Kinau*, or it may have been his nephew, *Kekuaokalani*, the son of *Keliimaikai*. It could not possibly have been *Pauli Kaoleioku*.

[2] The difficulty of judging the age of Hawaiians by their looks is well illustrated by the wellnigh random guesses, by which the navigators of those days expressed their opinion of the ages of certain prominent Hawaiians. In speaking of *Kaahumanu* in March 1793, Vancouver says that she was "about sixteen years old." It is now thoroughly well established that *Kaahumanu* was born in 1768 at Kauwiki, in Hana, Maui, and that *Kamehameha* took her as his wife in 1785, about the time of the campaign of Hapuu or Laupahoehoe Lope. She was consequently twenty-five years old when Vancouver saw her.

[3] *Vide* pp. 171, &c.

swine were deposited on the decks of the vessels, and a prodigious quantity of fruit and vegetables, besides feather cloaks and feather helmets; and during the entire stay of Vancouver hardly a day passed without some kind remembrance of similar kinds from *Kamehameha.*

It was at this time that Vancouver exerted himself to negotiate a peace between the two sovereigns of Maui and Hawaii. With what result has already been narrated on pages 252, &c.

On the 8th of March 1793 Vancouver left Hawaii, and after visiting the Leeward Islands, as already related in article " Maui," proceeded again to the north-west coast of America.

On January 9th, 1794, Vancouver returned from the American coast and came to off Hilo, Hawaii. The vessels being unable to enter the port on account of bad weather, *Kamehameha* and his suit went on board and accompanied them to Kealakeakua, where Vancouver anchored on January 12, and he and his ships became the national guests of *Kamehameha*, and were constantly and liberally provided with hogs and vegetables.

At this time Vancouver landed some more cattle for *Kamehameha*, and allowed the ships' carpenters to assist the foreigners[1] in the employ of *Kamehameha* to build a small schooner, which was named the " Britannia," the first vessel of the kind built on the islands.

Since the last visit of Vancouver an estrangement and separation had occurred between *Kamehameha* and his wife, *Kaahumanu*, occasioned by what appears to have been an unfounded jealousy of *Kaiana*, and she was now living with her father, *Keeaumoku.* Through the good offices of Vancouver a reconciliation was effected and the royal pair made happy. But as a strange instance of the manners of the time, even in high life, Vancouver narrates that, before quitting the ship where the reconciliation

[1] The principal of those foreign carpenters in *Kamehameha's* employ was named Boid.

took place, *Kaahumanu* insisted that Vancouver should exact a promise from *Kamehameha* not to whip her when they returned home.

We learn from Vancouver that at this time *Kaheiheimalie*, afterwards known as *Hoapiliwahine*, a younger sister of *Kaahumanu*, was still the wife of *Kamehameha's* brother, *Kalaimamahu*. Vancouver also mentions " a captive daughter of *Kahekili*," who was then residing at *Kamehameha's* court. The person referred to was either one of *Kahekili's* nieces and his sister *Kalola's* daughters, *Kalaniakua* or *Liliha Kekuiapoiwa*, or else *Kalola's* granddaughter, *Keopuolani*, which three ladies were brought from Molokai to Hawaii by *Kamehameha* after the death of *Kalola*, as related on page 238.

This may perhaps be the proper place to refer to some remarks of Mr. Jarves, in his " History of the Hawaiian Islands," touching events at this time.[1] He says, speaking of Vancouver's *séjour* at Kealakeakua Bay :—

" To confirm the general good-will and establish an amnesty for past troubles, *Palea*, the chief who stole the cutter of the " Resolution," was allowed to visit the vessels ; *Kameeiamoku*, the murderer of young Metcalf and his crew, having humbled himself, and urged in justification of his revenge the harsh treatment he had received from the father, obtained permission to come on board. He arrived at the bay in great state, attended by a thousand men. This act does not appear consistent with Vancouver's previous inflexibility in obtaining justice upon the death of his countrymen at Oahu. In this instance the property was American, and the principal actor a high chief, whom it would have been difficult to secure, and whose death would have caused a hostility which would have led to dire revenge. Impunity for crime where wealth and rank are engaged is not peculiar to the savage."

When Mr. Jarves penned the above lines he knew [2] that

---

[1] Jarves' History, p. 80.   [2] *Ibid.*, p. 59.

the ungrateful and barbarous treatment of *Palea* by an officer of the " Discovery " was never apologised nor atoned for, and that his unselfish exertions, in saving the crew of the " Resolution's " pinnace from being stoned to death by the natives, had not been noticed or acknowledged by Captain Cook, though he was present on the scene shortly after the occurrence. The provocations given by the civilised and enlightened side, what could be expected from the barbarous and ignorant side? If *Palea's* sum- mary settlement of his accounts with Cook, by abducting the cutter of the " Resolution," was not according to moral law, and contrary to the peace and dignity of His Majesty George III., yet Mr. Jarves might have done better justice to the memory of that injured chief than to brand him as a common thief, to be pardoned by the gracious amnesty of Vancouver. When Mr. Jarves speaks of *Kameeiamoku* in the same breath as of the murderers of Lieutenant Her- gest, of the " Dædalus," he evidently makes no distinction between the wanton unprovoked murder for robbery's sake by those lawless Oahu brigands, and the cruel pro- vocation that impelled *Kameeiamoku* to execute that vengeance on the tyrant Metcalf, which in his country, and from his point of view, was neither immoral nor illegal, the *Hoomauhala* being as cherished an institution with the ancient Hawaiians as the vendetta with some of the peoples in Southern Europe. And to such a mind, under such conditions, whatever belonged to Metcalf, from his child to his cat, would have been equally doomed to destruction in expiation for the wrong and the insult which *Kameeiamoku* conceived that Metcalf had inflicted upon him. We, writing in our peaceful parlours, whether in 1840 or in 1870, are naturally very much shocked at the killing of young Metcalf and his crew, and regret that the savage *Kameeiamoku* should have taken the law in his own hands; and perhaps we would have preferred that he should have gone and laid his complaint before *Kamehameha*, who at that very time was driving a lucrative trade with the elder Metcalf at Kealakeakua, and meditating how to kidnap Metcalf's boatswain, John Young. But the candid historian will judge men according to the standard of the times in which they lived, and will certainly not place *Kameeiamoku* in the same category with the Oahu ruffians who killed Lieutenant Hergest.

And, finally, when Mr. Jarves accuses Captain Vancouver of inconsistency in admitting *Kameeiamoku* to his presence, and being so inflexible in "obtaining justice upon the death of his countrymen at Oahu," and intimates that "in this instance the property was American, and the principal actor a high chief," &c., Mr. Jarves writes as a partisan and not as a historian, and commits a gratuitous libel on the good name of Vancouver, than whom no more judicious, high-souled, or kind-hearted man, in his dealings with the barbarous tribes that he encountered, ever sailed the high seas. There is no shadow of justification for assuming that the nationality of the sufferers in the least influenced Captain Vancouver in his treatment of the offenders. There may be a question how far Vancouver would have been justified in taking up the quarrels of other governments than his own with native chiefs. Vancouver expressly relates his personal repugnance to meet *Kameeiamoku* on account of the murder of young Metcalf; but, as Mr. Jarves puts it, *Kameeiamoku* "having humbled himself," and urged the extenuating circumstances above referred to, Vancouver received him as he did *Palea*. Of Vancouver's sense of fairness there is abundant evidence in the trial of the Oahu culprits, where they and their witnesses were again and again interrogated as to whether the captain and crew of the "Dædalus" had in the least manner committed any act that could possibly have been construed as an injury or a provocation, but they all admitted that the attack on the captain and the astronomer was unprovoked, wanton, and solely for the sake of plunder.

Many and sage were the counsels that Vancouver gave

Kamehameha and his chiefs touching their intercourse with foreigners, and in due time much of it bore good fruit. One thing, however, weighed heavy on *Kamehameha's* mind and that of his chiefs. They had heard and learned that there were other peoples on the earth with ships of war as powerful as those of "*Pelekane*" (Britannia); they had seen the armed merchant ships of the United States of America, of Spain, and Portugal; they had seen the French La Perouse and his squadron; and whether the idea arose in their own minds or was instilled by the foreigners residing among them, they felt an apprehension that at any unlooked-for moment some one of those other powers might pounce upon and take possession of their island. Who so likely to protect them as that power which had discovered and made them known to the others, and whose present representative had, by his judicious, generous, and unselfish conduct, won their fullest confidence and respect? From this germ of ideas sprang what by some writers has been called the cession of the islands by *Kamehameha* to the English Crown. In Vancouver's "Voyage," vol. iii., may be read his narrative of the whole transaction from his point of view. While *Kamehameha* and his chiefs became willing to acknowledge King George as their suzerain, in expectation of his defending them against foreign and outside foes, they expressly reserved to themselves the autonomous government of their island in their own way and according to such laws as they themselves might impose. It is not evident that Vancouver did or could hold out to the Hawaii chiefs anything more than the probability of such protection, the cession, from even his point of view, requiring the acceptance and ratification of the English Government, which it never received. That *Kamehameha* and his chiefs did not understand the full meaning of the word cession is plain from the reservations which they made. As it was, the so-called cession of the island of Hawaii was no doubt entered into by Vancouver with the very best intentions for the protection and advancement of the Hawaiians, and by *Kamehameha* and his chiefs with undisguised expectations of receiving material aid in their wars with *Kahekili* and *Kaeo*, and of certain commercial advantages not very well defined. The cession, however, was never accepted or ratified by the English Government, and no steps were taken by emigration or colonisation to make good use of the friendly disposition of the chiefs, and to secure by stronger ties the suzerainty thus loosely acquired. The disturbed state of Europe and the wars and troubles incident to this period diverted the attention of England, and a cession that might have become to Hawaii what the treaty of Whanganui fifty years later became to the New Zealanders quietly went by default and was lapsed by non-user.

To make the above cession as imposing and stately as possible, Vancouver sent Lieutenant Paget ashore to formally take possession and to hoist the English colours over the land that thenceforth was to have acknowledged King George IV. as its lord of lords—its protecting Numen, when badgered by insolent trading captains, or when bullying its own neighbours of the Leeward Islands. This ceremony was performed on the 25th of February 1794, and the parties present[1] on Vancouver's ship, who discussed and consented to the cession, were *Kamehameha*, his brothers *Keliimaikai*, and *Kalaimamahu*, the latter of whom Vancouver styles a "chief of Hamakua;" *Keeaumoku*, chief of Kona; *Keaweaheulu*, chief of Kau; *Kaiana*, chief of Puna; *Kameeiamoku*, chief of Kohala; and *Kalaiwohi*,[2] who is styled a half-brother of *Kamehameha*.

On February 26th, 1794, Vancouver left Kealakeakua, and on March 3d he left Kawaihae for the Leeward Islands.

---

[1] Vancouver, vol. iii. p. 54.

[2] I know of but one *Kalaiwohi* of that time, and he was the son of *Kalanikauleleiaiwi II.*, who was a half-sister of *Keawemauhili* of Hilo, their common mother being *Kekau-* *like-a-Keawe*. According to modern ideas of relationship he would have been called a second cousin of *Kamehameha*. *Kalaiwohi's* daughter, the venerable chiefess, *Kaunahi*, died in Lahaina, 1875, at a very advanced age.

After the departure of Vancouver nothing seems to have disturbed the tranquillity of Hawaii during the balance of the year 1794, though the Leeward Islands were profoundly moved by the events transpiring there. The death of *Kahekili;* the war between *Kaeokulani* and *Kalanikupule* on Oahu; the defeat and death of *Kaeo;* the seizure by *Kalanikupule* of the English vessels, "Jackal" and "Prince Le Boo," and the murder of their captains; the preparations for an invasion of Hawaii and its sudden frustration; the recapture of the vessels by their crews; all those events narrated on pages 268, &c.; each in its measure and each in due order, led up to the final act of Hawaiian ancient history, the consolidation of *Kamehameha's* empire, and the unification of the island group under one head, one will, and one system.

According to Hawaiian sources of information, the two recaptured vessels, after putting *Kalanikupule* ashore and leaving Oahu, made the Hawaii coast and acquainted *Kamehameha* with the state of affairs on Oahu, and, in exchange for refreshments and other trade, having delivered to him the guns, ammunition, and arms which *Kalanikupule* had collected and stored on board for the invasion of Hawaii. Acting on this intelligence, and having been thus fortuitously reinforced with warlike stores, *Kamehameha* and his chiefs determined that the time had come for the final struggle with the Maui dynasty for the possession of the group. Messengers were despatched to the great feudal lords to muster with their contingents of canoes and armed men.

The strength of *Kamehameha's* army, with which he invaded Oahu, has never been definitely stated by native historians. That it was not only unprecedentedly large, but also organised and armed according to all the latest instructions of Vancouver to *Kamehameha,* may be taken for granted. In the month of February 1795 *Kamehameha* left Hawaii with a fleet of canoes which, when it arrived at Lahaina, Maui, is said to have occupied the beach from Launiupoko to Mala. Refreshments alone being the object of stopping at Lahaina, the town was plundered, after which the fleet proceeded down the channel and came to at Kaunakakai, Molokai, being distributed along-shore from Kalamaula to Kawela. For some time previous to this great enterprise a coolness, that at any moment might become an open rupture, had been growing between *Kaiana* and *Kamehameha* and his aged chiefs and supporters. The latter were offended at the airs of superiority which *Kaiana* gave himself on the strength of his foreign voyages and foreign knowledge, and they were jealous lest his influence with *Kamehameha* should overshadow their own; while *Kamehameha*, on his part, deeply mistrusted the loyalty of *Kaiana*, whose ambition he measured with his own, but who had hitherto lived too circumspect to give an open cause to fasten a quarrel upon him and precipitate his ruin. *Kaiana*, on the other hand, had for some time been painfully aware that his influence was waning in the council of *Kamehameha*, and that his conduct was watched by no friendly eyes. His proud spirit chafed at his owing fealty and allegiance to *Kamehameha*, whom he looked upon as no greater chief than himself, a cadet of the younger branch of the royal house of *Keawe*, whom the fortune of Mokuohai and the, for the times, unexampled constancy of the great Kona chiefs had placed at the head of affairs on Hawaii. Still, when the summons was issued for the invasion of Oahu, *Kaiana* appeared at the rendezvous with his contingent of canoes, of warriors, and arms, as numerous and as well equipped as those of any other district chief. If he meditated defection or treason that was not the moment to show it. He knew full well that it might have delayed the expedition, but it would have ensured his utter and complete ruin to attempt single-handed to fight *Kamehameha* and the combined forces of the rest of Hawaii. And so *Kaiana* sailed with the other fleet to Lahaina and to Molokai.

What additional or later provocations *Kaiana* may have given to *Kamehameha* are not known; but after the arrival of the fleet at Molokai, at the very first council of war or of state that *Kamehameha* held at Kaunakakai with his chiefs to discuss and arrange the plans of the campaign against Oahu, it is certain that *Kaiana* was not invited to attend.

To a man like *Kaiana* this omission was not only a slight, that might be explained and forgiven, but an actual omen of danger, that must immediately be attended to and met or averted. He felt morally certain that his own death was as much a subject of discussion as the invasion of Oahu. Restless and annoyed, *Kaiana* left his quarters at Kamiloloa and went to Kalamaula, passing by Kaunakakai, where the council was held. Calling at the house occupied by *Namahana*, the mother - in - law of *Kamehameha* and the wife of *Keeaumoku*, *Kaiana* was invited in. After the usual salutations *Kaiana* said, "I have called out of affection for you all to see how you are, thinking some of you might be unwell after the sea voyage; and as I was coming along I find that the chiefs are holding a council, and I was considerably astonished that they should do so without informing me of it." *Namahana* replied, "They are discussing some secret matters." "Perhaps so," *Kaiana* said, and the subject was dropped; but *Kaiana* knew the men and their temper too well, and knew also that the only secret matter for their deliberation, to which he could not be a party, would be a question affecting his own fate.

Returning from Kalamaula, as he was passing Kapaakea, where *Kalaimoku's* quarters were, he heard a voice calling, "Iwiula E! Iwiula E! Come in and have something to eat." Recognising the voice of *Kalaimoku*, *Kaiana* entered and sat down.

The better to understand the relation of these two chiefs, it may be well to bear in mind that *Kalaimoku's* father, *Kekuamanoha*, was at this time still on Oahu, and supporting the interest of his nephew *Kalanikupule ;* and that *Kalaimoku,* having visited Hawaii in the train of *Kalola,* his aunt, and of *Kiwalao,* on their return from Maui, about a year or more before the death of *Kalaniopuu,* had remained at the court of *Kiwalao* until the battle of Mokuohai, when he was taken prisoner by the *Kamehameha* party ; that his life having been spared by the intercession of *Kamehameha,* he became firmly attached to the latter, who had taken a great liking to him, had employed him on many occasions of responsibility and trust, and on this very expedition had confided to him the command of a large portion of the invading army. On the other hand, *Kaiana,* though on his father's side a grandson of *Keawe* of Hawaii, appears to have set greater value on his connection with the Maui royal family, of which his mother was a near and prominent relative. Only by bearing this in mind can we rightly understand the peculiar yearning with which *Kaiana* accosted his Maui relatives, and the full drift of the conversation that occurred between him and *Kalaimoku* on this occasion.

Of that conversation, and the allusions therein occurring, I have been unable to obtain a very exact and reliable sketch, though it has been referred to by more than one native writer; but from what has been reported, it appears that *Kaiana* had made some appeal to *Kalaimoku,* on the strength of their common kindred to the Maui royal family, and that he had received evasive and unsatisfactory answers. So much was *Kalaimoku* impressed with the manner and purport of *Kaiana's* discourse, that, fearful lest some one should have betrayed the resolutions of the council to *Kaiana,* he went to Kaunakakai, as soon as the latter had gone, and informed *Kamehameha,* who, however, treated the matter with apparent indifference.

From his interview with *Namahana* and with *Kalaimoku,* it was now clear enough to *Kaiana's* mind that his ruin and death had been determined upon by the chiefs, and when he returned to his own quarters he informed

his brother *Nahiolea* of the state of affairs, telling him
that if they remained with *Kamehameha* they would
surely be killed secretly and suddenly; but that if they
joined the forces of *Kalanikupule*, the son of their brother,
as he called *Kahekili*, they might fall in battle, if so
should be, but they would die like men and like chiefs,
with their faces to the foe, and with numbers to accompany them in death.

Whatever may have been the resolution of *Kamehameha's* council as to the time and manner of despatching
Kaiana, its execution was apparently deferred, and the
invading fleet left Molokai in the same order and high
spirit as it had arrived.

Kaiana's resolution, however, had been taken, and his
plans formed. When that portion of the fleet which
carried the wives and daughters of *Kamehameha* and the
principal chiefs was ready to start, *Kaiana* goes to the
canoe, where his wife *Kekupuohi* was sitting, and, bidding
her a tender farewell, tells her of his intention to secede
from *Kamehameha* and join *Kalanikupule*. She expressed
some astonishment, but said that she preferred to follow
her chief (*Kamehameha*), and that thus, in case of unfore-
seen events, both their interests might be best subserved.

It has never been stated if the whole of *Kaiana's*
contingent to *Kamehameha's* army, or what portion of it,
followed him in his defection. The number must have
been considerable, however, including his own and his
brother's immediate friends and retainers. Neither has
it been stated whether the passage across the channel was
made in the night or in daytime. Certain it is, however,
that during the passage *Kaiana* and those who adhered
to him separated from the main fleet and landed on the
Koolau side of Oahu, whence, crossing the mountain, they
joined *Kalanikupule*.

In the meantime *Kamehameha* landed his fleet and dis-
embarked his army on Oahu, extending from Waialae
to Waikiki. Consuming but a few days in arranging

and organising, he marched up the Nuuanu valley, where *Kalanikupule* had posted his forces, from Puiwa upwards, occupying Kaumuohena, Kapaeli, Kaukahoku, Kawananakoa, Luakaha, Kahapaakai, Kamoniakapueo, and Nuuanu. At Puiwa the hostile forces met, and for a while the victory was hotly contested ; but the superiority of *Kamehameha's* artillery, the number of his guns, and the better practice of his soldiers, soon turned the day in his favour, and the defeat of the Oahu forces became an accelerated rout and a promiscuous slaughter. Of those who were not killed, some escaped up the sides of the mountains that enclose the valley on either side, while a large number were driven over the pali of Nuuanu, a precipice of several hundred feet in height, and perished miserably. *Kaiana* and his brother *Nahiolea* were killed early in the battle. *Koalaukani*, the brother of *Kalanikupule*, escaped to Kauai. *Kalanikupule* was hotly pursued, but he escaped in the jungle, and for several months led an errant and precarious life on the mountain-range that separates Koolaupoko from Ewa, until finally he was captured in the upper portion of Waipio, killed, brought to *Kamehameha*, and sacrificed to the war-god " Kukailimoku."

This battle, known as the battle of Nuuanu, after making all necessary allowances for preparations, journeys, and delays, could not possibly have been fought much earlier than the middle of April 1795. It made *Kamehameha* master of Hawaii, Maui, Kahoolawe, Lanai, Molokai, and Oahu, and though the acquisition of Kauai was delayed for several years, yet from this battle and the conquest of Oahu dates the unification and consolidation of the Hawaiian group under one government. It is the closing scene in the ancient history of the Hawaiian Islands. Though many things of the ancient regime survived for years, yet they were doomed to perish in the glare of the new era which that battle inaugurated. Of the transition period that followed—and which can hardly yet be said to have been passed—from feudal anarchy and general law-lessness to personal despotism and stringent repression, and from that to a constitutional monarchy; from social barbarism to a degree of civilisation that is unexampled in the history of mankind considering the time that has elapsed; from the most cruel and oppressive idolatry to the spontaneous repudiation of the idols and adoption of Christianity; of this period, which the battle of Nuuanu rendered possible, there are ample and documentary evidences to guide the candid and impartial historian. It forms the modern era of Hawaiian life—political, social, and religious—and as such has a history of its own, and formed no part of my design when I undertook to unravel the past of this people and, by critically collecting their legends and traditions, preserve the knowledge that they had of themselves, their origin, their migrations, their settlements, their national life, and its various episodes during ancient times.

If I have succeeded in showing that the Hawaiians had a history of their past, and a history worth preserving, my labour will not have been in vain. The dark shadows which flit across its pages are dark indeed, but they are no darker than those which, under even more favourable circumstances, have stained the annals of many a proud nation that formerly stood, or now stands, in the foremost rank of civilisation. I think it is Emerson who has said "that no nation can go forward that has no past at its back." The aphorism is pertinent, is one of the deepest lessons of humanity, and, if rightly used, a stimulus that leads to progress.

APPENDIX.

———◆———

No. I.

PRAYERS TO LONO (*Vide* page 63).

(1.)

Ua lewa mai ka Lani ;
Ua haule o Makakulukahi ;
Ke kau mai la na onohi i ka lewa.
Pili aku la na kapuai o Kahiki ;
5   *Nahae na lala Kamahele o ke Akua ;*
     Helelei-kia ka pohaku Eleku ;
Lele ka mamala i Haehae,
O komokomo kini o ke Akua
Haule ke kino o Lono i ka Hiwa.
10   *Kapu Kanawao i ka naele ;*
     Ku ke kino oia laau iloko o Lani wao ;
     Ua kau ka Aha kapu o Lono iloko a ka iuiu kapu.
Kapu ka leo o ke kanaka !
Eia kahoaka iloko o Kulu-wai maka-lani,
15 *O kahoaka iloko o ka iwi laumania o ke Akua.*
     Eia ka hoailona kapu o ka Aha ;
     Poha mai ka leo o ka hekili ;
     O mai ka maka o ka uwila ;
Nauwe mai ke olai i ka honua ;
20 *Iho mai ka alewalewa me ka anuenue ;*
Hele ino ka ua me ka makani ;
     Wili ka puahiohio ilalo a ka honua ;
     Kaa ka pohaku-pili o ke kahawai ;
     Iho ka omaka wai ula i ka moana.
25 *Eia ka wai-pui-lani ;*
Ke hiolo nei ka pae-opua i ka lani ;
Huai ka wai-punai ka pali.

Akahi maka o ke Akua ;
Alua, aha maka, i lele pono ka ike ma ka kua.
30   *Hoano nui ka leo o koú Akua i ka lani.*
Hahano o mai iloko o Papa-iakea,
Noho mai iloko o ka Makakolukolukahi.
Hoi ke kapu o Lono i Kahiki.
Hoi aku la e kulai i ke kapu o Kahai,
35   *Kau i ka lele ke kapu o Kahai,*
Hina e hio iloko o ka pilikua.
Make ka ia, moe i ka naholo ;
Hina kikepakepa iloko o Kahiki ;
Hoolale Kahai i ka paka o ka ua ;
40   *Hahau Kahai i ka papa o ka moku.*
Eia Lono ka iwi kaola a ka Hiwa ;
Ka iwi kau iloko o ka alaneo.
Paee mai ka leo o ke Akua,
Paee mai iloko o ka nalu alo kahi ;
45   *Ua hanau-mano koú Akua ;*
Hanau-mano iloko o Hinaiaeleele.
E ola áu i kaú waihona-pule !
E ola i ka Alana ola !
E ola i kaú pulapula !
50   *Ia oe e ke Akua !*

Unstable are the heavens ;
Fallen has Makakulukahi ;
The stars still stand in the upper space.
        Approaching are the footsteps of Kahiki ;
5   Broken are the Kamahele branches of the god ;
        Shattered is the brittle stone ;
Strewn are the pieces in Haehae,
And attached are they to the host of spirits ;
Turned has the body of Lono into glory.
10   The Kanawao grows in the moist earth ;
        The body of that tree stands where the gods reside;
        Established is the holy assembly of Lono in the far-
            off sacred place.
Forbidden be the voice of the native !
Here is the spirit within Kulu-wai maka-lani,
15   The spirit within the smooth polished bones of the god.
        These are the sacred signs of the assembly ;
        Bursting forth is the voice of the thunder ;
        Striking are the rays (bolts) of the lightning ;
Shaking the earth is the earthquake ;

20 Coming is the dark cloud and the rainbow ;
Wildly comes the rain and the wind ;
Whirlwinds sweep over the earth ;
Rolling down are the rocks of the ravines ;
The red mountain-streams are rushing to the sea.
25 Here the waterspouts ;
Tumbled about are the clustering clouds of heaven ;
Gushing forth are the springs of the mountains.
One eye has the god ;
Two, four eyes, that he may see clearly behind him.
30 Greatly revered be the voice of my god in heaven.
It has been inspired into Papa-iakea,
And it dwells with Makakolukolukahi.
The tabu of Lono has passed to Kahiki.
It has passed thither and overthrown the tabu of
Kahai,
35 The tabu of Kahai has been sacrificed on the altar,
It has fallen and tumbled into confusion.
Dead are the fish, fallen in their flight ;
Fallen disfigured all through Kahiki ;
Kahai is stirring up the heavy rainstorm ;
40 . Kahai is beating the surface of the land.
Here is Lono, the bone of salvation and glory ;
The bone set up in the serene sky.
Indistinct (softly) comes the voice of the god,
Indistinct through the one-billowed surf ;
45 My god has assumed the shape of a shark ;
Has assumed the shape of a shark in the month of Hina-
iaeleele.
May I be saved through my fulness of prayer !
Saved through my health-offering !
Saved through my devotion !
50 By you, O god !

(2.)

Kiekie e mai nei hoi ua Lani nei,
O ua Lani nei hoi keia ke hemo nei ka manawa o ka Lani;
Ke halulu nei ka piko i lalo ;
He api nei ka halo, ka maha, ka poo o ka honua ;
5 *Uwa mai kini, ka mano o ke Akua.*
Huli aku la ke alo o ke Akua i ka lewa ;
Huli aku la e keehi ia Kahiki.
O mai ka hoano kapu a Lono ;
O mai iloko o Kahiki a hoano.

10 *Oiliili mai ke kino lau o Lono;*
   Kahuli mai ke kino aka o ke Akua,
   Kahuli mai iloko o Maewa-lani;
   Kani ka poo iloko o Papa-ia-mea.
   Ua neoneo ka lani;
15 *Ua ikea mai e Kahiki na maka o Lono.*
   O mai na kukuna o ka malama;
   O Ikua la, o Makalii,
   O Hinaiaeleele, la, o Hilinehu,
   O Kaelo la, O Kaaona, ka malama.
20 *Ua hô iloli mai o Lono;*
   Ua haakokohi mai ka malama,
   Oili ka inaina,
   Hemo ke kuakoko iloko a Hinaiaeleele,
   Nauwe ka eha o Papa-ia-mea.
25 *Helelei ke kino lau o Lono;*
   Ua kau ke aka o Lono i ka molia,
   Ku, a hina i ka mole o ka moku;
   Opaipai lalo o ka Hiwa;
    Wahi ke Akua i ka lani;
30 *Ua paa ia lani.*
   Wahi ke Akua i ka papa o ka honua.
   Uina ka leo o ka Alae iloko o Kanikawi;
   Uina ka leo o ka hekili;
   Uina iloko o ke ao polohiwa;
35 *Naha ka umaka pali o lalo;*
   Hoi ke Akua, noho i ka hanono;
   Hele ke Akua, noho i ka pilikua;
   Hoi ke Akua, O Lono, noho i ka naele.
   Kani ke ka leo o ka pupu;
40 *Kani kaulele ka leo o ke kahuli;*
   Kani halale ka leo o ka manu;
   Uwi ka leo o ka laau i ka nahele;
   Eia ko kino manu, E Lono!
   Ke wili nei ka la i ka lani;
45 *Lele na maka o Lono i lele o Hoomo;*
   Ke noho mai la i ka wa o ka moku.
    Kupu ke kino a kiekie i ka lani,
    Haule na kikeao makini mua,
    Na makahiapo o Hinaiaeleele.
50 *E ola áu ia oe, e Lono, káu Akua!*
   E ola i kalele pule!
   E ola i ka wai oha!
   E ola i kanaenae ia oe, e ke Akua!
   Eia kanaenae la, he mohai leo.

Strangely lofty indeed is this heaven,
This very heaven which separates the seasons of heaven;
Trembling is the lowest point;
Moving are the gills, the fins, and the head of the earth;
5   Exclaiming are the hosts, the multitudes of spirits.
Turned is the bosom of the god to the sky;
Turned and treading on Kahiki.
Extended be the sacred worship of Lono;
Extended through Kahiki and worshipped.
10   Budding are the leaves of Lono;   .
      Changing is the image of the god,
      Changing within Maewa-lani;
      Sounded has the shell in Papa-ia-mea.
Silent are the heavens;
15 The eyes of Lono have been seen by Kahiki,
Extended be the rays of the light;
There is Ikua and Makalii,
There is Hinaiaeleele and Hilinehu,
There is Kaelo and Kaaona, the months.
20   Pregnant has Lono become;
      The light has been taken with the pains,
      The fœtus is coming,
      The birth is made in (the month) of Hinaiaeleele,
      Trembling with pains is Papa-ia-mea.
25 The leaves of Lono are falling;
Doomed is the image of Lono to destruction,
Standing it falls to the foundation of the land;
Bending low is the glory.
      Covered is the god by the heaven;
30   Fastened up is that heaven.
      Covered is the god by the shell of the earth.
      Squeaking is the voice of the Alae inside of Kanikawi;
      Cracking is the voice of the thunder;
      Cracking inside of the shining black cloud;
35   Broken up are the mountain springs from below;
      Passed away has the god, he dwells in the clefts;
      Gone is the god, he dwells in obscurity;
      Passed has the god Lono, he dwells in the mire.
Sounding is the voice of the shell-fish;
40 Sounding increasingly is the voice of the snails;
Sounding excitingly is the voice of the birds;
Creaking is the voice of the trees in the forest;
Here is your body of a bird, O Lono!
Whirling up is the dust in the sky;
45 Flying are the eyes of Lono to the altar of Hoomo;

And he dwells here on the land. '
    Growing is the body high up to heaven ;
    Passed away are the former blustering winds,
    The firstborn children of Hinaiaeleele.
50 May I be saved by you, O Lono, my god !
    Saved by the supporting prayer !
    Saved by the holy water !
    Saved by the sacrifice to you, O god !
    Here is the sacrifice, an offering of prayer (words).

No. II.

THE CHANT OF OHAI KAWILIULA (page 118).

O ke alialia liu o Mana,
Ke uhai la no.
Ke uhai la ka wai ;
Ke uhai la ka wai a Kamakahou.
5 Wai alialia,
Wai o Mana.
Mehe kai la ka wai,
Mehe wai la ke kai ;
Mehe kai la ka wai o Kamakahou.
10   O ka aina ko áu i ai a kiola, haalele,
    Hoi aku a mua,
    Hoohewahewa mai,
    Hoi ana i ke kua, i ke alo.
    O ka Iliau loha i ka la,
15   Puolo hau kakahiaka.
    Hele ke alia o Aliaomao,
    Hele kanu kupapau,
    O ke kaha i Nonohili.
    Halala na niu i kai o Pokii,
20   Hoakua wale la o Makalii.
      &c.   &c.

In English it would read as follows :—

The salt-pond of Mana
Is breaking away.
Breaking away is the water,
Breaking away is the water of Kamakahou.
5 Salt is the water,
The water of Mana.
Like the sea is the water,
Like water is the sea,
Like the sea is the water of Kamakahou.

10 The land which I enjoyed and rejected and forsook
It has gone before,
It is forgotten,
It has gone, both back and front.
The Iliau bush has faded in the sunlight,
15 (As) the plentiful dew of the morning.
Passed by have the emblems of the god of the year;
Gone to bury the dead,
(On) the barren sands of Nonohili.
Bending low are the cocoanut trees seaward of Pokii,
20 Doing reverence to Makalii.

&c.   &c.

NOTES.—*Verse 1. Mana* is a land on the south-west side of Kauai, celebrated for its salt-pond producing very perfect and really beautiful mirages.

Verse 15. "*Puolo hau,*" lit. "a bundle of dew;" a rather violent trope, but not uncommon.

Verse 16. "*Ke alia.*" The two staffs or wands, dressed with feathers, which were carried in procession before *Lono,* the god of the year, during the festival at the close of the year.

Verse 18. Nonohili or *Nohili.* Known as "the singing sands." A number of sandhills along the shore of Mana towards Poli-hale. which produce a soft, rather plaintive sound when a person slides down the hill, or in a similar manner disturbs the sand.

Verse 20. The cocoanut trees at Pokii and adjoining land are represented as bending low in homage to the new year—*Makalii.*

No. III.

DISCOVERY OF THE HAWAIIAN ISLANDS
(page 158).

1. *From the "North Pacific Pilot."* By W. H. ROSSER. London, 1870.

DISCOVERY OF THE ISLANDS, AND PROGRESS OF THE PEOPLE.— In the old Spanish charts taken by Anson from the Manilla galleon there is a group of islands called Los Majos, the different members of which are termed La Mesa, La Desgraciado, Los Monjes, Rocca Partida, La Nublada, &c. ; and they are placed between lat. 18° and 22° N., and between long. 135° and 139° W. ; but their existence in that position—at least as regards longitude—was disproved by the subsequent voyages to the Pacific of La Perouse in 1786, of Portlock and Dixon in 1786, and of Vancouver in 1793. The Spanish word *Mesa*, however, signifies *table*, and is sufficiently indicative of the island of Hawaii, the mountains of which do not, like most volcanoes, rise into peaks, but are " flat at the top, making what is called by mariners *tableland ;* " while other points of coincidence— such as an island-group extending through four degrees of latitude and longitude, the position as regards latitude nearly correct, &c.—would seem to refer to what is now called the Hawaiian Archipelago. The discrepancy as regards longitude (nearly twenty degrees) counts for little where *dead reckoning* was the means employed to determine that element ; as great an error was made by the Hon. East Indian Co.'s ship "Derby" in 1719, proceeding from the Cape of Good Hope to India, when the islands off the west coast of Sumatra were thought to be the Maldives.

The positions given above are, according to various authorities, those in which the Spaniards placed the islands of Los Majos ; but from a note, p. 116, in the second volume of "Voyage de La Perouse autour du Monde, redigé par M. L. A. Milet Mureau," published in Paris in 1797, it appears that Gaetano, in 1542, sailed from Navidad on the west coast of Mexico (lat. 20° N.) ; he steered a due-west course for 900 leagues, when he discovered a group of islands inhabited by savages nearly naked; the islands were fringed with coral, and grew cocoanuts and other fruit; there was neither gold nor silver; he named them Isles del Rey; the island twenty leagues more to the west he called Isle de las Huertas. It is also stated that the Spanish editor of Gaetano's account placed the islands between 9° and 11° N., a clerical error for 19° and 21°. Now Navidad is in lat. 19° 10' N., long. 104° 40' W.; 900 leagues in lat. 19½° in 28° 64' diff. long. (or 47° 44'), which added to the long. of Navidad gives 152° 24', or 2½° short of the long. of the nearest point of Hawaii, but 5½° short of the long. of Oahu; and the next island, Kauai, is sixty miles, or twenty leagues, distant. Thus, if the information conveyed in the note to La Perouse's "Voyage" is correct, it is more than probable that Gaetano *did* visit the Sandwich Islands; but it is extraordinary, as Cook observes, that, considering their favourable position, the Spanish galleons did not visit them.

2. Copy of the Official Communication from the Government of the Marianas Islands, and from the Colonial Office, Spain.

[*Translated from the Spanish.*]

GOVERNMENT OF THE MARIANAS ISLANDS,
AYANA, *January 27th,* 1866.

SIR,—I have the honour to acknowledge the receipt of your Excellency's esteemed communication of the 24th of April, ult., informing me that you had not yet received the notifications referring to the discovery of the Hawaiian Islands by Spanish navigators. It gives me great pleasure to transmit to you, herein enclosed, said notifications translated into the English and French languages, obtained from the archives of Spain, by order of Her Catholic Majesty. These documents will satisfy you that this long-contested discovery took place in the year 1555. These notifications reached me at the same time as your letter.

I am much gratified to comply with your desire on this subject, and I should be happy to have some other occasions to be agreeable to His Hawaiian Majesty, and to strengthen the ties of our good relations.

May God keep you in His guard.

(Signed)   FELIPE DE LA CORTE.

To His Excellency the Minister of Foreign
Affairs of His Hawaiian Majesty.

SIR,—The Marine Department communicated to this office on the 28th January, instant, that which follows. As there do not exist in the archives of this office any records whatever bearing dates previous to the year 1784, when all those of dates anterior to it were transmitted to the Archives Simancas, the Royal order of the 4th instant, communicated by your Excellency to this office, was referred to the Hydrographical Department, for obtaining particulars respecting the discovery of the Hawaiianas or Sandwich Islands, in order to ascertain whether there were to be found records that could elucidate in any way the date of that discovery, and the name of the discoverer. On the 25th instant the Chief of that Department replied as follows :

"SIR,—In fulfilment of the Royal order dated the 7th instant, for the purpose of ascertaining the historical information extant in this office regarding the discovery of the Hawaiianas or Sandwich Islands, I have the honour to send your Excellency the result of the investigations made with the diligence recommended to me in that Royal order. By all the documents that have been examined, it is demonstrated that that discovery dates from the year 1555, or 223 years before Captain Cook surveyed those islands ; and that the discoverer was Juan Gaetano or Gaytan, who gave names to the principal islands of that archipelago. It is true that no document has been found in which Gaytan himself certifies to this fact, but there exist data which collectively form a series of proofs sufficient for believing it to be so. The principal one is an old manuscript chart, registered in these archives as anonymous, and in which the Sandwich Islands are laid down under that name, but which also contains a note declaring the name of the discoverer and date of the discovery, and that he called them ' Islas de Mesa ' (Table Islands). There are, besides, other islands, situated in the same latitude, but 10° farther east, and respectively named ' La Mesa ' (the Table); ' La Desgraciado ' (the Unfortunate) ; ' Olloa,' or ' Los Monges ' (the Monks). The chart appears to be a copy of that called the chart of the Spanish galleon, existing long before the time of Cook, and which is referred to by all the national and foreign authors that have been consulted, such as the following :—' Batavian geography, 2d vol. of the geographical atlas of William Blaen, Amsterdam, 1663.' In the first map, entitled ' America Nova Fabula,' the neighbouring island, ' La Desgraciado,' and those of ' Los Monges,' are placed towards the 21st degree of north latitude, and 120° west of the meridian passing through the island of Teneriffe. ' Geographical Atlas of D'Auville, published in 1761, and revised and improved in 1786 by Barbie du Bocage.' In the second map, and in the hemisphere of the Mappa Mundi, the islands 'Desgraciado,' 'Mesa,' 'Olloa,' and 'Los Monges,' are found in the 20th degree of north latitude, and about $17°$ farther east than the Sandwich group, augmented by Barbie in this chart. James Burney, in the chronological history of the discoveries in the South Sea or Pacific Ocean, cites the atlas of Artelius, entitled 'Theatrum Orbis,' in which the same islands are found, and placed in nearly the same position. 'Alexander Findley's Directory for the Navigation of the Pacific Ocean, edition of 1857.' In the second part of this work, page 1120, the author expresses and recapitulates the ideas already brought forward respecting this matter by Mr. Flurien in his description of Marchand's voyage, and by Mr. Ellis in his voyage around Hawaii ; and conceives strong suspicions that the true discoverer must have been one of the Spanish navigators of the sixteenth century, because of the iron articles found by Cook in those islands, one of them being a fragment of a wide sword, whose existence there he could not satisfactorily account for. The author most explicit in regard to these surmises is the said Fleurien, who, on the 422d page of the first volume, says, 'By taking from Captain Cook the barren honour of the first discovery of the Sandwich Islands, I do not endeavour to diminish the glory he so justly merited ;' and he continues, on page 423, 'Lieutenant Roberts, who constructed the chart of the third voyage of the English navigator, in which are traced his three voyages round the world and towards both poles, has preserved the Mesa group of the chart of the Spanish galleon, and has placed it with its centre $19°$ east of Owhyhee, and in the parallel of the latter island. He doubtless thought that by preserving the group found by the Spaniards, none would dare dispute with the English the first discovery of the Sandwich Islands. But Arrowsmith, in his general chart of 1790, and in his planisphere of 1794, sacrificing his *amour propre* to the evidence, only lays down one of the two groups. Since 1786, La Perouse, desirous of ascertaining if such islands really existed to the eastward of Sandwich, passed over in the same parallel, 300 leagues from east to west, and in the whole of this expanse he found neither group, island, nor any sign of land ; and did not doubt that the island of Owhyhee, with its arid mountain in the form óf a table, was "La Mesa" of the Spaniards;' and he adds, at page 125, 'In the charts, at the foot of this archipelago, might be written : "Sandwich Islands, surveyed in 1778 by Captain Cook, who named them, anciently discovered by the Spanish navigators."' Perfectly in accord with this opinion, and strengthening it by an evident proof, is the log of the corvettes 'Descubierta' and 'Atrevida,' on their voyage from Acapulco to Manilla, which manuscript is preserved in this office, and apropos to this case, states, at folio 25, 'With a sea so heavy from N.W. and N., that while the rolling of the ship increased, and with it the irksome interruption of our internal duties, the speed decreased, with considerable delay to our voyage; scarcely by noon of the 20th could we consider ourselves to be at 72°, in the meridian of Owhyhee, about 55° longitude and 13° latitude; nevertheless we had not, according to our calculation, an error of less than 7° to the eastward, which, considering the long log-line we made use of, and that that error ought not necessarily to be the maximum to which it should be circumscribed on the voyage, strongly supported the suspicion that the Sandwich Islands of Captain Cook were Los Monges and Olloa of the Spanish charts, discovered by Juan de Gaytan in 1555, and situated about 10° to the eastward of the new position fixed upon by the English.' We thus see that the presumptive or circumstantial evidence as to the true discoverer of the Sandwich Islands is indubitable; having on its side the opinions of distinguished men, among whom figure countrymen of Cook himself, men who prefer justice and reason to a vain national pride. The last observation to be considered is the difference in the dates given to the first discovery. Foreign authors say that it took place in 1542, in the expedition commanded by General Rui Lopez de Villalobo; while the Spanish chronicles denote 1555. The latter date should be the more correct one, for Juan Gaytan wrote the narrative of the voyage of 1542, and mentions nothing respecting those islands, while he gives an account of Rocca Partida (Split Rock), and Amblada (Cloudy Island), and of all those he discovered on that expedition. To complete and terminate, therefore, these investigations, there is only wanting the narrative of Gaytan corresponding to the voyage in which he made that discovery; though in my opinion it is not required to make clear the truth of this fact. I have the honour to transmit this to your Excellency by Royal order, so that you may communicate the preceding information to the Government of the Sandwich Islands, and as being consequent to your Excellency's letter, No. 864, dated the 18th July ultimo. God guard your Excellency many years. SEYAS.

"MADRID, 21st February 1865.

"To His Excellency the Superior Civil Governor
of the Philippines.

"It is a true copy.   JOSE FELIPE DEL PAN,
"Acting Colonial Secretary.

"Es traduccion Inglesa
"FLORENCIO LAEN DE VIZMANO."

The remarks of La Perouse upon the effect of the westerly currents in the North Pacific, as regards the longitude of places discovered by the earlier Spanish navigators, are well worthy of attention by those who deny the discovery and identification of the "Los Majos" with the Hawaiian group. His remarks may be found in "Voyage de la Perouse autour du Monde," Paris, 1797, pp. 105–17. In coming up from the southward he found the current between the latitudes of 7° and 19° N., setting west at the rate of three leagues in twenty-four hours, so that when he arrived off the island of Hawaii, he found the difference between his observations and his dead-reckoning amounting to five degrees. Thus, by the latter alone the longitude of Hawaii would have been five degrees to the eastward of its proper place. Bearing this in mind, one has no right to be astonished that the early Spanish navigators, who calculated their longitude by dead-reckoning alone, should after crossing the Pacific from Mexico westward, have placed the island they discovered and named "Los Majos" some ten degrees too far to the eastward. And speaking of those very islands, La Perouse says, p. 106, "Mes differences journalières en longitude me firent croire que ces îles" (the Hawaiian group), "etaient absolument les mêmes" (as the Los Majos).

Vancouver, "Voyage," vol. iii. p. 3, remarks "that his dead-reckoning, on making the islands, coming from the American coast, was 3° 40' to the east of the actual position of Hawaii."

No. IV.

Page 179, *Note* 1.

I HAVE been led to offer a few remarks upon the etymology of the Polynesian word *Akua, Atua, Etua, Otua*—dialutial varia-tions of the same word—from noticing what so eminent a philo-logist as Professor Max Müller says on the subject in the November number, 1878, of "Nord und Lüd," a German periodical, published in Berlin, in an article headed "Ueber Fetischismus," p. 160. Professor Müller says :—

"Nichts ist schwieriger als der Versuchung zu widerstehen, eine unerwartete Bestätigung unserer Theorien, die wir in den Berichten von Missionaren und Reisenden finden, für einen Beweis zu halten. So ist das Wort für Gott im östlichen Polynesien *Atua* oder *Akua*. Da nun *Ata* in der Sprache der Polynesien Schatten bedeutet, was könnte natürlicher erscheinen, als in diesem Namen für Gott, der ursprünglich Schatten bedeutet, einen Beweis zu finden, dass die Vorstellung von Gott überall aus der Vorstellung von Geist entsprang, und die Vorstellung von Geist aus der Vorstellung von Schatten ? Es könnte wie blosse Streitsucht aussehen, wollte man Einwendungen dagegen erheben oder zur Vorsicht rathen, wo Alles so klar scheint. Glücklicherweise hat aber das Studium der Polynesischen Sprachen in der letzten Zeit schon einen mehr wissenschaft-lichen und kritischen Charakter angenommen, so dass blosse Theorien die Probe der Thatsachen bestehen müssen. So zeigt denn Mr. Gill ('Myths and Songs from the South Pacific,' p. 33) der zwanzig Jahre in Mangaia gelebt hat, dass *Atua* nicht von *Ata* abgeleitet werden kann, sondern dass es mit *fatu* im Tahitischen und Samoanischen zusammenhängt, und mit *Aitu*, und dass es ursprünglich das Mark eines Baumes bedeutete. Nachdem es nun zuerst Mark bedeutete, wurde es später, etwa wie Sanskrit, *sâra* zur Bezeichnung von Allem, was das Beste ist, bezeichnete die Stärke eines Dinges, und schliesslich den Starken, den Herrn. Das aublautende *a* in *Atua* ist intensiv, so das also *Atua* für einen Polynesier die Bedeutung von dem innersten

Mark und Lebenssaft eines Dinges hat, und hieraus entwickelte sich bei ihnen einer der vielen Namen für Gott.

"Wenn wir mit einem Manne von wirklichem Wissen zu thun haben, wie Mr. Gill ist, der fast sein ganzes Leben unter einem Stamme der Polynesier verlebt hat, so können wir uns wohl auf seine Darstellung verlassen."

The Rev. Mr. Gill, in the work above cited, says :—

"The great word for God through Eastern Polynesia is 'Atua' (Akua). Archdeacon Maunsell derives this from 'Ata' = *shadow*, which agrees with the idea of spirits being *shadows*, but, I apprehend, is absolutely unsupported by the analogy of dialects.

"Mr. Ellis (Polynesian Researches, vol. ii. p. 201) regards the first *a* as euphonic, considering 'tua' = '*back*,' as the essential part of the word, misled by a desire to assimilate it with the 'tev' of the Aztec and the 'deva' of the Sanskrit. Occasionally, when expressing their belief that the divinity is 'the essential support,' they express it by the word 'wi-mokotua' = *the back-bone*, or vertebral column; *never* by the mere 'tua' = back.

"That the *a* is an essential part of the word is indicated by the closely-allied expressions 'atu' ('fatu' in Tahitian and Samoan) and 'aitu;' in the latter the *a* is lengthened into *ai*.

"A key to the true sense of 'atua' exists in its constant equivalent 'io,' which (as already stated) means the '*core*' or '*pith*' of a tree.

"Analogically, God is the pith, core, or life of man.

"Again, 'atu' stands for 'lord, master,' but strictly and primarily means 'core' or 'kernel.' The core of a boil and the kernel of a fruit are both called the 'atu'—*i.e.*, the hard and essential part (the larger kernels are called 'katu'). As applied to a 'master' or 'lord,' the term suggests that his favour and protection are essential to the life and prosperity of the serf. By an obvious analogy, the welfare of mankind is derived from the divine 'Atu' or 'Lord,' who is the core and kernel of humanity. In the nearly-related word Atua = God, the final *a* is passive in form but intensive in signification, as if to indicate that He is 'the VERY core or life of man.'"

I am ready to accord all credit and praise to Mr. Gill's exceedingly valuable contribution to a better knowledge of Polynesian archæology, through its "Myths and Songs;" and I regret very much that I did not become acquainted with his work before the first volume of my own was sent to the press; but, in his analysis and explanation of the word *Atua*, I believe that his religious feelings have biased his judgment, and led him to a conclusion "absolutely unsupported by the analogy of dialects" and the hard matter of facts.

I entirely concur with Mr. Gill that the word *Atua* is neither referable to the Polynesian *Ata*, shadow; nor to the *Tev* or *Deva*, the Aztec and Sanskrit for God. But when he asserts that "the *a* is an essential part of the word, from the analogy of '*Atu*' and '*Aitu*,'" I would call his attention to the following considerations, which, I think, will be fully borne out by "the analogy of dialects," which Mr. Gill invokes in defence of his analysis.

Mr. Gill is aware that in the Hervey group (Rarotonga, Mangaia, &c.) the letters *H. F. S.* are not sounded; in fact, in that respect the Herveyans are the Cockneys of the Pacific. Now the Mangaia *Atu* occurs with the same or similar meaning in, I believe, all the other Polynesian dialects. Haw. *Haku*, "a hard lump of anything, a bunch in the flesh, ball of the eye;" with *po* intensive, *po-haku*, "a stone." Sam. *Fatu*, "seed, the heart of a thing, stone." Niua, Fakaafo, *Fatu*, "a stone." Tahit. *Fatu*, "gristly part of oysters, core of an abscess." Marquesan, *Fatu*, "breast of a woman," also "stone." N. Zeal. *Whatu*, "a nail," "*Ko-whatu*, "a stone," also *Patu* and *Patu-patu.* Figi, *Vatu*, "stone, rock;" *Vatu-ni-taba*, "shoulder-blade;" *Vatu-ni-balawa*, a whale's tooth put in the hands of a dead person. Tonga, *Fatu*, "the stomach." While in the Sam. Tong. *Fatu-titili*, Marqu. *Fatutii*, N. Zeal. *Watitiri*, Tah. *Pa-tiri* means thunder, probably thunderbolt or meteoric stone. Now in all these dialects the Mangaian *Atu* commences with a consonant, *F, H, V, Wh*, or *P*, which are more or less interchangeable, thus showing that the word originally was *Fatu, Haku, Whatu*, &c., and that the omission of the consonant *H* in the Hervey dialect is as much a later corruption of the original word, as the omission of the *L* or *R* in the Marquesan dialect is a later corruption of the original forms of the words containing them. If we now go to the Polynesian congeners in the Indian Archipelago, we find that the Sunda has *Batu*, "stone;" Amboyna (Liang), *Hatu-aka*, "belly;" Burn. (Wayapo), *Ulun-fatu*, "head," all showing that even there the word commences with a consonant similar to that of the Polynesian dialects.

Now if we look at the Polynesian word *Atua, Etua, Otua*, the first current in Samo. Tah., Rarot., Haw., Marqu., the second in Mangaia, the last in Tonga, there is no trace or indication that it ever commenced with either of the consonants that form the initial letter of the word *Fatu*, &c. There is no such word as *Fatua, Fetua, Fotua*. And as *Atua* is not a modern word, to be derived from the Hervey Islands' dialect, which is an historically late compound of the Samoan and Tahitian dialects, I see no possible ground for deriving the universal Polynesian *Atua* from the exceptional Mangarian *Atu.*

Neither do I see any good reasons for holding that *Aitu* is a lengthened form of *Atu,* or, as Mr. Gill says, that " *a* is lengthened into *ai.*" I question whether Mr. Gill can produce another word from the whole Polynesian language where the *a* has been lengthened into *ai.* It is true that in the Samoan and Tahitian, and in some from those derived dialects, *Aitu* means " spirit, god, supernatural being;" but in Hawaiian, where *Aiku* does not occur in that sense, we have *Iku,* one of the oldest royal appellatives of the highest tabu chiefs, thus showing what was its primary and simplest form before the euphonic *a* was added to it. In the Paumotu or Taumotu group this word with the meaning of " spirit " occurs in the form of *Maitu,* composed of the augmentative or intensive prefix *Ma* and *Itu.*

I do not deny, and think it very probable that both forms of the word, *Aiku* and *Itu,* were current at the same time in the Polynesian dialects ; and as there is no instance in the language, so far as I know, of the diphthong *ai* being shortened to *i,* I am forced to conclude that the initial *a* in *Aitu* is merely euphonic, a euphonism of too frequent occurrence in all the dialects, and which at this time should be too well known to mislead a comparative philologist. To what root and to what language the original form of *Itu* should be referred, and what may have been its primary sense, are questions for abler philologists than myself to settle ; and also whether the Hawaiian sense of " royalty and highest tabu " was anterior or posterior to the South Pacific sense of " spirit, god," or whether both were the outgrowths, in different directions, of an older, once common, then underlying, and now obsolete idea. On page 41 of the first volume of this work I have ventured to suggest a solution, and until a better is found I shall adhere to it.

In regard to *Atua,* as it cannot, as above 'shown, be referred to *Fatu, Haku,* &c., which undoubtedly are the original forms of the Mangarian *Atu,* I am inclined to hold with Rev. Mr. Ellis that the initial *a* in *Atua* is also euphonic. It is probable that the simple form *Tua* originally served to express a family relation. In the Indian Archipelago we still find it lingering in certain places. In the Sula Islands and in parts of Borneo *Tua* means " lord, master, husband." In Malay, *Tuan* or *Tuhan* means " god," and *Orang-tuan* a " grandfather." In the Fiji group, where so much of the archaic sense and forms of Polynesian speech still survives, *Tua* and *Tuka* means " grandfather] very old, immortal;" *Tua-na*, "elder brother or sister." In the Samoan *Tua'a*, in the N. Zeal. *Tuakana*, Tahit. *Tuaana*, Hawaiian *Kai-kuaana*, we have a "brother's elder brother," or a "sister's elder sister." In the Sam. and Tonga *Tua-fafine*, Tahit. *Tua-hine*, we have a word expressive of a brother's sister.

From this showing it is fair to infer that the word *Tua* was originally used to express a sense of age, strength, and superiority between the members of a family; and as men's thoughts travelled further beyond the narrow home circle, it came to express the ideas of "lord," "master," and "god." As the initial *a* in *A-tua*, or its equivalents, is common to the entire Polynesian family, it must have been adopted as a distinguishing sign of the supernatural, incomprehensible *Tua* from the ordinary family *Tua*, at a time when the Polynesians yet were a comparatively united and compact people, long before their exodus to the Pacific.

I think Mr. Gill is fully justified, "by the analogy of dialects," in considering the final *á* in *A-tu-a* as an intensive suffix; and the examples he quotes could be multiplied ad infinitum from every dialect of the Polynesian. That conceded, there remains *Tu* as the root of the words *Tua* and *Atua*. Does the meaning of *Tu* explain the derivation of *Tua?* In all the Polynesian dialects *Tu* or *Ku* means primarily "to rise up, to stand, be erect." In N. Zeal. *Tu-mata* was the name of the "first son, born of heaven and earth;" in Saparua and Ceram *Tu-mata* means "man;" in Fiji *Tu* is used interchangeably with *Ta*, to express the sense of a father when spoken to by his children. As I think there are many reasons to hold that the Polynesian language, deducting its many admixtures, was originally a form of Arian speech in Vedic or pre-Vedic times, I would refer to the Vedic verb *Tu*, "to be powerful, to increase;" a word occurring also in the Zend with similar meaning, whence *Tu-i* (Ved.), "much;" *Tavas* (Skrt.), "strong." From this root Benfey and Ad. Pictet derive the old Irish *Tuad*, *Tuath*, the Cymr. and Armor; *Tut*, *Tud*, the Goth; *Thuida*, the Lettic *Tauta*, all meaning "people, race, country."

As the Polynesian *Atua*, if I am correct, cannot be derived from *Fatu* or *Atu*, nor from *Aitu* or *Iku*, Mr. Gill's explanation, that the word refers to the "Lord, who is the *core and kernel of humanity*," and that it indicates that He is the *very* "core or life of man," cannot be maintained as a correct analysis and etymology. I think it more probable that men's ideas developed gradually from things natural to things supernatural, adapting the phraseology of the former to the exigencies of the latter, for the sake of distinction, and that thus from the original *Tu,* "to be erect, powerful, increasing, superior," were derived the expressions of *Tu* and *Tua* for "man, father, elder brother," subsequently "husband, lord, master;" and finally the Polynesian *A-tua,* "god, spirit," anything of a supernatural or incomprehensible character.

It is with some hesitation, and not without regret, that I have thus felt called upon to correct Mr. Gill's etymology and analysis of the Polynesian word *Atua,* and at the same time enter my protest against Professor Müller's endorsement of such an analysis. The Professor will again experience the sad truth of his own dictum, that "Nichts ist schwieriger als der Versuchung zu widerstehen, eine unerwartete Bestätigung unserer Theorien, die wir in den Berichten von Missionaren und Reisenden finden, für eines Beweis zu halten." The remedy, however, against such temptation ("Versuchung"), as regards the Polynesians, lies in a critical study of their language, which does not always come within the sphere or the ability of "missionaries and travellers;" and I may be permitted to refer Professor Müller to his own words in the same paragraph, where he says : —"Glücklicherweise hat aber das Studium der Polynesischen Sprachen in der letzten Zeit schon einen mehr wissenschaftlichen und kritischen Charakter angenommen, so dass blosse Theorien die Probe der Thatsachen bestehen müssen."

No. V.

KA INOA O KUALII (Page 279, *Note* 1).

He eleele kii na Maui,
Kii aku ia Kane ma,
Laua o Kanaloa, ia Kauakahi,
Laua o Maliu.
5   Hano mai a hai a hai i ka puu
Hai a holona ka puu o Kalani.
Ka Makau nui o Maui,
O Manaiakalani,
Kona aho, hilo honua ke kaa.
10   Hau hia amoamo Kauiki ;
Hania Kamalama.
Ka maunu ka Alae a Hina
Kuua ilalō i Hawaii,
Ka hihi kapu make haoa,
15   Kaina Nonononuiiakea
E malana iluna o ka ili kai.
Huna o Hina i ka eheu o ka Alae,
Wahia ka papa ia Laka,
Ahaina ilalo ia Kea,
20   Ai mai ka ia, o ka ulua makele,
O Luaehu kama a Pimoe, e Kalani o.
O Hulihonua ke kane
O Keakahulilani ka wahine,
O Laka ke kane, Kapapaiakele ka wahine,
25   O Kamooalewa ke kane,
O Nanawahine kana wahine,
O Maluakapo ke kane,
O Lawekeao ka wahine.
O Kinilauamano ke kane,
30   O Upalu ka wahine.
O Halo ke kane, O Koniewalu ka wahine.
O Kamanonokalani ke kane,
O Kalanianoho ka wahine.

O Kamakaoholani ke kane,
35   O Kahuaokalani ka wahine.
O Keohokalani ke kane,
O Kaamookalani ka wahine.
O Kaleiokalani ke kane,
O Kaopuahihi la ka wahine.
40   O Kalalii la ke kane,
O Keaomele la ka wahine.
O Haule ke kane, O Loaa ka wahine.
O Nanea ke kane, O Walea ka wahine.
O Nananuu ke kane, O Lalohana ka wahine.
45   O Lalokona ke kane,
O Lalohoaniani ka wahine.
O Hanuapoiluna ke kane,
O Hanuapoilalo ka wahine.
O Pokinikini la ke kane,
50   O Polehulehu la ka wahine.
O Pomanomano la ke kane,
O Pohakoikoi la ka wahine.
O Kupukupunuu ke kane,
O Kupukupulani ka wahine.
55   O Kamoleokahonua ke kane,
O Keaaokahonua ka wahine.
O Ohemoku ke kane, O Pinainai ka wahine.
O Makulu ke kane, O Hiona ka wahine.
O Milipo mea ke kane,
60   O Hanahanaiau ka wahine.
O Hookumukapo ke kane,
O Hoao no ka wahine.
O Lukahakona ke kane,
O Niau ka wahine.
65   , O Kahiko ke kane,
O Kupulanakehau ka wahine.
O Wakea la ke kane, O Papa la ka wahine.
     Hanau ko ia la lani he ulahiwa nui.
     He alii o Pineaikalani, ko Kupunakane;
70   Hanau ka lani he alii;
     Hua mai nei a lehulehu;
     Kowili ka hua na ka lani;
     Lele wale mai maluna
     Ka loina a ka lani weliweli.
75   He alii pii aku, koi aku, wehe aku,
     A loaa i ka lani paa ka ke alii.
     E Ku e, he inoa,
     Ina no ka oe, i o'na.

O Ku, o ke koi makalani !
80   Kakai ka aha maueleka, na Ku !
Kohia kailaomi e Ku !
Kai Makalii, kai Kaelo,
Kao ae Kaulua.
Ka malama hoolau ai a Makalii
85   O ke poko ai hele, ai iwi na
Ka pokipoki nana i ai ka iwi o Alaka—poki—e
O ka makua ia o Niele o Launieniele
O kanaka o ka wai,
     O Ku, ke Alii o Kauai.
90   O Kauai mauna hoahoa,
Hohola ilalo o Keolewa
Inu mai ana o Niihau ma i ke kai—e.
O Kiki ma ka-kai Keolewa.
O Kalaaumakauhi ma ka-kai luna—e—
95   O Hawaii.
O Hawaii, mauna kiekie.
Hoho i ka lani Kauwiki ;
Ilolo ka hono o na moku,
I ke kai e hopu ana.
100   O Kauwiki.
O Kauwike ka mauna i ke opaipai,
E kalai na a hina, Kauwiki—e—
     O Kauai
O Kauai nui Kuapapa,
105   Noho i ka lulu o Waianae,
He lae Kaena, he hala Kahuku,
He kuamauna hono i ke hau Kaala,
Noho mai ana Waialua ilalo—E—
     O Waialua-ia.
110   O Mokuleia, Kahala, Ku ipu
Ka loko ia mano lala walu
Hui Lalakea o Kaena
Mano hele lalo o Kauai—E—
Olalo o Kauai, kuu aina,
115   O Kauai.
Ke holo nei Ku i Kauai—e—
E ike i ka oopu makapoko o Hanakapiai.
Ke hoi nei Ku i Oahu-e-
I ike i ka oopu kuia, ia
120   Hilahila o Kawainui
Elana nei iloko o ka wai.
A pala ka hala, ula ka ai—e—

He hailona ia no Ku,
Ua pae mai la
125   O Kauai.
O Kauai nui moku Lehua,
Moku panee lua iloko o ke kai,
Moku panee lua ana Kahiki,
Halo Kahiki ia Wakea ka la,
130 Kolohia kau mai ana Kona i ka maka,
Hooulu ilalo Kumuhonua,
Makeke ka papa i Hawaii-akea,
O Kuhia i ka muo o ka la.
Ke kau la ka la i Kona, ke maele Kohala,
135 O Kahiki; ia wai Kahiki?
    Ia Ku.
O Kahiki, moku kai a loa,
Aina a Olopana i noho ai.
Iloko ka moku, iwaho ka la ;
140 O ke aloalo ka la, ka moku, ke hiki mai.
    Ane ua iko oe?
    Ua ike.
Ua ike hoi a'u ia Kahiki.
He moku leo pahaohao wale Kahiki.
145 No Kahiki kanaka i pii a luna
A ka iwikuamoo o ka lani ;
A luna, keehi iho,
Nana iho ia lalo.
Aole o Kahiki kanaka ;
150 Hookahi o Kahiki kanaka,—he Haole ;
Me ia la he Akua,
Me a'u la he kanaka ;
    He kanaka no,
Pai kau, a ke kanaka hookahi e hiki.
155 Hala aku la o Kukahi la o Kulua,
O Kukahi ka po, o Kulua ke ao,
O hakihana ka ai ;
Kanikani ai a manu-a !
Hoolono mai manu o lanakila !
160 Malie, iawai lanakila?
    Ia Ku no.
Ilaila ka ua, ilaila ka la ;
Ilaila ka hoku Hiki-maka hano he Alii.
O Kaulukahi ka la,
165 O Kaupukahi ka la,
O Puna, o Hooilo, o Hana, o Lanakila,

O Hooilo, ua ino Pele.
O ka makani; ia wai ka makani?
    Ia Ku no.
170 Puhia ka makani a Laamaomao
Ke ahe Koolauwahine ka makani olalo
O Kauai ka'u i ike,
O ke kiu ko Wawaenohu,
O ka hoolua ko Niihau,
175 O ke Kona ka makani ikaika,
O ke Aoa ka makani ino,
Ka makani halihali wai pua Kukui,
I lawea ia la e Lonomoku,
Pa ilalo o Hana—e—
180 Oia Koolauwahine olalo o Kauai
Ke pa la ka i Wailua la
O ka hoku, iawai ka hoku?
    Ia Ku no.
Iluna ka ua o Puanalua
185 Ku i ke Kao-Maaiku—hoolewa
Ka wae o ke kaina,
Oiliili lupea na hoku mahana elua.
Heua Kona me ka makani
Ku i ke Kao-Maaiku—hoolewa
190 Ka wae o ke kaina,
O ka ua; ia wai ka ua?
    Ia Ku no.
I moea ka ua i Kunaloa,
I pakakahi ka ua i ka ili,
195 I liki ka ua i Kananaola,
Pahee mahiki, ke ka la,
Ua luia ka ua e Hina,
Haalulu ai lalo o Maheleana.
O ka punohu o ka ua kai Kahalahala.
200 O ka pokii o ka ua,
E ua ka i ka lehua la,
O ka la, ia wai ka la?
    Ia Ku no.
I puka ka la ma Kauwiki,
205 Hawewe ka la i ka Upilialoula,
Ke kohokoho la kamalii,
Ke na'una'u la ka la,
Ka la kieke pua o Hilo,
O ke kua o ka la kai hulihia iluna,
210 O ke aloalo o ka la kai lawea ilalo,
O ka malu o ka la kai kaa iloko,

O ke aka o ka la kai hele iwaho,
O ka mahana o ka la ke hele nei
Maluna o ka aina—a
215　　Kau aku i Lehua la.
O ke kai; ia wai ke kai?
　　　Ia Ku no
I nui mai kai i Kahiki,
I miha kai i ka aina,
220　　I lawea kai i ka lima,
I kiki ke oho i ke kai,
I ehu ke oho i ke kai liu,
I pala ke oho i ke kai loa,
I lelo ke oho i ke kai kea.
225　　He kai kuhikuhinia ko ka puaa,
He kai lihaliha ko ka ilio,
He kai okukuli ko ka moa,
He kai ala ko ka anae,
He kai hauna ko ka palani,
230　　He kai heenalu ko Kahaloa,
He kai hului ko Kalia,
He kai hele kohana ko Mamala,
He kai au ko ka puuone,
He kai kaha nalu ko Makaiwa,
235　　He kai ka anae ko Keehi,
He kai alamihi ko Leleiwi,
He kai awalau kee Puuloa,
He kai puhi nehu, puhi -lala,
He kai o Ewa e noho i ka lai nei,
240　　Na Ewa nui a Laakona,
Ku i ka alai ka ua o ka lani,
Kai apukapuka Heeia,
Ke kai o hee ko Kapapa,
He kai oha i ke Kualoa,
245　　He kai aai ko Kaaawa,
He kai ahiu ko Kahana.
I wehe kai ia Paao,
Ikea Paao i ka wai—hi,
Ikea ka hiwa mai lalo Kona,
250　　O ka Hiwa ia mai lalo Kona,
He au, he koi, he aha, he pale,
E kii, e hoa, e lanalana,
E kua i kumu o Kahiki—e,
O ua mai Hilo.
255　　Ke kuee nei na opua ua o Maheleana—e,
Oua mai kanaka

Ilaila ka ua a malie,
He lala loa i ka makani,
Haiki ka make o ka ua,
260 Haakookoo ana Mahiki i ka pukalea,
Aia Mahiki, ke ka mai la.
O Opukahonua, O Lolomu, O Mihi,
O Lana ka wahine,
Noho Wakea noho ia Papa,
265 Noho ia Kananamukumamao,
Hanau ka Naupaka,
Ku i ke Kahakai,
O Ohikimakaloa ka wahine,
O Hoopio, O Hulumaniani,
270 Ku i Kaena, ana-iá i lalo.
O Mehepalaoa,
O Naholo,
Mehe kai olohia a Manu,
Oia alakai honua Ku.
275 O Lanipipili, O Lanioaka,
O Lanikahuliomealani,
O Lono, O Hekili kaaka,
O Nakoloailani,
O Kailolimoana, O Waia,
280 O Hikapoloa,
O Kapoimuliwaa,
O Kane,
O Ahulukaaala,
O Kanei Kamakaukau.
285 Alua ana hulu wau ia oe e Ku—e;
E ka'u Alii.
Eia ka paia ai o Kapaau,
He kanaka o Wawa-Kaikapua.
Keapua ko o Hawi,
290 Eia ke puhi kukui ai o Kukuipahu,
Ka wahine waha ula
Ke ai i ka ina o Makakuku,
Eia ke kanaka pii pali
Haka ulili o Nanualolo,
295 Keiki kia manu—e—
Kau kiakia manu o Lehua.
O Kuku, O Aa, O Naio,
O Haulamuakea ke koi; O Hinaimanau;
O Paepae
300 O Manau ka wahine,
Hanau ka Naenae noho kuamauna

Ka Hinihini kani kuaola,
Hakina iho i ka wae mua o ka waa.
O Molokai ua naha ke'na,
305 Haalele aku Kanaloapuna,
Kanaloa a Waia ;
O make holo uka, O make holo kai,
Hoonalulu ana Luukia,
Hoopailua i ka ilolo,
310 I ke kauhua o ke kamaiki
Hanau ka Ieie hihi i ka nahele,
O Makaaulii kana wahine.
Hanau ka Lupua me ka Laulama,
Ku i ke opu o Lono.
315 O Kapolei ka wahine,
O Kukaikaina i hope ka lanalana,
O Kukonaihoae, O Ku,
O ke kai mahuehue,
Mehe kai e haa aku ana Ku.
320   Eia ka wahine peeki
Uhi lepo o Keaau,
Ka umeke hoowali na lepo,
Mehe hako la ke ala,
Eia ka huakai hele
325   Alanui ka kanaka.
Wali ai ka lepo o Mahiki,
I ka paala a ka wawae.
O Kapapaiakea,
O ka nalu o ka inaina,
330 O Kauhihii kana wahine,
Hanau Koawaa ku i ka nenelu,
Kalaia ka ipu i ke kai aleale,
Kalaia o Hinakapeau,
Loaa mai o Ukinohunohu la,
335 Ukinaopiopio,
O Moakueanana,
O Kalei,
O Keelekoha,
O ke 'kua maka holo lalo,
340 O ke kau iluna Kahualewa,
Ako Lipoa o Kanamuakea,
O ke kai akea
O ka moana akea.
O Hulukeeaea
345 O Hauii, O Hauee,
O Hauii-nui naholoholo,

O Hauii kai apo kahi,
Kai humea mai ko malo o Ku.
No Ku ka malo i ke kaua, haa oe.
350   Oia i luia ka umu mehe awai la.
    Eia ka uhuki hulu manu,
    Kau pua o Haili,
    Na keiki kiai pua,
    Ka lahui pua o lalo.
355   Eia ka wahine ako pua,
    Kui pua lei pua, kahiko pua o Paiahaa,
    Ke uhai mai nei i ke 'kua,
    A pau mehameha Apua.
    Kau ia ka makani, hiamoe—la—e
360   .Moe ua makani, hiamoe la la—e—
    I ka papa o Kukalaula.
    O Uliuli, O Maihea,
    O Kahakapolani ka wahine,
    O Kaukeano, O Mehameha,
365   O po ka lani i ka ino;
    He ino ka lani, ke wawa nei ka honua,
    I ka inaina o kalani.
    Hoonaku, hookaahea, hoowiliwili,
    Hoonahu, hoomamae,
370   Hookokohi ana iloko o Hinaiaeleele,
    Hanau ka maua ku i ka nahele,
    Hanau ka ouou kani kuaola,
    Puka ke kama-hele
    Ku i ke alo o ka hakoko,
375   He pukaua, na ke Alii, he kaua,
    He wai kaua, o Ku no ke Alii,
    He kaua na Ku,
    E uhau ana iluna o Kawaluna.
    Ihea, ihea la ke kahua,
380   Paio ai o ke koa—a?
    I kahua i Kalena,
    I manini, i hanini,
    I ninia i ka wai Akua,
    I ko hana, i Malamanui
385   Ka luna o Kapapa, i Paupauwela,
    I ka Hilinai, i ke Kalele,
    Ka hala o Halahalanui-maauea,
    Ke kula Ohia, ke Pule—e,
    Ke 'kua o Lono o Makalii
390   Ka lala aala o Ukulonoku,
    No Kona paha, no Lihue.

No ka la i Maunauna,
No ka wai i Paupauwela,
I ulu Haalilo i Nepee,
395   A ka hau'na o Aui.
Kikomo kahuna i kakua laau,
Komo ku i kona ahuula,
Ka wela o ka ua i ka lani,
Ka la i Kauakahi-hale,
400   Ula ka lau o ka Mamane,
Ke koaie o Kauai;
Ke pili kai ihi ia e Ku,
Ka alo-alo o Kamaile,
Ka nalu kakala of Maihiwa,
405   Pani'a ka wai i Kalapo,
Ka naha i lalo o Eleu.
Huki ka ua a moa i ka lani,
Mehe hee nui no kuahiwi;
Ka hee'na o Hilo ia Puna,
410   Aia ma Hilo Peahi;
Ula ka wai i Paupauwela,
Ka Kilau o Malamanui,
Ka moo Kilau i Kapapa.
Kui ka lono ia Haalilo,
415   Haua aku la ko kaina;
Hahaki Haalilo i ka manawa;
I kai muku kahuna ia Ku;
I laa ka manawa ia Ku,
I Keiki a Haalilo.
420   Eia Malanai-haehae,
Kama a Niheu-Kalohe,
Ke pani wai o Kekuuna,
He mee nei no ke kanaka,
Ke pu nei i ka aahu,
425   Ke lapa nei i ka laau,
Ka laulau o ka palau,
Eia Haalilo—e!—
        O Ku no he Alii.
Aloha Kukui peahi i na leo Paoa;
430   Ua oa ka maka o ka ilima make,
Nonu i ka malama o Makalii;
Ia Makalii la pua ke Koolau,
Pau i ke hau o Maemae.
He mae wale ka leo o ke kai olalo,
435   Hoolono wale o Malamanui,
Ia ai Ku i ka uwala,

Kawewe Kupukupu ala o Lihue.
Kupu mai nei ka manawa ino e Ku—e—
Hanau mai, a me kalani wale la ;
440   O Ku no he Alii.
He pu hinalo no Ku i Kamakoa,
Oi lele Ku i ka pali,
Mai pau Ku i ke ahi,
O ke aha la kau hala—e Ku ?
445 O ke kua aku i ka laau,
O ka luukia ana o ka pau,
O ke ahina ana o ke oa,
O ko Ku ia o Kona hoa—hele
I ka ua, i ka la.
450 A ai ai Ku i ka unahi pohaku,
Ola Ku i ka ipu o Lono
I ka ipu a Kupaka,
      O Ku no he Alii.
O Kailua makani anea oneanea,
455 Makani aku a Hema,
He mama wale ka leo ke uwalo mai—e—
E o ia nei, o ka lahui-makani,
E ku mai oe i ka hea i ka uwalo,
Mai hookuli mai oe ;
460 O ke kama hanau
O ka leo kai lele aku la i waho,
Kai noa iwaho ka paio,
Pale aku la ilaila ;
Hoi mai i ka hale liliia,
465 Mehe leo la ko ka aha,
Ke kaunuia la ka moena,
Ke kapa me ka aahu,
Ke hea wale la i ka uluna—e—
Aole ia he kanaka.
470 O maua no na kanaka.

Ao ole i like i ka Hala wili,
Ke naio laau kekee,
Ka aukaahihi ku makua ole,
Ke kawakawa i keekeehia,
475 Ka hinahina i ka makani
Hele ana e hio, e hina la—
      Aole i like—Ku.
Ua like paha ka Ohia,.
Ka lehua i ka wao-eiwa,

480   Ka laau hao wale Ku i nahelehele,
      Aole i like—Ku.
   Aole i like i ka ekaha,
   I ka ekaha Ku i ka moena,
   Me ke kiele, me ke ala,
485   Me ka Olapa lau kahuli,
   Me ka pua mauu kuku,
   Hina wale—hina wale la—
      Aole i like—Ku.
   Aole i like i ka naulu,
490   Ia ua hoohali kehau,
   Mehe ipu wai i ninia la,
   Na hau o Kumomoku ;
   Kekee na hau o Leleiwi,
   Oi ole ka oe i ike
495   I ka hau kuapuu.
   Kekee noho kee, O Kaimohola,
   O Kanehili i Kaupea—la—
      Aole i like—Ku.
   Aole i like i ka Lipoa,
500   Ka Nanue, ai a ka ia,
   Ka Lipahapaha o Waimea,
   Ka limu kau i ka laau,
   Ka elemihi ula i ka luna o Kaala—la—
      Aole i like—Ku.
505   Aole i like i Kukui,
   I Kukui ili puupuu,
   Ili nakaka i ka la,
   Mehe kanaka iuu i ka awa la,
   Ka mahuna o Kukui o Lihue la,
510   Aole i like—Ku.
   Aole i like i ke Aalii,
   Ka poho lua laau ala,
   Ka Malie hoe hoi i Maoi,
   Ke Kaluhea o Kawiwi—la,
515   Aole i like—Ku.
   Aole i like i ke Kokio,
   I ka hahaka pua maoia,
   Ke kahuli pua i ka papa la.
      Aole i like—Ku.
520   Aole i like i ke Kawau,
   I ke Kalia ku ma ka waha,
   Ai mai ka mahele he kanaka,
   He moku, he au, he aina la,
      Aole i like—Ku.

525   Aole i like ka Naia,
        I Kona ihu i kihe i ke kai,
        Kona kino i kai ; O ka mano—la
            Aole i like—Ku.
        Aole i like i ke hokii,
530   I ka hawana ai pua Lehua,
        Ka Oo, Manu o Kaiona—la
            Aole i like—Ku.
        Aole i like i ka paaa,
        I ka weke lao a ke Akua,
535   Ka Ulu kanu a Kahai ;
        Oi ole ka oe i ike,
        Ka wahine pau mao
        I ka luna o Puuokapolei—la
            Aole i like—Ku.
540   Aole i like i ka Wiliwili
        Kona hua i kupee ia
        Ka oiwi ona i hee—a,
        Kona kino i kai o ka nalu la—Heenalu,
            Aole i like—Ku.
545   Aole i like i ka pa a ka makani,
        E nu ana i ke kuahiwi,
        Kakoo ana ka hale o Koolau,
        Lawalawa ana a hina i ka makani,
        Ka mokoi hoolou a ka lawaia,
550   Ka pa o Manaiakalani—la,
            Aole i like—Ku.
        Aole i like i ka Mamaki,
        I ka hialoa maka o ka nahele,
        Ka maka kohikohi laalaau ;
555   Ke a maka-ulii, maka-ehu,
        I ehu i ke alo o Kuehu,
        I ke ala ihi, i ke alaloa,
        I ke alaloa e hele ia la—la,
            Aole i like—Ku.
56c   Aole i like i na laki,
        I ka laki-pala o Nuuanu,
        I hehe ia e ka ua, e ka makani,
        A helelei,
        Ka laki-pala i ka luna i Waahila la
565   Aole i like—Ku.
        Aole i like i ka ua o Waahila,
        Ia makani anu o Kahaloa,
        E lu ana i ka pua Kou,
        E kui ana a paa ia,

570   E lei ana i ke kai o Kapua—la,
           Aole i like—Ku.
       Aole i like i ke Kamaniula,
       Ma ke kia ula o na manu—la,
       Me ka pa lei o ka hala—la,
575   Me ke pua o ke kaa,
       Lau kani o Ku—la
           O Ku no ke Alii
           Aole i like—Ku.
       Aole i like i ka makole,
580   Ia laau Kewai nui,
       E hihi ana e ka lihilihi—la
           Aole i like—Ku.
       Ua like ; aia ka kou hoa e like ai,
       O Keawe-i-Kekahi-alii-o-ka-moku,
585   O Keawe, haku o Hawaii la.
       He awaawa hoi ko ke kai,
       He mananalo hoi ka wai,
       He welawela hoi ko ka la,
       He mahana hoi ko kuu ili
590   No kuu kane o Nininini ke wai
       O Pulele la.   Ua like ?
           Aolo i like—Ku.
       Aole i like nei Lani,
       I ka hoohalikelike wale mai ;
595   He kanaka ia,
       He Akua Ku,
       He ulele Ku mai ka lani,
       He haole Ku mai Kahiki,
       He mau kanaka ia eha,
600   Ewalu hoi nei kanaka,
       O Ku, o Lono, o Kane, o Kanaloa,
       O Kane-makaiahuawahine,
       O Haihaipuaa, O Kekuawalu—la,
           Ua like.
605   O Kona la, ua wela ka papa,
       Ua ku ke ehu o ka la,
       Ua wela ka hua o Unulau,
       O Kalanipipili, o Hoolilo,
       E a'e e puka ae ka la,
610   Ka mana o Ku-leonui,
       Haawiia mai ai ka la
       Mahana ai na Lii aua o Kona.

Following is the English translation.

THE CHANT OF KUALII.

A messenger sent by Maui to bring,
To bring Kane and his company,
(Him) and Kanaloa, and (to bring) Kauakahi,
(Him) and Maliu.
5   To praise and to offer, to offer up prayer,
      To offer and decree the fortune of the chief.
The great fish-hook of Maui,
Manaiakalani,
 (And) its line, naturally twisted is the string that ties
      the hook.
10   Engulfed is the lofty Kauwiki,
      (Where) Hanaiakamalama (dwelt).
The bait was the Alae of Hina,
Let down upon Hawaii,
The sacred tangle, the painful death,
15   Seizing upon the foundation of the earth,
Floating it up to the surface of the sea.
(But) Hina hid the wing of the Alae,
Broken up was the table of Laka,
Carried away below (was the bait) to Kea ;
20   The fishes ate it, the Ulua of the deep muddy places.
      Luaehu, child of Pimoe, eh Kalani eh !
      O Hulihonua the husband,
      O Keakahulilani the wife.
      O Laka the husband, Kapapaiakele the wife.
25   O Kamoolewa the husband,
      O Nanawahine his wife.
      O Maluakapo the husband,
      O Lawekeao the wife.
      O Kinilauamano the husband,
30   O Upalu the wife.
      O Halo the husband, O Koniewalu the wife.
      O Kamanonokalani the husband,
      O Kalanianoho the wife.
      O Kamakaoholani the husband,
35   O Kahuaokalani the wife.
      O Keohokalani the husband,
      O Kaamookalani the wife.
      O Kaleiokalani the husband,
      O Kaopuahihi the wife.

40 O Kalalii the husband,
    O Keaomele the wife.
    O Haule the husband, O Loaa the wife.
    O Nanea the husband, O Walea the wife.
    O Nananuu the husband, O Lalohana the wife.
45 O Lalokona the husband,
    O Lalohoaniani the wife.
    O Hanuapoiluna the husband,
    O Hanuapoilalo the wife.
    O Pokinikini the husband,
50 O Polehulehu the wife.
    O Pomanomano the husband,
    O Pohakoikoi the wife.
    O Kupukupunuu the husband,
    O Kupukupulani the wife.
55 O Kamoleokahonua the husband,
    O Keaaokahonua the wife.
    O Ohemoku the husband, O Pinainai the wife.
    O Makulu the husband, O Hiona the wife.
    O Milipomea the husband,
60 O Hanahanaiau the wife.
    O Hookumukapo the husband,
    O Hoao indeed the wife.
    O Lukahakona the husband,
    O Niau the wife.
65 O Kahiko the husband,
    O Kupulanakehau the wife.
    O Wakea the husband, O Papa the wife.
        Born to that chief was a great purple fowl—
        A chief was Pineaikalani, your grandfather.
70   The chief begat a chief;
        Prolific he was, abundantly;
        Intertwined is the seed of the chief;
        Towering up on high
        Is the rank of the dreaded chief.
75   A chief ascending, pushing, breaking through,
        And reaching the solid heaven of the chief.
        Eh! Ku eh! (here is) a name,
        If it is you in that place.
    O Ku, the axe with heavenly edge!
80 Following is the train of clouds after Ku!
    Drawn (down) is the horizon by Ku.
    The sea of Makalii, the sea of Kaelo,
    The rising sea of Kaulua.
    The month that increases the food of Makalii;

85 The worm that eats crawling, eats to the very ribs.
The sea-crab that eats the bones of the shipwrecked,
That is the father of Niele and Launieniele,
The people of the water;
    O Ku, the chief of Kauai.
90 O Kauai with the ragged mountains,
Spreading out below is Keolewa;
Niihau and its neighbours are drinking the sea,
O Kiki, and those, following Keolewa;
O Kalaaumakauahi and those, following upwards.
95   O Hawaii!
O Hawaii with the lofty mountains,
Shooting up to heaven is Kauwiki;
Below is the cluster of islands;
In the sea they are gathered up.
100   O Kauwiki!
O Kauwiki, mountain bending over,
Loosened, almost falling, Kauwiki—eh!—
    O Kauai!
O Kauai, great and peaceful,
105 Situated under the lee of Waianae.
A cape is Kaena, (full of) hala is Kahuku;
A mountain ridge reaching up to the cold is Kaala;
Waialua is situated below:
    Oh, that is Waialua.
110 O Mokuleia, (with its) Kahala fish (and its) gourds,
(Its) fishpond of sharks to be roasted on coals.
The tail of the white shark is Kaena,
The shark stretching away under Kauai eh—
Below Kauai, my land,
115   O Kauai!
Ku is travelling to Kauai—eh—
To see the short-faced Oopu of Hanakapiai.
Ku is returning to Oahu—eh,—
To see the slow-moving Oopu,
120 The shameful fish of Kawainui,
Floating about in the water.
When the Hala is ripe the neck becomes red—eh:
That is a sign of Ku.
He has landed now.
125   O Kauai!
O great Kauai, island (filled) with Lehua,
Island stretching out into the sea,
Island stretching out towards Kahiki.
Kahiki looking at Wakea, the sun;

130 Creeping along, Kona stands forth to sight;
     Lifting up below is Kumuhonua;
     Shaking is the foundation of Hawaii—akea,
     Pointing to the rising rays of the sun.
     The sun stands over Kona, Kohala is in darkness.
135 O Kahiki; for whom is Kahiki?
                    For Ku.
     O Kahiki, land of the far-reaching ocean,
     Land where Olopana dwelt.
     Within is the land, outside is the sun;
140 Indistinct is the sun, and the land, when approaching.
               Perhaps you have seen it?
               I have seen it.
     I have surely seen Kahiki,
     A land with a strange language is Kahiki.
145 The men of Kahiki have ascended up
     The backbone of heaven;
     And up there they trample indeed,
     And look down below.
     Kanakas (men of our race) are not in Kahiki.
150 One kind of men is in Kahiki—the Haole (white man);
               He is like a god,
               I am like a man,
               A man indeed,
     Wandering about, and the only man who got there.
155 Passed is the day of Kukahi and the day of Kulua,
     The night of Kukahi and the day of Kulua.
     By morsels was the food;
     Picking the food with a noise like a bird.
               Listen, bird of victory!
160   Hush! with whom the victory?
               With Ku indeed.
     There is the rain, there is the sun,
     There is the star Hiki-maka-hano, the chief.
     O Kaulukahi the sun,
165 O Kaupukahi the sun;
     O Puna, O Hooilo, O Hana, O Lanakila;
     The winter season, very bad (has) Pele (become).
     And the wind; for whom is the wind?
               For Ku indeed.
170 Blown is the wind of Laamaomao;
     The gentle breeze of Koolauwahine, the wind from be ow
     Kauai—(as) I have known it;
     The north-west wind of Wawaenohu,
     The north wind of Niihau;

175   The Kona is the strong wind;
      The howling Aoa, a bad wind,
      The wind scattering Kukui blossoms
      That have been brought by Lonomoku
      And arrested below Hana—eh—.
180   Such is Koolauwahine below Kauai,]
      When it is stopped at Wailua.
      And the stars; for whom are the stars?
             For Ku indeed.
      Above is the rain of Puanalua,
185   Reaching up to Kao—Maaiku bringing along
      The drifts of low-hanging clouds.
      Stretching out as eagles are the two twin stars;
      There is rain in Kona and there is the wind,
      Reaching up to Kao—Maaiku—bringing along
190   The drifts of low-hanging clouds.
      The rain; for whom is the rain?
             For Ku indeed.
      Low-lying is the rain of Kunaloa;
      Pattering is the rain on the skin;
195   Pelting is the rain of Kananaola;
      Slippery is Mahiki, it causes (one) to fall;
      Poured out about is the rain by Hina;
      Causing (great) fear (when) below Maheleana;
      The storm-clouds of rain are at Kahalahala;
200   The younger children of the rain (the fine rain)
      Are raining on the Lehua (forests).
      The sun; for whom is the sun?
             For Ku indeed,
      Comes forth the sun at Kauwiki;
205   A humming sound (makes) the sun at Upilialoula;
      Challenging each other are the children
      To hold their breaths at the sun-(set).
      The sun is a net of flowers at Hilo;
      The back of the sun is turned above;
210   The changing face of the sun flits about below;
      The comfort of the sun takes effect within;
      The image of the sun is moving about outside;
      The heat of the sun is now passing
      Over the land—eh—
215   And rests upon Lehua.
      The sea; for whom is the sea?
             For Ku indeed.
      Great is the sea to Kahiki,
      Rippled is the sea by the land.

220.   Taken up is the sea in the hand,
       Painted white is the hair by the sea,
       Reddish (becomes) the hair by the very salt sea,
       Softened is the hair in the great sea,
       Brownish is the hair in the foaming sea.
225   Delicious is the soup of the (cooked) hog.
       Fat is the soup of the dog,
       Satiating is the soup of the fowl,
       Savoury is the soup of the Anae,
       Strong smelling is the soup of the Palani.
230   A sea for surf-swimming is Kahaloa,
       A sea for net-fishing is Kalia,
       A sea for going naked is Mamala,
       A sea for swimming is Kapuuone,
       A sea for surf-swimming sideways is Makaiwa,
235   A sea for catching Anae is Keehi,
       A sea for crabs is Leleiwi,
       A sea of branching crooked harbours is Puuloa,
       A sea for the Nehu eel and the Lala eel
       Is the sea of Ewa, basking in the calm ;
240   The great Ewa (lands) of Laakona
       Surrounded by the rain of heaven.
       A deceitful sea is Heeia,
       A sea for spearing Hee is Kapapa,
       A sea for nodding is Kualoa,
245   A sea of heavy surf is Kaaawa,
       A sea for the Ahiu wind is Kahana.
       Let loose was the flood by Paao,
       Seen was Paao in the waterfall,
       Known were the sacred things from below Kona ;
250   Oh, the sacred things from below Kona,
       A handle, an axe, a cord, a sheath,
       Take it, tie it, wind it around ;
       Cut down the foundations of Kahiki—eh,
       While Hilo is raining.
255   Contending are the rain-clouds of Maheleana—eh,
       While it rains on the people.
       There is the rain until it stops ;
       A long day in the wind ;
       Cramped (is he) who is (half-) dead with the rain ;
260   Mahiki is obstructing the great passage way ;
       There is Mahiki, striking one down.
              O Opukahonua, O Lolomu, O Mihi,
              O Lana the wife,
              Wakea dwelt with Papa,

265   Dwelt with Kananamukumamao
                Born was the Naupaka
                That grows by the sea-shore.
                O Ohikimakaloa the wife,
                O Hoopio, O Hulumaniani,
270   Stood at Kaena (and) were precipitated below.
                O Mehepalaoa,
                O Naholo,
                Like the (ever-) rolling sea of Manu,
                Over which the proper guide is Ku.
275   O Lanipipili, O Lanioaka,
                O Lanikahuliomealani,
                O Lono—O the rolling thunder.
                O Nakoloailani,
                O Kailolimoana, O Waia,
280   O Hikapoloa,
                O Kapoimuliwaa,
                O Kane,
                O Ahulu Kaaala.
                O Kaneikamakaukau.
285   Twice ten days I have been with you, O Ku—eh ;
                O my chief.
       Here is the pearl-shell fish-hook of Kapaau ;
       A man is Wawa-Kaikapua,
       A sugar-cane arrow is Hawi.
290   Here is the torch-lighter of Kukuipahu,
       The woman with the red mouth,
       Who eats the sea-eggs of Makakuku.
       Here is the man who climbs the mountains,
       The ladder of Nanualolo,
295   The child catching birds—eh—
       Reaching up the bird-catching pole on Lehua.
           O Kuku, O Aa, O Naio.
           O Haulanuiakea, the axe ; O Hinaimanau,
           O Paepae,
300   O Manau the wife.
       Born was the Naenae who dwells on the mountain,
       The Hinihini chirping on the hillsides,
       (Fed with) crumbs on the first division of the canoe ;
       O Molokai that has been torn in sunder,
305   Deserted by Kanaloapuna,
       Kanaloa and Waia ;
       It is death to go landward, death to go seaward.
       Suffering by headache is Luukia,
       Qualmish from her pregnancy

310 From her pregnancy with the child,
Born is the tangled Ieie in the forest,—
O Makaaulii is its wife,—
Born is the Lupua and the Laulama,
Placed on the stomach of Lono,—
315 O Kapolei was the wife,—
O Kukaikai 'na behind the spider,
O Kukonaihoae, O Ku,
O the rising sea,
As if the sea were dancing for Ku.
320   Here is the woman sent in haste
    To spreak the dirt of Keaau.
    (With) a calabash of mixed dirt.
    (Straight) as a sugar-cane leaf is the road ;
    Here is the travelling company ;
325   The great road of the people.
    Mixed is the dirt of Mahiki,
    Beaten up by the feet.
O Kapapaiakea,
O the roaring surf of angry feelings,
330 O Kauhihii his wife ;
Born was Koawaa of the muddy places,
Fashioned was the bowl for the billowy sea ;
Fashioned was Hinakapeau ;
Thus was obtained Ukinohunohu,
335 Ukinaopiopio,
O Moakueanana,
O Kalei,
O Keelikoha,
O the god with the downcast eyes,
340 O the turned-up (eyes of) Kahualewa ;
Gathering Lipoa is Kanamuakea ;
O the wide sea,
O the open ocean,
O Hulukeeaea,
.345 O Hauii, O Hauee,
O Hauii-nui the swift running,
O Hauii the sea-encircling,
Sea where your girdle is put on, O Ku.
When Ku puts on his girdle of war, you are humbled ;
350 He has scattered the oven like the (rush of) a watercourse ;
    He is the picker of bird feathers,
    (Of birds) lighting on the flowers of Haili,
    The young ones watching the flowers,
    The multitude of flowers below.

355   Here is the woman gathering flowers
Stringing flowers, making garlands, putting on the flowers
      of Paiahaa,
So as to drive away the spirits
And destroy the solitude of Apua.
Fallen has the wind, it is sleeping—eh—
360   Resting is the wind, sleeping indeed—eh—
  On the flats of Kukalaula.
      O Uliuli, O Maihea,
      O Kahakapolani the wife,
      O Kaukeano, O Mehameha,
365   O dark is the heaven by the storm,
      Stormy is the heaven, noisy is the earth,
      Because of the labour-pains of the chief.
      Trembling, crying, struggling,
      Travailing, shrinking (at the touch),
370   Lowering were the clouds in the month of Hinaia-
        eleele.
      Born was the Maua (tree) standing in the forest,
      Born was the Ouou (bird), singing on the hillsides ;
      Brought forth is the child,
      It stands before the face of the travailing (mother),
375   A chief of warriors for the king—a battle—
      A bloody battle ; Ku indeed is the chief,
      A battle for Ku,
      Fought on the heights of Kawaluna.
      Where, where was the field
380   (On which) the warriors fought ?
      Lo ! the field is at Kalena ;
      Scattered about, overflowing,
      Poured out is the godly fluid
      By your work at Malamanui,
385   Above Kapapa, at Paupauwela,
      At Hilinai (and) at Kalele.
      The Hala trees of Halahalanui-maanea,
      The upland Ohia trees, the strange prayer
      The spirit of Lono (and) of Makalii,
390   The fragrant branch of Ukulonoku.
      For Kona perhaps, for Lihue.
      For the day at Maunauna,
      For the waters at Paupauwela,
      That Haalilo's name may flourish at Nepee,
395   All the scourging of Aui.
      Enter the priests to dress the idol ;
      Ku is putting on his feather cloak ;

The rainbow (stands) in the heaven ;
The sun is over Kauakahi's mansion ;

400   Reddish are the leaves of the Mamane tree ;
And the Koaie tree of Kauai ;
The long grass has been removed by Ku,
The waving (grass) of Kamaile ;
The toppling surf of Maihiwa ;

405   Dammed up are the waters at Kalapo,
Bursting out (are they) below Eleu,
Drawn away are the rain-clouds and dried up, in
    the sky,
Like a great land-slide from the hills,
The falling of Hilo upon Puna,

410   Here in Hilo—Peahi.
Red are the waters of Paupauwela,
The Kilau of Malamanui,
The Kilau ridges at Kapápa.
Comes the report to Haalilo,

415   That your younger brother has been whipped ;
Troubled (broken up) is the mind of Haalilo ;
At the quarrelling of the priests with Ku ;
For the want of sympathy with Ku,
With the son of Haalilo.

420 Here is the Malanai-haehae,
Descendant of Niheu-kalohe,
The water-dam of Kekuuna,
A prodigy here among the people,
He is tying up his clothing,

425 He is swinging about his weapons,
The bundle of daggers ;
Here is Haalilo—eh !—
      Ku indeed is the chief.
Love to the Kukui trees wafting the voices of Paoa ;

430 Shattered are the buds of the withered Ilima,
Wilted in the month of Makalii ;
In Makalii blossoms the Koolau plant,
Wet with the dew of Maemae.
Faintly comes the sound of the sea below,

435 Heard only (perhaps as far as) at Malamanui,
Where Ku ate the potato,
Covered (in baking) with the sweet Kupukupu of Lihue.
Rising are bitter thoughts in the mind of Ku—eh—
They are born and with the chief they rest.

440   Ku indeed is the chief.
A bunch of Hala blossoms for Ku at Kamakoa ;

While Ku was leaping down the pali
Ku nearly perished in the fire ;
What could have been your fault, O Ku
445   (Was it) the cutting down of the trees,
The girdling on of the woman's garment,
The throwing down of the spear
That belongs to Ku and is his companion
In the storm and in the sunshine ?
450   Ku is reducing to powder the scales of the rock ;
Ku draws life from the bowl of Lono,
From the bowl of Kupaka.
            Ku indeed is the chief.
O Kailua with the hot and desolating wind,
455   The wind (coming over) from the south ;
Feeble is the voice that is calling out for help ;
When that one is calling the winds are answering ;
Stand up at the call, at the cry ;
Don't you turn a deaf ear,
460   The child is born.
The sound has gone forth abroad ;
Surely the struggle is outside,
And there is the delivery.
Return to the hated house ;
465   Vociferous becomes the company ;
Provoked to anger is the mat,
The covering cloth and the dress ;
He calls in vain to the pillow—eh—.
He is not a man ;
470   We too are the men.

Not like the twisted Hala,
(Nor) the crooked Naio tree,
(Nor) the Ahihi standing motherless inland,
(Nor) the deep pools trodden (by bathers),
475   (Nor) the Hinahina in the wind,
Moving, leaning, falling ;
          Not like these (is) Ku.
Perhaps like the Ohia,
(Like) the Lehua on the mountain side,
480   (Like) the big trees standing in the jungle ;
          Not like these (is) Ku.
Not like the Ekaha fern,
The Ekaha put on to mats,
With the Kiele, with the Ala,
485   With the Olapa of the changing leaves,

With the flower of the Kuku grass,
Falling hither, falling thither.
             Not like these (is) Ku.
       Not like the Naulu (shower),
490   The rain that brings the land breeze,
       Like a water-bowl that has been poured out,
       The land breezes of Kumomoku,
       The land breezes coming round to Leleiwi.
       Truly, have you not known
495   The mountain breezes, that double your back up,
       (That make you) sit crooked and cramped, the Kaimohala,
       The Kanehili at Kaupea ?
             Not like these (is) Ku.
       Not like the Lipoa seaweed,
500   (Or) the Nanue weed, food for fishes,
       (Or) the Lipahapaha weed from Waimea,
       (Or) the weed that clings to the trees,
       (Or) the red crab on the top of Kaala.
             Not like these (is) Ku.
505   Not like the Kukui tree,
       The Kukui with the rough bark,
       Bark that is cracking in the sun,
       Like (the skin of) a man drinking awa ;
       The scaly-(barked) Kukui trees of Lihue.
510   Not like these (is) Ku.
       Not like the Aalii tree,
       (Or) the Poholua, sweet-scented tree,
       (Or) the Maile, causing one to pant on Maoi,
       (Or) the flowering Kaluhea from Kawiwi.
515   Not like these (is) Ku.
       Not like the Kokio tree,
       With the many branches and wilted flowers,
       Dropping the flowers on the ground.
             Not like these (is) Ku.
520   Not like the Kawau tree,
       (Or) the Kalia (which), placed in the mouth,
       Consumes into morsels the people,
       The island, the district, the land.
             Not like these (is) Ku.
525   Not like the porpoise
       With his nose that spouts up the sea,
       While his body is in the sea, (and) the shark.
             Not like these (is) Ku.
       Not like one with the asthma,
530   The wheezing (bird) that eats the Lehua blossoms ;

The Oo, bird of Kaiona.

> Not like these (is) Ku.

Not like the rind of the banana,
(Or) the tattered sugar-cane leaves of the gods,
535   (Or) the breadfruit tree planted by Kahai;
Truly, have you not known
The woman with the faded garment
On top of Puuokapolei?

> Not like these (is) Ku.

540   Not like the Wiliwili tree,
Of whose fruit bracelets are made,
Whose trunk is gliding away,
Whose body is in the sea of the rollers surf-riding.

> Not like these (is) Ku.

545   Not like the blast of the wind
Moaning over the hill-tops,
Causing to be tied down the houses in Koolau,
Fastened down lest they fall by the wind;
The tricky hook of the fisherman,
550   The fish-hook of Manaiakalani.

> Not like these (is) Ku.

Not like the Mamaki shrub,
With its long tangling shoots in the forests,
The choicest buds of all shrubs;
555   With its fine mesh-like covering
Like spray of the surf on the breast of Kuehu,
On the sacred road, on the long road,
On the long road that must be travelled (by all).

> Not like these (is) Ku.

560   Not like the leaves of the Ti plant,
(Or) the leaves of the Wiliwili in Nuuanu,
Which wilt in the rain and the wind
And fall off.
The Wiliwili leaves on the top of Waahila.

565   Not like these (is) Ku.

Not like the rain of Waahila,
(And) the cold wind of Kahaloa,
Scattering the Kou blossoms
That have been strung and fastened up,
570   And worn as wreaths on the sea of Kapua.

> Not like these (is) Ku.

Not like the Kamaniula tree,
The bright catcher of birds,
(Or) like the garlands of Hala nuts,
575   (Or) like the blossoms of the Kaa vine,

The musical (singing) leaves of Ku.
　　　　For Ku is the chief.
　　　　Not like these (is) Ku.
　　Not like the Makole tree,
580　That tree of great moisture,
　　Which gathers thick on the eyelashes.
　　　　Not like these (is) Ku.
　　He is like; here is thy mate, thy equal,
　　O Keawe-i-Kekahi-alii-o-ka-moku,
585　O Keawe, Lord of Hawaii.
　　Bitter is the salt water,
　　Sweet is the fresh water,
　　Very hot is the sun,
　　Warm is my skin,
590　From my husband, Nininini (comes) the water.
　　O Pulele,—Is it like?
　　　　Not like these (is) Ku.
　　Not like these is the chief,
　　Under any comparison.
595　That was a man,
　　A god is Ku,
　　A messenger is Ku from heaven,
　　A Haole (foreigner) is Ku from Kahiki,
　　He is (equal to) four men,
600　Yes (to) eight men ;—
　　O Ku, O Lono, O Kane, O Kanaloa,
　　O Kane-maikai-ahua-wahine,
　　O Haihaipuaa, O Kekuawalu la.
　　　　To these he is like.
605　There is Kona, hot is its surface,
　　Rises the steam from (the heat of) the sun,
　　Warmed are the offspring of Unulau,
　　The rainy season and the winter,
　　Ascending, coming forth is the sun,
610　The glory of great-voiced Ku ;
　　Given (to us) is the sun,
　　To warn the selfish chiefs of Kona.

NOTES.—*Verses* 1–6 contain the introduction, or invocation, to the great gods acknowledged by the composers of the chant. It will be noticed that even so late as *Kualii's* time the original Hawaiian gods, "*Kane* and his company," *i.e., Ku* and *Lono*, took the lead of the southern gods, *Kanaloa*, *Kauakahi*, and *Maliu*, introduced during the migratory period referred to in the first portion of this volume.

Verses 7–21 give the Hawaiian version of the southern legend of how the earth was fished up from the ocean by the demigod *Maui*. The hook was called *Manaiakalani*; it was baited with the *Alae*, the mudhen sacred to *Hina*, the daughter or wife of *Kanaloa*, who hid one of the wings of the bird and thus defeated the purpose of *Maui*, so that "the table of *Laka*"—the bottom of the sea—was broken up into pieces and only came to the surface in the shape of islands. *Verse* 10.—"'Lofty Kauwiki" refers to a prominent hill in the district of Hana, island of Maui, where *Hanaiakamalama*, the reputed mother of the Hawaiian *Maui*, dwelt. The introduction of "Kauwiki" and "Hanaiakamalama" in this connection shows the confusion in which the legend had fallen at this time, and the attempts of Hawaiian bards and priests to localise a notoriously southern legend on Hawaiian soil. *Verse* 15. — "Nonononuiakea," the great wide place full of holes or gulfs —Poet. : the very foundation of the earth, the sea bottom.

Verses 22–67 contain the celebrated "Kuauhau Kumuuli," the Kumuuli genealogy, referred to in vol. i. p. 184.

Verses 82–83.—The months of "Makalii, Kaelo, and Kaulua" were noted for high tides, "Kaikoo," and rough seas. According to the generally received Hawaiian calendar, these months would correspond to January, February, and March. The reference to the "Poko" worm, which generally appears in the months of February and March, shows that the most ancient mode of computing the year was followed in this chant. At the same time there were other modes of computing in vogue both on Oahu and elsewhere on the group, some making the year commence at the vernal equinox, and calling "Welehu" the first month of the year; while others, commencing at the same time, called "Nana" the first month of the year.

Verse 117.—"Oopu," a small fish found in ponds and streams.

Verses 137–161.—The import of this portion of the chant has already been commented on, p. 285.

Verse 170.—"Laamaomao" was the Hawaiian Æolus who kept the winds imprisoned in his calabash or "ipu."

Verse 185.—"Kao-Maaiku." Kao was the Hawaiian name for the star Antares in the horns of the constellation Taurus. "Alaaeku" is evidently an epithet and a compound word, though its exact meaning has now been forgotten.

Verse 187.—"Na hoku mahana." The twin stars; referring to Castor and Pollux, also known by the name of "Nana-mua" and "Nana-hope."

Verse 196.—"Alahiki." The road from Waimea to Waipio on Hawaii.

Verse 243.—"Hee," the squid.

Verses 263–284.—Names of Aumakuas or deified ancestors.

Verses 328–347.—Names of more Aumakuas.

Verses 362–365.—Still more Aumakuas.

Verses 378–419.—Describing the battles of Kualii with the Ewa chiefs.

THE END.

www.ingramcontent.com/pod-product-compliance
Lightning Source LLC
Chambersburg PA
CBHW020817270326
41928CB00006B/376